1,000

Great Lives
Plantagenet Somerset Fry

D0310140

HAMLYN

LONDON · NEW YORK · SYDNEY · TORONTO

Illustrations by
Fred Anderson · Colin Andrew · Stephen Bennett · Terry Callcut
Mike Codd · Doughty · Mike Embden · Exell · Henry Fox · Gwen
Green · Roger Hall · Donald Horley · Angus McBride · Jan Nicholson
Ted Osmond · William Randell · Meg Rutherford · Rodney Shackell
Ray Sim · Jim Tate · Prue Theobalds · Jenny Thorne · Carlo Tora

Maps by Leigh Jones

First published 1975
Fifth impression 1980
The Hamlyn Publishing Group Limited
London · New York · Sydney · Toronto
Astronaut House, Feltham, Middlesex, England

ISBN 0 600 34411 8

Printed and bound in Spain by Graficromo, S. A. – Córdoba

Introduction

If you were asked to name the thousand most famous people in the history of the world, you would not really be surprised if your list was different from that of your friend next door. So it is quite possible that you will not agree with all the names in this book. There will be a few, perhaps many, of whom you have never heard. There may be some who are not included but whom everybody knows about.

How, then, was the list in this book arrived at?

To begin with, the book is essentially for English-speaking people, and so there are more British, Commonwealth and American names than any others. At the same time care has been taken to include at least some of the people who are generally considered the most famous in nearly every major country in the world, considered, that is, by those countries. For example, you may not have heard of John Sobieski, King of Poland in the 17th century, but in Poland he is still one of the country's most celebrated heroes of their long history, and so he has an entry in this book.

Another factor taken into account is the balance between statesmen, generals and admirals, artists, writers, scientists and philosophers. While the story of the world is inevitably bound up with the careers of men of action who succeeded, one way or another, in imposing their will and their personality upon other people, we cannot afford – nor would anyone want – to disregard the tremendous importance of art, science and scholarship in the progress of mankind.

There is something else that you will notice. Not one entry is of a living famous person. This is because if great men and women living were included, now that the population of the world is at least twice what it was at the beginning of the century, the book would be overloaded with people of this century, which would not allow a balanced distribution of people throughout the six thousand or so years in which man has been civilized.

The entries are arranged in order of date of death because the years of a famous person's greatest importance are usually the later ones. This arrangement makes it possible to find nearly all the great lives of one period of history together, and places them more accurately in relation to other prominent figures of the age.

It should never be forgotten that it is people, especially great people, who make history, and it is right that their achievements be recorded for succeeding generations.

Plantagenet Somerset Fry

Menes (between 36th and 33rd century BC)
Ancient Egyptian ruler (between 3500 and 3200 BC)

Menes was probably the first king of Upper Egypt, the kingdom on the Nile, some distance south of modern Cairo. He conquered the kingdom of Lower Egypt further north, and so united the two lands to form a much larger Egyptian kingdom. On the Nile, just below the Delta, he built a city. He is also said to have invented the nilometer, a gauge for measuring the levels of the Nile.

Imhotep (c.30th century BC)
Ancient Egyptian statesman and architect

The famous Step Pyramid of the Pharaoh Zozer was built in Egypt by the architect Imhotep in the 30th century BC. This wise man was also a great physician and he was one of the leading counsellors of state to the pharaohs. He seems to have made a great impression on ancient Egyptians, as in later centuries they were to worship him as a god.

Abraham (c.20th century BC)
Hebrew leader

Abraham was a Semite farmer living in Mesopotamia, who, according to the Old Testament, was called upon by God to take his family out of the country and go to settle in Canaan. He wandered for some time, accompanied by his family and some friends, and eventually settled in Hebron, a district in Lower Canaan, and their descendants came to be called Hebrews from this name. These first settlers mingled with other settlers of Semitic stock already there, who had emigrated from Mesopotamia. It is probable that Abraham was elected their chief.

Hammurabi (between 18th and 17th century BC)
Ancient Babylonian ruler (c.1730–c.1680 BC)

Hammurabi was the greatest of the ancient Babylonian kings. Perhaps his most important achievement was his Code of Laws, the very first of its kind in history. It was a list of rules on how to behave, and it covered an enormous range of areas of human conduct. If a house collapses, it said, and kills the owner, the builder is to be put to death; if the house kills the owner's son, the builder's son is to die. If a gentleman breaks another gentleman's bone, he shall have his own bone broken. But if he breaks the bone of a commoner, he shall pay one mina of silver.

It was a severe code, but they were hard times, and the code ensured a high degree of law and order in a land which had been fraught with internal strife for a long time. The laws were inscribed on a pillar of black rock, and this has survived and is now at the Louvre in Paris.

Hammurabi built canals, temples, roads, and libraries. He enlarged his kingdom, kept it intact and made his neighbours fear his power.

Ahmose I (16th century BC)
First pharaoh of the 18th dynasty of ancient Egypt (c.1580–c.1550 BC)

For about a century (c.1680 to c.1580 BC) Egypt was ruled by kings, with their advisers and armies, who came from Syria and Palestine. They were called the Hyksos (foreigners) by the Egyptians and they were very tyrannical. It was Ahmose, an Egyptian noble from the city of Thebes, who organized an army of patriots and eventually drove the Hyksos out. Ahmose then reorganized the Egyptian kingdom as a military state, with the idea that in future the kings (or pharaohs) would also be generals in command of armies.

Hatshepsut (c.1500–1482 BC)
Ancient Egyptian queen (1503–1482 BC)

Hatshepsut was the queen of Thutmose II (c.1512–c.1504 BC), of the 18th dynasty. It seems that her husband was deposed for a few years, but by 1493 BC they were both back in power. For the next twelve years she devoted her energies and Egypt's resources to building roads, houses and temples, to improving the country's domestic condition and to trying to keep out of war with Egypt's neighbours. One of her great works was a tomb to her father in the Valley of the Kings, near Thebes. She also patronized artists and craftsmen. Her son was Amenhotep II (c.1447–c.1420 BC).

Akenhaten (Amenhotep IV)
(14th century BC)
Ancient Egyptian ruler (c.1375–c.1358 BC)
Amenhotep IV of the 18th dynasty has often been called the 'Religious Revolutionary' because he spent so much of his time trying to upset the established religious order in his kingdom. To break the hold the high priests had on the government, he introduced a new cult, whose followers would worship Aten, the Sun God. To show he meant his subjects to accept the new worship, he changed his name to Akenhaten, which means 'Aten is satisfied', and built a new capital city called Akehtaton, on whose site Tell-el-Amarna stands today.

Akenhaten is believed to have introduced the first civil service in Egypt. He was succeeded by his young son-in-law, Tutankhamen.

Suppululiumas (14th century BC)
Ancient Hittite king (c.1380–c.1346 BC)
This great Hittite king rebuilt the imperial capital of the Hittite Empire, Hattusas, and fortified it. Then he took an army outside his country's borders and advanced against Syria, conquering it. By the last years of his reign, his empire stretched from western Turkey down to Jerusalem. He was so strong that other kings would invite him to arbitrate in disputes. He died of the plague in about 1346 BC.

Moses (13th century BC)
Hebrew leader
Moses was the leader of the Hebrews who suffered many hardships in Egypt under the pharaoh, Rameses II (*p. 8*). He organized them into a close band of followers, whom he promised to lead back to Palestine. Then he began to badger Rameses incessantly, begging him 'Let my people go!' The Old Testament

Temple of Amon at Luxor, and Akenhaten with an Offering Tablet

records that Moses also caused certain disasters to befall Egypt, such as a plague of locusts which destroyed crops, and an epidemic that caused death to the new born. Although it is not likely that this was Moses' own work, one may be sure that he did take advantage of such natural disasters as did occur and persuaded Rameses that he was responsible.

Rameses ordered him and the Hebrews to go. So a long trek began across the awful Sinai desert, a journey that took forty years and which Moses did not live to complete. On the way he gave his people a simple code of behaviour by which to live. It was said to have been dictated to him by God and inscribed on tablets; there were ten commandments, which to-day are still the basic rules for Christians all over the world.

Rameses II (13th century BC)
Ancient Egyptian ruler (c.1290–c.1220 BC)

Possibly Rameses II is the best known of all the ancient Egyptian rulers. If this is so, it is in no small part due to the great belief he had in himself and his enthusiasm for self-advertisement. He fought a great battle with the powerful Hittite Empire, at Kadesh in Syria, in about 1288, and he claimed it as a victory. It was, however, more a victory for the Hittites, and in the peace negotiations which eventually followed, in c.1272 BC, they certainly preserved their empire.

Thereafter, Rameses spent most of his reign adorning Egypt with grand temples and other public building schemes. Among these were major additions to the temples at Karnak and Luxor and a temple cut in rock at Abu-Simbel. He was the pharaoh who oppressed the Hebrews and whom Moses begged 'Let my people go!', when he asked for the Israelites to be allowed to return to Canaan.

Joshua (13th–12th century BC)
Hebrew leader

Moses led his people out of Egypt, but after many years in the wilderness with them, he died before he could take them into Canaan. One of his chief lieutenants was Joshua, the son of Nun, and he became the new leader of the Hebrews. In a campaign splendidly described in the first chapters of the Book of Joshua in the Old Testament, he conquered much of Canaan and settled his people there.

Samson (12th century BC)
Hebrew leader

Everyone knows the story of Samson and his almost superhuman strength, how he routed an army of Philistines by crushing their skulls with the jawbone of an ass, how he slew a lion with his bare hands, and of how, at the end of his life, blinded through the treachery of his lover, Delilah, he pulled down the pillars of a great temple in which many leading Philistines were gathered and destroyed them all.

David slaying the Philistine champion Goliath with a stone

There is no reason to disbelieve the existence of a man of immense strength who could, like many professional weight lifters and 'muscle men', do things which ordinary folk could not. Perhaps the stories about Samson were exaggerated, because as a leader of men he defeated the Philistines in several battles after a long period in which the Hebrews had always been beaten.

Saul (11th century BC)
First king of the Hebrews (1025–1013 BC)

Saul was a descendant of Benjamin, the youngest of Jacob's sons. In the 11th century BC the Hebrews in Palestine had been struggling for independence against the Philistines who had conquered them in about 1050. What they lacked was a military leader, for they had put the leadership in the hands of legal experts

one occasion). He was disrespectful to his father-in-law and was outlawed. He went to war sometimes unnecessarily. But for all that, David gave his people good government and instilled in them a great sense of national pride, largely by his conquests of his neighbours. He defeated the Philistines under their champion Goliath, whom he is said to have slain personally by slinging a stone at him. He overcame many neighbouring tribes, such as the Moabites and the Ammonites. He enlarged the boundaries of his kingdom so that at his death it embraced an area between Sinai in the south and Syria in the north.

David made treaties with some neighbours, and these included clauses encouraging trade and commercial exchanges. One was with the great Hiram of Tyre (*p. 9*). He also tempered the power of the chief priests and judges. He created a national capital city at Jerusalem, on a hill which could be seen from miles away. There he erected many splendid buildings and the city was thereafter always known as the Holy City.

Hiram of Tyre (10th century BC)
Ancient Phoenician ruler (975–936 BC)

Hiram was king of the Sidonian state, a small but prosperous Phoenician kingdom, whose capital was the sea-port city of Tyre. In the last years of the reign of David I, King of the Hebrews (*p. 9*) Hiram formed an alliance with him which was continued by the latter's son, Solomon (*p. 10*). This was to organize a fleet of ships for trading in the Mediterranean, in the Red Sea and as far away as the Indian Ocean, and both Hebrews and Sidonians profited enormously from the arrangement. They also exchanged artists, craftsmen and builders, and Solomon's famous Temple at Jerusalem (since destroyed) was designed and built by Hiram's architects. This period of peace between Tyre and the Hebrews enabled Hiram to spread his territory north and south and thus unite many of the Phoenician states, which for a while were glad to accept his leadership.

and thinkers like Samuel. In the end, Samuel appointed Saul as king in 1020, and gave him full authority over the people.

Saul led an army against the Philistines and had some success, but in 1000 BC he was utterly defeated at Gilboa and died in battle.

David
King of the Hebrews (c.1013–c.973 BC)

This splendid warrior king ruled for about forty years. He was the son-in-law of Saul, the first king of the Hebrews, and such was his achievement that he became perhaps the greatest figure in all Hebrew history.

David was by no means without faults, as the Old Testament chroniclers are quick to point out. He tried to steal other people's wives (successfully on at least

Solomon (10th century BC)
Hebrew king (973–933 BC)

Solomon was the son of David I, king of the Hebrews, and he was in many ways as splendid a ruler. He was not as warlike as David, and though he was a good commander when it came to battle, he preferred dealing with his enemies by converting them into friends. He continued the good relationship between his father and Hiram of Tyre (*p. 9*) and employed artists and craftsmen from Tyre on his building projects, notably the great Temple at Jerusalem.

This remarkable king was a law-giver who introduced taxation reforms which relieved the poorer parts of his country. He was a student of many things and wrote several works, one or two of which are included as chapters in the Old Testament and the Apocrypha. His policy of encouraging trade and mining made his country rich. It also made him very wealthy indeed, so that his riches became legendary. But he neglected many aspects of government.

Soon after his death, his great kingdom was split in two, to form Israel and Judah.

Homer (9th century BC)
Greek poet and story-teller

Homer's life is a mystery. He is credited with two great books on the war between the Greeks and the Trojans, of the thirteenth century BC, the *Iliad* (the story of the ten years of struggle) and the *Odyssey* (the tale of the ten years of wandering of the Greek commander, Odysseus). But there is a school of thought that considers the texts to have been the result of collaboration between many poets. (The same has been said of Shakespeare's works.) Herodotus (*p. 19*) appeared quite convinced that there was a story-teller called Homer and that he lived in the 9th century. Judging from the great respect that is felt for Herodotus, it seems certainly possible that Homer, said to have been a Greek from Smyrna, did indeed collect the facts of the Trojan war (which we know from archaeological evidence was fought) and weave them into a tale which he decorated with much legendary and magical detail. Behind the stories of giants like Ajax and Achilles, there must lie some truth.

Romulus (8th century BC)
First king of Rome (753–716 BC)

Most Romans accepted that Romulus and his twin brother Remus were found as abandoned babies and suckled by a she-wolf. When they grew up they founded the city of Rome, on a hill overlooking the river Tiber, later called the Palatine Hill. As the walls were being put up round the crude huts and sheds, Remus laughed at their absurd height and showed his contempt by jumping over them. Romulus is said then to have slain his brother on the spot, and to have exclaimed that no one was to laugh at the new town.

Romulus went on to rule Rome for nearly forty years. In that time he enlarged the boundaries and took in some more fields for crops. He is said by some to have been murdered.

Sennacherib
Assyrian king (c.705–c.681 BC)

Sennacherib was a warlike king of Assyria, who carried on the national policy of conquest and dominion in the Near East. He captured the state of Sidon, invaded and sacked many towns in Judah, and defeated the Babylonians in several battles, destroying the city of Babylon in 689. Eight years later he was murdered by one of his sons, Esarhaddon. It is said that Sennacherib made many improvements to the great Assyrian capital of Nineveh.

Ashurbanipal (7th century BC)
Assyrian king (c.669–c.640 BC)

Ashurbanipal was the grandson of Sennacherib (*p. 10*). Such was his fame as a conqueror and ruler that he was known as 'King of the World'. He raised Assyria to a greatness that it had not known before, but he is especially remarkable for his great interest in, and encouragement of, more peaceful achievements. He built a splendid palace

The Greeks and the Trojans at the battle of Troy

at Nineveh. On some of the interior walls were wonderful sculptures in relief. He built a library and collected together many clay tablets, of various shapes, which contained records, poems, histories, laws and all kinds of written matter. He set up schools and he built roads and public buildings.

Towards the end of his reign (when the events were well documented on clay tablets) his empire came increasingly under attack from the Chaldeans.

Solon (c.640–c.560 BC)
Athenian lawgiver
Solon has been called the founder of democracy. In 594 he was elected chief magistrate of Athens at a time when the conditions of the poor were very bad.

Up to then the rich farmers and businessmen, who were known as aristocrats, (aristocracy means rule by the best), had had things all their own way. They even made and unmade laws to suit their own interests.

Solon determined to sweep all that away. He put an end to the system by which a debtor who could not pay became the slave of the man to whom he owed money. He re-ordered the constitution of Athens by dividing the population into four classes, each having defined rights. The most important was that members of all four could be elected to the popular assembly, which meant that more people could have a real say in government – the beginnings of democracy.

Nebuchadrezzar II (6th century BC)
Babylonian king (c.600–c.560 BC)

In the sixth century BC the ancient Babylonian empire, which had enjoyed periods of power and magnificence, followed by times of depression and conquest, once more flourished as a strong and aggressive dominion, most particularly under its great king, Nebuchadrezzar II (sometimes called Nebuchadnezzar). This interesting ruler was both conqueror and builder. He led an expedition against Egypt and defeated the pharaoh. He conquered the Hebrew kingdom of Judah and sacked Jerusalem, in about 586, sending all the leading Hebrews into captivity in Babylon. He besieged and captured the great city of Tyre. Thus he made himself the greatest ruler of the Near East of the time.

But he was not always at war. The new Babylon was to be beautiful and magnificent. So he rebuilt it, surrounding it with a huge wall several miles long. Inside, he erected the famous Hanging Gardens, which were later included as one of the Seven Wonders of the Ancient World.

Nebuchadrezzar is believed to have suffered from a curious type of mental illness, lycanthropy, which means occasionally imagining that one is a wild beast and promptly behaving like it. It is mentioned in the Book of Daniel.

Cyrus the Great (6th century BC)
First Persian king (560–529 BC)

There is always something romantic and exciting about the great Persian empire of bygone days, and none of its rulers was more fascinating than the first one, Cyrus, who built up an enormous empire and laid down excellent principles for governing it. First, he conquered many neighbouring kingdoms, Lydia, Media and then Babylon, which he overthrew in 539. In the last city he found the exiled Hebrews imprisoned by Nebuchadrezzar II (*p. 12*) half a century earlier and allowed them to go home to Judah if they so wished.

By 530, Persia was the largest empire in the world. Then Cyrus began the process of allowing the conquered regions considerable powers of self-government, which was to be a characteristic of Persian imperial policy for many generations. It was a good way to hold together an empire of greatly differing peoples and customs.

Tragically, Cyrus was killed in 529, during a skirmish with the Massagetae, a barbarous race living east of the Caspian Sea.

Pisistratus (c.590–c.527 BC)
Athenian popular leader

Solon's reforms were not allowed to remain unchallenged for long, and he was driven out by the aristocrats whose powers he had clipped. They tried to cancel much of his legislation, but the people, having had a taste of political power, decided to take matters into their own hands. They elected Pisistratus chief magistrate, calling on him to restore Solon's programme.

Pisistratus had been a successful general in the war between Athens and the city state of Megara (570–565) and when he came home he entered politics, on the side of the people. His first attempt to control the city, in 560, was thwarted despite popular support, but in 554 he was more successful, and he held power for a quarter of a century. In that time he did restore Solon's laws and he developed them. He stimulated the Athenian economy by getting the gold and silver mines working properly again, after years of disuse.

Miltiades (c.540–489 BC)
Athenian general

To Miltiades belongs the credit for the Athenians, with the help of the little city state of Plataea, defeating the great hosts of the Persian king, Darius I, at the battle of Marathon in 490 BC. This proved to be a turning point in history, for it prevented the Persians from gaining a foothold in Europe. Miltiades' life story is hardly known at all, but just before the great battle he was picked as one of the ten generals to resist Persia. And on the great day his superior tactics, his great courage and inspiration brought about the rout of the enemy.

Darius I (the Great)
Persian king (521–486 BC)
When Cyrus died, he was succeeded by his son, the gloomy and self-centred Cambyses who conquered Egypt and had himself acknowledged as pharaoh. Cambyses, as might have been expected, committed suicide (in 522). A year later, after a struggle for power, Cyrus' son-in-law, Darius, became king. This great ruler was much like Cyrus, determined to expand the empire and anxious to introduce new schemes into the government and the country. One was the construction of a long road for swift communication between the outer limits of the empire. It was called the King's Highway and it ran from Ephesus, on the West Coast of Asia Minor, to Susa in central Persia, not far north of the Persian Gulf, and it was over 2,400 kilometres long.

Darius divided his empire into twenty regions, called satrapies, which were managed by governors (satraps) usually selected from among local people. Each governor was responsible to the king, as head of the central government, but had a fair measure of self-determination. Darius kept watch on the governors, however, with a well-organized secret police.

In the 490s, Darius went to war with the Athenians because they had been helping the Ionian Greeks in Western Asia Minor to rebel. A huge army under two generals, Artaphernes and Datis, was defeated at Marathon by the Athenians in 490, under Miltiades (*p. 12*). This did not deter Darius from trying again, but on his next expedition to Greece he died.

Gautama Buddha (c.563–c.483 BC)
Indian religious teacher
This founder of one of the world's great religions, Buddhism, began life as a Nepalese prince, living in the lap of luxury. Right to the age of 30 he never had to worry about a thing. All his wants

The founder of Buddhism, Gautama Buddha

were provided for out of court funds, and for most of these years he enjoyed an idle and useless existence. Then he began to grow tired of it all, and in about 533, he decided to study philosophy and religion so as to find out how men could best use the comparatively short lives they had on this earth. He visited many scholars, some of whom told him that he should renounce all worldly pleasures and live the life of a hermit. But this was not for him.

The legends say that one day he was sitting under a pipal tree near a place called Buddh Gaya, when he had a startling vision of what he had been seeking. He had by that time collected around him a troop of followers and to them he announced that he was now completely happy. He had become 'enlightened'. Buddha actually means The Enlightened One. He now knew what men should be seeking. They should be searching for the state of inner peace and freedom from suffering, which is called Nirvana.

Buddha claimed that everybody has been alive in an earlier existence, many times, and that they will be born again, also many times. Events in a life are thus but punishments or rewards for things done in those earlier lives. Bad deeds can be wiped out by doing good deeds and by meditating, and Nirvana should in the end be reached.

Brutus, Lucius Junius (6th century BC)
First Consul of Rome

The seventh king of Rome, Tarquinius Superbus (Tarquin the Arrogant) (534–509) was so bad that a number of senators got together and drove him out, vowing never to have another king in Rome. To give effect to this they created a new structure of government. Two of their number, each year, were to be elected to the office of consul, with equal powers. The first consul was Lucius Junius Brutus, who had led the senators against Tarquin in 509. His colleague was Gaius Collatinus.

This Brutus was a very severe man. When he heard that two of his sons had been conspiring to bring Tarquin back to the throne, he ordered them to be executed. There was no mercy to be seen in his eyes as the sentence was carried out.

Pythagoras (flourished 6th century BC)
Greek mathematician

Pythagoras is, of course, renowned for his famous theorem which most school-children find hard to prove, because it is so long. But he was much more than just a geometrician. He was a brilliant thinker who settled in the Greek colony of Croton in Italy in about 530 BC and there set up an academy for colleagues to come and consider abstract subjects, such as what happens to the spirit when the body dies.

Pythagoras was deeply interested in many scientific subjects. He is said to have suggested that the earth moved round the sun, some 2,000 years before the Polish astronomer Copernicus (*p. 122*). He also demonstrated that tightening or slackening a piece of wire between two clamps varies the musical note it produces when it is plucked, and that by doing this at regular intervals, a harmonic scale is produced.

Cleisthenes (6th–5th century BC)
Athenian popular statesman

Pisistratus had been succeeded as chief magistrate by a son who proved hopelessly unworthy of so great a father. So, the popular party, dreading a restoration of aristocratic power, elected Cleisthenes as their leader. Their faith was justified, for Cleisthenes ruled well for many years. He expanded Solon's new popular assembly into a Council of Five Hundred, all of whose members were to be elected by the people, and this meant every free man. The new Council was divided for easier working into committees of fifty, which managed the government for a tenth part of the year. This arrangement was astonishingly advanced for 2,500 years ago, even for a hundred years ago: the U.K. did not grant suffrage to all men until the 1880s.

Confucius (c.551–c.480 BC)
Chinese philosopher

Confucius is the Latin rendering of the Chinese name of the great philosopher, Kung Fu Tzu, which means Philosopher King. Confucius' early years, like those of many founders of religions or beliefs, are obscured by myth. He was said to have been the ugliest boy in all China, with huge, flapping ears, a boxer's squashed nose, and sharp, protruding teeth. He was also said to have been astonishingly clever at a very young age.

In manhood, he entered the Chinese civil service and for many years followed a worthwhile career. But as he grew older he began to want to improve the quality of life among his fellow men. He did not think this should necessarily be done by a benevolent government handing out favours and gifts, but rather by men improving their way of life and their attitudes to their neighbours; in short, developing a better sense of social responsibility.

At the age of about 60 he retired from government service and set up a school of pupils whom he sought to instruct in his ideas in order to send them out into the Chinese countryside to pass on his teaching. The syllabus was a wide one: morals, family duties, social reform, and individual personal relationships. He is said not to have put many of his ideas to writing, but of course his followers did, and among the works attributed to his

The Battle of Thermopylae

teaching are the *Analects* (or *Conversations*), which are a record of his lectures.

Confucius was greatly respected in his lifetime and is the best known of the Chinese philosophers.

Leonidas
Spartan king (c.490–480 BC)
When the Persian king, Xerxes I (*p. 16*) launched his invasion of Greece in about 480, he had to go through the narrow pass at Thermopylae to chase the main Greek army retreating into central Greece. There, he found an unexpected obstacle, a picked force of some 300 Spartans noted for their cool bravery and endurance. They were led by their king, Leonidas. The Persian king ordered the front troops of his army to charge through the pass, and a desperate battle followed. Wave after wave of Persians were sent in, and were severely mauled by the Spartans. By evening time, Leonidas and all his men had been slain, but the Persians had been greatly delayed and the Greek army had been given a respite.

Euripides (5th century BC)
Greek playwright
Euripides was a contemporary of the Greek playwrights Aeschylus (*p. 17*) and Sophocles (*p. 18*), and the three of them were probably the finest dramatists of ancient Greece. Euripides had been a painter, but took up literature in later life, and he produced many plays. About twenty believed to have been written by him have survived, and these have had a profound and lasting effect on Western theatre. They include *Alcestis*, *Medea*, *Hippolytus*, *Orestes* and *Electra*, all well-known figures of Greek mythology or ancient history. These plays are notable for the skill of their plots, the drama and simplicity of their dialogue, and their tragic content.

Xerxes's bridge across the Hellespont

Xerxes I
Persian king (486–465 BC)

Son of Darius I, Xerxes determined to carry on the struggle against the rebellious (as he regarded them) Greeks. In 483 he led another huge Persian expeditionary force against Athens. To get to the mainland of European Greece, he constructed a huge bridge across the Hellespont, made of ships tied together side by side in a long row. Then he marched his armies across it and took them through Thrace and Macedonia. He defeated the Greeks under Leonidas of Sparta (*p. 15*) at Thermopylae, but his navy was almost destroyed at Salamis (480).

Xerxes left for Persia and put the army under the command of his leading general, Mardonius, who, the next year (479) was defeated and killed at Plataea. Xerxes lost interest in the war and resigned himself to bad living, neglecting the government. Eventually, his captain of the guard, Artabanes, murdered him.

Themistocles (c.527–c.460 BC)
Athenian statesman, general and admiral

Themistocles was one of the most interesting of all the Greek leaders. Brave, cunning, treacherous, skilled alike in war and in politics, he seemed a man of mystery and has baffled historians ever since his day. After the defeat at Marathon, the Persians tried again. Themistocles appreciated the very great danger, and he urged his countrymen to build a huge fleet of ships. When the Persians did attack Greece again in about 480, Themistocles persuaded the Athenian magistrates to evacuate the city, so that much of it would be saved from the kind of destruction that resistance would bring.

Meanwhile, he would lead the fleet against the Persian ships, which he did, and at Salamis he destroyed them. It was the end of the Persian danger.

After the war, Themistocles continued to badger the Athenians to keep a strong fleet ready, just in case there was a revival of Persian aggression. He also tried to get them to fortify Athens, but they would not, partly because of the growing influence of the Spartans, who were contending with Athens for the leadership of the Greek city states. Themistocles was eventually banished, and after many adventures arrived – of all places – at the court of the Persian king, Artaxerxes, who received him with honour.

Aeschylus (525–456 BC)
Greek tragic playwright
Aeschylus is believed to have fought at the battle of Marathon, and possibly at Salamis, too. After the Persian wars, he took to writing plays, all with a strong dramatic and tragic content. His plots, taken either from legend or from Greek history, are well constructed, and the drama was invariably heightened by his effective use of stage props, huge masks for the choruses, mythical beasts, and so forth. One suspects that he would have used artificial thunder and lightning and other more modern stage effects with devastating impact, had they been available to him.

Although he wrote nearly seventy works, only a handful has survived. These include the *Suppliants*, the *Seven against Thebes* and the trilogy of the *Oresteia*, which comprises the *Agamemnon*. Aeschylus was the creator of a new type of dramatic presentation that was followed by many playwrights after him.

Myron (flourished 5th century BC)
Greek sculptor
Myron is best known for his sculpture of the Discobolos, or the Discus-Thrower. This very fine action-sculpture has been copied several times, and there are replicas in the British Museum and at the Vatican.

Myron was a pupil of Ageladas, in whose classes the great Pheidias also studied.

Pheidias (flourished 5th century BC)
Greek sculptor
The age of Pericles (*p. 18*) produced many sculptors in Greece, but none is considered to have excelled the supreme craftsmanship of Pheidias. He was taught by Ageladas, and when Pericles became the first man in Athens, he commissioned Pheidias to undertake several works. One was a series of sculptures on the great Parthenon building. Another was a fine statue of Zeus, the king of the gods, at Elis.

Pheidias is believed to have got into trouble with some of Pericles' enemies and to have died in prison.

Cimon (507–449 BC)
Athenian general and statesman
Cimon was the son of the great Miltiades (*p. 12*) and he was in command of the Athenian fleet in its continuing war with Persia after the battle of Salamis (480). You will remember that Themistocles (*p. 16*) got into trouble with the Spartan element in Greece. Cimon was one of the Athenian statesmen who favoured closer links with Sparta. For a while his views prevailed, as he was one of the leading commanders, but a new political figure, Pericles (*p. 18*), began to make his name as a keen Athenian patriot who wanted Athens as leader of the city states. Although Pericles was largely responsible for Cimon's banishment, the two men were eventually reconciled.

Cincinnatus, Lucius Quinctius (c.519–c.430 BC)
Roman general
Although this great Roman soldier lived for many years, we know very little about him other than the fact that when he was nearly sixty and had retired from high office, he was called upon to save the state in the war with the Aequi. The deputation from the Senate that called upon him found him in his fields on his small farm, ploughing. They begged him to accept the office of dictator. Grudgingly, murmuring something about being retired now, Cincinnatus said he must finish the strip first. Then, as the sun set, he went back to his humble cottage, took down some arms from the wall and allowed himself to be conveyed to Rome.

There, he accepted the office on the clear understanding that it was only a temporary one. Then he put himself at the head of the army and led it to victory (458). Immediately afterwards, he resigned the dictatorship and went back to his farm. Scarcely a fortnight had passed since the deputation arrived. Several years later, he was again called upon to save the state and he crushed a rebellion at the age of 80.

Later generations used to quote his simple, direct and virtuous life as a model of how a Roman ought to be.

Pericles, the leader of a splendid age

Pericles (c.490–429 BC)
Athenian statesman

Dominating the ancient city of Athens, in Greece, is a splendid temple called the Parthenon. It stands on a hill called the Acropolis and it is a permanent memorial to the man who had it built, Pericles, the greatest of all the ancient Greek statesmen.

This much-loved man, reputedly handsome, kind, firm when necessary, courageous in battle and generous in victory, rose to power as leader of the popular party in Athens in about 460 BC. He had been elected a member of the board of commoners, which governed the state in those days. Very soon he established a reputation for high political skill, for total honesty (one could never under any circumstances bribe Pericles), and within two years he was the leading man in the government. Thus he remained for the next thirty years.

Pericles' rule was noted for its peaceful achievements, although he had perforce to go to war from time to time. The Greeks had of course been experimenting with variations of democratic government for a long time. Pericles tried to make it work still better. Elected members of the governing councils had to have their backgrounds examined to see if they were qualified to serve. All those dealing with public money were carefully watched, so that the temptation to steal or to 'fiddle' the accounts was cut down. Pericles really believed that all men were good at heart, and only needed guidance.

At the same time, Pericles was determined to make his age a splendid one, and he adorned Athens with beautiful buildings like the Parthenon. He encouraged arts of all kinds and among his many friends were the sculptor Pheidias (*p. 17*) and the playwrights Aristophanes and Sophocles (*pp. 19, 18*). He encouraged philosophers to speak their minds, however controversial they might want to be, like Socrates (*p. 19*) whose troubles only began after Pericles' death.

To the great grief of all Athenians, this splendid statesman died of the plague in 429 BC.

Sophocles (c.495–c.406 BC)
Greek tragic playwright

Sophocles' output of tragic plays was somewhat greater than that of Aeschylus (*p. 17*) but, again, only a handful has survived. Of these, *Oedipus Rex*, *Antigone*, and *Electra*, are perhaps the best known to-day.

This interesting man was a commander of the Athenian army in the time of Pericles, and he was also a great conversationalist and thinker, and counted amongst his close friends Socrates, Plato, Aristophanes and Herodotus (*pp. 19, 20*). In some ways his play construction may be said to be like that of Aeschylus, but for the most part he was an entirely original writer. He is credited with introducing, for the first time, a third actor on the stage in a single scene. Up to then, there had never been more than two, except for the chorus or silent crowds. This idea made the play move more swiftly and gave it depth.

Herodotus (flourished 5th century BC)
Greek historian

Herodotus is often called the 'Father of History'. He was an Asian Greek who travelled very widely around the known world, living for a time in Athens and finally settling in Italy, in the Greek colony of Thurii. On his travels he visited all kinds of battle scenes associated with the series of wars between the Greeks and the Persians over the years 500 to 470, and he was most probably at some of the battles like Marathon or Salamis.

When he settled, he wrote long, action-packed, detailed and always gripping accounts of the wars, which were punctuated with splendid descriptions of peoples, cities and empires. His consistent, graphic and often grand style of writing, together with his sound head for detail, rightly earned him the reputation of being the first serious historian.

Socrates (c.470–c.400 BC)
Athenian philosopher

Socrates is often said to have been the wisest man of the ancient world. After an early career as an artist, he turned to philosophy, and soon established himself as a thinker of great originality. He developed a method of inquiry and instruction which was a series of questions aimed at obtaining a clear and consistent expression of something supposed to be implicitly understood by all reasonable human beings. He was always searching for the truth, always anxious to make the complex problems of life easier to understand. In pursuit of this end he had perforce to question many accepted beliefs and conventions and this made him enemies.

While Pericles was alive, Socrates was safe, for the great statesman admired him. But after Pericles' death, Socrates' enemies began to put the pressure on to get him to revoke much of what he said. He would not do this, but continued working on what he thought needed to be questioned. Eventually, he was tried for corrupting the young and sentenced to death by drinking the deadly poison hemlock.

Aristophanes (c.450–c.385 BC)
Athenian playwright

Ancient Greece produced many first playwrights during the 5th century BC, especially in the days of Pericles. But none was so amusing and at the same time so penetrating as Aristophanes. This master of the comic play with the undertone of serious political or social criticism is said to have written more than forty works, only a quarter of which have come down to us. In these he poked fun at all kinds of people, including well-known figures like Socrates whom he counted as a friend. Much of his language was disgracefully rude to people of the time, although it was cleverly dressed in highly comical terms.

One of his plays to be frequently produced today in the twentieth century is *Lysistrata*. It is about the women of a certain Greek city who refuse to let their husbands come home to them, unless they decide to give up the whole career of soldiering for good. It is extremely funny, but it is also a lecture on the futility of war.

Camillus, Marcus Furius (flourished 4th century BC)
Roman dictator and saviour

Camillus was always revered in Roman times as one of Rome's early great heroes. It was he who saved the Capitol from the Gauls, when they invaded Rome in 390, and he prevented the Gallic leader, Brennus, from devastating the city. He also besieged the city of Veii, a dangerous neighbour, for ten years and finally captured it. And there were other occasions when he came to the rescue of Rome, by taking command and extricating Roman armies from disasters.

Camillus was created dictator at least four times in national emergency. It was an office of short duration, but which carried absolute powers while it was in being.

Although he was an aristocrat, Camillus, in his old age, in about 367, urged the senate to grant more rights and more say in the government to the common people. It is believed he died of plague in about 365.

Xenophon (c.434–c.355 BC)
Greek historian and general

Xenophon studied philosophy under the great Socrates (*p. 19*). Then he fought in Persia and reached high rank, leading an army of 10,000 Greeks back to their country. After his war service, however, Xenophon settled down to a life of serious historical writing, and he wrote an account of the Persian expedition of Cyrus the Younger, called the *Anabasis*, a history of Greece from about 400, called *Hellenica*, and a book on Socrates called *Memorabilia*. He also wrote a *Symposium*, a record of discussions with Socrates.

Plato (c.427–c.347 BC)
Athenian philosopher

Plato was the celebrated pupil of Socrates (*p. 19*). He had been born into an aristocratic family and had served in the army against the Spartans. He studied under Socrates and wrote down accounts of their discussions, which was as well, for Socrates left no works himself. When the Master, whom he loved so greatly, was put to death, Plato left Athens in disgust and travelled to many parts of the Near East, probably visiting schools of philosophy. Then he came back in 387 and founded his own school, known as the Academy, which was to develop into a university – possibly the first ever in world history.

During this time he produced a number of learned books. Perhaps the best known was *The Republic*, a dialogue (or discussion) in which his great master was represented as the leader. This book was an attempt to outline an ideal state, how best to run a government, how individuals should behave towards one another. It was not unlike the *Analects* of Confucius (*p. 14*) although it is very unlikely that Plato would have been aware of the existence of the Chinese thinker. Plato died at the age of about 80.

Alexander the Great (356–323 BC)
Macedonian ruler (336–323 BC)

The career of Alexander the Great was one of the most amazing in all history. In

Alexander the Great

ten years he expanded his small kingdom into an empire covering all the lands between Greece and India.

Alexander was the son of Philip II of Macedon, a small state in northern Greece. Philip was an aggressive ruler who warred with his neighbours and eventually conquered all Greece. Although much of his time was taken up with fighting, he did not neglect his family, and young Alexander was especially favoured by being taught by the great Aristotle (*p. 21*).

When he was twenty, in 336, Alexander became king. By that time he had accompanied his father several times in battle and had commanded detachments of the army with great skill and bravery. It was particularly noticeable how Alexander would rough it with his men, sharing their toils and discomforts, and this won their love and reverence.

Hardly had he assumed the throne

when he decided to fulfil his father's ambition to conquer Asia Minor. He assembled a huge army which he equipped with the best weapons and supplies available, and led it into Asia. In a series of breath-taking campaigns he overcame Syria, the Phoenician cities and even Egypt. When he was in Egypt he founded a new city which was called Alexandria, in 332. There he established a university, and among the earliest teachers there was the geometrician Euclid (*p. 22*).

The following year Alexander marched through Mesopotamia and down into the heart of the Persian Empire, which at the time was the biggest in the world known to the Greeks. But it was not the tough, well-organized Persia that Cyrus (*p. 12*) and Darius I (*p. 13*) had created. At Arbela, Alexander utterly routed the Persians under king Darius III. Then he expelled Darius from the throne and had himself declared king. He moved on to take many Persian cities, Babylon, Susa, Persepolis and Ectabana. To make his conquests a little more acceptable, he married a Persian princess, Roxana. Then he expelled many of Darius' officials and gave their jobs to Macedonians and other Greeks, for he was anxious not only to conquer but also to spread Greek civilization and culture in the East.

After a short respite, Alexander marshalled a fresh army and set out for India. It was his ultimate ambition to reach China, of which he had heard and wanted to know more. By the summer of 326 his advance troops had reached the banks of the river Indus and had overrun what is known now as the Punjab. Then he was brought news that rebellion had broken out back in Persia, and he left to put it down. He reached Babylon in 323, but was taken ill with a dangerous fever, possibly malaria. There was no cure and he died, aged only 33, master of the largest empire the world had yet known.

Unfortunately, Alexander had no sons, and the empire was left to his leading generals, who divided it up between them and promptly fell out with one another.

Aristotle (384–322 BC)
Greek philosopher

Aristotle's father was a doctor at the court of Philip II of Macedon. When Aristotle was about 17, he left home and set off for Athens, where he wanted to study philosophy under the great Plato (*p. 20*). He stayed in Athens for twenty years, studied all manner of subjects including biology, philosophy, mathematics and astronomy, and he also taught pupils. Then, in 342 he was invited back to Macedon to become tutor to young Alexander, Philip's son. Aristotle taught Alexander for about five years, and he inspired the young prince with his enthusiasm for wisdom and for the free expression of ideas. In 336 Alexander became king and his tutor went back to Athens. There he opened his own school of philosophy. The students used to walk about under trees, discussing this or that philosophical argument, and this led them to become known as the Peripatetics, for peripateting means walking around, in Greek.

Aristotle's basic thinking was about how to solve the problems that men actually came across in their lives. Plato, on the other hand, had been much more concerned with what man's life ought to be like. Thus, Aristotle was like a modern scientist; he looked at facts and tried to work out new ideas from those facts. This gave rise to the science of logic, or rules of reasoning. Aristotle had a profound influence upon mediaeval writers and scholars, and he is still an important influence to-day.

The Lion Capital on Asoka's Pillar at Sarnath

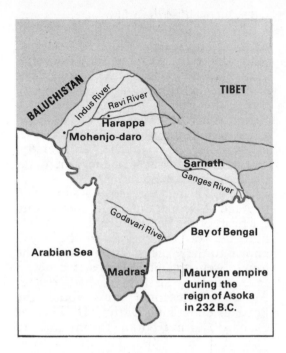

Harappa
Mohenjo-daro
Sarnath
Ganges River
Godavari River
Bay of Bengal
Arabian Sea
Madras
BALUCHISTAN
Indus River
Ravi River
TIBET
Mauryan empire during the reign of Asoka in 232 B.C.

Euclid (c.350–c.300 BC)
Greek mathematician

Most of the geometrical theorems that one has to learn at school were propounded by the Greek mathematician, Euclid. He lived for some years at Alexandria and taught scientific subjects at the new university set up there by Alexander the Great (*p. 20*). Possibly it was there that Euclid worked out his theorems, added some discovered by earlier generations, and put them all together in his series of books called *Elements*.

Praxiteles (flourished 4th century BC)
Athenian sculptor

While Pheidias (*p. 17*) is probably rightly entitled to first place in the ranks of the ancient Greek sculptors, many experts place Praxiteles a close second. It seems that the Romans, no mean judges of taste and beauty, considered him supreme for the delicacy with which he portrayed human bodies in all manner of postures. Many of their own craftsmen modelled their works on his style.

It is sad that there is only one surviving work that can be said with any probability to have been created by Praxiteles, and that is the statue of Hermes with the child Dionysus, now in the Olympia Museum.

Mencius (c.370–c.290 BC)
Chinese philosopher

Confucius may have been the greatest of the Chinese philosophers, but he was by no means the only one. After him came a succession of them, and one was Meng-Tzu (or in Latin form, Mencius). He was born in the same Chinese province as Confucius, and as a boy was taught by one of the great man's grandsons. Mencius became a teacher of Confucianism and may have written some books about the Master's ideas. He also had some of his own, one of which was that government ought to have a policy of welfare services for the poorer elements of a country.

Chandragupta I (c.340–c.286 BC)
First Mauryan emperor of India (322–297 BC)

Chandragupta I was the first emperor of the Mauryan Dynasty of rulers in India, and he ruled from about 322 to about 297 BC. As a young man he had met Alexander the Great (*p. 20*), when that magnificent world figure had led his armies as far as the river Indus. Alexander's empire broke up soon after his death in 323, and Chandragupta was one of the first eastern princes to break away from Greek dominion. In a short time he created a new empire, the Mauryan, which covered the land between the Ganges and the Indus and which included what is now Afghanistan.

Chandragupta gave his dominion strong central government. He based it on ideas taken from the Greeks, and mixed them with those more familiar to Indians. To keep the wide-spread empire under control, he used a professional army which had already proved itself in successful fighting against Seleucus, one of Alexander's heirs. Such was his fame that at the end of the fourth century, in about 300, the Greeks sent an ambassador to his court at Patna.

Chandragupta abdicated in 297 and committed suicide, presumably in a fit of depression, in 286.

Asoka (3rd century BC)
Mauryan emperor of India (273–232 BC)
Asoka was for many centuries – and is still now in some Indian circles – regarded as the greatest of all their many kings and emperors. He ruled the Mauryan Empire from about 273 to about 232. Asoka united large parts of India into an empire which corresponded to nearly all Moslem India, Pakistan and Afghanistan today. But in the effort, Asoka became increasingly sickened by the horrors of warfare. He had become devoted to Buddhism, and he longed to help all his people to know the great teacher's ideas of living. So he spent the best part of the next thirty or so years in spreading the faith, through meetings, national councils and regional discussions.

Asoka made Buddhism the state's religion, and he signalled this by engraving religious instructions on rocks and pillars in many parts of India, some of which have been found and deciphered in recent years. At the same time, he did not neglect the business of government, nor did he miss the chance of adorning his capital, Patna, or other towns, with splendid buildings. It was he who encouraged architects to construct buildings of stone so that they should last. And many of them have – up to the present day.

Pyrrhus (c.318–272 BC)
King of Epirus (Greece) (307–272 BC)
When one talks about a Pyrrhic victory it means a victory achieved only at great cost to the winners. This comes from the battle of Asculum in southern Italy at which Pyrrhus, the king of the Greek state of Epirus, defeated the Romans in 279, but said afterwards that he had never encountered such tough and brave troops. 'With men like those I could have conquered the world.'

Pyrrhus wanted to make his small kingdom a great empire, and he got involved in the war between the Greeks in Tarentum in southern Italy and the Romans. He decided to support Tarentum and at Heraclea in 280, by using a charge of elephants, he routed a Roman army and chased it off the field. When he fought them again at Asculum, they had learned how to deal with elephants. But they were nonetheless defeated, although they inflicted heavy casualties on Pyrrhus.

Regulus, Marcus Atilius (d. c.250 BC)
Roman general
Regulus was one of those splendid Roman generals who, made of the old virtues of courage, hard-work and rectitude, refused to take the easy way out in problems. In the first war with Carthage he smashed a Carthaginian fleet, invaded Africa and defeated a Carthaginian army in the field. But a year later, in 255, he was himself beaten in battle and captured.

The Carthaginians offered to let him go back home provided that he would agree to negotiate peace and then return with an exchange of prisoners. When he got to Rome, however, the Senate would not hear of peace terms. They were out to break Carthaginian power. So Regulus kept his word, went back to Carthage and said he had failed. They arrested him and tortured him to death.

Hamilcar Barca (c.270–228 BC)
Carthaginian general

Hamilcar Barca was one of the leading field commanders on the Carthaginian side in the first Carthaginian War with the Romans (264–241). He developed an intense hatred for everything Roman, and in his later years, although technically the two powers were not at war, Hamilcar made his sons Hannibal, Hasdrubal and Mago all swear eternal enmity against Rome. He was killed in Spain in 228.

Archimedes' helical screw

Archimedes (c.287–212 BC)
Greek mathematician

Archimedes is always associated with the story in which he is said to have jumped out of the bath and to have run down the streets, naked, shouting 'Eureka!', the Greek for 'I have found it!' Whether it is true or not, what he had proved was that when a solid is weighed in air and then in liquid, the apparent loss in weight in the liquid is equal to the weight of the liquid displaced. He was trying to show the king of Syracuse, Hiero, that the gold coronet he was wearing was in fact made partly from some baser metal, with a gold covering. When it was dipped in water it did not displace as much as it should if it had been all gold.

This Syracuse-born scientist introduced many other ideas. One was the helical screw for raising water from one level to another. One was a magnifying glass which directed the sun's rays on to an object and set it alight. He also devised a system of levers for moving heavy loads with little effort. And he worked out how to calculate the volume of a sphere.

Archimedes is said to have been killed during the siege of Syracuse by the Romans in 212. He had been in charge of the fortifications.

Shih Huang Ti (259–210 BC)
Chinese emperor of Ch'in dynasty (246–210 BC)

This great emperor was a man of contrast. He successfully beat off attacks on Chinese territory by barbarians from Mongolia, united the several regions of the land, and arranged the building of the Great Wall of China to keep the new nation safe from attack. This astonishing engineering feat, probably the most amazing in all world history, was accomplished between 218 and 204. It was over 2,240 kilometres long, with large, square, castellated turrets positioned regularly along its entire length. Then he built roads and canals and generally improved the condition of towns and the countryside.

But he was also a cruel man. The wall was built not so much by teams of willing workers as by gangs of cowed peasants and political prisoners. He developed a great hatred of Chinese scholars and philosophers, seeing in them implacable opponents to his ideas and ambitions to build a new imperial dynasty. So he ordered the arrest and execution of

A pottery watchdog and pleasure pavilion of early Chinese dynasties

hundreds of scholars, and to prevent others from following their ideas, he instigated the wholesale destruction of their works. This included the writings of Confucius, Mencius and many others, and up and down the land his troops built bonfires of scrolls and texts. This was a great tragedy, for many of the original works were lost and they had to be written down again from memory in later years when Huang Ti was dead.

Hasdrubal (c.245–207 BC)
Carthaginian general

Hasdrubal was one of Hamilcar Barca's sons and so brother to the great Hannibal. When Hannibal re-opened the war with Rome in 219, and marched up through Spain across the Alps and into

Italy, he left Hasdrubal in charge of the Carthaginian forces in the peninsula. Hasdrubal succeeded in keeping large numbers of Romans tied down in Spain, and this helped his brother who had crushed several Roman armies but had not brought Rome to total defeat.

In 207, Hannibal sent for Hasdrubal to bring reinforcements for another attempt to get the Romans to fight a pitched battle. On the river Metaurus, Hasdrubal was surprised by the Roman general, Tiberius Claudius Nero, and his army was utterly defeated, losing his life on the field. A messenger is said to have taken Hasdrubal's head over to Hannibal's camp and thrown it over the wall. It was the first news Hannibal had of the disaster.

Fabius Maximus, Quintus, called Cunctator (d.203 BC)
Roman general

After the Romans had suffered such catastrophic defeats at the Trebia, Lake Trasimene and at Cannae (*see Hannibal, p. 26*) in which their best generals were killed or driven off the field, the Senate gave the command to Quintus Fabius Maximus, an elderly man who had been consul in 233 and again in 228. Fabius decided that the Romans must not get involved any more in direct confrontation with the brilliant and seemingly invincible Carthaginian. Instead, they should organize raids on Hannibal's camps and on his army, when it was on the move. These delaying tactics proved successful. They exhausted Hannibal's resources while recovering from the awful losses of the campaigns of 218–216.

The Senate gave Fabius the title 'Cunctator', which means 'the delayer', and today military strategists talk about using fabian tactics when they want to describe this type of warfare.

Antiochus the Great (242–187 BC)
King of Syria (223–187 BC)

The Seleucid kingdom of Syria and its neighbouring lands had been founded by Seleucus, one of Alexander the Great's leading generals, in the late 3rd century. In 223, Seleucus' great grandson, Antiochus, had become king, and he set out on a policy of expanding the power of Syria and of resisting the more powerful nations of Europe and the Near East, namely, Rome, Parthia and Egypt. He conquered Parthia and Bactria (Afghanistan), defeated the Egyptians and even invaded Greece. But in Greece he ran up against the Romans who, after the defeat of the Macedonian king, Philip V, at Cynoscephalae in 197, had guaranteed the Greeks their independence.

Twice Antiochus took on a great Roman army, and twice he was thoroughly beaten, at Thermopylae in 191 and at Magnesia in 190. He had to give up nearly all his conquests. Two years later he was slain while plundering a sacred temple.

Hannibal (c.247–183 BC)
Carthaginian general and conqueror

The name of Hannibal is one of the best known in all history. In his time, for fifteen or more years, it struck terror in the heart of every Roman who heard it.

This very great military genius was a son of Hamilcar Barca (*p. 24*), one of the leading generals on the Carthaginian side in the first war between Rome and Carthage (264–241). As a lad, he had been compelled by his father to promise that he would fight the Romans whenever he could.

By about 220, the Carthaginians felt strong enough to renew the war with Rome, and they appointed Hannibal to command a large army and sent him to Spain. There he quickly established himself as a splendid leader of men, especially gifted in the art of surprising his enemies and, having done so, ramming home his advantage in a crushing victory. He captured Saguntum, a Roman town on the north-east coast, and immediately marched on, out of Spain and up the Alps. He had with him some 50,000 troops and fifty elephants.

Then he began to cross this cold, treacherous, formidable group of mountains. Everyone had to go on foot. It was a terrible journey. The elephants slipped and slithered down the mountain sides or into great drifts of snow, screaming and trumpeting, and by the time the army reached the plains of Italy on the other side, the animals were dead. So were thousands of men. But many thousands survived and, invigorated by a rest in the foothills, and freshly encouraged by their intrepid commander, they marched on into Italy itself. There, under superb leadership and guided by brilliant strategy, they crushed every Roman army sent against them, at the Ticinus, the Trebia and Lake Trasimene in 218, and finally at Cannae in 216 where, it is said, 80,000 Roman cavalry and infantry were destroyed. These four victories were devastatingly complete. Cannae remained one of the worst disasters ever to befall a Roman army in twelve hundred years of history.

At that point, the gates of Rome were unprotected and there were hardly enough men left to make any but a token resistance. But Hannibal's men were tired, too, and he needed reinforcements. So he did not attack. Instead, he ravaged the countryside far and wide and kept what was left of the Roman army on its toes. The Roman senate had appointed Quintus Fabius Maximus (*p. 26*) as dictator and he kept the army from fighting pitched battles with Hannibal.

After a few years of this inconclusive kind of warfare, Hannibal was called home to defend Carthage against a Roman force which had landed there from Italy under Publius Cornelius Scipio (*p. 28*). At Zama, the armies met and for the first time Hannibal was defeated. It was total surrender for Carthage.

Hannibal left Carthage and wandered about in the Near East. He had not forgotten his oath to fight Rome, and he looked around for other enemies of Rome whom he might help. He acted as adviser to Antiochus the Great (*p. 26*), who was defeated at the battle of Magnesia in 190. He then fled to Bithynia, where a few years later he took poison and died. It was a sad end for a once invincible military leader. But his fame has remained largely untarnished, for the crossing of the Alps and the succession of victories against Roman arms have seldom been equalled as achievements in world history.

Hannibal crossing the Alps

Scipio Africanus, Publius Cornelius (237–183 BC)
Roman general

Scipio was one of the most celebrated generals of Roman history. This is because he finally and decisively defeated the hitherto unbeatable Hannibal (*p. 26*) who had, more or less, done as he wanted in Italy for nearly 20 years, during the Second Carthaginian War (221–202 BC).

Scipio came from an aristocratic and military family in Rome. His ancestors had commanded armies. His father was a competent general, who was, however, defeated by the superior strategy of Hannibal at the battle of the Trebia in 218, but who beat a Carthaginian fleet the following year. Scipio entered politics in the usual way open to young aristocrats and became an aedile, which is a junior magistrate, in 212. Then he hankered after army command and was sent to Spain where he proved his worth as a leader of men. In 205 he won the consular elections and the next year he took a Roman army over to Carthaginian territory in North Africa, where he defeated all forces sent against him. This prompted the Carthage government to recall Hannibal from Italy. At Zama, in 202, the two men met in battle, and after a long and arduous fight all day the Carthaginian ranks broke up.

Scipio's peace terms for Hannibal and Carthage were on the whole reasonable and were put to Hannibal with generosity and good will. The victorious Roman then went home to a splendid triumphal reception. He was called Africanus in honour of his victory.

A few years later, Scipio accompanied his brother, Lucius, who was in command of the Roman army sent to Asia Minor to deal with Antiochus the Great (*p. 26*) and at Magnesia in 190 the two brothers utterly defeated the Syrian king and brought his power to an end.

Flamininus, Titus Quinctius (c.230–c.174 BC)
Roman general

This very able commander was remembered by Romans for two crushing victories against the Macedonians under King Philip V of Macedon in Greece, at Antigonea in 198 and at Cynoscephalae in 197. But the Greeks of that century remembered Flamininus for something else. His second victory had put an end to Macedonian dominion over the Greek states and soon after he had won it, he held a meeting in the stadium at Corinth, on the occasion of the Isthmian games for 196. Thousands of Greeks attended, and before the games began, Flamininus announced through the medium of heralds' voices that Rome guaranteed Greek independence. Almost at once a tremendous roar went up among the great surging crowd, rising to a crescendo that could be heard at sea, several miles away.

Cato the Elder, Marcus Porcius (234–149 BC)
Roman statesman

Cato the Elder was a very highly principled and austere statesman, who bitterly regretted the effect the Roman conquests in the Near East had on the character of the Roman people. From being stern, simple and hard-working people, they had been changed by the Eastern luxuries and wealth pouring into the city, into lax, pleasure-seeking spendthrifts and layabouts who were, for the most part, quite unfit to govern the vast new territories their armies had won. In the Senate he sought to get men to turn back to the old virtues, to be perhaps more like Cincinnatus (*p. 17*), and he set an example by the austerity of his own life.

Cato also developed an intense fear of Carthage. Although Hannibal had been defeated, he dreaded the resurgence of Carthage, and time after time he urged the Senate to attack and root out this menace once and for all. He ended every speech he made with the sentence 'I say Carthage ought to be destroyed,' even if it had nothing to do with the rest of the speech. He lived just long enough to witness the outbreak of the Third Carthaginian War (149–46), which actually culminated in the total destruction of the city of Carthage.

Gracchus, Tiberius Sempronius (163– 133 BC) and Gaius Sempronius (153– 121 BC)
Roman statesmen; brothers

Tiberius Gracchus and his brother Gaius were two extremely able political leaders who sought to reform the serious abuses which afflicted the central government of Rome and its provincial government machinery. Tiberius was elected tribune of the people in 133 and in his year of office he introduced a revolutionary proposal to restore land to small farmers bought up by rich city tycoons, who had grown fat on the plunder in the provinces. The proposals included a limit to the amount of land that could be held by any one person, which was an ancient law, and they also allowed for large areas to be broken into small allotments for the poor and for army veterans.

As soon as his term of office was over, his enemies in the big landlord class – and there were many – engineered a riot in which he was killed.

Ten years later his brother Gaius got himself elected tribune of the people. His programme was even more revolutionary. Not only would he fully restore his brother's laws and make them work (they had not entirely failed); he would also introduce free corn hand-outs to the poor from state granaries. He would try to extend Roman citizenship to the Latin tribes living around the city, as a reward for their loyal service in Roman armies. Gaius, in fact, wanted to alter the whole structure of government by taking power out of the hands of the aristocracy.

At the end of his term he, too, had to reckon with his enemies and was driven to commit suicide in 121.

The Gracchi brothers were grandsons of Scipio Africanus (*p. 28*).

Han Wu-Ti (c.169–c.87 BC)
Han emperor of China (140–87 BC)

Han Wu-Ti was one of the greatest emperors of the celebrated Han Dynasty in China. He ruled western China from about 140 to about 87 BC. During his reign he conquered Manchuria, Korea and parts of southern China and added them to the empire. He also re-structured the central government, curbing the powers of the landlord class by monopolizing the striking of coinage. He accepted much of the teaching of Confucius (*p. 14*), which of course made him popular with scholars and other educated people. But it was a large empire and it could only be held together by a firm and dictatorial hand.

Jade head of a horse from the Han Dynasty

Gaius Marius

Marius, Gaius (157–86 BC)
Roman general and statesman

There is always something romantic about a man from humble origins, who makes good and rises to the top position in his country. Gaius Marius, a simple farmer's son from the small town of Arpinum, rose to become the greatest general in the Roman world of his time and to be seven times consul.

Marius first saw high military command in the campaign against King Jugurtha in North Africa, 113–107. He was second-in-command to the haughty aristocrat Metellus, but he felt he could do a better job at putting an end to Jugurtha than his superior. So, while he appeared to support Metellus in the field, he kept up a barrage of correspondence with friends at Rome, saying Metellus was no good and ought to be succeeded. Eventually, the senate recalled Metellus and Marius stood for the consulship. He won it, and after his term of office he was sent to Africa to continue with the war. Jugurtha was caught, though not by Marius but by one of his senior officers, Sulla (*p. 31*).

In about 105 some barbarian tribes, notably the Cimbri and the Teutones, in central Europe, began to threaten the borders of Italy. It was a serious danger for there were well over one hundred thousand of them. Marius was elected consul to deal with the problem. What he did was to rebuild the Roman army and put it on a professional basis. Hitherto, troops were raised from the farms and the businesses of Italy and they served only for the duration of the war concerned. Marius made the army a career. Men served for a fixed term, and then retired with a gratuity. He also re-modelled the structure of the army. In five successive years he was elected consul, 104–100, and in that time he brought the army into a condition which enabled him to crush the barbarians at Aquae Sextiae in 102 and again at Vercellae in 101. These were two of the most glorious victories in all Roman history.

But though he was a brilliant commander and organizer, Marius was hopeless as a politician. Romans looked to him to re-order the state after the barbarian menace had gone, but he made one blunder after another.

In 88 he was driven out of Rome by his rival, Sulla, but returned the next year when Sulla had gone east to deal with Mithradates. Marius, by now 70, was tired and given to prolonged drinking bouts. This made him gloomy and aggressive, and filled with thoughts of revenge on Sulla and all his supporters, he went round the streets of Rome with a gang of executioners. If he nodded in the direction of a particular house, the owner was dragged out and executed. This orgy of bloodshed went on for two weeks, during which time the old man was elected consul for the seventh time. Then he caught pleurisy and died, in 86.

Sulla, Lucius Cornelius (138–78 BC)
Roman statesman and general

It is said that when Sulla was dying, he ordered that on his monument it should be inscribed 'No friend or enemy ever did anything for me that I have not repaid in full.' This cynical comment summed up his character, for he was ruthless, cruel, cold and calculating. He was also clever, forceful and methodical. His whole career, spectacular as it was, seemed geared to no end other than the brutal exercise of power for its own sake.

Sulla was one of Marius' *(p. 30)* senior officers in the war against Jugurtha and it was he who actually succeeded in capturing the African king, although Marius took the credit for it. Sulla served with Marius again in the war against the Cimbri and Teutones. At about that time, a terrible rivalry grew up between the two men and it coloured Roman politics for a generation.

Sulla was elected consul in 88. A year later he drove Marius out of Rome and then accepted the command of the army against Mithradates of Pontus. In four years he drove the Pontine king back to his kingdom and enforced his obedience to Roman dominion. When Sulla came back to Rome, he was made dictator, for matters had deteriorated badly in his absence and civil war had developed. He published long lists of those he considered his enemies, and these included many senators and members of old Roman families, numbering nearly one thousand. They were all executed and their families deprived of their rights.

Sulla then reconstructed the machinery of government by taking away the powers of the tribunes of the people. He increased the authority of the Senate. In fact he put the clock back, and the disorders that followed his rule were unavoidable. In this, perhaps more than in anything else, he showed his dreadful cynicism. He had the chance and the power to reform Roman government and cure the ills of the state, but he chose to confirm the wretched and unworkable current system.

Then, in 79, he showed this cynicism

A Roman infantryman

again when he resigned from the dictatorship and retired, to a life of vice and extravagance.

Sertorius, Quintus (d.72 BC)
Roman general and statesman

If circumstances had been different, Sertorius might well have become one of the very greatest of all Romans. As it was, his gifts were spectacular. A brilliant leader of men, a skilful negotiator, a progressive politician, he was a supporter of Marius in his quarrel with Sulla and in the 80s he took an army to Spain to continue the war against the Sullan party. For several years Sertorius defeated every army sent against him by Rome. He also created a new republic there, with its own senate and government. The native Spanish people benefitted enormously from his mild but effective rule.

Then, in about 76, he was joined by Marcus Perpenna, who claimed to be a member of the popular party in Rome, but who was really an agent of the aristocratic party which had supported Sulla. Perpenna bided his time and at the right moment had Sertorius assassinated at a banquet. It was a tragic end for a splendid Roman who could have brought order to the state.

Gladiators in the Roman arena

Spartacus (d.71 BC)
Roman slave and rebel leader

Spartacus was a slave of Thracian origin who worked in a school of slaves who were taught how to fight as gladiators in the arenas of Italy for the amusement of the Romans. In 73 he organized a rebellion of slaves in the school, and news of its success spread rapidly round the countryside. Soon, thousands and thousands of slaves had flocked to his colours and accepted his leadership. The Roman senate sent several armies against him, but he beat them all.

Then Marcus Licinius Crassus (*p. 34*) was given the command, and in 71 he defeated Spartacus in a battle in which the rebel was killed. It is said that Crassus lined the road from Rome to Capua with crucifixes, on which were hanged several thousand survivors of the battle, as a lesson to others.

Mithradates VI (c.132–63 BC)
King of Pontus (120–63 BC)
Mithradates succeeded to the throne of the kingdom of Pontus in Asia Minor, in 120, when he was only twelve. No sooner was he old enough to take over power than he did so, and began his policy of breaking up the growing Roman Empire. In 88 he occupied parts of Asia Minor that were in Roman hands. This brought the wrath of the Roman republic down on his head in the shape of Sulla (*p. 31*), who crushed him in a battle and forced him to leave the territory. But the Romans whom Sulla left behind behaved so badly that the native Asians begged Mithradates to come and help throw them out. This resulted in the Second Mithradatic war in which he was very successful. In 68, however, he was badly defeated by Lucius Licinius Lucullus (*p. 33*) at Artaxata, and again, two years later, he was beaten by Gnaeus Pompeius Magnus (*p. 34*) on the Euphrates.

Mithradates committed suicide in 63. It was an inglorious end to a remarkable career. He had been a man of some culture, who spoke over twenty languages, and had a fine collection of pictures.

Catilina, Lucius Sergius (Catiline) (c.108–62 BC)
Roman politician
Catiline was a man of high birth but low morals, who aspired to reach the highest position in the state. In 67 he was governor of North Africa, but because of his extremely expensive tastes he found he had to stoop to all sorts of corruption to raise money (as many governors did) and in doing so he brought hardships to the province. When he returned to Rome, he was prosecuted for extortion.

A year or so later, he stood for the consulship, but was defeated. To campaign he had borrowed vast sums, and now he could not pay. So he got together with some other discontented and impoverished men and plotted to murder the consuls and seize power.

His plans were betrayed to the consul Cicero (*p. 38*) who had Catiline's associates arrested. Catiline got away, but was hunted down in Etruria where he had gone to join a friend with a small gang of armed men, and in a battle in which he fought desperately, Catiline was slain.

Lucullus, Lucius Licinius (b. 2nd century BC, d. c.60 BC)
Roman general and art connoisseur
Lucullus was consul in 74. At the end of his term he went to Asia Minor in command of the army to deal with Mithradates of Pontus and his ally, Tigranes of Armenia. In a series of sound campaigns, Lucullus defeated both men several times, but he seemed unable to bring the war to an end. Worse, his aristocratic upbringing and his natural haughtiness made him very unpopular with the troops and although they were doing well in the matter of rewards in Asia they mutinied. The Senate sent Pompey (*p. 34*) out to replace him.

Lucullus returned home laden with riches and thereafter devoted his life to the pursuit of pleasure, always of a tasteful kind. He encouraged poets, artists and craftsmen. He gave magnificent feasts. He built a beautiful home and lavished money on its decoration. Later ages have used the word Lucullan to describe luxurious but tasteful living.

Catullus, Gaius Valerius (c.84–54 BC)
Roman lyric poet
This young and handsome poet wrote some of the loveliest romantic verse in the Latin language. He was a very emotional person, sad and introspective, who for some years was desperately in love with a notoriously loose-living woman, Clodia, the sister of Publius Clodius Pulcher, a Roman political agitator. Clodia did not return his love – she loved only pleasures and vice and this broke Catullus' heart.

Catullus wrote more than one hundred lyric poems, many of them addressed to 'Lesbia', his pet name for Clodia. He also wrote stingingly insulting verses about well known political figures whom he did not like. One of these was Caesar, who forgave him because he, also a man of letters, admired his lyric poetry.

A Roman nobleman's house at the time of Crassus

Crassus, Marcus Licinius (115–53 BC)
Roman financier, statesman and general

Great wealth does not always bring one happiness, and Crassus' enormous riches brought him no happiness at all. His ability to make money was natural and seemingly effortless, and yet he craved, above all else, to be liked by the masses. To this end he devoted his varied career, but he was not successful.

Crassus came from the ranks of the aristocracy, and he entered politics in the orthodox way. In the time of Sulla (*p. 31*), he proved a good general who took decisions firmly and cared for his men. It was he, rather than Pompey, who crushed the dangerous revolt of Spartacus. While he was following his career as soldier and politician, he was also building up his large fortune in property deals, trading and money lending. He did well in the proscriptions of Sulla (82), buying up properties confiscated when the owners had been executed. One of those he lent money to for many years was Caesar – in our money it amounted to over £2 million – and he got it all back with interest. This was some testimony to his faith in Caesar's potential greatness.

Crassus' wealth did not endear him to the masses, although he supported the popular party and put his riches at its disposal. Perhaps people were put off by the way he became rich. He gave several monster banquets in Rome, with seats for ten thousand a time, but while many ate and drank their fill, few were grateful.

Crassus joined Caesar and Pompey in the First Triumvirate in 60–59 BC, and in Caesar's absence in Gaul, he watched over his interests in Rome. In 54 he was given the command of a large army with which to deal with the Parthians in the Near East, but the following year he was utterly defeated at Carrhae and killed. His head was taken to the Parthian king, Orodes, who ordered molten gold to be poured down the throat.

Pompey (Gnaeus Pompeius Magnus) (106–48 BC)
Roman statesman and general

The career of Pompey was an unusual one in Roman history. Long before he was thirty, he had been saluted 'Imperator' by his troops and had been called 'the Great' by the dictator Sulla (*p. 31*) in 83. He was elected consul without having to stand for the lesser magistracies first. Then he was given exceptional powers, in 69, to clear the Mediterranean Sea of pirates, who had been crippling the trade between Rome, its colonies and its friendly commercial neighbours. No sooner was this done, than he was sent to Asia to supersede Lucullus (*p. 33*) in the war against Mithradates of Pontus, and in a series of brilliant victories, he smashed the power of the Pontine monarch, and in the process captured many cities and towns, acquiring huge quantities of booty for Rome. He also annexed Syria and Palestine for the empire. His triumph, when he returned to Rome in 61, was the most magnificent yet seen by Romans.

Pompey was extremely good-looking, bold, daring and cruel; he was also vain and politically naive. Because his military career had been so spectacular he could not grasp why politicians would not instantly do what he asked of them.

In 60, Pompey, Caesar and Crassus joined together to run affairs at Rome, and later ages called the committee the First Triumvirate (rule by three men). To cement the alliance between himself and Caesar, he married Caesar's only daughter Julia, and it was a love match.

Once Caesar had left for Gaul, the aristocratic party in the senate did all it could to try to detach Pompey from the Triumvirate, but it was unsuccessful until 54, when Julia died, thus breaking the bond between Pompey and Caesar. Added to that, Caesar's sensational military successes in Gaul and Britain had overshadowed Pompey's own military renown and he did not like it.

When Caesar left Gaul to come home, in 49, the Senate prevailed on Pompey to lead their forces against him. Thus the civil war began and Pompey took the senatorial party and its forces over to Greece. At Pharsalus, however, in 48, he was defeated by Caesar's superior generalship and his men's greater fighting qualities. Pompey fled to Egypt where he was murdered at the orders of the young Ptolemy XIII, Cleopatra's brother.

Cato, Marcus Porcius, The Younger (95–46 BC)
Roman statesman
Have you ever known anyone who always thought they were right and that everybody else was wrong if they did not agree? This great-grandson of Cato the Elder (*p. 28*) was just that kind of person. He was a lawyer of average intelligence, who entered politics as a supporter of the aristocratic party. He soon made a reputation for himself as the arbiter of what was the correct way to behave or react to this or that situation. He took violent dislikes to people, especially to Catiline, Crassus and Caesar (*pp. 33, 34, 35*). For years he opposed Caesar, during his consulship of 59, and his tenure of command in Gaul. When the Senate wanted to give Caesar a thanksgiving for his conquest of the Germans, Cato said Caesar should be handed to the Germans for them to do what they would with him.

When Caesar and Pompey went to war, Cato joined Pompey, and at Utica, in 46, he committed suicide rather than surrender to Caesar, who had just defeated the Pompeian generals at Thapsus.

Caesar, Gaius Julius (100–44 BC)
Roman dictator, general, statesman, writer, lawyer, orator, founder of the Roman Empire
That Julius Caesar was the greatest man of the ancient world few historians would deny. Many of them, moreover, rate him as the greatest man of action of all time. And when you look at his career and the magnitude of his achievements, it is not hard to see how this extraordinary man has become perhaps the best known man in history. The combination of his talents stands unparalleled: command in battle, statesmanship, oratory, writing, the law, government, friendship with his fellow men, conversation, appreciation of art, he excelled in every one. He was witty, handsome, kind, and forgiving. He had immense will power, great personal courage, and a total absence of hatred or rancour of any kind.

Caesar gave the Roman republic a system of imperial government, though it was his great nephew and adopted son, Octavian, who became its first emperor. All succeeding emperors of Rome were called Caesar. Several later empires in other parts of the world were also to call their rulers by names derived from the name Caesar, like the Czars of Russia, the Kaiser of Germany, and the Shahs of Persia. Caesar entered politics when Rome was a Mediterranean empire; by his conquest and absorption of France, Belgium and parts of Spain (Gaul and Hispania) he made it a European empire and so laid the foundations of the Western Europe we know to-day.

He was worshipped as a god in his own lifetime and when he was brutally murdered Romans believed he ascended into the heavens.

The first forty years in Caesar's life were sad times for Rome. The republican system was breaking up. Ambitious generals could threaten the city with armies and create governments of their own. Corruption and bribery were the order of the day. Caesar had not achieved much as yet, other than a magistracy or two and a command in Spain, where he demonstrated his coolness in battle, his bold leadership and his readiness to endure all the hardships he expected his men to put up with. But he learned a great deal, and he had enough experience in the Roman law courts to become the second greatest orator in the city (Cicero, *p. 38*, was the greatest), while among the political clubs he showed himself the most brilliantly clever manager of them all.

In 60 BC Caesar decided to make a bid for real power. The two leading men in the state, Pompey (*p. 34*) and Crassus (*p. 34*) were at daggers drawn. Caesar befriended them both, made them come to terms and offered to manage them as a pair as head of the government, with him as a third member of the team. Then he won an election as consul largely by his unique political skill in managing elections but also by holding the most magnificent entertainments electors had ever seen. At the end of his term of office, which had been filled with practical and necessary reforms, he was appointed to command the Roman armies in Gaul, for five years.

For two terms of office he led his men through this hitherto wild and unknown land, conquered it, invaded Britain and Germany, and brought most of the tribes under the dominion of Rome. They resisted bitterly at first, but once they were thoroughly beaten, they welcomed Roman civilization. During this time Caesar wrote a history of his campaign, and this has since been regarded as one of the best historical works to have been written by a Roman.

He came home to the Italian border to receive honour and reward for himself and his tough and loyal army, or so he thought. But instead, he was told he must disband his troops and give himself up for trial for the beneficial acts he passed when he was consul ten years before. He refused, and his troops backed him. Civil war followed, in which in a series of masterly campaigns which were not without moment of personal danger to him he crushed the opposition. He pardoned the survivors every time, probably without realizing that in so doing he was building up resentment against him. By 45 BC he was master of the Roman Empire.

Among his more constructive reforms which followed were the re-shaping of the calendar, the organization of local government, the founding of colonies, the beginning of the codification of Roman law, and the enlarging of the governing Senate so that it contained members of the provinces which had been conquered. In 44 he planned to take a huge army to Parthia in the East to deal with that continual border menace, but before he could leave he was struck down in the theatre of Pompey, on the Ides of March (15th) by the daggers of several jealous and greedy senators many of whom, ironically, owed everything, even their lives, to him. More than anyone he shaped the Europe we know today.

Caesar had felt that the one hope for the Roman state was a successive monarchy. But this meant in effect restoring the kingship, something Romans had, for centuries, been brought up to abominate. When some of them thought about it more deeply, they came to the conclusion that whatever good Caesar was to the state, as king he just was not accept-able. So they plotted to murder him. As an historian, he has never been surpassed for his simplicity, directness, and dignity.

The death of Caesar

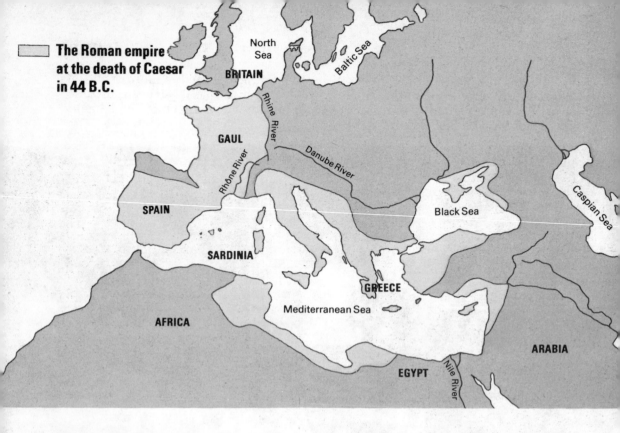

The Roman empire at the death of Caesar in 44 B.C.

North Sea
Baltic Sea
BRITAIN
Rhine River
GAUL
Danube River
Rhône River
SPAIN
Black Sea
Caspian Sea
SARDINIA
GREECE
Mediterranean Sea
AFRICA
ARABIA
EGYPT
Nile River

Vercingetorix (mid 1st century BC)
Gallic chief

Vercingetorix – the very name rings of courage and daring leadership – was chief of the Arverni tribe of Gauls. By about 53 BC, Caesar had more or less completed his conquest of Gaul, but in that year the Arverni tribe rose in revolt against Roman dominion. They were led by their fiery young chief, Vercingetorix, who was already known among Gauls for bravery and for the iron discipline with which he controlled his troops.

By 52, many of the beaten tribes rose in his support and he assembled a huge army with which to confront Caesar. The great Roman surrounded Vercingetorix with a series of huge earthwork fortifications around the Arverni town of Alesia and besieged it. Vercingetorix eventually surrendered and the revolt was over. Gaul was pacified and became a Roman province.

According to custom, Caesar sent Vercingetorix to Rome in chains, where he languished in prison until Caesar could exhibit him at his triumph, which he did in 46.

Cicero, Marcus Tullius (106–43 BC)
Roman statesman and orator

Cicero was born in the town of Arpinum and he rose in his time to be consul in Rome and the greatest orator of Roman history. He had many gifts, but he also had fatal flaws to his character, for he was vain, stubborn and often very naive.

He came of humble parents, but he had a quick mind and soon got to the top of his profession as a lawyer, helped of course by his marvellous powers of oratory which he cultivated by studying for some time on the island of Rhodes, where the world's leading tutor of oratory, Apollonius Molo, resided. Cicero's rise to fame brought him in contact with the leading men of the day. For a while he was glad to join the more revolutionary elements in politics, but deep down he had a devotion to the aristocracy, even though most of its members had shown themselves corrupt, inefficient and incapable of governing.

In 64 he was elected consul and he crushed a revolt against the government led by Catiline (*p. 33*). Cicero believed the revolt – and his prompt suppression of it – to be more important than it really was, and thereafter he continually boasted about how he saved the state.

Cicero was a close friend of Caesar because they had a common interest in poetry, oratory and literature, but he could not bring himself to support Caesar's schemes to rebuild the state. When Caesar was murdered, Cicero declared the deed a glorious one, which it was not. But he also said that Caesar never forgot anything, except an injury – a generous remark.

Cicero was executed by Octavian (*Augustus, p. 42*) after the battle of Philippi.

Brutus, Marcus Junius (c.85–42 BC)
Roman politician

This moody, thoughtful and humourless aristocrat was the son of one of Julius Caesar's favourite mistresses, Servilia, and her husband. It was often said that he was Caesar's illegitimate boy, but there is no evidence of this, except that Caesar was extremely fond of him and gave him all sorts of promotions and favours.

Brutus was said to have been descended from that Lucius Junius Brutus (*p. 14*) who expelled the last king, Tarquin, from Rome in 509. Certainly, young Brutus grew up to be a staunch republican, ready to overlook the obvious failings of the republican system of government. He married Porcia, the daughter of Cato the Younger (*p. 35*) and so it was little wonder that while he felt great affection for Caesar, he nonetheless disapproved of all that the great man stood for.

When Gaius Cassius Longinus and other discontented Roman senators, all of whom had good reason to be grateful to Caesar, plotted his death because they thought he was going to restore the monarchy, Brutus at first refused to join the plot. But they worked on his historic connection with the first Brutus and soon he convinced himself that he must sacrifice his benefactor for his idea of how Rome should be governed. When he plunged his dagger into Caesar's breast, on 15 March 44 BC, it was, as Shakespeare's Mark Antony said, 'the most unkindest cut of all.'

Brutus and the others paid the price of their crass folly and treachery, when they were defeated at Philippi in 42. Brutus fell upon his own sword, probably regretting his part in the terrible deed.

Mark Antony (Antonius, Marcus) (83–30 BC)
Roman statesman and general

One of the most famous names of Roman history, Mark Antony, was Caesar's friend, and he was also Cleopatra's lover. This boisterous, good-natured, handsome, devil-may-care Roman was a mixture of talents and defects. He was a good general, an excellent second-in-command, popular with his men; a fiery and bold politician who did not mind what he said. But he was in some ways unpredictable. Caesar more than once had to rebuke him for getting above himself, and yet no man adored Caesar more.

Antony attached himself to Caesar's cause in about 54 BC, and the great man helped him to win several important magistracies.

When Julius was murdered, it was Antony who harangued the stunned populace in Rome and urged them to get their revenge on the conspirators. Then he joined forces with Caesar's great-nephew and heir Octavian (later Augustus, *p. 42*) and Lepidus and formed the Second Triumvirate to divide the Roman world between them and govern it. Antony was allotted the eastern provinces.

One of these was Egypt and in about 40 he met Cleopatra again and this time fell to her charms, although he had only just married another woman. Soon he and Cleopatra were living together and ruling Egypt jointly. This made him neglect the other provinces, and when he did stir himself to go to war with the Parthians, he was defeated.

Octavian was concerned about the gradual crumbling of order in the east and he dismissed Antony. War followed, in which Antony was crushed at the great battle of Actium in 31. All was lost and he committed suicide.

Antony and Cleopatra on a barge on the Nile

Cleopatra (c.69–30 BC)
Queen of Egypt (51–30 BC)

Cleopatra was the daughter of Ptolemy XI of Egypt. She succeeded as queen in 51, sharing the throne with her brother, Ptolemy XIII. She has been described as beautiful, but from known portraits it is clear that she was not. Men were more attracted by her strong and lively personality and her wits.

She and her brother quarrelled incessantly and eventually he drove her out of Egypt. At this time, Egypt was a kingdom under Roman protection and was a main source of grain for the Roman people. Caesar came to Egypt after the defeat of Pompey at Pharsalus in 48 and arrived to find the civil war still going on. Cleopatra was trying to make a comeback and she had herself smuggled into Caesar's presence, rolled up in a carpet, it was said, so that she could appeal to him for help in her cause. She won him over, whether by her charms or by the obvious logic that she would be a better ruler than her brother, one cannot say. Caesar helped her to defeat Ptolemy, who was drowned at the end of a battle.

Cleopatra ruled for some years. In about 40, her kingdom was part of the allotment of the empire given to Mark Antony (*p. 39*) when he, Octavian and Lepidus shared the Roman world after the murder of Julius Caesar. Cleopatra and Antony became lovers. Their liaison caused him to lose favour in Rome.

Antony was eventually defeated by Octavian at Actium in 31 and committed suicide. When Cleopatra heard, she poisoned herself.

Virgil (Publius Vergilius Maro) (70–19 BC)
Roman poet

Virgil was another Latin poet who enjoyed the patronage of Maecenas (*p. 41*), and who endeared himself to Augustus. His kind of verse was different from that of Horace (*p. 41*), for it was often written in long, ballad lengths, and in what is called heroic language. One of his most remarkable works was a long narrative poem, called by us today the *Aeneid*. This was the imaginary story of the wanderings of Prince Aeneas, one of the sons of Priam, King of Troy. Aeneas escaped from the holocaust of the fall of Troy in about 1200 BC and came to Italy to found, it was said, what we now know as the Latin race.

Virgil also described in some detail the life of a peasant farmer in Italy of his time, in a series of poems known as the *Georgics*.

Agrippa, Marcus Vipsanius (63–12 BC)
Roman general and statesman

In his own way, Agrippa was one of the most wonderful men of Roman history. He was one of those very rare individuals who have many first rate qualities, but who are prepared to devote them solely to the advancement of their fellow men, with no thought of being the 'boss'.

Agrippa made Augustus (*p. 42*) what he later became – absolute and supreme head of the Roman state. This he did by staying tactfully in the background at the right times, pushing his friend forward, guiding him and taking on many arduous jobs, like running the government. He also led Roman navies very successfully into sea battles and destroyed the fleet of Antony (*p. 39*) and Cleopatra (*p. 40*) at Actium in 31.

Agrippa came from comparatively humble beginnings, and he rose to the highest ranks of government almost entirely by his love of hard work and his great organizing genius. For about ten years, 23–12 BC he was chief minister to Augustus, and in that time he never once was heard to say that he wanted his friend's position as Emperor, or that he could do it better himself. The success of Augustus' long and peaceful reign was largely due to Agrippa.

Maecenas, Gaius (c.70–8 BC)
Roman statesman

Maecenas was a statesman friend of young Octavius, who became the Emperor Augustus (*p. 42*). He looked after affairs in Rome while Octavius and Agrippa were fighting Pompey the Younger, the son of Pompey the Great (*p. 34*). And after Octavius and Agrippa had beaten Antony and Cleopatra's forces at Actium in 31, Maecenas persuaded Octavius to assume the rank of emperor. He did not at first, for he became Princeps, which really meant first among equals, but when he accepted the title Augustus, which meant 'revered', he was in fact becoming emperor, something his great uncle Julius Caesar had considered.

Maecenas made a lot of money in his career, and when he was about 50, he retired to private life, continuing to patronize artists, poets and writers. All the same, he was always ready to give Augustus his advice if it was sought.

Horace (Quintus Horatius Flaccus) (65–8 BC)
Roman poet

'I loathe the uneducated man in the street and keep him at a distance.' So runs the translation of the opening line of one of the most famous poems written by the Latin poet, Horace. He had evidently forgotten his own very humble origins, for he was the son of a freed slave!

Horace did remarkably well in his career. At about 23, he was in command of a detachment of the army of Brutus (*p. 39*) and Cassius, who were defeated by Antony (*p. 39*) at Philippi in 42 BC. Despite this, he was received back in Rome, where he was patronized by Maecenas (*p. 41*) and later introduced to Augustus. The Emperor enjoyed his verses, many of which were satirical, often extremely funny.

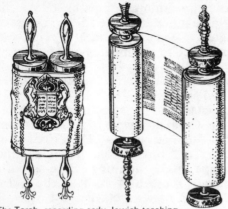

The Torah, recording early Jewish teaching

Hillel (1st century BC)
Jewish teacher and legal authority

Hillel was a Hebrew teacher who came to Palestine from the Babylonian Jewish community. In about 30 BC he was elected head of the Jewish council of advisers to the Pharisees. A man of magnetic personality, a wise thinker, and endowed with great personal courage, Hillel soon came to dominate Jewish thinking of the time. He aimed to give the Jews an enduring code of laws, for up to then their law had become a jumble of statutes and sayings of elders and judges. So he had the laws written down, stating that this code was supreme. All other laws were to be based upon the supreme code.

Hillel's code became the basis of all future Hebrew law-making. It also influenced very greatly the teaching of Jesus Christ (*p. 44*).

Augustus Caesar (Gaius Octavius) (63 BC–14 AD)
First emperor of Rome (27 BC–14 AD)

Gaius Octavius was born in 63 BC, the son of Octavius and of Atia, who was the daughter of Julius Caesar's sister, Julia. As a boy he was sickly and delicate; he was also moody, cruel and not very brave. But he had an excellent brain and did not mind hard work. When he was in his teens, his great uncle (*p. 35*), then master of the Roman world, watched his growth with interest, for he had it in his mind that young Octavius might one day inherit his power.

In 45 Julius formally adopted Octavius, who became known as Gaius Julius Caesar Octavianus. He also made Octavian principal heir to his will. When the great man was assassinated in 44, Octavian was away in Greece. He came back to Rome to sort out his great uncle's will, and soon joined up with Mark Antony (*p. 39*) to defeat Julius' murderers at the battle of Philippi, in 42.

After this, Octavian, Antony, and another friend of Julius, Marcus Aemilius Lepidus, formed the Second Triumvirate, divided the huge Roman world between them and ruled together. For a while the arrangement worked. Then Lepidus retired. Antony, meanwhile, had been neglecting his duties, and eventually he and Octavian went to war. At Actium Octavian and his great friend, M. Agrippa (*p. 41*), defeated Mark Antony in 31. Octavian became master of the Roman world.

The Roman world was tired of war. It longed for stable government, order and prosperity, all of which Julius Caesar was beginning to give to it when he was murdered. So Octavian set out to complete his great uncle's work and to modify it with his own ideas, together with ideas from colleagues like Agrippa (*p. 41*), Maecenas (*p. 41*) and, later, Tiberius (*p. 46*). In 27, Octavian was offered the title Princeps, which meant first man in the state. It was a good compromise. It did not say 'King' or 'dictator' (although that is of course what it really meant), for those words were not really liked by Romans. Julius was in fact finally murdered partly because he was thought to be planning to have himself declared 'King'.

Octavian also took the title 'Augustus', which means 'revered', and from that time onwards that is how he was known, as Augustus Caesar.

Over the next forty years Augustus brought the stability that Romans yearned for, strengthened the boundaries of the empire and provided an age of peace in which trade, industry, art and literature flourished. He did much to make Rome beautiful, coming, as he

Cameo of Augustus Caesar by Dioscorides

Germanicus Caesar (15 BC–19 AD)
Roman general

Germanicus Caesar was the son of Drusus, Livia's elder son (*p. 44*). He became one of the most popular military commanders of his time, possibly of all Roman history. Tall, extremely good looking, brave as a lion, a brilliant strategist and a great leader of men, Germanicus proved himself a top class army general before he was thirty.

In 16 AD he completely defeated the German chief Arminius who, seven years earlier, had crushed the Romans under Varus and captured their precious eagle standards.

When Germanicus came home, he found that his uncle Tiberius (*p. 46*) was extremely jealous of his military gains, and he was sent out East to Syria. There he died under mysterious circumstances, but most Romans believed he had been poisoned by the orders of The Emperor Tiberius.

Germanicus was the father of the emperor Gaius (Caligula) (*p. 47*).

Wang Mang (33 BC–23 AD)
Chinese emperor (9–23 AD)

Wang Mang was born in about 33 BC. He was the nephew of Yuan T'i, who had been Han Emperor from 48 to 32, and by the end of the first century, Wang was in a strong position in the counsels of the emperors. In about 9 AD, the year that Varus, the Roman general, was defeated and killed in Germany by Arminius, Wang seized power, offering the Chinese a revolutionary programme of reform. This included restructuring the system of tax raising, nationalizing all land and distributing it on a fair basis to peasants, fixing prices and incomes, and curbing monopolies of business and trade. He made loans available to farmers to improve their holdings. It was about as revolutionary a programme as any offered by a 20th century socialist party, but it was 1,900 years too early.

Strange to relate, many people of all classes, including those who stood to benefit most, were frightened by the radicalism of his reforms and they rebelled. In 23 AD Wang was assassinated.

said, to the city of brick and leaving it clad in marble. People looked back to the Augustan Age with pride, but without undervaluing his achievement, it is necessary to remember that without the career of Julius Caesar, the life work of Augustus would not have been possible.

Livy (Titus Livius) (59 BC–17 AD)
Roman historian

Livy was very fortunate to get noticed by Octavian (Augustus, *p. 42*), who became the first emperor of Rome. Octavian patronized him and encouraged him to get on with an enormous project, a full history of the Roman people, from the foundation of the city in 753, to the year 9 BC. This remarkable work apparently filled one hundred and forty two volumes, of which only thirty four have survived in their complete texts. Fortunately, however, Livy also wrote digests of each of the one hundred and forty two books and so we do have an idea of the scope of this vast and invaluable work.

Livia Drusilla (c.56 BC–29 AD)
Roman empress
Livia was the wife of Augustus (*p. 42*). She had previously been married to Tiberius Claudius Nero, a Roman senator of ancient family, and their son, Tiberius, was to succeed Augustus as Emperor in 14 AD.

Livia was almost literally taken away from her husband by Augustus, who fell violently in love with her and virtually ordered Tiberius Claudius to divorce her. This was surprising, for by all accounts Livia was not beautiful. She was rather handsome in a matronly sort of way, and she was also very bossy. Perhaps Augustus wanted to be dominated by his wife. In the earlier years of their long marriage, she played an important part in the running of the state. But when it became clear that she was pushing her two sons by Tiberius Claudius, Drusus and Tiberius, up to the front, Augustus, no doubt egged on by enemies of Livia, tried to cut down her influence in state affairs.

However, when Augustus died and Tiberius, her son, did after all succeed, Livia acted for a while as one of his principal advisers.

Jesus Christ (?4 BC–?33 AD)
Jewish religious leader
Jesus of Nazareth was born at the end of the reign of Herod the Great, King of Judah (37–4 BC). Christians believe that he was the son of God. In his youth he discovered that he had certain healing powers which occasionally he used to alleviate illnesses. He also studied Hebrew law and learnt about many Jewish writings, including the works of Hillel (*p. 42*).

When he was about thirty, Jesus decided to give up his job as a carpenter, and set out to preach and to heal. Before long he had a following, and as it grew he began to organize a band of the leading men. These he regarded as his disciples, and it was their job to manage the meetings at which Jesus preached or healed.

Jesus' message was a simple one, based on the brotherhood of man. However, it was not in accordance with strict Hebrew doctrine. The Sadducees, then the ruling party in Palestine, objected to his teachings and they cast doubts on his healing powers. So they summoned a meeting and put Jesus on trial. They had already secured the agreement of the Roman governor, Pontius Pilate, who above all wanted peace and quiet in this trouble-ridden Roman province.

Pilate allowed the Jews to crucify Jesus for blasphemy (which is really saying that they punished him for disagreeing with them). His death did not affect many at the time, except his followers, but within twenty-five years his teachings were being spread all around the Roman world, albeit secretly, because the Roman government had prohibited Christianity in any form. Much of this teaching was due to the Cilician tent-maker, Saul, who changed his name to Paul and devoted his life to building up a new faith, that of Christianity (*p. 44*).

St. Peter (1st century AD)
Jewish disciple of Jesus Christ
St. Peter was one of the original twelve disciples of Jesus Christ (*p. 44*). Not long before he was put to death, Jesus Christ had said that Peter would become the first of the twelve to go out and spread his teachings abroad. And so, not long after Jesus' death, Peter began to preach all around Palestine, saying that Jesus was not dead at all, but was waiting to come back to earth in glory.

Several times Peter was arrested by the authorities for disturbing the peace, but he escaped, and continued to spread the gospel, though he kept it among the Jews.

There is a belief that he eventually finished up in Rome with Paul, and that he was crucified there after the fire by the imperial guards.

St. Paul (1st century AD)
Jewish religious leader and Christian saint
St. Paul began life as a Hebrew, born in Tarsas in Cilicia, and called Saul. He became a tent-maker, but he was also interested in teaching Jewish law, and

The birth of Christ

soon acquired a reputation as a tough opponent of all those who were not strict Hebrews. Consequently, he persecuted Christians, a new sect which had broken away from the main Hebrew religion and followed the doctrines taught by Jesus Christ (*p. 44*).

But one day, he announced that he had been struck down on the road to Damascus by the Christian God, who said he must give the rest of his life to spreading Christianity far and wide beyond the borders of Palestine. Saul was converted to the new faith, met some of the original disciples of Jesus, including Peter, and changed his name to Paul. Then he soon became one of the most enthusiastic supporters of the faith. In the next years he made numerous voyages around the Roman world, preaching and writing about the new religion, founding new churches, and gradually persuading men to accept that they were all equal.

When Rome was disastrously burned in the great fire of 64, while Paul was on a visit there, the Emperor Nero blamed the Christians and had many of them put to terrible deaths. They were mauled by lions and gladiators in the arena. It is thought that Paul was one of the victims.

Boadicea leading her Celtic troops into battle

Tiberius (Tiberius Claudius Nero Caesar) (42 BC–37 AD)
Roman emperor (14–37 AD)

Tiberius was the step-son of Augustus (*p. 42*). He was a sour, sad-faced man, mean, cruel, humourless and suspicious by nature. But he was also an excellent administrator and commander of troops in battle, and Augustus was glad enough to give him several important commissions. In about 4 AD, Augustus officially recognized him as his heir to the imperial throne.

Augustus died in 14 and Tiberius succeeded him. It was a hard job to follow in the footsteps of one who had become revered throughout the Roman world, but at first Tiberius governed wisely and with tolerance. Then, as he got older, his natural disposition to be gloomy grew worse, and so did his suspicious nature. Soon he began to think that everyone was plotting against him, and he retaliated by having all sorts of people arrested and imprisoned or put to death, without cause or trial. 'Let them hate me,' he used to say, 'so long as they fear me.'

In 27 he retired from Rome to live out the last ten years of his reign in the island of Capri where, according to the historians, he followed a life of debauchery and vice.

Boadicea (1st century AD)
British (Celtic) queen

When Britain was invaded by Aulus Plautius in 43 AD, the king of the Iceni, (from what is now East Anglia) Prasutagus accepted the sovereignty of Rome and ruled in peace. Prasutagus died in 60, and the Romans took over his kingdom. It appears that in the process they insulted and ill treated his widow, Boadicea, a fine looking Celtic woman of tremendous spirit and courage.

A little while later, the main Roman army moved westwards, in order to conquer Wales. Boadicea took advantage of their departure to stir up a national revolt of Celtic Britons. Support came swiftly, and in 61 she was strong enough to descend upon the Roman garrison towns of Camulodunum (Colchester) and Verulamium (St. Albans) where her troops slaughtered the inhabitants and burned down the buildings.

The Roman governor, Suetonius Paulinus, heard about the rising, marched swiftly back from Wales and surprised Boadicea in a battle somewhere in the East Midlands. Her people fought with stubborn bravery, and she did especially, but were completely overcome by superior Roman discipline and scattered.

Boadicea took poison and died almost at once.

Caligula (Gaius Caesar) (12–41 AD)
Roman emperor (37–41 AD)
Caligula is the Latin for little boot. When Gaius Caesar was a young boy, his father, Germanicus (*p. 43*), used to take him to the wars and dress him up in miniature uniform – hence the nickname. But no sooner had Gaius succeeded his uncle Tiberius (*p. 46*) as Emperor in 37, than he showed himself to be a cruel and insane tyrant of the worst kind. The affection felt for the little boy in army boots turned quickly to hate and fear.

For four years this madman ruled Rome absolutely. At the slightest whim he would order someone or other, no matter how senior, how respected, and most of all how innocent of any crime, to be put to death for no better reason than that he enjoyed the power to give such orders at will. 'Make him feel he is dying,' was one familiar cry Caligula would utter, as some unfortunate man or other was tortured to death before his eyes.

His madness was so extreme that he is said to have created his favourite horse, Incitatus, consul, for the year 41. By that time, he had made enemies everywhere. One was Cassius Chaerea, commander of his bodyguard, and this rough old soldier stabbed the Emperor to death during a session of the gladiatorial games in 41 AD.

Claudius (Tiberius Claudius Drusus Nero Germanicus) (10 BC–54 AD)
Roman emperor (41–54 AD)
Claudius was the brother of Germanicus (*p. 43*) and so uncle to the tyrant Caligula (*p. 47*). He was reported to have been born somewhat deformed, with a limp, a stutter and a twitch. If he did have such disabilities, they may have saved his life,

for he was the butt of his nephew's jokes and taunts. Caligula, who was quite capable of ordering his uncle's death, may have spared him because of his apparent uselessness. But when Caligula died and was hardly cold, the troops in Rome declared Claudius Emperor.

One of the first achievements of Claudius' reign was the conquest of Britain. The Emperor himself visited Britain in about 44.

Claudius was a scholar, and he was also a builder. In fact the aqueduct he erected in Rome is still partially standing. He also enlarged the harbour at Ostia and made it into a major port, a project already planned nearly 90 years earlier by Julius Caesar.

Claudius had very little luck with his wives. The first, Urgunilla, was tall and hideous. The second, Messalina, betrayed him and committed adultery with many senators, and the third, his niece, Agrippina, poisoned him, in 54.

Agrippina (The Younger) (c.15–59 AD)
Roman empress
Agrippina the Younger was the daughter of Germanicus (*p. 43*) and his wife, the virtuous and beautiful Agrippina the Elder, who was the daughter of Agrippa (*p. 41*) and of Augustus' daughter, Julia. Agrippina the Younger was thus the sister of Caligula (*p. 47*) and it is now thought that she was in many ways like him, cruel and unpredictable.

She married first a Roman aristocrat, Domitius Ahenobarbus, by whom she had a son, later called Nero (*p. 48*). Her third husband was her father Germanicus' younger brother, Claudius, who was emperor of Rome from 41 to 54. From the start, she set out to humiliate Claudius and to advance the claims of her son, Nero, as heir, against Claudius' own son, Britannicus. When Claudius died in 54, it was believed by most that she had poisoned him.

Nero became emperor, but very soon showed his mother that he was not going to have her bossing him about. He made several attempts to murder her, and in 59 one such effort was successful.

Nero, (Nero Claudius Caesar Drusus Germanicus) (37–68 AD)
Roman emperor (54–68 AD)

Nero was the son of Agrippina the Younger (*p. 47*), and the stepson of Emperor Claudius. As a boy he had been brought up by the great philosopher and statesman, Lucius Annaeus Seneca, who managed to exert a good influence on him. And when in 54 Nero, aged 17, became Emperor, Seneca became his principal adviser. Another steady influence was Sextus Afranius Burrus, commander of the imperial guard. For a few years these two men managed to keep Nero more or less in control of his vicious and insane passions.

In 59, however, Nero succeeded in having his mother murdered, for he resented her advice. Then he murdered his wife, Poppaea by kicking her when she was pregnant. After that, his self control collapsed altogether and he spent the remainder of his reign behaving as wildly as Caligula (*p. 46*). He took part in games and theatrical performances in the circus at Rome. He had innocent people put to death, so that he could confiscate their wealth to help pay for the extravagant way of life he was all the while pursuing.

Then in 64, a disastrous fire broke out in Rome which, after raging non-stop for a week, burned down over half the entire city. Nero was credited with having started it, and it was even said that he played the lyre while watching the flames. There is evidence, however, that in fact he did much to help control the conflagration.

In 68, some of his generals rebelled against him and he was driven out of Rome. On the way, he committed suicide.

Vespasianus, Titus Flavius Sabinus (9–79 AD)
Roman emperor (69–79) AD)

Vespasian was one of the better Roman emperors. Despite humble beginnings, he had held most of the usual offices like aedile and praetor. When the Emperor Claudius ordered the conquest of Britain, Vespasian accompanied the expedition, and he conquered and brought the Isle of Wight (Vectis) under Roman rule. In

Nero reputedly started the fire which ravaged Rome for over a week in 64 A.D.

64 he was governor in Africa, and three years later he was sent to Palestine to deal with the Hebrews, who were in revolt.

Vespasian reached Antioch in Syria and marched down through Palestine. Early in 68 he captured Jericho and by the summer he was in control of the whole countryside, except for Jerusalem. At this point he heard that the emperor Nero had committed suicide after a revolt. One general after another tried to seize the imperial dignity. Then he heard that most Romans wanted him as Emperor, so he returned to Italy and there defeated the last rival, Vitellius.

As Emperor, Vespasian ruled well, earning a reputation for being mean with money. But this was not a bad thing, for his predecessors had one after the other squandered fortunes and almost bankrupted the state treasury. He had a great sense of humour. As he lay dying, he suddenly stood up and cried out, 'An emperor should die on his feet.' A few minutes later he gasped, 'Dear me! I think I am turning into a god!' and dropped dead.

Vitruvius Pollio, Marcus (1st century AD)
Roman architect
Vitruvius was a Roman architect and engineer, who flourished in the early years of the first century AD. We know little about him, but his great work, *De Architectura*, written in ten books, tells us a lot about the principles of design and building that governed Roman engineers and constructors. He is thought to have been given an important post in the household of the Emperor Augustus.

Vitruvius' designs for buildings were lost to the world for many centuries, but were re-discovered in some form during the Renaissance, and they guided European architects for many years.

Plinius Secundus, Gaius (The Younger) (62–113 AD)
Roman statesman
Pliny was a statesman who flourished during the splendid reign of the Emperor Trajan (98–117). He was the nephew of another Pliny, called the Elder, who wrote about many historical, scientific and natural things, and who died during the great eruption of Vesuvius in 79, which completely enveloped Pompeii in lava and dust. He was trying to observe how the volcano worked when he was caught off his guard.

Pliny the Younger became governor of the province of Bithynia in about 111. During this time he kept up a lengthy correspondence with the Emperor Trajan, much of which has survived and which throws a fascinating light on many aspects of Roman life and provincial government. One letter also mentioned Christians and Trajan replied to this one by saying that Pliny was not to persecute them, providing they were willing to give up believing that their God was superior to the Emperor of Rome.

Trajan (Trajanus, Marcus Ulpius) (52–117 AD)
Roman emperor (98–117 AD)
Marcus Ulpius Trajanus was a bold general, hard-working and able statesman, patient and kindly father of his people, tolerant and interested in many things outside his own particular capabilities. Even the elaborate name conjures up a picture of this great Emperor of Rome. Trajan had attracted the attention of the Emperor Nerva who, as he had no son, adopted him, confident that Trajan would prove a good ruler. His faith could not have been better justified.

Trajan guaranteed the safety of the imperial boundaries by crushing enemies along the borders, including the Parthians, the Germans and the Dacians. At home he worked for prosperity in the empire. He restored the power of the Senate by giving the members more work to do and more say in the administration of the government. The national finances were run properly, and cuts in expenditure were achieved by Trajan setting an example himself at his own court.

Finally, he selected as heir Hadrian (*p. 50*), who proved to be a remarkable man.

Part of Hadrian's wall which ran from the river Tyne in Northumberland to the Solway Firth

Tacitus, Cornelius (c.55–c.117 AD)
Roman politician and historian

Tacitus was one of the most distinguished of all Roman historians. He had had a full career as statesman and army commander, and he was also the son-in-law of the great Julius Agricola, governor of Britain, who defeated the Picts in Scotland and nearly led an expedition to Ireland. This put him in a good position to write detailed histories of the various peoples against whom Rome fought in his time.

Tacitus' main works were his *Histories*, an account of the political, domestic and military affairs of the Emperors from Galba (68 AD) to Domitian (81–96), his *Germania*, which was about the German tribes and their neighbours, and finally the life of his father-in-law, Agricola. This gives a good picture of Britain towards the end of the 1st century AD.

Hadrian (Hadrianus, Publius Aelius) (76–138 AD)
Roman emperor (117–138 AD)

Hadrian is famous most of all for the great wall he had built from the mouth of the river Tyne in Northumberland to the Solway Firth, creating a strong barrier between what was then (in 122 AD) Britain and Caledonia. But he achieved much more than that.

Hadrian was the nephew of the splendid emperor Trajan (*p. 49*), and by the time he succeeded his uncle in 117, he had experienced many years of high command.

One of the first things he did was to contract the eastern boundaries of the empire set by Trajan, largely because he felt this would make it easier to police the borders. He also travelled throughout the whole of his dominions and was one of the very few Roman rulers to do so. On his prolonged journeying he relieved grievances, confirmed statutes and privileges, founded buildings and towns, and generally showed the huge, many tongued nationalities of the empire that their emperor cared about them.

In Rome itself he added many fine buildings, including the Hadrian Mausoleum (known now as the Castel Sant' Angelo) and the Aelian bridge.

Antoninus Pius (86–161 AD)
Roman emperor (138–161 AD)

Titus Aurelius Fulvus Boionius Arrius was of a Gallic family. He rose through the ranks to become governor of Asia and in 138 was adopted by the emperor Hadrian (*p. 50*). Hadrian then died almost at once and Titus succeeded him, taking the name Antoninus.

His reign was a peaceful and interesting one, in which the arts, literature, trade and building all flourished under his encouragement and patronage. The only real trouble he had was with the Picts in Scotland (then northern Britain) and he had a huge earthen wall built across the land, from the Forth to the Clyde. Men remembered his reign and he was nicknamed Pius, which means blessed.

Marcus Aurelius Antoninus (121–180 AD)
Roman emperor (161–180 AD)

Marcus Aurelius was Emperor of Rome from 161 to 180 AD. He was the nephew of Emperor Antoninus Pius (137–161) whom he succeeded.

His life was not altogether a happy one. Much of his reign was taken up with fighting one barbarian race after another, on the borders of the empire. This distressed him, for he was by nature peace-loving and kindly. During his free hours, and there cannot have been many of them, he studied philosophy and science. He thought a lot about human conduct, and produced a series of rules of human behaviour, which came to be called his *Meditations*. This book, written in Greek, is among the most famous Roman works of the 2nd century AD.

Marcus Aurelius contracted the plague on one of his campaigns, this time in Austria, and he died while in command of his armies.

Suetonius Tranquillus, Gaius (2nd century AD)
Roman historian

Suetonius was a Roman historian who worked with Pliny the Younger (*p. 49*) in Bithynia, and who later became private secretary to the Emperor Hadrian (117–138). This last post gave him access to all sorts of confidential records in Rome, especially in government offices, and he used his unique skill to write the lives of the first of the twelve Caesars, starting with Julius Caesar. These biographies are blunt, on the whole un-sympathetic, colourful and probably accurate in a great deal of detail. They are extremely amusing, often scandalous and occasionally even horrifying. But whatever else they may be, they are worth reading, for they show all twelve men to have been, above all else, human beings afflicted by frailties like everybody.

Ptolemy

Ptolemy (Claudius Ptolemaeus) (2nd century AD)
Egyptian astronomer

Ptolemy was a celebrated geographer and astronomer who lectured at the university of Alexandria. He suggested that the sun and the planets of our solar system moved round the earth in an ellipse. This was accepted for centuries, until Copernicus (*p. 122*) disproved it in the 16th century. He also wrote a Geography, which gave precise details of the earth, guessed at its size, pin-pointed many important features and places, and suggested lines of longitude and latitude.

Kanishka (2nd century AD)
Indian king

Kanishka was lord over a great empire of Indian territory which encompassed Afghanistan, Kashmir, and much of India itself between the Ganges and Bokhara. His capital was at Peshawar. His great fame, however, was his devotion to Buddhism and he built numerous monuments to the faith. He also convened many councils to discuss the faith which was more a way of life than a belief in any one person. Kanishka also opened up contacts with Rome, resulting in trade and in a free exchange of ideas.

51

Galen (Claudius Galenus) (c.130–c.201 AD)
Greek doctor

Galen is one of the greatest names in medical history. He was a Greek-born physician who spent much of his life in Rome. He attended the emperors Marcus Aurelius (*p. 51*), Commodus and Septimius Severus (*p. 52*). He also wrote a lot about medical and philosophical matters, and nearly 100 of his treatises on these subjects have come down to us. They were so comprehensive that for centuries the medical world was dominated by what Galen had thought or observed. He is said to have been the first doctor to diagnose complaints by feeling the pulse.

Septimius Severus, Lucius (146–211 AD)
Roman emperor (193–211 AD)

Septimius Severus was a most remarkable emperor of Rome. Believed to have been black, he came from North Africa, and in a reign of some 17 years, achieved many conquests and administrative reforms.

Septimius Severus was a quaestor under Marcus Aurelius, and later became commander of the Roman forces in what is now Yugoslavia. When Commodus, the irresponsible son of Marcus Aurelius, was murdered in 192, a succession of generals persuaded their armies to elect them emperor, as when Nero died in 68 (*p. 48*). In the end, Severus was elected by his troops and succeeded in defeating his rivals.

Severus covered himself with military glory during his reign. He defeated the Parthians, for which an arch, still standing, was erected in the Roman Forum. He also defeated the Picts, and he died in York at the end of the campaign.

Ardashir I (3rd century AD)
Sassanid Persian ruler (226–241 AD)

Ardashir was the grandson of Sassan, a Persian noble. In about 224 AD he led a revolt against the Parthian government which had been ruling Persia for many years, and the last Parthian king was killed. Ardashir seized the vacant throne and thus began a new dynasty of kings, known as the Sassanids. These were more truly of Persian origin, and under their dynasty the great country made great progress.

Persia became a powerful state, balancing that of Rome in the Near East. Ardashir himself encouraged the building of towns and roads to connect them. He also strengthened the ties between the central government and the local authorities in the Persian provinces. He captured several cities in the western part which had been lost to Rome, including Nisibis and Carrhae. He made the empire powerful enough that his son, Sapor I, was actually able to defeat the Romans in a major battle and capture the emperor Valerian in person, in 260.

Diocletian (Diocletianus, Gaius Aurelius Valerius) (245–313 AD)
Roman emperor (284–305 AD)

Diocletian was one of the greatest of the long list of Roman emperors. Born the son of a freed slave in Dalmatia, he rose through the ranks of the army to become a general under a succession of short-lived emperors. These were Aurelian, Florian, Probus, Carus, Carinus and Numerianus (270–284). Then in 284, his army proclaimed him emperor. At once he realized that the empire was too big to be managed by one man, and he created a Board of Emperors. This was to consist of two Augusti (himself and his friend, Maximianus) and two Caesars (Galerius and Constantius). Between them they governed four main areas, and each area was sub-divided into smaller dioceses.

To maintain the system he enlarged the army and established a mobile force, which could be rushed to any danger point. But this cost money, as did many other reforms, and he was faced with the same sort of inflation that we know in the 20th century. So he took measures similar to ours to curb it. This led him to fix a series of maximum prices for food, clothing and other necessities.

Diocletian's new order made Rome a

dictatorship not unlike those of Hitler or Mussolini in the 20th century, but it saved the empire from collapse. Then, suddenly, in 305, he resigned office and retired to his magnificent palace at Spalate (in Yugoslavia). He went there, as he said, to grow cabbages.

Constantine (Constantinus, Flavius Valerius Aurelius) (c.280–337 AD)
Roman emperor (306–337 AD)

Constantine the Great was a very strange figure of Roman history. He spent much of his younger days fighting to win the sole imperial crown of Rome, which he finally obtained by 324, when he crushed the last of his rivals, Licinius, and had him executed. No sooner had he won the imperial throne, he decided to move the capital of the empire to the East, and he selected Byzantium, a small port on the Bosphorus, which was the most easternly edge of Europe. The idea was not new: Julius Caesar had contemplated moving the capital eastwards in 45 BC. But Constantine fought one of his greatest battles actually near Rome, on the Milvian Bridge, and perhaps one could be forgiven for thinking he loved the city.

In six years the new city was complete. Called Constantinople, it was decorated by trophies, statues and works of art taken from all corners of the empire, most of them from Rome itself!

Having defeated all his rivals, Constantine made himself sole Emperor, built a new capital, and allowed Christians to live unpersecuted throughout the empire. He finally died, leaving the empire divided between three sons, thus almost ensuring that his work would be undone.

Garlands and birds surround scenes from the Gospels and everyday life, in paint on plaster, on this catacomb of the mid-4th century

Julian (Julianus, Flavius Claudius) (331–363 AD)
Roman emperor (361–363 AD)

Julian is known as 'The Apostate' because he refused to believe in a Christian God, and when he was Emperor from 361 to 363, he discouraged Christians wherever he could, largely by granting freedom of expression to believers in other religions.

As a young man and nephew of Constantine the Great, he stood in some danger when the civil war between Constantine's sons broke out in 337. He spent years in quiet and devoted study of philosophy, Greek, science and other things, so that he became known as a 'swot'. Then in 355, when he was 24, he was appointed Caesar, that is, deputy Emperor. All of a sudden he demonstrated amazing powers of leadership, not unlike those of the great Julius Caesar himself, and won several major battles against the Germans.

In 361 he became Emperor, and led an expedition against Persia, but he was killed after a great battle near Ctesiphon. It is thought he may have been murdered by one of his generals who was a Christian and did not like Julian's toleration of other sects.

Sapor II (309–379 AD)
Sassanid Persian king (309–379 AD)

When Sapor's father, Ormizd II, died, his advisers murdered his eldest son, blinded his second son and imprisoned his third son. One of his wives was expecting a fourth child, and when this was born it was Sapor. Thus he was actually born king. When he came of age he demonstrated remarkable strength and independence, setting out to make Persia a truly great nation. This meant incessant warfare with Rome which, in the end, severely sapped the strength of both empires and made them easier prey to barbarians. On the whole his struggle was a successful one, however, especially when in 363 he managed to force the Roman emperor Jovian to accept a humiliating peace treaty. Sapor then went on to conquer Armenia.

Persia had not known such strength for centuries.

Stilicho, Flavius (c.359–408 AD)
Roman general

Stilicho was a Vandal barbarian by birth, but he won his way into the counsels of the Eastern Roman Emperor, Theodosius I, who in 384 sent him to Persia as an ambassador. Stilicho came home a few years later and married Theodosius' niece, Serena, and in 394 he was sent to Italy to look after young Honorius, who had become emperor in the West at the age of ten. He managed the government well, and he also successfully fought off an invasion attempt by Alaric the Goth (*p. 54*) in Greece in about 400. Alaric invaded North Italy in 403, but Stilicho again defeated him, and three years later when the Gothic chief, Radagasius, brought a huge host of barbarians against North Italy, Stilicho defeated him, too.

Then, when Stilicho suggested that Alaric be invited to combine with the Romans to defend themselves against another barbarian host, some of those around Honorius who were jealous of Stilicho, accused him of treason. Honorius weakly gave in and allowed the great soldier to be murdered.

Alaric (c.370–410 AD)
Gothic chief

Alaric was a barbarian Goth leader who spent some years in the service of the Roman army. In those hard times for the Roman empire it was customary for Europeans to employ one lot of barbarians to help beat off another lot. But this policy proved dangerous, for the first barbarians grew to like the luxuries of Rome and were liable to turn on their employers.

Alaric was extremely disappointed not to receive preferment after he had helped the Emperor Theodosius. So he left Rome and got himself made chief of the Visigoths. He invaded Greece, but was temporarily held off by the Romans. Then he served again in the Roman army under the Emperor Honorius. One would think the Romans would have learned, but they did not, and in 410 Alaric, upset once again, turned on the capital and sacked it.

Theodosius II (401–450 AD)
Emperor of Rome in the East (408–450 AD)

Theodosius II was Emperor of the Roman Empire in the East from 408 to 450 AD. This interesting man was a scholar, who specialized in the complexities of Roman law. And yet, although he was no soldier or administrator, his reign was an important one.

One of his early acts was to fortify Constantinople with a vast wall, about a mile to the west of the boundary. This astonishing engineering project stretched for miles, from the Sea of Marmora to the Golden Horn. It was about 5 metres thick, with an inner wall 12 metres high and an outer wall 9 metres high. Along it were about one hundred towers 6 metres high, with battlements. Much of it is still standing today.

Theodosius started to codify Roman law, a task completed by Justinian a century later. He also founded a university at Constantinople.

Attila (c.406–453 AD)
Hun chief

Attila was the ferocious chief of a large horde of Hun tribes, who came into Western Europe from Russia in the 5th century AD. They were looking for living space and they were, like so many other barbarians of the times, attracted by what they heard of Roman luxury. In about 447, Attila reached the very gates of Constantinople, which was then the richest city in the world. As his men prepared to surround the huge walls, there was a terrifying earthquake. The men were extremely frightened.

The Byzantine Emperor Theodosius II used this 'heaven-sent' opportunity to try to bribe Attila, and envoys were sent out to the Asiatic warrior with three tons of gold ingots. Attila accepted, and moved off.

Five years later, he stormed through Italy and came to Rome, threatening to siege it. This time there was no earthquake. But nor were there any bribes. The Pope, Leo I, merely asked him to go away – and he did.

The chief of the Huns, Attila

St. Patrick (c.389–461 AD)
British saint

St. Patrick is the patron saint of Ireland. But he was not Irish at all. He was a Romano-British boy, son of a military officer, and he was captured on a raid on Wales by marauding Irish pirates, who sold him as a slave in Antrim. After six years he escaped to Gaul, and then by his initiative, made his way back to his family in Wales. He is said to have had a vision that it was his job in life to bring Ireland into the fold of Christianity. So he went back to Gaul to study in an early monastery.

In 432 he was sent to Ireland by Pope Celestine I and made a bishop. He landed at Wicklow, was insulted by the local druids, but was received at the court of King Laoghaire, who gave him protection and allowed him to preach.

Over the next generation, Patrick founded many churches, created bishops and started monasteries and schools. He also introduced Latin as the church language. When he died in about 461,

St Patrick was kidnapped as a boy in Wales by marauding Irish pirates

much of Ireland was under the influence of Christianity.

Odoacer, (or Odouacer) (d.493 AD)
Barbarian German warrior
Odoacer was a barbarian warrior of German descent. He led the revolt which resulted in the expulsion of Romulus Augustulus, the very last Western Roman Emperor, in 476. He then became ruler of the rest of the empire and it seems he governed well. Meanwhile, the emperor of the Eastern Roman empire, Zeno, concerned at Odoacer's success, encouraged Theodoric, chief of the Ostrogoths, to invade Italy in 489. Odoacer was besieged in Ravenna for nearly three years, and then he had to surrender because of shortage of food. Soon afterwards he was murdered.

Cerdic (end of 5th century AD)
Saxon chief
Cerdic was a Saxon chief who came over to Hampshire in 495 and after defeating the British, set up the West Saxon kingdom later called Wessex. Cerdic's life seems to have been much the same as Hengist's (*p. 57*) for in the Anglo-Saxon Chronicle there are references to battles in which Welsh (British) were slain. It seems that in 530 Cerdic captured the Isle of Wight which, on his death in 534, was handed on to his nephew, Stuf, and to his grandson, Whitgar.

Hengist (5th century AD)
Jutish chief
Hengist came to Britain with his brother, Horsa, from Jutland in 449 AD at the invitation of the British chief, Vortigern, who wanted help to drive off Pict invaders. Hengist liked the country, though he did not have much time for the British people. He persuaded some more of his friends to come over, and they began to settle in Kent. They turned on Vortigern, and at Aylesford they defeated him. For the next thirty years Hengist continued to fight against the British, and in 473 he defeated them and killed twelve nobles. Hengist, who made himself king of Kent, died in 488.

Clovis

Clovis (465–511 AD)
Merovingian king of Salian Franks (481–511 AD)
Clovis was one of the earliest of the Frankish kings, and he was keen to unite all the Franks under one dynasty. He defeated the Gauls at Soissons and occupied all the land between the river Somme and the river Loire. In 493, he married Clothilde, daughter of the king of Burgundy, who after Clovis' death became a nun and was made a saint. Clovis fought the Alemanni near Cologne and promised his wife that if he was victorious he would accept Christianity. He was, and on Christmas Day he and many of his troops were baptized.

Clovis settled in Paris and continued to strive to unite the Franks.

Anastasius I (c.430–518 AD)
Emperor of Rome in the East (491–518 AD)
Anastasius I was an Italian noble who married the widow of Emperor Zeno I. He was a man of great honesty as well as ability, and he was also extremely careful with money, especially state finances. This was a very unusual characteristic, for most Byzantine emperors were recklessly extravagant. But it was advantageous to the Empire at the time, because its very frontiers were being threatened by hordes of barbarian invaders from central Asia and Russia.

One of Anastasius' acts was to build a new wall about 48 kilometres west of Constantinople. This stretched from the coast on the Black Sea down to the Sea of Marmora. It was constructed not of stone but of compressed earth, and little of it remains today, although it certainly served its purpose in the 6th century AD.

Boethius, Anicius Manlius Severinus
(c.475–524 AD)
Roman statesman and scholar

This remarkable Roman was a political adviser to the barbarian Gothic king, Theodoric, who ruled Italy from Ravenna at the turn of the 6th century. Boethius is said to have been responsible for preventing Theodoric becoming an oppressive ruler, so that for a generation Italians enjoyed a relatively mild government. But in 524 some of Theodoric's friends accused Boethius of treason, and the king accepted the allegations. The great Roman was stripped of his titles, put in prison and finally executed.

In prison, Boethius is said to have written his famous *De Consolatione Philosophiae*, in which the author holds a conversation with Philosophy, concluding that nothing is secure except virtue and good behaviour. Boethius was also a teacher, and his manuals on arithmetic and music were used in schools all over Europe in later years.

Theodora (508–548 AD)
Empress of the Byzantine Empire (527–548 AD)

Theodora was the wife of Justinian (*p. 59*). She had been a small time actress whose beauty exceeded her talents in the theatrical art. He fell in love with her, as many other men must have done, and when he succeeded as Emperor in 527, she had acquired a strong hold over him. For the next twenty years she more or less dominated Justinian, but thankfully, as a rule, to the advantage of the empire. Her influence was not entirely good, however, and she did favour some very unworthy people. Many mosaic pictures of the time feature her standing near her husband.

The magnificent cathedral of Saint Sophia in Constantinople was built by Justinian I

Justinian (Justinianus, Flavius Petrus Sabbatius) (483–565 AD)
Emperor of Rome in the East (527–565 AD)

Justinian I has been called the 'Last of the Romans', because in his reign there was a move to make Greek the language of the Byzantine Empire. He resisted it, setting an example by producing a large amount of his famous works on law in Latin. His reign was often referred to as the Golden Age, and not without reason.

First, large tracts of the old Western Roman Empire, lost to barbarians in the 5th and 6th centuries, were recovered by his able generals, especially Belisarius (*p. 59*) and Narses. Then, Justinian organized the re-framing of Roman law, continuing the start that had been made by Theodosius II (*p. 55*) and finishing splendidly with his great books.

Justinian also built what came to be the most magnificent cathedral in history, Saint Sophia, in Constantinople. Today, it is a museum in a city long since occupied by Moslem Turks (Istanbul).

This strange man, weak-willed at times, cruel and dominated by his forceful wife, Theodora, was also generous, learned and patient. Possibly without his reign, Byzantium might not have withstood the first onslaught of the Moslems, which took place in the 7th century.

Gelimer (6th century AD)
Last Vandal king (530–533 AD)

Gelimer was the last of the barbarian Vandal kings of North Africa. In 530 he deposed his cousin, Hilderic, who had been pro-Roman, and he ignored the objections of the Byzantine emperor Justinian I (*p. 59*). So Justinian sent Belisarius (*p. 59*), his great general, to Africa to put Gelimer in his place. In 533 there was a great battle fought not far from Carthage and Gelimer was defeated. He had been so confident of victory that he had prepared a huge feast in a large tent to celebrate. As it was, Belisarius and his men went into the tent instead, to the consternation of the servants and chefs.

Gelimer was not put to death. He was exiled to Asia Minor, where he died a year later.

St. David (6th century AD)
Welsh bishop

St. David is the patron saint of Wales, the one nation in Britain to become Christian in Roman times and to remain so even afterwards. He was a Welsh priest, who in the middle of the sixth century made an effort to unite the Welsh churches. Though most of his life story is shrouded in mystery, we do know that he presided over an important meeting of church leaders at Caerleon-on-Usk, when it is thought he himself was archbishop of the southern part of Wales. He is said to have moved his seat of church government to what is now the little city of St. David's, in Pembrokeshire.

Clearly he brought a sense of unity and purpose to Christians in Wales in the troubled years that followed the departure of the Roman forces from Britain. David was made a saint in 1120.

Belisarius (505–565 AD)
Byzantine general

Belisarius was a brilliant military leader, who several times won great victories against the enemies of the Eastern Roman Empire. He defeated the Persians in 530. Two years later, when his emperor, Justinian I (*p. 59*), was threatened with a very dangerous revolt in Constantinople, Belisarius crushed it by putting to death a large number of supporters. The very next year he defeated Gelimer, King of the Vandals, in North Africa, and so recovered that part of the old Roman empire. In 535 Belisarius fought the Ostrogoths in Italy and captured their capital, Ravenna, in 540.

Justinian then sent him to Persia again, and in 542 Belisarius defeated Chosroes I, the Persian king. In 559 he beat off a serious attack by the Huns on Rome.

In 562 some of his enemies suggested to Justinian that Belisarius was plotting to overthrow him, and Justinian put his famous general into prison. But the conspiracy collapsed and the next year Belisarius was restored to honour.

St. Columba (c.521–597 AD)
Irish missionary

Saint Columba was an Irish missionary who brought Christianity to the heathen Picts and Scots in the northern districts of what is now Scotland. He had become a priest in his native Ulster and began by setting up churches in unconverted parts of Ireland.

Then in about 560, with twelve followers who were well versed in Latin, Greek and the scriptures, he sailed to the island of Iona, off the coast of Argyll in Scotland. There he built a small monastery, and from it he and his men set out to bring Christianity to the Picts. In the north he was befriended by the local Pict chief, Brude, who encouraged him a great deal. Soon, many of the savage Pict warriors began to learn the advantages of Christian beliefs and standards of behaviour, and in a while, Columba had converted these fierce men.

By the time Columba died in 597, a large part of Scotland (and some areas of northern England, too) had become Christian.

Gregory the Great (c.540–604 AD)
Pope (590–604 AD)

Gregory was born in Rome. He served the emperor as a civilian, but longed to enter a monastery. One day he was walking in the streets of the city when he was shown some young Anglo-Saxon children in the slave market. He is reported to have exclaimed, 'Non Angli, sed Angeli,' which means, 'They are not Angles, they are Angels.' He wanted to bring Christianity to England, but it was not until 597, by which time he was Pope, that he could send Augustine to Canterbury with the express charge of converting the Anglo-Saxons to the Church.

Gregory's reign as Pope is considered to have provided the best administration the church ever had in nearly two thousand years. He was responsible for the complete organization of public services and rituals, and for the introduction and simplification of sacred chants. He was also instrumental in lessening slavery.

Chosroes II (d.628 AD)
Sassanid Persian king (591–628 AD)

Chosroes began his reign by trying to keep peace with Byzantium. He was friendly with the Byzantine emperor, Maurice, but when the latter was murdered in 602, Chosroes decided to avenge his friend and he invaded Syria and Asia Minor. By 608 his armies were almost at the gates of the capital Constantinople itself.

Chosroes ravaged far and wide in the Near East. He captured Damascus in 614 and then took Jerusalem, where he found and carted away the True Cross, on which Jesus Christ was said to have been crucified. In 616 he captured Alexandria. Chosroes was not finally beaten until 628, when he met his match in the emperor Heraclius (*p. 61*).

Mohammed (570–632 AD)
Arabian prophet

It would always be a great mistake to underestimate the importance of Mohammed in world history. He may not have predicted what his ideas would lead to, nor could he have known that in the 20th century more than 600,000,000 people would accept his teachings. Nor could he have known that the conquests carried out in his name in fact saved many aspects of Greek and Roman civilization from extinction, and that they benefited the world to an inestimable degree.

Mohammed was an Arab merchant who had been born at Mecca in about 570. Like Jesus Christ, he spent the first years of his life quite ordinarily, and then suddenly gave up this normal life to concentrate on prayer and meditation. Mohammed began to preach about a new code of living which was based on kindness and the worship of one God, Allah. When he acquired a following the authorities expelled him from Mecca. He fled to Medina, and in 622 began to preach again. Soon he built up a band of his disciples round him, who gathered his teachings together to form a book called the *Koran*. By 632, when he died, many thousands of Arabs were his followers, and the faith that he preached, called Islam, was to be launched upon the world by a series of organized raids on Byzantine and Persian territory.

Abu-Bakr (573–634 AD)
First Moslem caliph
Abu-Bakr was the right hand man and leading general of the prophet Mohammed (*p. 60*). He was also the father of one of Mohammed's wives. When the prophet died in 632, Abu was chosen as caliph of the new empire which the prophet's followers were beginning to build up in the Near East and in the Mediterranean. Abu defeated the Byzantine emperor, Heraclius (*p. 61*) in 633 and he also crushed a Persian army.

Isidore of Seville (c.560–636 AD)
Spanish historian and saint
Isidore was archbishop of Seville and was considered to be the most learned man of his time. He was notable for organizing the Council of Seville in 618 and that of Toledo in 633, at which the fundamental principles of the constitutional law of Spain were worked out. He collected the decrees of the councils and other church laws made before his time and put them in a great encyclopaedia, which also contained a vast amount of information about many other scientific, religious and historical things. He was a prolific and learned writer.

Heraclius (c.575–641 AD)
Emperor of Rome in the East (610–641 AD)
Heraclius was much like the ancient Greek hero, whose name his so closely resembled, Heracles (Hercules), for both were tall, handsome, tough and bold. He came to Byzantium in about 610 and seized the imperial throne, in order to save the empire from collapsing before the onslaught of its enemies, the Persians, the Avars, and the Slavs.

For some years he endured defeats, though none were too severe to sustain. All the while he was building up Byzantine strength until he could strike the decisive retaliatory blows.

In about 627, Heraclius was ready to strike and in a few months he recaptured all lost territories, and even invaded Persia itself. In 628, Ctesiphon was taken by storm, and the Holy Cross, stolen from Jerusalem by the Persians under Chosroes in 614, was recovered.

Omar I (581–644 AD)
Moslem caliph
Omar became the second caliph of the newly formed Moslem empire when the caliph, Abu-Bakr, Mohammed's great friend and second-in-command, died in 634. Omar extended the empire over a vast area in a short space of time. The Persians were crushed in 637, Syria and Palestine fell in 641 and Egypt a year later. It was an astonishing series of victories.

Omar was murdered in 644.

Harsha (c.590–647 AD)
King of India (606–647 AD)
India had several periods of greatness interspersed with days of decline and periods of anarchy. Harsha was a strong and resolute king who in about 610 took hold of the northern part of India and brought to it some order. He set up a capital at Kanauj, and there, when he was not involved fighting or repressing rebellion, he patronized the arts, and even wrote some good poetry himself. It was a great period for India, though regrettably it did not last long after his death.

Harsha

Callinicus (7th century AD)
Egyptian born scientist
Callinicus was an Egyptian architect and scientist who was born at Heliopolis. He invented Greek Fire, a devastating weapon which enabled the Byzantines to ward off their enemies for a century or more. And it was as well that he did so in the middle of the seventh century, for this invention came just at the time that the followers of the prophet Mohammed, led by Abu-Bakr, began to overrun the Eastern Mediterranean. In the space of a few years Persia, Syria, Palestine and Egypt had all fallen.

Callinicus' invention was a chemical liquid like naphtha, which could be enclosed in a case of stone or metal. This would explode when the case was discharged at an enemy target, creating the same sort of burning that follows the use of napalm today. It was particularly effective when used by the Byzantines against Arab ships.

Caedmon (7th century AD)
English poet
Caedmon was a shepherd in Yorkshire, who lived in the seventh century AD. He had no education whatever and could neither read nor write. Then, suddenly, when he was asleep one evening, he had a vision. In it, an angel invited him to sing. Caedmon asked what he should sing, for all he knew was the odd, rough farming song. The angel replied that he should sing about God, how the world was created, and so on.

When he woke up, Caedmon remembered the dream vividly. He also remembered the verses that he had sung in it, telling of things he knew nothing about, in language he had never heard. So he rushed to the priory at Whitby, near where he lived, and began to sing these to the prior in comprehensible verses. There the abbess Hilda took down all his words, and was amazed at their force, clarity and accuracy. When she read him parts of the Bible, he immediately transformed them into verse.

Clearly, this young man was a fine poet, but how could he develop, if he could not read nor write? So the abbess took him in as a member of the community, where he learned to write down the verses that kept tumbling out of his thoughts.

He was the earliest English poet.

Bede, The Venerable (673–735 AD)
English scholar
The Venerable Bede, as he has long been known in English history, was a brilliant scholar and theologian, who spent practically all of his long life in the famous monastery of Jarrow in Northumberland. This had been founded by Benedict Biscop, who took Bede into his care as an orphan of seven.

Bede became a priest in about 703, but stayed on at Jarrow where he taught Greek, Latin, Hebrew and theology. During his years he also studied a great deal of history very closely, especially that of England, of Britain before the Anglo-Saxons, and of Rome. He produced several works, which have become among the most important histories of Britain of all time. One was his Ecclesiastical History of the English Nation.

Charles Martel (c.689–741 AD)
Frankish king (720–741 AD)
Charles Martel was duke of the Austrasian Franks and in 720 he became ruler of the Franks. In that year he began his campaign to drive the Saracen Arabs out of France, and this was crowned with glory when he crushed the forces of the caliph Abd-er-Rahman at Tours, near Poitiers, in 732. It is probably as a result of his great victory that he acquired the nickname Martel, which means 'the Hammer'. Certainly, European historians have noted this battle as a turning point in west European history. Charles Martel was the father of Pepin the Short (*p. 62*) and so grandfather of Charlemagne (*p. 63*).

Pepin the Short (c.715–768 AD)
King of the Franks (751–768 AD)
Pepin was the younger son of the great Charles Martel (*p. 62*) and he was the

father of Charlemagne (*p. 63*). He also founded the Frankish dynasty of Carlovingians. Pepin became king in 751, and led an army into Italy to protect the Pope from the attacks of the Longobards. This was the beginning of the creation of the Papal state as a temporal empire.

Pepin spent the rest of his rule fighting the Saracen Arabs and the Saxon Germans.

Offa's dyke

Offa (d.796 AD)
King of Mercia, England (757–796 AD)

Offa was a great English king who ruled Mercia for nearly forty years (757–796). In that time he made Mercia the dominant kingdom of England, and his power and influence were felt outside Britain as well, as far afield as Europe, where he kept up a correspondence with Charlemagne, then the greatest ruler in Europe.

Offa is famous for having built a huge dyke between his kingdom and Wales. It ran from the mouth of the river Wye, right up to the river Dee, between Cheshire and Denbighshire. This was to keep the Welsh cattle raiders out of the prosperous districts of Herefordshire, and Shropshire.

Although he ruled for a long time, Offa did not ensure that Mercia would remain the principal kingdom of England. Within twenty years, the supremacy had passed to Ecgbert of Wessex (*p. 64*).

Alcuin (735–804 AD)
English scholar

Alcuin was the adviser of Charlemagne (*p. 63*) in educational and literary matters. He introduced schools and colleges in the empire of the Franks, with Charlemagne's help, and he served at the emperor's court as tutor to his children and those of the senior courtiers. In 796 Alcuin settled at Tours as abbot of the monastery there. In his time he wrote a number of important works including manuals of grammar, poetry books and studies of theology. He also amassed a library of the best works available anywhere, and this library was said to be the best outside Italy.

Charlemagne (742–814 AD)
First emperor of the Holy Roman Empire (800–814 AD)

Charles, who was the son of Pepin the Short (*p. 62*), became King of the Franks in 771 when his brother died. His great qualities were personal courage, an ability to lead men, and the capacity to wield a sword better than most warriors. But he also had a vision of a big Frankish empire embracing most, if not all of Western Europe, and he devoted his considerable energies to achieving this.

He overcame large tracts of Italy and expelled the Lombards. By 800 he was master of Central and Western Europe, and the Pope crowned him first Emperor of the Holy Roman Empire. His campaigns were fought in God's name.

Charles was a man of practically no education and he could hardly read or write. He had to learn late in life, but he was extremely fortunate in having the services of Alcuin (*p. 63*) who not only taught Charles to write letters, but also reconstructed the educational system in the empire by organizing schools and colleges. In later years, Charles kept up a correspondence with many rulers and scholars, including Offa of Mercia, and made treaties wherever possible to secure peace along his borders.

Astonishingly, this great man's empire broke up on his death, when it was divided among his children. But the idea of a united Europe had been born, and many European figures have since revived it, though without much lasting success.

Ecgbert (d.839 AD)
King of England (828–839 AD)

In the ninth century a man who was king of one of the English kingdoms and who could make most, if not all of the other kings accept him as overlord, could regard himself as king of England. Whether Ecgbert actually thought of himself as such we do not know, but history has looked upon him as the first effective king of all England. As the *Anglo-Saxon Chronicle* put it, he was 'Bretwalda' or 'Ruler of Britain'.

Ecgbert had become king of Wessex in 802. He spent several years establishing order in the south-west, which had suffered, along with nearly all other parts of the country, from the Vikings. He then turned his attention to Mercia and at a great battle at Ellandun he defeated the Mercian king, Beornwulf. Almost at once other English kings recognized him as their overlord, and when, three years later, in 828, Beornwulf died, Mercia submitted as well. Ecgbert was now Bretwalda.

The greatest of his victories, however, was against the Vikings, in 837, when he overwhelmed huge numbers of them at Hingston Down.

Kenneth McAlpine (d.860 AD)
First King of Scotland (843–860 AD)

Kenneth McAlpine was made King of Dalriada, the area of Scotland embracing Argyll and the islands, in 834. He was a Christian and he longed to see all Scotland turn Christian and united under one king. In about 843, he turned on the Picts in the north and dealt them a series of crushing blows that brought them to submission. He was then master of half of Scotland, and was regarded as the first king of the Scots. He moved his seat of administration from Argyll to Scone in Perth, a place ever afterwards hallowed in Scottish royal history.

In about 859, Kenneth set out to try to win the Lowland part of Scotland, below the river Forth, but he died before making any real progress. Every king of Scotland following him was in some way or other descended from him.

Michael III (839–867 AD)
Byzantine emperor (842–867 AD)

Michael III is known in Byzantine history as Michael the Drunkard. This is because of the stupendous drinking bouts he had indulged in as a young man, and the nickname stuck, although in his more mature years he proved a good administrator, chose good generals to command the Byzantine armies and took a close personal interest in the arts and in building.

Michael was the first emperor to try to recover the Byzantine lands. These had been lost in the seventh century to the crusading Arabs in their path of conquest for the glory of Allah and Mohammed throughout the Mediterranean. He organized a major offensive campaign in Asia Minor and drove the Arabs out of part of their gains there.

He was eventually murdered by one of his humble grooms, Basil, who seized power and managed to make himself emperor Basil I.

Erigena, Johannes Scotus (c.815–c.877 AD)
Irish born scholar and philosopher

This Irish born scholar has come to be known as John the Scot, because in those days the Scots were a race occupying part of Ireland. He was invited to become head of the school at the court of the French king, Charles the Bald. There he got into trouble when he declared that evil is 'simply that which has no existence, and that therefore damnation consists only in the consciousness of having failed to fulfil the divine purpose.' This theory was condemned at various meetings as 'Irishman's porridge'.

John the Scot became abbot at Malmesbury in Wiltshire, and was said to have been killed by his students, who stabbed him with their quill pens. In his time he wrote many important works. One was *De Divisione Naturae*, a treatise which tried to reconcile authority with reason. But the work was condemned by the Church. Erigena translated into Latin the writing of the pseudo-Dionysius, the Areopagite.

Rhodri Mawr (The Great) (d.878 AD)
Prince of Wales (844–878 AD)

This masterful Welsh leader became Prince of Gwynedd, in North Wales, in 844 and he galvanized his people into fighting off the Vikings. He also tried to persuade other Welsh chiefs that Wales would benefit by being united, even if it meant their accepting one prince as overlord of them all. Some saw it his way, but others were too jealous of their local authority and resisted. So he went to war with them, and by about 860 he had crushed the prince of Ceredigion (Cardigan) whereupon the other chiefs accepted him as their overlord.

For a while Rhodri maintained his supremacy, but in 878, the very year that England's Alfred the Great (*p. 65*) smashed the Danes under Guthrum near Chippenham, he was killed in a war with the Vikings off Anglesey, his home island. The unity of Wales broke up on his death, but the idea of a ruling house in Wales was born. All the princes of Wales, right up to the last one, Llywelyn II (*p. 92*) were descended from Rhodri.

Alfred the Great (849–900 AD)
King of England (871–900 AD)

There have been more than sixty kings and ruling queens of England, but only one has been known as the Great. And no man better deserved the title than Alfred, son of king Aethelwulf (839–856) and grandson of Ecgbert (*p. 64*).

This splendid ruler was a statesman, war leader, scholar, lawgiver, writer and inventor, all rolled into one. In 878 he crushed the Viking army of Guthrum the Dane at a great battle at Slaughterford, near Chippenham, and made the defeated survivors accept Christianity. Then he allowed them to live in an area that came to be called the Danelagh, part of England north of a line running from Chester to London. He also built a fleet of ships and defeated several Viking raiding squadrons in the Channel.

On the domestic front, Alfred busied himself with education and literature. He founded schools. He had several important Latin works translated into Anglo-Saxon, some of which he actually

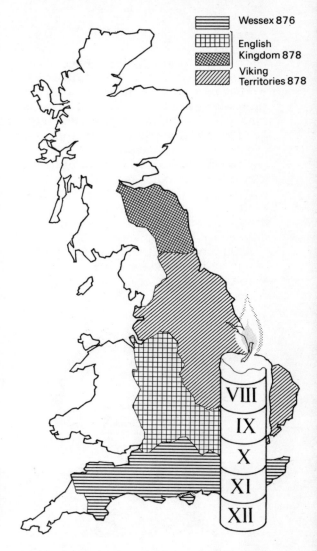

Wessex 876

English Kingdom 878

Viking Territories 878

undertook himself. He started the *Anglo-Saxon Chronicle*, a comprehensive history of England starting from the invasion of Britain by Julius Caesar (*p. 35*) in 55 BC. This was continued after his death right up to the year 1154.

Alfred's inventions included a candle clock and a lantern made of translucent ox horn panels.

One of his many activities was arranging for the laws of England to be codified, and for generations people talked about the laws of Alfred, when they really meant the law of England.

Many of Alfred's descendants proved almost as able as he was.

Asser (late 9th and early 10th century)
Welsh monk
Asser was a brilliant scholar from Wales, whom Alfred the Great of England (*p. 65*) encouraged to work at his court. He probably gave a lot of help to the English king who, though he eventually translated several important Latin works into English for the people to read, may not have been educated himself until he was grown up. Possibly, too, Asser advised Alfred in political matters and may have drafted the various treaties the king drew up with the Viking Danes who plagued his country in those times.

Asser was appointed bishop of Sherborne, and it could have been in his last years there that he wrote his biography of Alfred.

Rollo of Normandy

Rollo of Normandy (c.869–932 AD)
Viking chief
Rollo was a Viking chief who brought a band of his fierce warriors down to France at the beginning of the tenth century in search of space for making a new life. He was given an area in northern France by the king, Charles the Simple, probably in the hope that Rollo would thus stop any of his compatriots from Scandinavia coming to claim land again. Rollo also had to agree to accept Christianity and to recognize Charles as his overlord.

This land became the duchy of Normandy, and one of Rollo's descendants was William the Conqueror (*p. 74*).

Athelstan (894–940 AD)
King of England (924–940 AD)
Athelstan once met his grandfather Alfred the Great (*p. 65*) who gave him a purple cloak with a jewelled belt. It was said that the great king predicted a splendid future for the boy, and so it indeed turned out. Athelstan was the son of Alfred's son, Edward, who reigned from 900 to 924. Almost all of his young life was spent in an atmosphere of warfare, for Edward, bold and skilful leader as he was, had to spend his time fighting the Danes. In the end he triumphed, and when Athelstan succeeded, he set out to consolidate his father's work.

Athelstan did so with magnificent success, culminating in a splendid victory over a combined army of Vikings, Scots, Irish and Welsh, at Brunanburgh, where he drove the whole host off the field, sending many thousands to their death.

This victory won him the admiration of many rulers in Europe.

Hywel Dda, The Good (d.950 AD)
Prince of Wales (916–950 AD)
Hywel was the grandson of Rhodri Mawr (*p. 65*). He was never master of all Wales as his grandfather had been, but his work as a lawgiver made him respected throughout the country, and towards the end of his time as prince of Ceredigion (Cardigan) he was generally accepted as the foremost prince in the land. Hywel in fact summoned an assembly of all the Welsh princes and their legal advisers so that they could sift through all the conflicting laws in Welsh, many of which varied from principality to principality. Out of this muddle he arrived at a kind of code which could be applied throughout Wales.

The value of this code was especially important in fostering the spirit of Welsh nationalism, which has lasted, despite the Normans and the English, right to this day.

Otto the Great (912–973 AD)
Emperor of the Holy Roman Empire (962–973 AD)
Otto was King of Germany from 936 to

973. He spent most of his reign in an attempt to rebuild the empire of Charlemagne (*p. 63*), which fell apart soon after that great man's death in 814. Otto defeated the Hungarians in a decisive battle in 955, and then overwhelmed the Italians six years later. He had himself crowned as Holy Roman Emperor and became the first of the German kings to occupy the position.

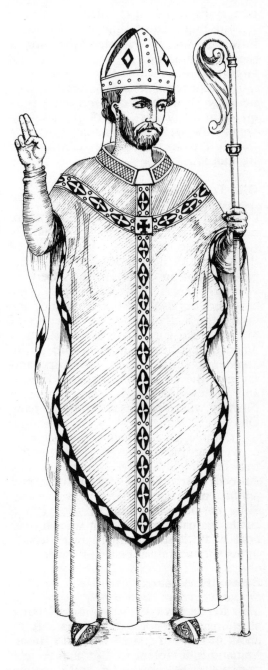

St. Dunstan (c.925–988 AD)
English archbishop and statesman

Dunstan was brought up at Glastonbury in Somerset by Irish pilgrims. He entered a monastery, and before he was twenty, he was so gifted that he was made abbot of Glastonbury by King Edmund (940–946). Dunstan rebuilt the monastery there, and made it a centre of learning.

The next king, Eadred (946–955) was so taken with Dunstan's scholarship and wisdom that he made him his chief adviser. And Dunstan remained in this principal post for the next generation, with one short interval. Thus he decisively influenced the development of the country. He was made bishop of Worcester, then of London, and finally, in 961, Archbishop of Canterbury. On the whole his influence was good, for he encouraged learning, worked hard to make the country's laws operate effectively and fairly, and to get English and Danes to live peacefully together.

Hasdai-ibn-Shaprut (c.915–c.990 AD)
Hebrew scholar

Hasdai ibn Shaprut was a Jewish doctor who became greatly favoured by Caliph Abdar Rahman III of Moslem Spain, in the middle of the tenth century. He was highly educated, spoke several languages, and was extremely useful to Abdar for interpreting the conversation of foreign visitors. In time, Hasdai became the Caliph's principal adviser.

Hasdai was a devout Jew who loved his race and watched over their interests in Spain. He was a fine physician, and among his great works was a translation into Arabic of the works of the Greek scientist, Dioscorides (1st century AD), which dominated medical ideas in Europe and the Near East, right up to the 15th century.

Hugo Capet (c.940–996 AD)
King of France (987–996 AD)

Hugo Capet was elected king of France in 987. He was the first of the Capetian line of French kings which ruled until 1328. Being king of France at this time, however, was a thankless job, for it meant containing, as overlord, several large dominions whose rulers were notoriously independent and aggressive, particularly Normandy, Aquitaine, Burgundy and Lorraine. We do not know in detail how well Hugo managed, except that he appears to have kept control over Burgundy.

Olaf Tryggvason (969–1000)
Norwegian king (995–1000)

Olaf had a most fascinating life before he became King of Norway in 995. He was born and brought up at the court of the Grand Prince of Russia, while his parents were in exile. He then went to Ireland where he married an Irish princess and he also lived in England. He visited the Scilly Islands where he is said to have been converted to Christianity. Then in 994 he organized a raid in the manner of his Viking ancestors and ravaged the coasts of England, France and Wales. Finally, he went home to Norway where he was accepted as King Olaf I.

At home Olaf began the process of converting his people to Christianity, but he did not have much success. Abroad, he quarrelled with the tough and almost unbeatable Sweyn Forkbeard, King of Denmark, and in 1000 lost a battle against him. When it was all over Olaf is said to have jumped over the side of his ship and disappeared forever.

Sweyn Forkbeard (d.1014)
King of Denmark (985–1014)

This fierce, savage and ruthless Viking chief, who was King of Denmark from about 985 to 1014, first descended upon England in a violent raid in 994. A year or two later he came again, and this time he attacked London, but though he did a lot of damage he failed to capture it. In 1000 he waged war against Olaf Tryggvason (*p. 68*), King of Norway and defeated him, making himself king of Norway.

Aethelred II (the Unready) of England ordered a massacre of Danes in various parts of England in 1002. Among the victims were relatives of Sweyn, and the Viking chief became determined to have revenge. For the next twelve years he descended upon England in force, staying a little longer each time and burning and pillaging all the more, so that in 1013 he seized the throne in place of Aethelred whom the English Council forced to abdicate. Sweyn died the following year in Lincolnshire.

Brian Boru (926–1014)
King of all Ireland (1001–1014)

Ask any Irishman if he knows who were the two greatest Irishmen of all time, and as likely as not he will reply Michael Collins (*p. 267*), the great leader in the war against Britain, 1918–1921, and Brian Boru, king of Ireland, from whom your Irishman will also say he is descended. Nearly all Irishmen claim Brian as their ancestor.

This tremendous personality that was to impress so many Irishmen for so many centuries was King of Munster, one of the five Irish kingdoms, in the 10th century. He had a vision to unite all Ireland under himself, and he set out to achieve it with dogged determination. In 984 he conquered the kingdom of Leinster, and a few years later overwhelmed Meath and Connaught. By 1001 he was master of all Ireland, except for a small enclosure around Dublin that remained occupied by the Vikings.

Brian had himself recognized as Ard Rí, or High King, at St. Patrick's Church at Armagh, and then set out on a tour of his dominions, compelling the underkings to pay him tribute. That is how he came to be called Boru, for the name means Taker of Tributes. He was by now 75, but was still vigorous and active.

In 1014 the show-down with the Vikings came at Clontarf, not far from Dublin, where a great battle was fought. Brian carried the day, but as the sun went

The Ardagh Chalice and Tara Brooch. Irish artefacts of the 8th century AD

down and the enemy fled from the field in panic, one of them saw the old king standing in his observation tent. He went up behind him and split his head open with an axe. Thus Ireland's greatest king fell in the hour of one of the nation's finest victories.

Edmund Ironside (c.980–1016)
King of England (1016)
This great martial prince ruled for only a few months, but such was his courage in battle and his mercifulness to the vanquished afterwards, that his exploits were talked about for generations after his death. His whole reign was taken up with fighting the Danes, chiefly under his rival – and later friend – Canute (*p. 70*) whom he admired. They fought

several battles with more or less equal success. Then, at Ashingdon, in Essex, Canute beat Edmund but allowed him to share England with him. But Edmund was tired out, and in November 1016 he died. Canute then became king of all England.

Aelfric Grammaticus (c.955–1020)
English scholar
Aelfric probably studied at the monastery of Abingdon. Then he became abbot at the new monastery at Cerne Abbas, in Dorsetshire, after which he went to Eynsham, near Oxford, also as abbot. In his time as a cleric, he wrote many works, the most important being a Latin and English grammar, with a glossary of words, not unlike a dictionary.

Basil II (c.958–1025)
Byzantine emperor (976–1025)

Basil was a short, thick-set man of bull-like courage and determination. He was often stern, but as a leader of men and as a military strategist, he ranks among the greatest of the Byzantine leaders. His long reign was largely devoted to warfare with the Bulgarians whom he ultimately crushed, and with the Arabs whom he defeated on several occasions.

Basil drove the Bulgarians out of Greece altogether and also out of the lands south of the Danube. For this he became known as Basil Bulgaroctonus, or Basil the Bulgar-Slayer, presumably because of the enormous number of enemy men left dead on the field. Then he turned his attention to the East and there made heavy raids on Arab territory beyond Asia Minor and Syria. It is said that he even persuaded the caliph of Baghdad (in what is now Iraq) to recognize his superiority.

These military successes resulted in a great upsurge in commerce, and Constantinople once more became the Mediterranean's main market and supply depôt. Before long the royal treasury was full, and Byzantine fleets again dominated the seas.

It is sad to relate that Basil's successors did not maintain the splendid dominion that he had built up.

Malcolm II (d.1034)
King of Scotland (1005–1034)

Malcolm was a splendid victorious warrior who fought against the Vikings and the English for the part of Scotland called Lothian. At the battle of Carham, on the river Tweed, he smashed a combined Viking and English army and drove it off the field. This cleared them out of the territory and Lothian was annexed to Scotland. Then he moved over to the south-west part of Scotland, Strathclyde, which was also in the hands of English and Vikings, and he expelled them from that, too. This made Scotland one country as it is to-day, and Malcolm gave it good government up to the time of his death.

Avicenna (980–1037)
Arab physician and philosopher

Avicenna was born in Afghanistan, and grew up to become a physician. He secured appointments as physician to several sultans in the Arab world, and even became vizier in Persia. Apparently, he made himself unpopular with the Arab army in some way, because they forced him to resign. After this he travelled far and wide, and also wrote a number of important scientific and philosophical works. His work on medicine was for a long time reckoned to be a standard book on the subject.

Sancho III (970–1035)
King of Navarre (1027–1035)

Sancho was the grandson of Sancho I, first King of Navarre, a province in the north of Spain, along the French border. He became king in 1000 and spent much of his reign trying to conquer and unite the various small kingdoms in the Spanish peninsula. He overcame Castile and Leon, and declared himself Sancho III of Castile, in 1027. Before his death he had announced that he was King of Spain, but on his death he divided his new empire among his four sons.

Canute the Great (c.994–1035)
King of Denmark, Norway, England and Sweden

Canute was the son of Sweyn Forkbeard, the savage ruler of Denmark. In his time he became King of England (1016–1035), Denmark (1018–1035) and Norway (1028–1035) and he claimed overlordship of Sweden in his last years.

His career in England was remarkable. He began as a young Viking leader under his father and was every bit as ruthless and warlike as the older man. Then, when Ethelred the Unready died in 1016, the English Council in London elected his son, Edmund Ironside (*p. 69*) to succeed. But Canute, now heir to his father Sweyn, had conquered parts of England, and some councillors at Southampton elected him Ethelred's successor. So he and Edmund fought it out over the next few months, eventually agreeing to divide the kingdom between them. And when Edmund died, Canute became king of the whole land.

In a very short time this fierce, tall, blond warrior changed into a wise, firm, civilized ruler. He adopted Christianity and encouraged the Church to build more schools and monasteries. He no longer used his Danish bodyguards and gave the senior posts of government in England to Englishmen. He brought the nation's laws up to date and added some good new ones, himself governing with great justice.

English and Danes alike revered him almost as a god. Indeed, the famous story about him and the waves illustrates this. His courtiers flattered him by saying he could make the sea recede on the shore, so he ordered them to set a chair down by the water's edge, knowing full well he would get his feet wet. In no time, of course, the waves splashed over his toes, regardless of any commands from him, and with an eye that seemed to say 'I told you so,' he chided his courtiers and said, 'God is the only king whom all things obey. It is him you should honour.'

Canute died aged only 40 in 1035. The Scandinavians called him The Great, and indeed he was perhaps the best ruler anywhere in Western Europe in the 11th century.

'God is the only king whom all things obey. It is him you should honour,' said King Canute

Stephen I (c.975–1038)

First king of the Arpad dynasty of Hungary (1001–1038)

Stephen was crowned King of Hungary in 1001, with the blessing of the Pope who sent him a crown for the ceremony. He strove to make his country Christian and to give it good government.

At the start of his reign, the area that is now Hungary was split up into several smaller chiefdoms ruled by fierce Magyar warriors. Stephen welded these all into one kingdom, introduced them to Christianity and gave the new nation the foundations of institutions that have lasted up to the present time. He was made a saint in 1087.

Godwine (d.1053)
Earl of Wessex

Godwine was one of the most powerful men in the kingdom of England during the reign of Edward the Confessor (1042–1066). He first came to the notice of the great Canute (*p. 70*) who made him an earl and gave him Wessex as his earldom. When Canute's son, Hardicanute, died in 1042, Godwine exerted the required pressure to have Edward, the son of Ethelred the Unready (King, 978–1016), elected to the throne. He gave his daughter, Edith, to Edward as wife. But Godwine – and many Englishmen, too – were soon to regret this election, for Edward, who had spent much of his youth in Normandy, began to fill his court and the higher offices of state with Normans.

Godwine resisted, but was finally banished. In 1052 he returned with a large following, and before many days passed, a large number of the English people joined him in his revolt against the king who had to re-instate him in all his titles.

Godwine died at Winchester in 1053. His son was Harold, who became Harold II and was killed at Hastings in 1066.

Macbeth (d.1057)
King of Scotland (1040–1057)

This fine Scottish ruler has received rough treatment from historians taking their cue from Shakespeare, who portrayed him as a veritable monster of crime. The facts show otherwise. Mediaeval historians from Scotland spoke highly of his reign and of his character. For example, they show that King Duncan (1034–1040), said by Shakespeare to have been invited as a guest to Macbeth's house and then murdered in his bed, was in fact one of the country's worst rulers. He had led a raid into England which was so unsuccessful that his people rose up against him when he got back, and he was slain in an ensuing battle.

Macbeth succeeded Duncan, his cousin, and in seventeen years brought a measure of law and order to Scotland that was remarkable enough for the his-

torians to note it. He encouraged trade and farming, both of which benefitted by the peace he brought to his realm. He supported the Church and gave it lands. He also dealt with the pressing problem of highway robbers by organizing local police forces to seek out and arrest these terrorists.

At the end of his reign there was a civil war, led by Duncan's son, Malcolm (*p. 75*) and Macbeth was slain in battle.

Macbeth

Casimir I (1015–1058)
King of Poland (1040–1058)

Poland was for centuries a great kingdom in East Europe, situated between the German states and the far-flung Russian kingdoms and duchies. It was strongly religious and its people were very proud of their race. One early king was Casimir I, called 'the Peaceful'. He was elected king in 1034, but clearly not with a big majority, for a revolt by the nobility which took place in the next few years, drove him into exile.

Six years later, with the assistance of Henry III, emperor of the Holy Roman Empire, he was restored, and from 1040 until his death he ruled Poland wisely. In his absence, the people had almost abandoned Christianity and Casimir regenerated their faith. From that time to the present the Polish people have been among the staunchest Christians in all Europe.

Edward the Confessor (c.1002–1066)
King of England (1042–1066)

Edward was the son of Ethelred the Unready, and as a very small boy was sent to be brought up in Normandy, for his father considered England too dangerous a place for him at the time. As a result, Edward grew up under Norman influence, and when the house of Canute ended with the death of Harthacanute in 1042 and Edward was elected king by the English Council, he immediately filled up his court and government with Norman friends. The English lords, like Godwine of Wessex (*p. 72*) and Leofric of Mercia objected strongly and rebelled. Eventually, Edward agreed to admit some Englishmen, including Godwine, to the top posts in the government.

Edward's reign was marked by the

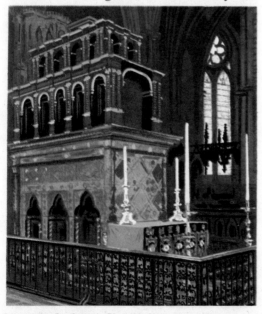

Edward the Confessor's Chapel in Westminster Abbey

building of Westminster Abbey, a small part of which survives in the more magnificent arches, aisles and chapels that can be seen to-day.

Harold III, Hardraada (1015–1066)
King of Norway (1047–1066)

Hardraada was present as a boy at the battle in 1030 in which his popular brother, Olaf, later canonized as St. Olaf, was killed. Hardraada fled to Russia to stay with a relative, Yaroslav, who was Duke of Novgorod. Then he went to Constantinople to join the Varangian bodyguard of the Byzantine emperor. He helped to defeat the Saracens in Italy, went back to Novgorod and married Yaroslav's daughter, and finally, after these adventures, returned to Norway, in 1045, where his nephew Magnus was king. Magnus agreed to divide the kingdom, and in two years, Hardraada became sole ruler.

When Tostig, a half-brother of Harold II of England, invaded England in 1066, Hardraada agreed to come with him to help the expedition, but both men were defeated and killed at the battle of Stamford Bridge.

Guiscard, Robert de (c.1015–1085)
Norman adventurer

Guiscard was a Norman soldier and adventurer who won great fame as a captain in Italy. He conquered Calabria, and became the Pope's champion. He waged endless wars with the Saracens in south Italy and in Sicily, and even attempted to march against Constantinople itself. When he was on this bold expedition, he heard news that the Holy Roman Emperor, Henry IV (*p. 77*) had invaded northern Italy. The Pope Gregory VII (*p. 74*) was in some danger, and Guiscard returned at once and drove Henry out. The Pope had in fact been imprisoned in the great fortress of Castel Sant' Angelo in Rome, and Guiscard rescued him.

He then returned to Epirus in eastern Europe where he defeated the Greeks. He then tried again to attack Constantinople, but died suddenly as the expedition set out.

Gregory VII (c.1020–1085)
Pope (1073–1085)

Gregory VII was a Benedictine monk who entered the papal service in about 1050. For twenty-three years he played an important part in many papal decisions, and in 1073 it was his turn to be elected. Once in office as head of the Church, he set out to make the authority of the popes supreme throughout Christendom. He also aimed to make national governments and rulers bend to the Church in ecclesiastical appointments. When the Emperor Henry IV refused to accept this particular decree, Gregory excommunicated him in 1076. A year later, the Emperor was overcome with remorse and begged forgiveness, at a meeting at Canossa, often referred to as the Humiliation of Canossa. But a few years later Henry resisted papal decrees again and this time Gregory was imprisoned in Rome by an army of the Emperor.

Gregory retired to Salerno, where he was protected by Robert de Guiscard (*p. 73*).

William I, the Conqueror (1027–1087)
King of England (1066–1087)

William was indeed a conqueror, and few men have overrun a country and so completely bent its people to his ways. This great ruler was one of the most masterful men of European history. Long before he actually set out with his ships, in late September 1066, to invade England, he had planned to add England to his dominion. He planned well, too, for he enlisted the support of the Pope. He obtained the services of some of the best knights in Europe by promising them big land grants in England. He trained his men rigorously. And he even prefabricated the parts of several wooden forts which were to be shipped over to England and erected on raised mounds of earth, to act as garrison and police depots. Even in the last days he waited cunningly to see the result of the fight between Harold II of England and the Norwegian Viking king, Hardraada,

which was a victory for England. Whichever of the sides had won, William thought, they would have to come down the length of England and would be tired out when they met him on the Sussex downs.

And so it was, for though Harold and his Englishmen fought desperately they were half exhausted and no match for William's rested and exercised troops.

Once William was king he imposed his ideas of government and society on the country with firmness, skill and thoroughness. Norman and Saxon alike were made to feel the weight of his authority and the justice of his laws. Even the biggest lords had to do homage to him, at the Oath of Salisbury, and thereby admit that they held their lands from him. Every village and manor was taken over by the king and new loyalties were affirmed. Even the contents of his new land were surveyed and catalogued, in the great *Domesday Book*, a wonderful achievement of administrative work for those days.

This handsome, bold and on the whole, good-natured man with a notable sense of humour, died in 1087 as a result of a fall from his horse at a siege.

Lanfranc (c.1000–1089)
Archbishop of Canterbury

When William the Conqueror (*p. 74*) planned to re-shape the country after conquering England in 1066, one of the organizations which received his attention was the Church. He cleared it of nearly all the Saxon bishops, and in 1070 he appointed Lanfranc, an Italian scholar, as Archbishop of Canterbury. Lanfranc held this office for the rest of his life, and he and William drastically re-ordered the church. Among many other things they did was to abolish bishoprics in small towns like Dorchester-on-Thames and Sherborne, and install them in bigger centres like Chester and Norwich.

Like many archbishops before and after him, Lanfranc was deeply interested in education, and at Canterbury his school became well known throughout Europe. He also acted as one of William's

74

A saxon soldier wielding a battleaxe at the Battle of Hastings

chief political advisers, as in those days churchmen were often as worldly and skilled in statecraft as anyone else.

Malcolm III (died 1093)
King of Scotland (1057–1093)

Malcolm was a short, thick-set young man when he became king, with an unusually large head, so that he was nicknamed 'Ceanmor' or 'Big Head'. He was the elder son of Duncan (1034–1040) who had been killed in a civil war, and he had to leave Scotland when Macbeth (*p. 72*) became king. Malcolm grew up to hate Macbeth. It was not hard to find support among exiled lords who had been banished when Macbeth had tried to restore order in Scotland.

Eventually, Malcolm was powerful enough to invade Scotland, in 1057, and he defeated Macbeth at Lumphanan, where the great king was killed. But Malcolm's long stay in England had made him almost more English than Scottish, and while the Lowland half of his country was willing to accept new English ideas, the Highland part was not. Macbeth might have been dead but his spirit lived on, and much of Malcolm's reign was vexed with opposition from the Highlands. Matters were not helped when he married an English princess, Margaret, granddaughter of Edmund Ironside, for though she was a cultured and beautiful woman, her ideas were not welcome in Scotland.

Malcolm invaded England in 1093 but was killed at a siege of Alnwick castle.

St. Wulfstan (c.1012–1095)
English bishop

Wulfstan was bishop of Worcester when William the Conqueror came over to England. He submitted to the new king, but, although it was William's policy to replace Anglo-Saxon bishops with Norman ones, he left Wulfstan in office. Probably he believed all that he had heard of this remarkable man who was said to have put an end to the slave trade in Bristol harbour by preaching a series of cautionary and obviously effective, sermons to the traders.

Wulfstan also supported William Rufus, which is interesting because William ran foul of the Church. This led to his being constantly maligned in the histories of the times. Wulfstan was canonized in 1203.

Urban II (c.1042–1099)
Pope (1088–1099)

Urban, whose real name was Udo, was French born, and he became a Benedictine monk. In about 1080 he was appointed a papal ambassador to Germany, and when Gregory VII died in 1085 and Victor II followed, Udo was tipped to succeed him. And so it happened, in 1088. He took the name Urban II, and his reign was an important one. The principal event was the announcement he made to Western Christendom that it should arm itself and go to the Middle East to attack the infidel Turks, who were molesting Christian pilgrims to the Holy Land. He aroused a crusading spirit with his eloquence and an army was formed and the campaign launched. It was to be called The First Crusade. Sadly, Urban died before he received the news that Jerusalem had been captured by the Christians.

Adam of Bremen (11th century)
German historian

Not much is known about this historian who wrote *Gesta Hammaburgensis Ecclesiae Pontificum*, a history book which tells us much about the church and about military and political history in north-western Europe in the period 700 to 1050.

Eriksson, Leif (11th century)
Norwegian explorer

Leif Eriksson was the son of Eric the Red, a Viking Norwegian chief who had founded the colony of Greenland in about 985. He had also established Viking dominion in Iceland. Eriksson had all of his father's thirst for discovery and his ability to lead men through dangerous waters.

In about 1000, after growing up in the colony of Greenland, Eriksson set out with several colleagues in some ships to chart the western side of the great landmass. But the winds took them out to sea and for days they were at the mercy of the Atlantic. When the wind dropped, Eriksson sighted land and steered towards it. They all scrambled out of their ships across the sand and found themselves among a mass of wild vine bushes. The land came to be called Vinland, but it was in fact America, probably Labrador. Without appreciating it Eriksson and his friends had anticipated Columbus by nearly 500 years!

William II (Rufus) (c.1056–1100)
King of England (1087–1100)

William was the Conqueror's second son. He was called Rufus because of his fiery complexion, which in some degree matched his temperament. He was more quick-tempered than his father, which led him to commit unjust acts, that in more sober moments he would probably have regretted. But he was by no means as black as history has painted him, a history incidentally written almost entirely by churchmen – and Rufus spent most of his reign quarrelling with the Church. He has, in fact, had a bad press, for he was both a loyal friend and a generous enemy, and he had also been a stout supporter of his father's cause.

Rufus was determined to see his father's new order work in England. He governed firmly, but his tempers led him to quarrel with those most able – and most willing in some cases – to help him. It was a pity, for example, that he fell out with the wise and saintly Anselm, his Archbishop of Canterbury, and even drove him into exile. As his chief adviser, William appointed Ranulf Flambard, an arrogant Norman bishop, who made himself unpopular with Saxons and Normans alike.

William was fond of hunting, and one day in the New Forest, not far from Winchester, he was accidently killed by a friend who was shooting at a running stag.

Godfrey de Bouillon (c.1061–1100)
French noble and Crusade leader

Godfrey de Bouillon was duke of Lorraine, on the eastern border of France. He was a bold, handsome and deeply religious leader of men who, when Urban II announced the organization of the First Crusade, in 1095, immediately offered his services as a commander. They were readily accepted, and Godfrey, together with a troop of knights, set out for Constantinople.

The campaign against the Turks at first ran into trouble, but by 1097 Jerusalem was within their grasp, and Godfrey was one of the commanders who led his men through its gates. The Holy City was therefore saved from the Turks. When the Sultan of Egypt attempted to displace the Crusaders in Palestine, Godfrey defeated him at Ascalon, in 1099.

Henry IV (1050–1106)
Holy Roman Emperor (1056–1106)

Henry IV was King of Germany and Holy Roman Emperor from the age of six. His minority years of rule were supervised by his mother, Agnes of Poitou, a French princess who had married his father, Henry III. When he came of age, he became involved in a long quarrel with Pope Gregory VII (*p. 74*) on the question of who should invest princes and dukes in the Empire. He was excommunicated, and then grovelled for forgiveness before the pope at the 'Humiliation at Canossa'. He continued, however, to quarrel with Gregory and to assert his rights, and in 1084 he drove the Pope off the papal throne, setting up a rival pope, Clement III, in his place.

Leif Eriksson at the helm of a Viking longship

77

St. Anselm (1033–1109)
Italian born theologian

Anselm was born in Piedmont in north Italy. He was a fine scholar and became abbot of the well known monastery at Bec in 1078. There he attracted the attention of William the Conqueror (of England) who gave him preferments, but it was William's son, Rufus (William II) who appointed him Archbishop of Canterbury.

Anselm quarrelled with William and left England in fear of his life. He was restored to the position when Henry I (1100–1135) succeeded, but he quarrelled with Henry, too, and had to escape the king's wrath. But they made it up and Anselm remained Henry's wisest adviser.

Peter the Hermit (c.1050–1115)
French monk and Crusade leader

Towards the end of the 11th century the Church, encouraged by Pope Urban II, preached war against the Turks who were harassing pilgrims visiting Palestine, especially the Holy City of Jerusalem. Among those who spread the message was the French monk, Peter of Amiens, and he was as good as his word, for he set an example by forming an army of crusaders to join the main forces of the First Crusade, assembling at Constantinople.

At first, Peter's army was not successful, and it was dispersed by the Turks. But then he went to fight with Godfrey de Bouillon (*p. 77*) who in 1097 captured Jerusalem.

Abelard, Peter (1079–1142)
French thinker and theologian

Peter Abelard is often described as one of the boldest thinkers of the 12th century. His life was both romantic and tragic.

He taught philosophy in Paris, and among his pupils was Héloise, the niece of a canon of the church. She was seventeen and Abelard was thirty-eight, but they fell deeply in love. They fled from Paris to Brittany, where they were married and had a son. However, her uncle caught up with them and sent a group of very tough men to attack Abelard. Their blows were brutal and the unfortunate Abelard was castrated. He had to return to a monastery where he began again to teach. Soon, pupils came from far and wide to learn from him.

Ordericus Vitalis (1057–1143)
French historian

Ordericus was the son of a French priest and an English housewife, and was born at Shrewsbury. When he was young he was taken to the abbey at St. Evroult where he spent his life as a monk. He wrote several major works, in particular, the *Historia Ecclesiastica*, which is a history of England and Normandy. It is full of useful facts, but it is also punctuated with much gossip, like the biographies of the early Caesars written by Suetonius.

William of Malmesbury (c.1090–1143)
English historian

William became a monk at Malmesbury in Wiltshire, and in time he ran the monastery's library. He wrote many books, including volumes about the lives of English bishops, for this was of popular taste in mediaeval England. But his most useful work was his *Gesta Regum Anglorum*, or Deeds of the English Kings. This was the story of the kings from about 449, when Hengist (*p. 57*) came to Kent, up to the time of Henry I. It was an important work, largely because it destroyed many myths, rumours and exaggerations about various kings. In particular William deflated the legend of King Arthur.

Conrad III (1093–1152)
Holy Roman Emperor and King of Germany (1138–1152)

Conrad was the first of a dynasty of German rulers who were also Emperors of the Holy Roman Empire. This was the Hohenstauffen line, and it ruled from 1138 to 1254. Four of its house were never actually crowned by the Pope, but they held the power, which of course is what mattered.

Conrad, like many other German kings,

sought to unite Germany with Italy, but his attempts were not successful. In 1147 he joined Louis VII of France on the Second Crusade to the Holy Land.

David I (1084–1153)
King of Scotland (1124–1153)

Scotland has had many excellent rulers, and one of the best was David I. He was the youngest son of Malcolm III (*p. 75*) and though he spent much of his youth in England, he was very proud of being a Scot. This did not, however, prevent many Normans obtaining high posts in the government of Scotland. But all the same David quarrelled often with the English rulers, and although he lost the Battle of the Standard at Northallerton to the English in 1138, he did well out of the following peace treaty. Northumberland and Cumberland, excepting one or two castles, were recognized as Scottish territory. This was probably due to the weakness of the English king, Stephen.

David was deeply religious, and he sponsored the building of several splendid abbeys in Scotland, notably Kelso, Jedburgh and Melrose, whose magnificent ruins can still be seen to-day. He increased the number of bishoprics and he financed schools.

When he died in 1153 a contemporary historian wrote that he was 'the best of all his kind'.

Kelso Abbey built under the patronage of David I

Turlough O'Connor (d. 1156)
King of all Ireland (1121–1156)

Turlough O'Connor was King of Connaught, one of the four principal kingdoms of Ireland, and he was determined to make himself Ard Rí, or High King of all Ireland. When Domhnall O'Lochlainn, King of Ulster (who had claimed to be Ard Rí), died in 1121, Turlough announced his claim. He gave a huge quantity of gold to St. Patrick's Church at Armagh, in return for which the archbishop recognized the claim.

But to claim was one thing: to get it accepted by the other kings was another. Much of his reign was taken up with fighting to establish his supremacy. But despite this, Turlough was able to do much for Irish learning, art, buildings and towns. He was also interested in bridge construction and built several across the Shannon, which divided Connaught from Meath.

Adrian IV (c.1100–1159)
Pope (1154–1159)

Adrian IV was the title taken by Nicholas Breakspear, an English-born prelate who, as bishop of Albano in Italy, was the only Englishman ever to be elected pope. His reign was a short one, from 1154 to 1159. During that time he quarrelled with Frederick I (*p. 82*) about the question of papal supremacy over all rulers in Europe. He also authorized Henry II (Plantagenet) of England (*p. 81*) to invade Ireland, so as to bring its church under Roman dominion.

Matilda (1102–1167)
English queen (1135–1154)

Matilda was the daughter of Henry I. When he died in 1135, his will ordered that she should be his successor. But the barons of England did not want her, and chose her cousin Stephen, count of Blois, instead. He was Henry's nephew. The result was a reign of nineteen years (1135–1154) during which Matilda and Stephen struggled incessantly for the throne. On one occasion, Matilda escaped from Oxford Castle, running through the snow in bare feet.

Matilda's second husband was Geoffrey Plantagenet, Count of Anjou, and they had a son, Henry II (1154–1189).

Owain Gwynedd (d.1170)
Prince of Wales

Owain was the son of Gruffydd ap Cynan, Prince of North Wales. In 1136 he invaded the principality of Ceredigion and captured its capital, Cardigan town, a centre of Norman power in west Wales. Then he went on to take Carmarthen, and by the end of the year he had all south-west Wales in his hands. Gruffydd died happy, having been cheered in his last weeks by the news of his son's exploits.

Although Owain became prince of much of Wales, the first years of his rule were taken up with war against other princes, but by 1152 he had defeated them all and was effectively prince of Wales, except for the marcher pockets. This was extremely exciting for Welshmen. Owain embarked on a programme of building, including abbeys like Valle Crucis and Strata Florida. He encouraged the arts, especially literature, and two of Wales' best poets of the Middle Ages, Gwalchmai and Cynndelw, flourished in his day. He also introduced the idea of the eisteddfod, a gathering of Welsh people at which poets and musicians recited and played in a competitive manner for prizes awarded by the prince.

St. Thomas Becket (c.1120–1170)
Archbishop of Canterbury

Becket was a scholar and lawyer, who in 1155 was appointed chancellor of England by young Henry II (*p. 81*). For seven years Henry and he worked together to administer a land which had recently endured a generation of civil war under Henry's predecessor Stephen (1135–1154). Then, in 1162 the archbishopric of Canterbury fell vacant, and Henry offered Becket the job. Becket was unwilling to accept at first, because he knew that his duty to the church would clash with the sense of loyalty and friendship that he felt for the king. Henry was bent upon reforming the church, in particular the privileges which churchmen claimed in order to avoid the penalties of the law.

From the start, Becket became a changed man. He had been gay, rumbustious, fun-loving, and had hunted and feasted with the king day after day. Now he became morose, argumentative, dictatorial, and wore hair shirts next to his skin. He vehemently defended the church in all the king's attempts to reform it, and in doing so the two men quarrelled frequently. Henry drove him into exile in 1164, but invited him back again in 1170. Becket came, but he had not learned his lesson. Again he opposed the king, whereupon Henry lost his temper and exclaimed that surely there was someone among his friends who would rid him of this 'turbulent priest'.

Four knights took the king's words seriously, and on 29 December they brutally murdered Becket on the steps leading to the high altar in Canterbury Cathedral. It was a dreadful crime and Henry had to repent of it grievously. Some people, however, now claim that Becket sought a martyr's death and deliberately provoked the king's loss of temper.

John of Salisbury (12th century)
English scholar

John of Salisbury was a scholar who studied under Abelard (*p. 78*) in Paris. He was appointed secretary to Theobald, archbishop of Canterbury, in the first years of the reign of Henry II (Plantagenet, *p. 81*). When Becket (*p. 80*) succeeded Theobald, John supported

The Archbishop of Canterbury, Thomas Becket and Henry II

him in his stand against the king who wanted to reform church privileges. So he was banished. He came back and was said to have been present when Becket was actually killed on the steps of the high altar at Canterbury in 1170. His biography of Becket was received with great interest and enthusiasm.

Henry II (Plantagenet) (1133–1189)
King of England (1154–1189)
At the age of 21, this red-haired, thick-set Angevin noble, with grey eyes that flashed when he was angry, became King of England. He was also lord of vast areas of land in France, more even than the King of France himself owned. And he ruled them well, for above all else Henry believed in the majesty of the law.

First of the House of Plantagenet, so-called because his father used to wear a sprig of broom (*planta genista*) as a badge, Henry was the greatest lawgiver England ever had. He also tried to curtail the powers of the church by challenging its right to release its members accused of crimes, by dealing with the cases in

church courts. This brought him into conflict with the archbishop of Canterbury, Thomas Becket (*p. 80*) whom he had appointed in 1162.

In 1171, Henry invaded Ireland and in a short campaign brought the country under his rule, taking the title Lord of Ireland. The Irish High King, Roderic O'Connor, was allowed to retain his throne, but his powers were greatly reduced.

Henry II was a man of immense energy and endurance. He never sat down for a moment, except to eat a quick meal or a snack, and indeed he often ate while on horseback. He travelled ceaselessly about his domains, taking the royal household and the assize courts with him.

The last years of his reign were filled with rebellions by his sons, who could not wait for their inheritances. When he heard that his youngest and favourite son, John, had taken up arms against him, in 1189, he exclaimed that he had nothing else to live for. So, turning his face to the wall he died of a broken heart.

Saladin on the right, fighting with a Crusader

Frederick I (Barbarossa) (c.1123–1190)
Holy Roman Emperor (1152–1190)
Frederick was known as Barbarossa because of his red beard, which was an instant clue to his fiery temperament. Yet this sensitive ruler, who often did things in a most dramatic manner, was a cultivated and enlightened man, who brought many benefits to the German people.

He was King of the Germans and Holy Roman Emperor from 1152 to his death. He aimed to make Germany strong, free and prosperous. He encouraged the arts, fostered trade, and took a keen interest in the development of towns and ports. He also set out to expand his dominions, and was for a time King of Italy.

When the Third Crusade to the Holy Land was announced in 1189, Frederick joined it as one of its leaders. But out in Asia Minor he was accidentally drowned as he crossed a river, while marching through Cilicia.

Saladin (1138–1193)
Arab Sultan
Salah-ed-din Yusuf ibn Ayub had been made vizier, or governor, of Egypt in 1169, by the caliph of Baghdad. He governed well, but he was ambitious, as well as able, and in 1171 he rebelled against his master. He seized power and created himself Sultan of Egypt. Then he conquered Syria and attacked the Christian army near Tiberias in 1187 and defeated it. Pushing on, he took Acre, Jerusalem and other towns and effectively cleared Palestine of Christians.

This sparked off the Third Crusade, led by Richard I of England (*p. 83*). Saladin was defeated at Acre in 1190, but managed to prevent the Crusaders from taking Jerusalem. A treaty between the two sides in 1192 was favourable to both.

Saladin was renowned for his generosity and humanity, and the Crusaders admired him greatly. He allowed Christians to visit the Holy City in peace.

Bela III (d.1196)
King of Hungary (1173–1196)
Bela III became King of Hungary in 1173. He had been educated at Constantinople, and had introduced Byzantine customs to his kingdom which at that time was struggling for unity. One of his wives was Margaret, the sister of Philip Augustus of France (*p. 86*).

Roderic O'Connor (c.1116–1198)
Last King of all Ireland (1166–1198)
Roderic O'Connor was the son of Turlough O'Connor (*p. 79*) and he claimed the title Ard Rí, or High King of Ireland, in 1166. He even had himself proclaimed as such in a splendid ceremony held at Dublin.

When Henry II of England invaded Ireland in 1171, and swiftly made the Irish recognize him as Lord of Ireland, he came to terms with Roderic whereby Roderic was to continue as Ard Rí on the understanding that Henry's new title of Lord of Ireland was clearly seen as meaning what it said. Roderic agreed with this somewhat humiliating condition, but in 1186 he retired to a monastery.

Richard I (Plantagenet) (1157–1199)
King of England (1189–1199)
It seems a pity to say that Richard, known as Lionheart, who is one of the greatest heroes of English history, was perhaps the worst king in the story of England. In ten years he spent less than a year in England. He bled the country white with taxes for money to finance the Third Crusade, which was to be campaigned in a part of the world most Englishmen had not even heard of. He left his kingdom in the hands of one of the most arrogant men ever to have authority in the island, William Longchamp. This self-opinionated and oppressive man succeeded only in turning everyone in the land against him, and Prince John rightly threw him out.

Richard started the business of selling charters or rights to towns. In principle this was not a bad thing, but he did it willy-nilly, without discretion, and some towns received charters when they ought to have waited.

All this said and done, however, Richard was bold, generous to his enemies, chivalrous to ladies and fair to his friends, even to those who let him down. On his deathbed he forgave the archer who had shot the fatal bolt which entered his shoulder.

Chrétien de Troyes (12th century)
Mediaeval French poet
This poet used to write verses out of the songs sung by wandering troubadours in France. He also took famous legends, such as Arthur and the Knights of the Round Table, Tristan and Isolde, and wove them into fine ballads and poems. His works include *Erec et Énide*, *Cligès*, *Lancelot*, *Yvain* and *Perceval*.

Petrus Waldus (12th century)
French religious thinker and reformer
It is easy to think that the movement for reform of the church began only in the 16th century. Many, especially Wicliffe and Huss, were questioning the very doctrines of the church in the 14th century. In the 12th century Peter Waldo, or Petrus Waldus, who had been a merchant, gave up all worldly pleasures, just as Mohammed (*p. 60*) had done, and retired to study. He sooon gathered round him a group of disciples, who questioned many of the church's teachings and interpretations of the Scriptures. These disciples came to be known as the Waldenses.

Eleanor of Aquitaine (c.1122–1204)
Queen of Henry II of England
Eleanor of Aquitaine was the daughter of William X, Duke of Aquitaine. She became owner of this vast territory in 1137. Then she married Louis, son and heir to the King of France, who became Louis VII a few weeks later. They had two daughters but no son, and they did not like each other very much. Eleanor was difficult to get on with, being very self-opinionated, and men of these days did not like that. However she was famed as a patroness of the arts, and her court had an extraordinary influence on the cultural life and social customs of Europe at this time. The marriage ended in 1152. Eleanor then married Henry Plantagenet, Count of Anjou, who two years later was to become Henry II of England. The marriage frightened the French king and it is said the rivalry between France and England began at this time.

Eleanor had several children, Henry, Richard (Richard I), Geoffrey and John (King John), but she was no more happy with Henry than with Louis. She set her sons against their father, encouraged them when they were old enough to rebel, and gave him a great deal of trouble. He had to put her into confinement to keep his realm in order.

An allegorical portrayal of William the Lion

Maimonides (Moses ben Maimon)
(1135–1205)
Jewish scholar

Maimonides is regarded by many Jewish people as the greatest scholar that their magnificent race has produced in a long history of brilliant people. He was a boy of thirteen living in Cordoba in Spain when an army of Moorish Arabs overran the whole area and carried him off to Morocco. There, he grew up under the influence of Mohammedanism, and he liked some of its teachings.

When he was about twenty he went to Egypt to join a Jewish community there, that had been welcomed and given freedom to live in its own way. He studied medicine, and like Hasdai (*p. 67*) he was appointed physician to the viceroy of Egypt. He was still in office when the viceroy, Saladin, (*p. 82*) seized control and set himself up as Sultan. Yet Saladin treated Maimonides well.

Maimonides was also a philosopher and he wrote down much of what he believed and thought. He produced a compendium of Hebrew law and he

84

gathered round him a number of pupils who carried his ideas further afield. One thing he did was to re-state the principles of the Jewish faith, relating them to principles of reason. This meant rejecting much that was old and illogical, and it offended some more orthodox Jewish religious leaders, but the majority accepted his ideas.

Walter Map (c.1140–1209)
Welsh poet and prelate
Walter Map studied in Paris after a childhood in Herefordshire and his parents were Welsh. He returned to England and was made a clerk to the royal household. Later he was sent on missions abroad, just as Chaucer and Marlowe were.

When he was at court, Map compiled a book of the gossip that he had heard about the various comings and goings of the lords and ladies. This was very amusing, even if at times scandalous. He also worked on the Arthurian legends, and is thought to have been the first to link Arthur and the Round Table with the quest for the Holy Grail.

William the Lion (1143–1214)
King of Scotland (1165–1214)
This was an ideal name for a king who was indeed bold to the point of recklessness, but King William was in many ways a disaster for Scotland. In 1174, on one of his many foolhardy raids across the English border he was surprised at Alnwick and captured. Henry II of England, then in France, ordered William to be brought to him – in chains. The English king allowed him to return, but only on condition that he accepted Henry as his overlord. He also had to surrender several important castles.

When Richard I of England was raising money in 1189 for the Third Crusade, he offered William exemption from the stiff conditions imposed by Henry for a cash sum. The Scottish king accepted. Scotland was free again, but it was not long before it was suffering under the stress of civil war.

Innocent III (1161–1216)
Pope (1198–1216)
Among the many popes who have been at the head of the Roman Catholic Church since the time of St. Peter (*p. 44*), Innocent III was one of the most forceful, and his reign was one of the most eventful.

He was elected pope in 1198. From the start he determined to make the papacy supreme over the state, just as Gregory VII (*p. 74*) had done before him, and certainly in his time the papal power was at a very high point. He called for the Fourth Crusade, in the years 1202–1204, which ended in the shameful sacking of Christian Constantinople by Christian knights and soldiers from Western Europe. It was something that Innocent probably had not bargained for. He intervened in England when King John (*p. 85*) refused, in 1207, to allow his nominee, Stephen Langton (*p. 89*), to take up his appointment as Archbishop of Canterbury, and he put the country under an interdict for five years. But this same pope told John, in 1215, that he need not keep to his promise to abide by the terms of Magna Carta. This was said because the terms had been forced on John by the barons, whose leader was Stephen Langton!

John (1166–1216)
King of England (1199–1216)
Few kings can have been so maligned as John, who was the youngest son of Henry II (Plantagenet, *p. 81*). It is true he was quick tempered, given to being lazy, and probably not always a man of his word. But when one considers the general statement that his reign of seventeen years was a catalogue of disasters, one has also to recall that in that time there was no revolt until the very last year, and then it was a baronial one. One has also to record that John loved England, and that many of his actions were motivated by this.

During his brother Richard I's reign (*p. 83*) he led the revolt which got rid of the hated William Longchamp, a Norman whose arrogance was exceptional even for a Norman. In the early years of his own reign he lost most of his father's possessions in France, but it could be said they were more of a burden than an asset. When he refused to allow Stephen Langton (*p. 89*) to take up his appointment by the Pope as Archbishop of Canterbury, it was because he wanted his friend, the Bishop of Norwich, whom England would have preferred. And even his resistance to Magna Carta was a stand for the rights of the ordinary people as much as for the dignity of the king. He was certainly wise enough to know that the charter was little more than a written certificate for the barons to continue to have things all their own way.

John encouraged the growth of local government by extending the process of granting charters to towns. He understood the need for town planning, and the origins of the port of Liverpool may be put down to his royal interest. He also saw that the new stone bridge across the Thames in London was finished: it had been taking far too long under his predecessors.

John died at Newark in 1216, fighting for his throne against the barons who had invited the aid of Louis, Prince of France and son of Philip Augustus (*p. 86*).

William the Marshal (c.1150–1219)
English statesman

England was fortunate that when King John died in 1216 there was an able and popular statesman in William the Marshal, capable of smoothing over the first years of the next king, Henry III, who was then only a boy. This great military leader and statesman, who was Earl of Pembroke, was also highly educated. He was at one time a tutor to Prince Henry, eldest son of Henry II. Richard I appointed him Justiciar of England while he went off to the Holy Land on the Third Crusade in 1189. When Richard died in 1199 some of the barons elected to have the boy prince, Arthur, son of Richard's next brother, Geoffrey, as king, but Marshal, a supporter of John, persuaded them that an adult king was a safer bet.

John is said to have treated him ungratefully, but we find William supporting him throughout the reign, especially during the struggle over Magna Carta and the ensuing civil war. It therefore came as no surprise when the English council made William Regent during Henry III's minority.

Saxo Grammaticus (1150–1220)
Danish historian

Known as 'the Scholar', Saxo was the author of a huge work of sixteen volumes, called *Gesta Danorum*, which was the history of Denmark up to the end of the 12th century. Much of it is legend, mingled with Viking sagas, a splendid combination of what happened and what people wanted to happen. Among the legends was the story of Hamlet, Prince of Denmark, which Shakespeare used for his famous play.

Philip Augustus (Philip II) (1165–1223)
King of France (1180–1223)

Philip Augustus was a proud, aggressive and bold Frenchman who, from the moment he became king, in 1180, determined to throw the English out of all their French possessions. He had little success against Henry II and Richard I, but in the first years of the 13th century he drove John out of Normandy, Maine, Anjou and Touraine, and succeeded in capturing the impregnable fortress of Chateau Gaillard, on the river Seine. This concentric castle, built on rock by Richard I, fell to Philip's troops, some of whom climbed inside by scrambling up the drains.

The last ten years of his reign were devoted to domestic matters. Philip commissioned the building of Notre Dame Cathedral, granted a charter to the University of Paris, and reformed the law.

St. Francis of Assisi (1182–1226)
Italian friar

Giovanni Francisco Bernardone was a young merchant from Assisi, in Italy. An illness and a military expedition which disgusted him, made him give up his life

as an ordinary man of the world. He renounced everything, even his clothes, to live a life of poverty in which he would help the poor, the sick and the disabled. It was not long before he gathered round him a number of followers, each man donning a simple grey cloak. They called themselves brothers (*fratres* in Latin, from which the word friars eventually stemmed).

Francis founded an order which the Pope approved. It grew rapidly all over Europe, for it offered a higher standard of behaviour and devotion than monks in other monasteries could set, for monastic life had recently been growing lax. Francis himself set a fine example. He lived entirely by begging for alms for support while he healed the sick and tended the crippled. He even loved and talked to the animal kingdom and to all of nature, to birds and beasts, and to flowers and trees.

On his death bed, he is said to have spoken to Death saying 'Welcome, sister.' He was canonized in 1228.

St. Francis of Assisi

Genghis Khan (1162–1227)
Mongol ruler and conqueror

It is all too easy to regard Genghis Khan as an uneducated savage who, by sheer force of personality and superb military flair, conquered nearly all Asia, in the 13th century. This is only half the truth, for the great Mongol chief was a man of considerable political skill as well, and it is known that once he had conquered Asia he devised a comprehensive scheme for governing it. It was his tragedy, and perhaps Asia's too, that he died before this could be put into effect. It was also unfortunate that his successors were not as able as he.

Genghis Khan's real name was Temujine. He was the son of a Mongolian chief who died in 1175, leaving his thirteen year old son as heir. It was a rough inheritance. Few of the old chief's associates wanted to be ruled by a mere boy, but Temujine was no ordinary child. He was grown up for his age, extremely tough and brave, and in a short while he proved himself worthy of his elders' respect.

Temujine began to build up a powerful fighting force of armed horsemen, for he was already thinking about extending his father's territory, and by the end of the 12th century he was lord over a great part

The Mongol ruler, Genghis Khan, breaching the Great Wall of China

of Mongolia. His followers called him Genghis Khan, which means 'Lord Absolute'.

In 1206 Genghis Khan launched the first of his great wave of invasions in Asia. He attacked China, breached its famous Great Wall in several places and soon occupied the whole of the north. Then he turned westwards and over the next decade overran a great part of Asia, including Persia, Afghanistan, Armenia, most of India and huge areas of Russia. By about 1223 he claimed to be lord of Asia and admitted that it took a year to ride from one end of his dominions to the other and back.

In 1227 he embarked upon yet another raid, but died on the way.

Langton, Stephen (c.1150–1228)
Archbishop of Canterbury

Langton was educated abroad and spent some time at the University of Paris. He was a friend of Innocent III who made him a cardinal in recognition of his scholarship. For Langton had divided the Old Testament into books, and had published various papers on bishops' powers.

In 1207 Innocent appointed Langton Archbishop of Canterbury, but John of England objected. He wanted his friend, the Bishop of Norwich, to be appointed. The result was that England was placed under an interdict for five years, until John relented. In 1213, Langton came to England to take up his post. It is not surprising, therefore, that we find his name at the top of the list of those barons who forced John to accept Magna Carta, in 1215.

Llywelyn Fawr (Llywelyn the Great) (c.1175–1240)
Prince of Wales

Greatest of all the independent princes of Wales, Llywelyn ap Iorwerth was grandson of Owain Gwynedd (*p. 80*). He drove his useless uncle, Dafydd I, off the throne in 1194 and ruled all Wales, except for a few isolated pockets controlled by the Norman marcher lords. This splendid, martial leader of Welshmen was a bold and skilful general, and a very astute statesman. By marrying a daughter of John of England he overcame English attempts to resist his supremacy in Wales. When John was forced to agree to Magna Carta, Llywelyn managed to get clauses into it which recognized his independence. From 1215 until his death his rule was never seriously challenged. And in that time of peace he encouraged learning and art, trade and agriculture. He endowed churches and monasteries generously.

Not long before his death, he ordered the Welsh council of lords to accept his son Dafydd as his heir.

Waldemar II (1170–1241)
King of Denmark (1202–1241)
Waldemar was one of Denmark's greatest rulers. Known as 'the Victorious', he conquered substantial areas of north-west Germany, and reached as far as Estonia, on the eastern side of the Baltic Sea. By 1227 he was probably the most powerful king in north-west Europe. At home, he ruled well and gave his people a code of laws.

Ogdai Khan (1185–1241)
Mongol chief
Ogdai was the third son of the great Genghis Khan (*p. 88*). He inherited a large part of his father's huge conquests, and he tried to carry out some of Genghis' ideas about governing these areas. He was greatly helped by a brilliant Chinese-born statesman, Ye-lu-Ch'u-Tsai, whom Genghis had brought back from northern China. But Ogdai was very fond of drink, and for some of the time his wits were befuddled.

In about 1237 Ogdai sent a huge army against Russia, and thus burned Moscow, Kiev and other towns and ravaged far and wide in Poland and Hungary. Western Europe was terrified, but in the middle of this great drive Ogdai died, possibly as the result of drink.

Frederick II (1194–1250)
Holy Roman Emperor (1220–1250)
Frederick II became King of Sicily when he was only four, and was Holy Roman Emperor before he was twenty-one. He wanted to unite Germany and Italy, although there were numerous differences of character, outlook and ambition, quite apart from language and culture. But he was strongly resisted by the Italian states.

In 1228 he organized and led the Fifth Crusade, capturing Jerusalem in the following year and assuming the title of King of Jerusalem.

Frederick was a cultured man, who patronized the arts and encouraged science, at that time subjects which few people understood. His wisdom and his learning earned him the reputation of being one of the cleverest men in Europe, as well as the nickname 'Stupor Mundi', or Wonder of the World.

Grosseteste, Robert (c.1175–1253)
English scholar and prelate
Grosseteste means Big Head. This fine scholar was leader of one of the earliest friars' schools at Oxford in the 1220s. Then in 1235 he became bishop of Lincoln. He incurred the wrath not only of his own fellow bishops, but also of Rome when he attacked the age-old practice of giving English church livings to foreigners, which resulted in money going out of the kingdom. This was something Henry III and his favourites were doing and Grosseteste rightly saw it as a danger to England's economy. This opposition led to his being suspended as bishop, but his pupils and supporters continued to visit him. In some ways he was also generally defending the rights of Englishmen.

Matthew Paris (c.1200–1259)
English historian
Matthew Paris was an historian who spent much of his life in the monastery at St. Albans. There he compiled his *Chronica Majora*, which is a detailed history from the beginning of Man to 1259. The work had been started by another chronicler, Roger of Wendover, but Paris wrote much of it and completed it. In 1248, the Pope, Innocent IV, sent him to Norway to reform a large abbey.

It is by consulting Matthew Paris' work that we discover that King John was not as black as he has been painted in in other sources.

De Montfort, Simon (c.1208–1265)
English statesman
The British are justly proud of having been the first to introduce a form of parliament similar to the kind the world knows today. And the man who initiated it, in 1265, was Simon de Montfort. He was Earl of Leicester, married to the king's sister. Henry III had been ruling badly for years, and the barons rose up against him. Led by Simon, they insisted

Simon de Montfort

upon more participation in the government of the land. Simon therefore summoned a parliament not only of lords, but also of bishops, four knights from each shire and two citizens from each major town. It was the first gathering of its kind to be elected. Although of course the representatives were not elected by the whole community in every case, it was nevertheless a start.

Simon was killed a few months later at the battle of Evesham, where Henry's son, Edward (later Edward I), fought to restore his father's honour and power.

Bracton, Henry (d.1268)
English judge

Bracton is famous for having compiled a systematic treatise on the laws of England in his day, called *De Legibus et Consuetudinibus Angliae* (Concerning the Laws and Customs of England). He had been an itinerant judge and also archdeacon of Barnstaple (in Devonshire) and Chancellor of Exeter Cathedral. Bracton is often quoted in historical works and occasionally in courts of law.

Louis IX (St. Louis) (1215–1270)
King of France (1226–1270)

Louis was one of the most revered of all the kings of France. His mother ruled during his first years, as he was only ten when he succeeded to the throne, but once he came of age he set out to make France a great country. He also wanted to break the English grip on large parts of the mainland.

In 1248 Louis accompanied the Sixth Crusade (1248–1254) and took an army to Egypt, where he captured Damietta. At El Mansura, however, he was defeated and captured, and he languished in confinement until a large ransom of 100,000 marks was raised for his release. He returned to France in 1254, where he made peace with England. This transferred some of the English possessions to France.

Louis improved relations between the French church and Rome, which had been quarrelling for some time. He regionalized the courts of justice and organized a new code of laws. He also expanded the University of Paris at the Sorbonne.

In 1270 he set out on another Crusade to the Holy Land, but died in North Africa on the way. Twenty-seven years later, he was canonized.

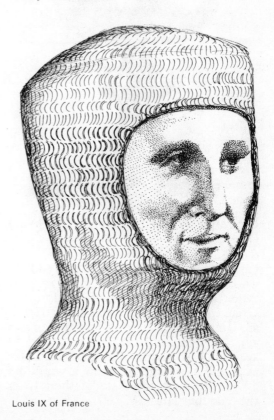

Louis IX of France

St. Thomas Aquinas (c.1225–1274)
Italian scholar

Thomas Aquinas entered the Dominican order of friars in 1243, and he went to Paris in 1252 to study theology and other subjects. In six years his quick thinking, his clarity of reasoning and his ability to set out arguments well, earned him a great reputation as a philosopher, and in 1258 the pope invited him to teach at various centres in Italy. His opinions thereafter began to carry enormous weight in the Church, and quite often his views on certain disputes or points of doctrine were regarded as decisive. His comments on the Bible were read widely to such an extent that they influenced Catholic thought for generations to come.

Thomas would not accept any preferment or office, and he turned down many rich appointments, including archbishoprics. He was canonized in 1323.

The Dolgellau Chalice, an artefact of the time of Llywelyn

Llywelyn Yr Ail (Llywelyn the Last)
(13th century)
Prince of Wales (1246–1282)

Llywelyn was the nephew of Dafydd II, who was Prince of Wales from 1240 to 1246, and grandson of Llywelyn the Great (*p. 89*). He was intensely patriotic, at a time when his uncle seemed to prefer alliance with England, and he strove to keep the English out of as much of Wales as possible, though he knew it would be all but impossible to dislodge them from the Marcher lands.

When Edward I of England came home to his coronation in 1274, he summoned Llywelyn to the ceremony, ordering him to pay homage. Llywelyn refused, so the king invaded North Wales, in 1276, and a year later forced the prince to surrender. The terms were fair; Llywelyn must recognize Edward as his overlord; otherwise, most of his lands were left in his charge.

In 1281 Llywelyn broke the peace, for he knew that his countrymen resented English sovereignty and did not like the English officials that Edward sent in to various parts. The war was renewed, and Llywelyn was again defeated. He fled into the mountains. He travelled across large areas of Wales trying to whip up support for another attempt to throw the king's forces out, but at Builth Wells he was spotted by an English guard, one Adam Frankton, who killed him.

It was the end of Welsh independence, until the brief interlude in the time of Owain Glyndŵr (*p. 104*).

Rudolph of Hapsburg (1218–1291)
First Hapsburg Holy Roman Emperor (1273–1291)

Rudolph was elected king of Germany in 1273. In that year he also became Emperor of the Holy Roman Empire. The family name had come from the ancestral castle Hapsburg, in Aargau, Switzerland, and the Hapsburgs were to produce, over the next seven hundred years, rulers in most of the countries of Europe, including Germany, Austria, Hungary and Spain.

Rudolph strengthened his power in Austria and overcame the Bohemian prince, Ottokar, in battle in 1278.

Bacon, Roger (c.1214–1294)
English scholar and chemist

One of the most brilliant scholars in thirteenth century Europe was the friar, Roger Bacon. He was a teacher at Oxford and specialized in chemistry. In about 1250 he discovered that gunpowder (that is, saltpetre, sulphur and charcoal) would, if packed tightly in a powder mix and ignited by a taper, explode with great force. It was not long before his discovery was taken up by engineers in warfare, though the earlier cannons which fired large cannon balls at enemy buildings had a high rate of self destruction. Many of them blew up in the hands of those who were operating them.

Bacon experimented in many fields, and invented the magnifying glass. But his work aroused the suspicions of the church, and he was imprisoned more than once for long periods. During these times he wrote many papers on mathematics, physics and grammar.

Khubilai Khan (1216–1294)
Mongol ruler of China

Khubilai Khan was the grandson of Genghis Khan (*p. 88*) and like him was a great conqueror. He was particularly interested in southern China, which Genghis had not conquered, and when he was ruler of the eastern part of his grandfather's empire, he led an expedition against the Chinese and conquered them. He treated these people with great humanity, largely it is said because he was so impressed with their civilization and culture. From then onwards Khubilai devoted his energies to building up a strong Chinese empire, and in the course of this he overran Burma and Korea.

Khubilai Khan built a capital city at Peking and ruled China from it. He retained the old customs, except where they were harmful to the country, kept quite a few Chinese government servants in office, and generally assumed the character of a genuine Chinese emperor. He also encouraged greater contact with the Western world, and when the famous Italian explorers, the Polo family, visited Peking in the 1260s, he gave them a great welcome.

Khubilai Khan became a Buddhist, but he allowed his people to follow other beliefs, so long as they did not threaten the stability of his order.

John Baliol (1249–1315)
King of Scotland (1292–1296)

Baliol was a remote descendant of David I (*p. 79*), but he was recognized as King of Scotland by Edward I of England who had been asked by the Scottish lords to decide who was to succeed the child queen Margaret (1286–1290). This sad little girl had been brought home from Norway in 1290 and had died on the way. As it turned out, Baliol was not Scotland's first choice, and if the Scots hoped he would stand up to Edward, their hopes were not altogether realized. When finally Baliol did make an effort, by forming an alliance with France, Edward marched against him and at Dunbar routed him (1296).

Baliol resigned and went into exile. Edward then called himself King of Scotland, and governed as such for ten years.

Wenceslaus II (1271–1305)
King of Bohemia (1278–1305)

Wenceslaus began his reign as a boy and the throne was dominated by German courtiers. But when he came of age he took hold of the reins of power and governed himself. He started by crushing the nobles who had too much influence in the government. Then in 1300 he got himself elected King of Poland as well. This, however, proved a bigger job than he expected and after five years he resigned the Polish crown.

93

Wallace, Sir William (c.1272–1305)
Scottish leader

William Wallace, or le Walays, or Wallensis, meaning 'the Welshman', was the son of Welsh parents who emigrated to Scotland during the occupation of Wales by Edward I of England (*p. 94*). Born in Scotland, he grew up to love the Scots. Perhaps it was when he heard about Edward I capturing the Scottish throne in 1296 (*p. 94*) and about the arrogant and brutal manner in which the English lords and soldiery treated the Scots that he determined to give his life to expelling them from his beloved land. He would doubtless have heard sad tales of English behaviour in Wales from his father.

When only twenty-five, Wallace organized a select band of tough patriotic fighters, and they attacked English army encampments and garrisons all over the Lowlands, in raids carried out swiftly and with surprise. Then when the English sent an army against him at Cambuskenneth, near Stirling, he defeated it in the open field. Armed with this success, he marched down to the English border, crossed it and ravaged Cumberland and Northumberland.

Edward I of England raced northwards, drove Wallace back into Scotland and at Falkirk crushed him. Wallace got away and for the next few years continued with the raids, trying to raise foreign help to throw the English out, but to no avail. In 1304 someone betrayed his hideout to the English and he was taken. Edward had him tried and not surprisingly he was found guilty of high treason. The sentence, carried out in all its awfulness, was to be hanged, drawn and quartered.

But his cause lived on in the efforts of Robert Bruce (*p. 97*).

Edward I (Plantagenet) (1239–1307)
King of England (1272–1307)

Son of Henry III (1216–1272), this tall, robust, handsome king stood about 1.85 metres in his shoes, a giant in those days, so that historians called him Longshanks. Edward was bold, dashing, fierce-tempered, hard-working and on the whole, just, and he was imbued with a great sense of national pride. He fought for his father in the latter's wars with the barons under Simon de Montfort (*p. 90*) and when he came to the throne in 1272 he set out to make England strong.

At home he introduced many important law reforms and measures. One was to regulate the amount of land the church held. Another was to accept the principle that taxes should not be raised without the consent of parliament. He sought to deal with highway robbery by having all roadsides cleared to a distance of sixty metres from the edges, so that highwaymen could no longer hide so easily and spring out on travellers.

Edward determined to unite the four countries of Britain, under the English crown. Accordingly, he invaded and conquered Wales, on the grounds that the last prince, Llywelyn (*p. 92*), had refused to pay him homage. Then he marched against Scotland when the Scottish king, John Baliol, whose homage he had accepted in 1292, made an alliance with France, England's enemy. Baliol was defeated and deposed, and Edward took over the throne for about ten years. He was resisted by many Scots, led by Wallace (*p. 94*) and Robert Bruce (*p. 97*).

On a journey towards Scotland, where he intended to attack Bruce, the old king died in 1307.

Philip IV (1268–1314)
King of France (1285–1314)

This French king quarrelled with the Popes for much of his reign, to such an extent that one of them, Boniface VIII, challenged his very authority to rule France. So Philip summoned an estates-general, the French equivalent of a parliament, in order to win the support of the nation. When a new Pope succeeded, in 1305, Philip managed to gain his support.

Philip believed that you could only govern a country like France if you had absolute power. So he set out to break the grip on the country held by the feudal lords, and to cut down their privileges.

He also raised forced loans from many rich lords and used the money to dress up the new monarchy, employ tough fighting men as royal bodyguards and build strong stone castles all over the land.

Dante Alighieri (1265–1321)
Florentine poet

Perhaps the finest – and certainly the most famous – of all Italian poets, Dante, was one of the spearheads of the Renaissance in Italy. He was a contemporary and friend of the painter Giotto (*p. 97*). He appears to have studied at several seats of learning, such as Bologna, Paris and Oxford, to have fought in the wars between the Guelphs and the Ghibellines, and to have been employed on state business.

But he is of course celebrated for his *Divina Commedia*, a long philosophical poem telling the story of an imaginary journey through Hell, Purgatory and Paradise. In Hell he saw the Devil with Judas Iscariot on one side and Brutus and Cassius (Caesar's murderers) on the other. In Paradise he describes a pure association with Beatrice Portinari, the wife of a real-life nobleman whom he knew and loved – from a distance.

Dante wrote several other important works, including a set of beautiful love poems collected under the heading *La Vita Nuova* (the New Life).

Dante and the beautiful Beatrice Portinari about whom he wrote in his philosophical poem, *Divina Commedia*

Marco Polo at the court of Khubilai Khan

Polo, Marco (1254–1324)
Italian explorer

Marco Polo was the son of a Venetian merchant, Niccolo Polo. The two set out on a long journey across Asia, along with Maffeo Polo, Marco's uncle, in about 1260. They followed the famous Caravan Route for some of the way, and headed for Peking in China where Khubilai Khan (*p. 93*) the emperor ruled. This great man welcomed the visitors, for he was anxious to improve contacts with the western world.

The Polo family returned to Venice in about 1270 with marvellous tales about the splendid things they had seen. Two years later, they set out again, by which time Marco was about 18. They went by a different route and it took about four years to get to Peking. Again they received a welcome from Khubilai Khan and this time Marco was given a job in the Chinese government. He stayed there for nearly seventeen years.

In about 1290 Marco returned home and sat down to write about his travels and his amazing career in China, which had included being appointed a provincial governor. The stories had an important effect on Europe. They opened European eyes to the wonders of China and to the fact that the Chinese were every bit as civilized – if not more so – as they.

Othman I (1259–1326)
Founder of the Ottoman Empire
Othman, or Osman as he is also known, became chief of the Seljuk Turks in Bithynia in 1288. He conquered most of Asia Minor and established himself as ruler of all the Turks. He founded a dynasty of sultans (or rulers) which lasted until after the First World War, in 1919.

Robert I (Bruce) (1274–1329)
King of Scotland (1306–1329)
There have been many splendid kings of Scotland in that great land's long history, but none can vie for top place with Robert Bruce. He was a bold and fierce, sometimes cruel, often patient, always intensely proud man. As a Scotsman he gave his whole energy to two things; the throwing off of the yoke of English rule and the creation of a strong, independent kingdom for the Scots. There is no doubt that he finally succeeded on both counts. And that Scotland remained independent until the Act of Union in 1707 is largely due to Robert's groundwork.

In 1306, despite the fact that Edward I of England (*p. 94*) was technically sovereign of Scotland, Robert, as the nearest claimant to the throne, had himself crowned king at the traditional coronation site of Scone. Edward died a year later, and was succeeded by his son Edward II who had little heart for war with Scotland. This was Bruce's opportunity and he fought a long drawn out campaign to rid his country of the English. In 1314, he completely routed an English army several times bigger than his, and this effectively put an end to English dominion. The English, however, refused to recognize Scottish independence, until Edward's son, Edward III (*p. 100*) did so at the Treaty of Northampton in 1328.

Bruce was first and foremost a soldier, but he did not neglect the domestic needs of his kingdom. He encouraged the building up of the national navy and merchant fleet. He ensured that the machinery of the law worked fairly. And he fostered building, especially of churches and monasteries. He also destroyed several stone castles erected in Scotland by the English, as well as a few built by rebel barons.

Giotto di Bondone (1267–1337)
Florentine painter
Giotto was said to have been found at the age of ten by the Italian painter Cimabue, painting animals on stones in the open fields. Cimabue took him to Florence to teach him art, especially his new ideas of painting in a natural style rather than heavily and mechanically. Giotto soon acquired the same enthusiasm as his master, and he carried through Cimabue's ideas, by representing nature closely and by using a greater lightness of colouring. During the seventy years of his full life Giotto produced numerous works, and he exerted a powerful influence on artists of the next few generations, who were creating wonderful works for the period known as the Renaissance.

Marsilius of Padua (c.1290–1343)
Italian philosopher
Marsilius was a teacher of philosophy at the University of Paris from about 1311, which meant that he was very young to begin. He became the university's rector, which is the administrator, in 1313. His most important work was a book arguing against the temporal powers of the Pope. This was a thorny problem for many years in the Middle Ages. The book earned him the hostility of the church and Pope John XXII excommunicated him.

Pisano, Andrea (c.1270–1348)
Italian sculptor
Andrea Pisano was one of the earliest and greatest of the Renaissance sculptors. He was a fine worker in bronze and he was also very skilled in marble work. He superintended the interior decoration in the cathedral at Florence and also of that at Orvieto. The bronze door on the baptistery at Florence Cathedral has twenty reliefs depicting scenes from the story of John the Baptist, and these are among the very best bronze reliefs of the whole Renaissance.

William of Ockham (1300–1349)
English thinker

William of Ockham was known by several flattering titles, such as Doctor Invincibilis, and Venerabilis Inceptor. He became a Franciscan friar at Oxford and led the order's attack against the papacy, under Pope John XXII, who had condemned the poverty of the Franciscans. William was imprisoned for a while, escaped and settled in Munich where he was protected and encouraged by the Emperor Louis of Bavaria. There he led an attack on the papacy for its involvement in temporal matters, such as state business in other lands and who was to appoint archbishops. This led him to write an important work on civil government in general, *Super Potestati Papali,* and he returned to this subject in his *Dialogues.* These are regarded as the foundation of modern ideas about the independence of civil rule.

Stephen Dusan (c.1308–1355)
King of Serbia (1335–1355)

In the 14th century Serbia was a large empire in south-east Europe. It acted as a sort of buffer between western Europe and the Russians and Turks. Stephen Dusan became king of Serbia in 1335 and embarked on a programme of empire building. He conquered Bulgaria, Macedonia (in northern Greece) and Bosnia. He called himself Emperor, or Tsar, and even launched an expedition to capture Constantinople itself. But on the march there he died. In his time he had reformed Serbian law and had given the Church considerable powers.

Pedro the Cruel (1334–1369)
King of Castile and Leon, in Spain (1350–1369)

Pedro became king in 1350 and his reign began well, for he had a strong sense of justice. But a series of revolts against his authority, organized by his brothers and supported by foreign powers, led him to build up a powerful dictatorship. He remained a just ruler, but his severity in dealing with rebels when he caught them earned him the title 'the Cruel'.

One of his brothers was in fact beaten to death. Eventually, another brother, Henry, defeated and killed him in battle at Montiel, in 1369.

Casimir III (The Great) (1310–1370)
King of Poland (1333–1370)

Casimir was one of the most splendid kings of Poland. He put an end to the age-old struggle between the Poles and the German Teutonic knights. He overcame Galicia and Lithuania, two large states on the Polish borders, and he persuaded Hungary to work together with him for peace.

He carried out many domestic reforms. One was to codify the laws of Poland and another was to found the University of Cracow. He also introduced measures to alleviate the distress of the poor, for whom he had great sympathy.

Petrarch (Francesco Petrarca) (1304–1374)
Italian poet

Petrarch is regarded as one of the leading poets of the Renaissance. He studied law and classical subjects for some years and then entered the church. When he was at Avignon, where he was the favourite of Pope John XXII, he met a French woman of exceptional beauty, Laure de Noves, or Laura, as she later became known. She was the wife of a nobleman. Petrarch fell violently in love with her, but it was not returned for she was perfectly happy with her husband and bore him eleven children. Nonetheless, Petrarch wrote a great number of lyrics dedicated to her, collected under the heading *Canzioniere*, and these are among the loveliest Italian verses of all time.

Petrarch won widespread fame for his verses and other works, and he was invited to all manner of high places in Europe as guest of honour. Pope Clement VI employed him on diplomatic missions and he was created poet laureate of Rome. But he was not happy with the high living and corruption of the church, and in 1353 he left the papal entourage and lived simply in the north of Italy.

Boccaccio, Giovanni (1313–1375)
Italian author

Boccaccio is of course famous for his work, the *Decameron*, a collection of one hundred short stories. They are extremely imaginative, full of both pathos and debauchery, and are written in the finest Italian prose. Boccaccio was a contemporary and friend of Petrarch (*p. 98*) whom he admired, and like Petrarch, he was also employed in diplomatic work.

Apart from the *Decameron*, Boccaccio wrote many other important books. These included a life of Dante (*p. 95*) and some very beautiful sonnets. His works were later drawn upon by many playwrights and poets, notably Chaucer, Shakespeare and Tennyson.

Edward Plantagenet, The Black Prince (1330–1376)
Famous English soldier

Edward the Black Prince, so called because of the colour of his armour, was only fifteen when his father, Edward III, allowed him to take command of a division of cavalry at Crécy, in 1346. The king's trust was amply justified. Edward carried the day and helped to rout the enemy in one of the greatest victories ever to attend English arms. When Edward III instituted his Order of the Garter as a reward to field commanders, the Black Prince was at the top of the list of the new knights.

Edward covered himself with glory again at Poitiers in 1356, when he not only smashed a French army several times bigger than his own, but also captured the French king himself.

But after this victory, the great soldier was not so successful, nor did he always behave with the chivalry which had characterized his earlier career. In 1370 he stormed Limoges in central France, and when it surrendered he massacred the inhabitants. Then he became ill with some lingering fever which he could not throw off. For years he languished at home in a state of semi-invalidity, trying now and again to help in the government. But in 1376 he collapsed altogether and died.

Effigy of the Black Prince, and a small figure showing armour of the 14th century

Edward III (Plantagenet) (1312–1377)
King of England (1327–1377)
Edward III came to the throne with a tragedy hanging over him. His mother and her lover, Roger Mortimer, had arranged for the murder of his father, Edward II, in a particularly brutal manner, at Berkeley Castle in 1327. As soon as he was of age, his first act was therefore to arrest and execute Mortimer, who had been acting as Regent, and to put his mother into prison, at Castle Rising in Norfolk. For the rest of his reign violence and misery were not very far away, although he was not always responsible.

Edward was of medium height, red-haired, with a longish and untidy red beard, large brown-grey eyes and a kindly mouth. In his younger days he loved warfare, and believed he had a mission to make himself King of France; he was nephew of the last king, whereas the present king of France was only the cousin of the last. Edward was also guided by economic motives, for English wool and cloth were in some danger from French competition. So he went to war and at first covered himself and English arms with glory. A French fleet was smashed at Sluys in 1340. In 1346 a French army was destroyed at the battle of Crécy. To celebrate the victory and to represent the campaign as a kind of historic and mystical mission, reminiscent of the wars of King Arthur, Edward created the Order of the Garter, a knighthood for the principal commanders in the field.

But in 1349 England was devastated by the Black Death plague which carried off a third of the population. When it was over, the whole order of feudal society was in danger of collapse. An acute shortage of labour meant that lords could not compel labourers to stay on their lands, so Edward allowed the Statute of Labourers to be passed, which rectified this. Yet it caused a good deal of discontent.

In 1356, Edward's son, the Black Prince (*p. 99*), crushed the French at Poitiers and a treaty at Bretigny, in 1360, gave Aquitaine to England. Edward's star was at its height. Thereafter it went down hill. His beloved wife died and he fell under the influence of a selfish mistress, Alice Ferrers. Meanwhile, his fourth son, John of Gaunt (*p. 102*), mismanaged the government, for which the king had to take the blame. When he died in 1377, he was but a shadow of his former self, and he was regretted by no-one.

Tyler, Wat (d.1381)
English leader of rebellion
Wat Tyler was a Kent man, who in 1381 organized a peasants' revolt against landlords and the authorities over a new poll tax, and over grievances against the feudal system in general. This was at almost exactly the same moment as when a similar rising broke out in Essex. These were agitated by people like John Ball, the Essex clergyman, who went round preaching to the text 'When Adam delv'd and Eve span, who was then the gentleman?'

Wat led his angry followers into London and presented a petition of demands to the young king, Richard II, at Smithfield. These included the abolition of serfdom, freedom of movement for labourers, and pardon for all rebels. As the two men grew closer together to discuss the matter, the Mayor of London, Walworth, thinking Tyler was going to harm the king, struck him with his sword and killed him. The crowd got angry, but with great presence of mind, Richard stepped forward and offered to be their new leader.

The rebels broke up and went home, carrying on pieces of paper their pardons, hastily written out by a troop of scribes. A few days later the government revoked the pardons, for they said they were extracted from them under duress.

Wicliffe, John (c.1320–1384)
English religious reformer
Wicliffe was known as the Morning Star of the Reformation. This was because his thunderings in church against the abuses of the higher clergy and the

Wat Tyler slain by the Lord Mayor of London with the young Richard II in the background

neglect they showed towards their parishes were the first real protests to be heard in Europe. What was more interesting is that he was protected from the vengeance of the church by the powerful John of Gaunt (*p. 102*) who ruled England in the last years of his father, Edward III (*p. 100*) and first years of his nephew, Richard II.

Wicliffe condemned archbishops, bishops, high clergy and abbots alike for their expensive tastes, their apparent ungodliness, their greed for wealth, and also for their departure from the simpler teachings of Jesus Christ. The Church had become a vast, organized state within a state and he believed this to be wrong.

He attracted a number of followers and while he was alive they remained unharmed. But when in the next century these people continued to urge a return to proper church attitudes, the king, Henry IV ordered them to be tried and burned at the stake.

Hung Wu (1328–1398)
Chinese emperor (1368–1398)

Hung Wu was the title taken by the great Chinese administrator, Chu Yuan-Chang, who in 1368 seized power in the area north of the river Yangtze, called Wu, and had himself declared emperor. He was the founder of the Ming dynasty, in whose years some of the finest Chinese porcelain of all time was made. Hung Wu built a beautiful city at Nanking and made it his capital.

John of Gaunt (Plantagenet) (1340–1399)
English Duke (of Lancaster)

John of Gaunt was the fourth son of Edward III (*p. 100*). He was filled with the same warlike spirit as his father and his brother, the Black Prince (*p. 99*), but he did not have their military skill, although he certainly had their courage. John's military adventures were nearly always disastrous. In Spain, France and even Scotland he was generally defeated. And these adventures cost England money.

As Edward III stopped taking an active share in governing the land, in the 1370s, and the Black Prince became too ill to continue, John tried his hand at administration. But in this he was as ill-fated as in the battlefield. He alienated nearly everybody and when Edward III died in 1377 and Richard II, his grandson, succeeded, England groaned when it knew that John's weak government would continue.

In about 1385 Richard asked him to resign, and John left for Spain to pursue another unsuccessful campaign.

John was married three times. His son by his first wife became Henry IV. His great-great-grandson by his third wife became Henry VII.

Hafiz (14th century)
Persian poet

Shams ed-Dín Mohammed, or Hafiz, as he became known, was one of the greatest of the Persian poets. He was probably born at Shiraz, lived there all his life and was buried there. He was a mystic and his poetry was devoted to natural subjects such as flowers, beautiful women, wine and gardens. The common people thought of them as songs and they called him 'Sugar mouth' (Chagar-lab) because of the sweetness of his words.

Langland, William (c.1332–c.1400)
English poet

This is the name given by history, if it was not his real name, to the author of *The Vision of Piers Plowman*, the famous 14th century allegorical poem which reveals the humbleness of a peasant's life. It is a long work and was said to have been drafted over some thirty years, after a long time spent in poverty. Scholars are still not agreed as to whether it is the work of a single man or of several, but the nobility of much of the verse is widely acknowledged.

Langland was believed to have been born in Herefordshire, to have been educated at a monastery at Malvern, and to have lived in London. He may well have met and conversed with Chaucer.

Froissart, Jean (c.1333–c.1400)
French historian

This interesting historian was a contemporary and friend of both Petrarch (*p. 98*) and of Chaucer (*p. 102*). He came to England in 1360 and was welcomed by Edward III's queen, Philippa, who made him a clerk in her bedchamber. He visited the King of Scotland and also went to Aquitaine with the Black Prince (*p. 99*).

During these years he compiled a chronicle of the history of England, Scotland, France and Spain, which covered the years 1326 to 1400. The work is impartial and probably fairly accurate. It also tells much about European lands other than those already mentioned.

Froissart became a priest in 1372 and took a living near Liège in Flanders, where he completed his book. Richard II invited him to England in 1395.

Chaucer, Geoffrey (c.1340–1400)
English poet

This splendid Englishman, the first great poet to write in the English tongue, wrote some marvellous stories in verse. These were the *Canterbury Tales*, a collection of stories told by imaginary people while they were on a joint pilgrimage to the shrine of St. Thomas Becket at Canterbury. The stories are filled with details of everyday life in mid-14th century England. They contain humour, variety, great beauty of style and penetrating, realistic observations of human character, and the descriptive power of the *Tales* makes them unique in all literature.

Chaucer was married to the sister of John of Gaunt's wife. As well as enjoying Gaunt's patronage, Chaucer was employed by the government on many important missions, and even received pensions from Edward III and Richard II. Nevertheless, the poet complained a great deal about being poor and underpaid.

Bayazid I (1347–1403)
Sultan of the Ottoman Empire
Bayazid, who succeeded his father, Murad I, in 1389, earned the nickname Yilderim, or Lightning. This was for the speed with which he marched into countries and overran them. In three years from his accession he had conquered Bulgaria, part of the Serbian Empire, and much of Asia Minor. Then he blockaded Constantinople for about ten years. He was unable to take the great city, however, because in 1402 he was diverted by the invasion of his own territory in Asia Minor by the Mongol chief Timurlaine (*p. 103*). He hurried off with an army to drive the Mongols out, but was utterly defeated at a great battle at Angora. Bayazid was captured by Timurlaine who treated him with generosity. He did not, as the legend claims, keep him in an iron cage.

Bayazid died in 1403 in Timurlaine's camp, despite the best efforts of the Mongol chief's doctors to keep him alive.

William of Wykeham (1324–1404)
English statesman and prelate
This very versatile English scholar was Hampshire born and became a chaplain to Edward III in 1349, the year of the Black Death. He was a man of many gifts and skills. It was William who superintended the construction of the interesting circular castle at Queensborough, on the Isle of Sheppey off Kent, in 1361, and surveyed the royal castles in general between 1356 and 1360. He became a priest in 1362 and he was then appointed Keeper of the Privy Seal in 1364 and bishop of Winchester in 1367. Edward picked him as Lord Chancellor in 1368, one of the top posts in the realm.

But William was not merely a king's man. He had a proud, independent mind and he objected to the corrupt government run in the king's name by John of Gaunt (*p. 102*), who in 1373 dismissed him.

Thereafter, William devoted himself to good works of a more public nature. He founded New College at Oxford, Winchester College, and superintended the building of part of Winchester Cathedral. Richard II restored him to favour in 1389 and made him Lord Chancellor again, but in 1391, already an old man for those days, he retired.

Timurlaine (1336–1405)
Mongol conqueror
Timurlaine was a Mongol chief, and a descendant of the great Genghis Khan (*p. 88*). He grew up with a burning ambition to re-create the vast empire of his ancestor. He was gifted with many of the same great abilities and was said to have had more personal charm. He trained and equipped a large, mobile army of cavalrymen and foot-soldiers and set out on a path of conquest. It was a good time to do so, for many of the states in Asia were weak and unprepared, and in no time he conquered Persia, Afghanistan and much of India. Delhi, the Indian capital, fell in 1398. He then took Asia Minor, and began to prepare for the biggest campaign of all, the conquest of China.

At the moment of his departure eastwards, in 1405, he was taken ill and died. Unfortunately, he left no heir capable of holding his empire together, and a great dream was ruined.

Huss, John (c.1369–1415)
Bohemian religious reformer

John Huss was educated in Prague, and after receiving his doctorate he stayed on as lecturer in theology. In 1402 he was made rector of his college, having been accepted as a priest.

Huss had read all of Wicliffe's works (*p. 100*) and was very much influenced by them. The state of the church in Bohemia was no better than it was in England, and Huss soon came to realize that the church needed reform throughout Europe. So he preached to congregations in Bohemia, thundering against a great deal of abuse. Before long he was forbidden to preach any more, and the church opened an enquiry into his works. The papacy had already banned Wicliffe's writings, but Huss continued to preach, whereupon in 1410 he was excommunicated. This did not stop him either, and in 1412 the pope threatened to put Prague under an interdict unless Huss could be forced to leave. The king persuaded him to go.

In 1415, the Council of Constance put Huss on trial for heresy, and he was condemned to be burned at the stake, a sentence carried out on 6th July, for he refused to abandon his preachings.

Glyndŵr, Owain (c.1360–c.1416)
Welsh national leader

This wonderful Welsh patriot, descendant of the last prince of Wales, Llywelyn (*p. 92*) revived the spirit of nationalism among the Welsh during the reigns of Henry IV and V. He took advantage of the troubled times of the former, and organized raids across the border into Cheshire and Shropshire. He grew stronger as more and more Welshmen flocked to join his cause, and he managed to beat off every army sent against him by the English.

Glyndŵr captured the allegedly impregnable castle of Harlech in 1404 and held a parliament there. He held another at Machynlleth, and there declared Wales an independent sovereign state.

When Henry V came to the English throne in 1413, Owain continued the struggle, but shortly after the king's great victory at Agincourt against the French, Owain's cause declined in the general jubilation. He disappeared and is believed to have died in 1416.

Albany, Duke of, Robert Stewart (c.1340–1420)
Scottish leader

The Duke of Albany was the third son of King Robert II of Scotland. His father had grown senile in the last years of his reign, and his brother, who became Robert III in 1390, was deranged as a result of an accident. So it happened that Albany had to manage the government both in his father's and brother's reigns. And he managed it extremely well.

Albany was absolutely fearless; he seemed to dread nobody. This in many men would make them unbearable, but Albany remained a popular hero. Bold, brilliant, cunning in council and tough but fair in the administration of the law, he gave constant encouragement to all those classes of people who suffered from the endless squabbling between the feudal lords in Scotland, in particular the merchants, craftsmen, farmers and common folk.

He fought and controlled the wild Highland clan chiefs and their fierce hordes who had been the bane of many Scottish rulers. He fought the English, though not successfully. And throughout his regency he kept his control of the government, right up to his death at nearly 80 years of age. During this time he sponsored the foundation of the University of St. Andrews.

Henry V (1387–1422)
King of England (1413–1422)

Henry V is famous for his great victory over the French at Agincourt in 1415. He was certainly a fine general, and he was very popular among the troops, but his ambition to win France re-opened the age-old rivalry between the two countries, and it was his heir who had to suffer the eventual humiliation of being driven out of France altogether.

Henry was the eldest son of Henry IV

Henry V at the battle of Agincourt

(1399–1413), first king of the House of Lancaster. As a young man, Henry was fun-loving, irresponsible and always up to pranks of one kind or another. He quarrelled continually with his father.

In 1413 he succeeded to the throne, and almost at once he became far more responsible. He had many good ideas for government, but very little was done for he was first and foremost obsessed by the desire to conquer France and make himself its King. After Agincourt, he got the French to agree that he should succeed the French King Charles VI. Then he married Charles' daughter, Katherine, and their son became Henry VI of England and France, an arrangement that did not last long.

Yung Lo (1359–1424)
Chinese Emperor (1403–1424)

Yung Lo, whose royal name was Ch'eng Tsu, was the third of the great Ming dynasty of Chinese emperors. He was the son of Hung Wu (*p. 102*), and proved to be one of the best Emperors in centuries, particularly in respect of his encouragement of the arts. Under him porcelain manufacture and colouring reached its zenith, and today pieces of his period are priceless. Perhaps the greatest achievement was the Yung Lo La Tien encyclopedia, a vast compilation of some 10,000 manuscripts of all kinds, including legal documents, selected works of prose and poetry, geographical surveys, and so on.

Yung Lo moved the capital built at Nanking to Peking, where today some remains can still be seen, in a fine state of preservation.

Martin V (1368–1431)
Pope (1417–1431)

The Great Schism which rent the Church between 1378 and 1417, when there were Popes at Rome and at Avignon, came to an end when, at the Council of Constance, Oddone Colonna was elected Pope Martin V at Rome and the bulk of the Church accepted him. This was in 1417. He spent his reign making agreements between the papacy and various countries in order to heal the breach.

Joan of Arc at her trial

St. Joan of Arc (1412–1431)
French national leader

One of the most famous and tragic women of all time, Joan, was a peasant girl from the French village of Domrémy. From quite an early age she believed she had been called by God to deliver the French from the dominion of the English, whose Henry V had crushed their army at Agincourt. So she set out to visit Charles, the son of the King of France, to persuade him to let her lead the French army against the English.

In 1429, Charles let her put on some armour and lead the French against an English force which was besieging Orleans, and she succeeded in driving it off. Then she persuaded Charles to go to Rheims to be crowned as King of France. After that she led other armies to success, so restoring to the French their national pride.

But in 1430 she was captured in a skirmish, and handed over to the English who burnt her at the stake as a witch, after a trial that was nothing more than a mockery of justice. Joan was made a saint in 1920.

John (Joao) I (1357–1433)
King of Portugal (1385–1433)

This splendid Portuguese king ruled from 1385 to 1433. His reign was filled with achievements, not only in war and politics, but also in exploration and science. He fought off a claim to his kingdom by the King of Castile. He made a valuable treaty of friendship with England, which has never been broken in nearly 600 years and he sealed this by marrying the daughter of John of Gaunt (*p. 102*).

In 1415, John sponsored a Portuguese invasion of the Moorish province of North Africa. Ceuta was captured, a strategic town and port which the Moors had long been using as an embarkation base for raids on Spain and Portugal. It was the first major victory against the Arab Moors on their own ground for centuries.

In the last years of his reign, John and his son, Henry the Navigator (*p. 108*), organized a series of voyages of exploration to find an alternative route by sea round the African coast to India and China.

Jagiello of Lithuania (c.1351–1434)
Founder of the Jagellon dynasty

Jagiello was Grand Prince of Lithuania from 1377 until his death. He was baptized a Christian and married Jadwiga, Queen of Poland, thus becoming King of Poland as well. He took the name Vladislav II. His territories included Poland and Lithuania, and also large areas of Russia, stretching from the Baltic to the Black Sea. Poland was at its height as an empire.

Brunelleschi, Filippo (1377–1446)
Italian architect

One of the leading architects of the High Renaissance (the fifteenth and early sixteenth centuries) was Brunelleschi. He had studied the styles adopted in mediaeval Europe over the centuries and found that he did not like the current domination by Gothic styles, especially in churches and cathedrals. He wanted to return to the simpler yet grander classical Roman styles, and so in the various buildings which he designed, he reintroduced the kind of styles that Vitruvius (*p. 49*) had advocated in the early days of the Roman Empire.

Perhaps Brunelleschi's best building was Florence Cathedral.

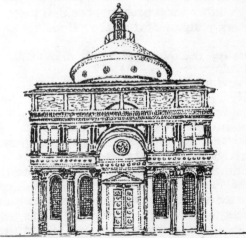

A Renaissance building by Filippo Brunelleschi.

Constantine XI (1404–1453)
Last Byzantine Emperor (1448–1453)

Constantine became Emperor of Byzantium in 1448. By that time, the Empire was no more than the great city of Constantinople and some small amounts of land around it. Already, the whole Empire was doomed, and there was nothing he could do to stop it. Although a skilful general, he was no match for his adversary, Mohammed II, the Turkish Sultan. In 1453, the Turks moved by land and sea against the city. One weapon they used was a huge cannon which fired a ball weighing about 7 kilogrammes over a distance of more than a kilometre.

The city was surrounded by a huge and almost impregnable wall, and it had several massive gates. In the fighting for one of these gates Constantine was killed. When the news spread that their Emperor was dead, the Byzantines lost heart and resistance collapsed.

Ghiberti, Lorenzo (1378–1455)
Florentine metalwork sculptor

Ghiberti is remembered for his bronze sculpture of doors for the baptistery of the cathedral of San Giovanni, in Florence. These were made to supplement those executed by Pisano (*p. 97*), and they took nearly half a century to complete. They are magnificent metalwork, well deserving the phrase describing them that was uttered by Michaelangelo, 'the gates of Paradise'.

Ghiberti was probably the best metalwork sculptor of the entire Renaissance.

Henry the Navigator, Prince (1394–1460)
Portuguese patron of explorers

Henry was a son of King John of Portugal (*p. 107*), and he devoted the best part of his life to promoting and financing voyages of exploration by Portuguese navigators down the West African coast, principally to search for a sea route to the East. These navigators also wanted to see what it was like hundreds of leagues south of the Equator where, it was believed, the water boiled, one fell off the earth's surface, and all kinds of grotesque animals, some half-human, roamed about.

Henry set up a college of navigation at Sagres, on Cape St. Vincent, and there employed the best geographers, astronomers, and boat builders he could find. The first voyage of any importance was one led by Gil Eannes, who rounded Cape Bojador and sailed into the Gulf of Guinea, to find that it was not a boiling sea at all.

James II (1431–1460)
King of Scotland (1437–1460)

James became king when he was only six, and for the first ten years Scotland was ruled by a succession of inadequate regents acting in the boy's name. Finally, in 1447 he took control himself. He soon proved a good leader of men, for in battle he shared the men's hardships, sleeping rough if necessary.

Much of his reign was taken up suppressing powerful and unruly Scottish nobles, who often behaved little better than their primitive ancestors, whom the early kings had tamed. In particular, the king was troubled by the wild Douglas family. In the end, James had to resort to a trick to despatch the most dangerous of them, William Douglas – and this was regrettable, for William was very popular.

In 1460 James was killed when a cannon by which he was standing at the siege of Roxburgh Castle blew up, a hazard endured by many in those early days of cannons and gunpowder.

Donatello (1386–1466)
Florentine sculptor

Donato di Betto Bardi, known as Donatello, has been called the father of modern sculpture, inasmuch as he was the first since the days of Greece and Rome to produce sculptures of people complete in themselves, and not as part of some building or architectural surroundings. He was particularly skilled at reproducing dramatic action or emotion in the features of his figures. In a long life he produced many statues, including figures of St. Peter, John the Evangelist, and David, King of the Hebrews (*p. 9*).

Warwick the Kingmaker slain at the battle of Barnet in 1471

Donatello was a contemporary and friend of Brunelleschi and Ghiberti (*p. 108*), and was the leading sculptor of the early Renaissance.

Gutenberg, Johann (c.1400–c.1468)
German printer

Gutenberg is generally said to have been the first European to make any kind of printing press. The Chinese had developed moveable type centuries earlier, but, strange to relate, the invention never reached Europe. Nor did Gutenberg know about it. His first press was working in about 1430. If he had known he could have printed a leaflet condemning the English for burning Joan of Arc!

We are not certain if there are any books still surviving printed by Gutenberg, but there is a Bible, named after him, which was found in a French library in 1760. And in 1901 someone else discovered a fragment of a Calendar said to have been printed by him.

Warwick the Kingmaker (1428–1471)
English soldier and statesman

Richard Nevill, Earl of Warwick, was in his time the wealthiest landowner in England. He was also the most popular, and his tenants loved him. This splendid soldier, brilliant general and skilled statesman, loved above all things hard work. Of course he was ambitious and he owned a tenth of all England. He made and un-made kings, which is why he was known as the Kingmaker. He fought and won the battle of Towton in 1461, during the civil war known as the Wars of the Roses, which put Edward IV on the throne. He fought and defeated Edward in 1469 and drove him out of England, putting Henry VI back on the throne again.

Richard Nevill was determined to make England great, and he sought alliances with foreign countries. To make these it was sometimes helpful to arrange for the king or a member of his family to marry a princess in the country with whom you wanted a treaty. Warwick tried to match Edward IV with a French princess, and nearly succeeded, only to find that the king had, behind his back, married an English widow, who was not even of noble birth. This was the cause of the quarrel between them.

Edward returned in 1471 and defeated Warwick at Barnet where the great man was slain.

Mohammed II (1430–1481)
Conqueror of Constantinople

Constantinople, for over a thousand years the grandest city in the world, was finally besieged and taken by the Turks under their Sultan, Mohammed II, in 1453. There was a strange coincidence about the two main opponents in the siege. Constantinople had been founded by the Roman Emperor Constantine I. It was defended in 1453 by the Emperor Constantine XI. The city was taken by Mohammed II, whose namesake, the prophet Mohammed, had been the source of the age-old rivalry between the Byzantine Empire and the Arabs.

Mohammed II was a brilliant general, a lover of beauty and an ardent follower of Allah. When he captured the city, he had one of his soldiers flogged for breaking up the mosaic floor of the wonderful Christian cathedral of St. Sophia, which he had turned into a mosque for the glory of Allah.

Mohammed also conquered Serbia and Greece.

Richard III (1452–1485)
King of England (1483–1485)

This king has the worst reputation of any British monarch. Tudor children were led to believe that he spent two years in his mother's womb before birth, and had hair down to his shoulders and a huge hump back when he was born. This portrait was meant to make it easier for them to accept the allegations that he murdered Henry VI and his son, George, Duke of Clarence (Richard's brother), Ann Nevill (his wife) and Edward V and Richard, Duke of York (his nephews).

There is no evidence against Richard on any of these charges, and in some of them we now know what really happened. His physical appearance was handsome enough, to judge from portraits painted in his time.

In two years as king, Richard had the laws of England written in English, passed more statutes than any king before him, founded the College of Heralds, and patronized Caxton (*p. 110*). In the south, it is true, he was not understood and so was regarded with some suspicion, but he was adored in the north. When he was killed at Bosworth in August 1485, the City of York recorded its great grief at the news. You can see the note of it in the City Library today.

Caxton, William (c.1422–1491)
First English printer

Caxton began his career as a merchant dealing – quite successfully – in silk. Then he started to manufacture it himself, and he made money. This enabled him to travel, and on his wanderings he came across a printing press in Cologne, which fascinated him. He thought how good it would be to have one in England.

In 1476 he returned to England and in Westminster he set up a press. The first book of the press was not very exciting, though scholars will have appreciated it. It was the *Dictes and Sayings of the Philosophers.* He had previously printed a book on chess and another, on the siege of Troy, abroad.

After 1476, he was overwhelmed with commissions. Many of the works he published were dedicated by him to kings, like Edward IV, Richard III and Henry VII. One book he printed was *Le Morte d'Arthur*, by Sir Thomas Malory (*p. 112*).

William Caxton and his printing press

Lorenzo the Magnificent

Lorenzo the Magnificent (1449–1492)
Florentine statesman

Lorenzo dei Medici, a member of the powerful, rich, influential merchant family which dominated the state of Florence for a century and a half (c.1390–c.1540) was probably the most interesting of them all. His life was a very full one. He ruled Florence from about 1478 to 1492. It was a period of dictatorship, with police spying, torture and imprisonment without trial. But it was an age of brilliant art and building, encouraged and often financed by Lorenzo, who was himself a writer of excellent prose. It was also an age of prosperity for merchants, bankers, businessmen and many craftsmen, if not for the poorer classes. Lorenzo made Florence the dominant art centre in Italy. He also made Florentine Italian the principal dialect of Italians.

Torquemada, Thomas de (c.1420–1498)
Leader of the Spanish Inquisition

The name Torquemada is now almost synonymous with the Spanish Inquisition. Ferdinand V of Aragon (*p. 115*) decided to try and rid Spain of all Jews, Arabs and even not strictly orthodox catholics, by setting up the Inquisition. This was to hear cases against heretics and non-believers brought by a variety of informers, and he appointed Torquemada as inquisitor general.

Torquemada, a Dominican monk who was stern and uncompromising, was an ideal person to head these enquiries in which most victims were believed to be guilty before they were even heard in front of the tribunals. Torquemada soon became notorious for the severity of his judgements and sentences.

Savonarola, Girolamo (1452–1498)
Italian religious reformer

Savonarola was a Dominican friar who became prior of St. Mark's, Florence. He was appalled at the corruption and loose living of many high dignitaries of the established church, and of the way this worldliness was spreading out through the lower clergy. It was nothing new, but it was the scale that frightened him, and he attacked it soundly and repeatedly in sermons. This brought him considerable support in the state of Florence, and before long he was able to assume the position of head of the Florentine government. There he tried to construct an ideal Christian state.

But the forces of reaction were very strong. Too many people of power and influence liked the old order, and when Savonarola started to attack the character of the Pope, Alexander VI (Borgia) (*p. 113*), these men captured him, put him on trial and found him guilty. His sentence was severe: he was tortured, hanged and then burned at the stake.

Charles VIII (1470–1498)
King of France (1483–1498)

Charles was a young soldier king who aimed to make the state of Naples, in southern Italy, a French possession, as it had once been. In 1495 he succeeded in seizing the city and had himself installed there in great pomp. But very shortly afterwards a coalition of European powers drove him out again.

Malory, Sir Thomas (late 15th century)
English writer

We do not know much about Malory's career, but as a writer he was an important figure of the 15th century. His fame rests on his *Le Morte d'Arthur*, a long book about King Arthur which Caxton (*p. 110*) printed in 1485. He said Malory was a knight who died in about 1471. This book was an attempt to crystallize in one volume all the legends about Arthur, including those written in French.

Diaz, Bartholomew (c.1450–1500)
Portuguese explorer

Diaz was too young to have gone to Henry the Navigator's college at Sagres (*p. 108*), but he did join the movement for further exploration which took fresh heart a few years after Henry's death. In 1486, John II commissioned Diaz to search further down the African coast, and in 1488 he got as far as the southern tip of the African continent. He turned back because of terrible weather, passing the cape he called The Cape of Storms.

When he got home, King John cheered him up and said, 'Let's call it the Cape of Good Hope': and so indeed it proved, for a few years later Vasco da Gama (*p. 118*) rounded it successfully and continued to India.

Christopher Columbus at the Court of Queen Isabella

Alexander VI (Borgia) (1431–1503)
Pope (1492–1503)

Rodrigo Borgia, a Spanish born priest, was the nephew of a pope. In 1476 he was made a cardinal and was elected Pope in 1492. His times were said to have been vicious, corrupt and utterly irreligious. They may well have been: he may have had several mistresses; his family (especially Cesare and Lucrezia) may have been given all sorts of preferments. But he also made important contributions to the Europe of the day.

In 1493, following the discovery of the West Indies by Columbus (*p. 113*) he sanctioned a dividing line in the New World, allotting part to Spain and part to Portugal. He broke the power of several Italian families which had for years monopolized many of the best jobs in the states, the Orsini, the Colonna and the Sforza. He patronized Renaissance artists like Michelangelo and Raphael.

Isabella I (1451–1504)
Queen of Castile (1474–1504)

Isabella the Catholic was Queen of Castile, one of the largest kingdoms in Spain. She married Ferdinand V of Aragon (*p. 115*) and between them they ruled most of Spain. She is remembered for her support of Christopher Columbus on his voyage to the West Indies in 1492, and for her fervent devotion to Catholicism.

Columbus, Christopher (1451–1506)
Italian born navigator

This brave, determined, and on the whole unhappy man, is probably the most famous name in the history of exploration. Although he did discover the first route to America, when he sailed westwards in 1492 and reached the West Indies in October, he was in fact looking for China and India. And the islands (Bahamas) which he found were not filled with gold, jewels and spices. So it is a matter of surprise that he has become more famous than other men who made more substantial discoveries, like Vasco da Gama (*p. 118*). But he had found a new world, and opened up the way for others to follow, which they did in quick succession over the next few years.

Columbus himself made several more voyages to the West Indies, and touched the main lands of both North America and South America, probably without appreciating it. But he stirred up much resentment, not least by his habit of boasting of his achievements in an age when men of this kind were wont to let their achievements speak for themselves. It was nonetheless tragic that he died in poverty.

Cesare Borgia

Borgia, Cesare (1475–1507)
Italian adventurer

Cesare Borgia was a swashbuckling soldier of fortune, son of Pope Alexander VI (Borgia) (*p. 113*), and he conceived the idea of uniting all the states of Italy in one confederation. It was a vain effort: the states did not want it. Cesare got into all kinds of trouble through his warlike behaviour, and was often saved from his fate by his father. When Alexander died in 1503, the next Pope, Julius II, was not so understanding. Despite his attempts to get the states together, Cesare was forced to leave Italy altogether, and was killed at a siege in Navarre.

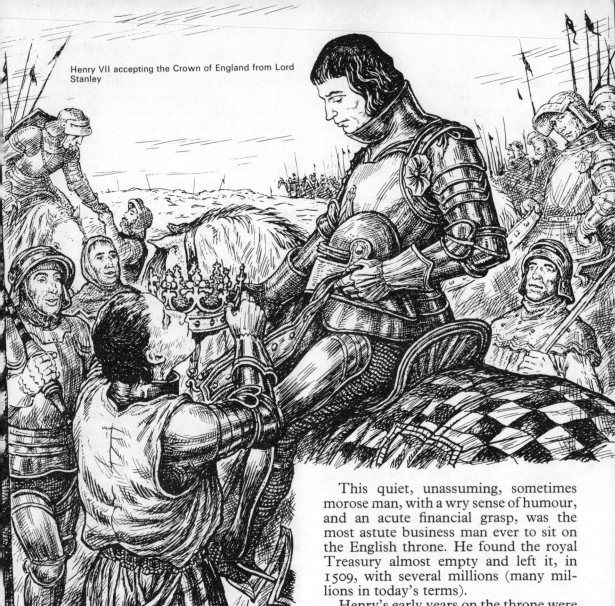

Henry VII accepting the Crown of England from Lord Stanley

Henry VII (1457–1509)
King of England (1485–1509)

Henry Tudor, Welsh born and descendant of the ancient princes of Wales, won the battle of Bosworth in 1485 and took the crown of England offered to him by Lord Stanley. He had a claim to the throne, since his mother was a direct descendant of John of Gaunt (p. 102). But he always claimed he had won the throne by battle.

This quiet, unassuming, sometimes morose man, with a wry sense of humour, and an acute financial grasp, was the most astute business man ever to sit on the English throne. He found the royal Treasury almost empty and left it, in 1509, with several millions (many millions in today's terms).

Henry's early years on the throne were almost constantly disturbed by attempts to deprive him of it. Several rebellions broke out, often in support of real heirs to the old Plantagenet line of kings or of pretenders, and it was not until 1499 when he defeated and executed Perkin Warbeck who pretended to be Richard, Duke of York, the younger of the two Princes in the Tower, that he was safe.

In the meanwhile, Henry tried to keep England out of trouble with her neighbours, especially Scotland and Spain, by arranging marriages between his relatives and members of their royal families.

He encouraged the wave of exploration in the New World by supporting

John and Sebastian Cabot (*p. 126*) on their voyage to Newfoundland in 1497. He also patronized Caxton, banned the great lords from having private armies, nationalized all supplies of gunpowder, and instituted the Court of Star Chamber in which even the highest noble in the land could be tried by the normal processes of English law.

Botticelli, Sandro (c.1444–1510)
Florentine painter

Botticelli was employed by many rich Florentine families to decorate their homes and paint pictures. He helped to paint some in the Sistine Chapel. But his fame rests on many pictures, including the *Madonna of the Magnificat*, at Florence, and some illustrations for the *Divine Comedy* of Dante (*p. 95*). Towards the end of his life his popularity declined as the new ideas of Leonardo and Michelangelo spread.

Vespucci, Amerigo (1451–1512)
Italian explorer

Amerigo Vespucci was an Italian sailor who joined expeditions to the New World after Columbus' celebrated travels to the West Indies (*p. 113*). In 1500, he was an officer on the Ojeda expedition which reached the mainland of South America, and he claimed to be the first man to discover the spot. His claim was hotly contested.

In 1507, Vespucci explored the Gulf of Mexico, and a German geographer of the period, Waldseemuller, suggested that the continent should be called America, after Vespucci – and the name became generally accepted.

Julius II (1443–1513)
Pope (1503–1513)

Giuliano della Rovere succeeded Alexander VI (Borgia) (*p. 113*) as Pope in 1503. He was a secular statesman who had no piety, but a 'decided talent for intrigue and hard fighting', and his short rule was given over to expanding papal territory and influence. He formed leagues of European nations against other nations whom he thought too rich or powerful, and encouraged open war with them. At the same time he patronized great Renaissance artists like Michaelangelo and Bramante.

Bramante (1444–1514)
Italian architect

Bramante, whose real name was Donato d'Agnolo, was one of the leading architects of the High Renaissance. He worked in Milan in north Italy and in Rome where he was employed by Popes Alexander (Borgia) and Julius II. One of his principal assignments was to redesign St. Peter's Cathedral, but the work did not get far before he died, in 1514.

Ferdinand V (1452–1516)
King of Aragon (1479)
King of Sicily (1468)

Ferdinand was King of Sicily from 1468 until his death. He married Isabella of Castile (*p. 113*) in 1469 and five years later became joint sovereign of Castile with her. In 1479 he succeeded his father as King of Aragon. These titles gave him great power, and they enabled him to raise armies big enough to drive the Arabs out of Spain, after a ten year campaign which ended in a battle near Granada in 1492. All Spain was now united under him and his wife.

For the next twenty years they set out to make Spain truly Catholic. They formed the Inquisition which dealt with heresy very severely. It was largely aimed at Jews and Arabs.

Ximenes, Francisco (1437–1517)
Spanish statesman

Ximenes was a Franciscan prelate who in 1495 was elevated to be archbishop of Toledo in Spain. The queen, Isabella (*p. 113*), trusted him absolutely and left much of the running of the nation's affairs to him. When she died, he was selected as chief adviser to the heir, Joana the Mad. And when Ferdinand V (*p. 115*) was dying in 1516 he appointed Ximenes Regent for the minority of his grandson and heir.

Ximenes was also a military leader, and in 1509 he successfully conquered Oran in North Africa.

Leonardo da Vinci at work in his studio

Leonardo da Vinci (1452–1519)
Italian artistic and scientific genius

This astonishing Italian has been described as a universal genius. He dominated the world of art as a painter, sculptor and architect, and was only equalled by Michelangelo (*p. 128*). Over and above that he excelled as an inventor, mathematician, engineer, naturalist and anatomist. There seemed nothing he could do that he did not do better than anyone else.

Leonardo was years ahead of his contempories in many fields. In scientific research he disregarded what had been found before and accepted only what he could observe and test for himself. In painting he used new materials and produced some wonderful works, like the *Mona Lisa* and the *Last Supper*. He was absorbed by nature and loved to draw animals, fishes and birds, chiefly because he was fascinated by their movement. And since he was also a very skilled engineer he thought a lot about adapting these movements to machines, and thus dreamed up the idea of aeroplanes and submarines.

He left behind a large number of pencil and crayon sketches of his many ideas, which well illustrate the amazing versatility of his genius.

Tetzel, Johann (c.1465–1519)
German monk
Tetzel might never have been heard of in history but for the fact that it was he who was ordered by the archbishop of Mainz to go round selling indulgences to people. These were bits of paper granting people forgiveness of their sins in return for cash contributions to the building of the new St. Peter's Cathedral in Rome.

Indulgences were not new, but it was with this figure that resentment of the malpractice came to a head. The monk Martin Luther (*p. 123*) used this opportunity to make public objection, and he published his 95 Theses on the door of Wittenburg Cathedral, in 1517. This started off the Reformation.

Colet, John (c.1467–1519)
English scholar
John Colet was a brilliant scholar, who, after graduating at Oxford, travelled to foreign universities for further learning, where he came under the influence of

arola (*p. 111*).
In 1504 he was appointed Dean of St. Paul's Cathedral in London, and here he used his great position to preach thundering sermons against all manner of church abuses, such as the sale of bishoprics. He founded a school at St. Paul's.
people like Erasmus (*p. 122*) and Savon-
Balboa, Vasco Nunez de (1475–1519)
Spanish adventurer
Balboa is best known for being probably the first Spaniard – or European – to espy the Pacific Ocean from the mainland of America. He emigrated to Hispaniola, an

early Spanish colony in the West Indies, in 1500. In 1510 he was sent to the Darien, in central America, and given the post of governor. On 25th September, in 1513, he saw the Pacific from a spot on the western shore of the Darien, and formally declared that it belonged to Spain. He little knew that it was a vast ocean, bigger than all the others of the world put together. He came to a sad end. He was arrested for treason and executed.

Borgia, Lucrezia (1480–1519)
Lucrezia Borgia has been maligned for centuries: accused of murdering husbands, relatives and enemies by poisoning, of having numerous lovers, of interfering in state matters in many Italian states, Lucrezia for a long time seemed a monster of iniquity. But recent research has cleared her of most of the allegations.

She was the beautiful, witty, intelligent daughter of Pope Alexander VI (Borgia). He married her off three times for political reasons. The last was to the heir of the Duke of Ferrara, one of the d'Este family. Lucrezia may not have loved him, but she used her power and his money to establish a brilliant court where she could entertain the greatest people in Europe, especially artists such as Titian.

Lucrezia had no children that we know of, and seems to have devoted much of her time to charitable work, especially among children of the poor.

Raphael (1483–1520)
Italian painter
Raphael, or Raffaello Santi, was a leading painter and architect of the Renaissance. He was employed by Pope Julius II and Pope Leo X, two holders of the papal crown who cared much more for art than for God, and who patronized many leading artists of the time. Raphael was appointed chief architect to St. Peter's Cathedral in Rome, and he also designed several major palaces in Italy.

His paintings include *St. George and the Dragon* (now in the Louvre), *The Adoration of the Trinity* (Perugia) and *Coronation of the Virgin* (Vatican gallery).

Leo X (1475–1521)
Pope (1513–1521)

Leo was the son of Lorenzo the Magnificent (*p. 111*) and he became Pope in 1513. He, too, loved the arts much more than God, and is on record as having said that 'Christianity was a profitable superstition for Popes'. It is little wonder that the Church was racked with the tremors of the Reformation when you consider the lack of godliness of the three successive popes Alexander VI, Julius II and Leo.

Leo was a fine administrator of the church and the Vatican state. But he could not grasp the fact that although the church was in dire need of reform, this could be effected from within. It did not need Luther and his contemporaries.

Magellan, Ferdinand (1480–1521)
Portuguese navigator

Magellan served the King of Portugal for some years as a sailor, but in 1517, when he wanted to embark on a voyage round the world, the Portuguese king would not support him. So Magellan went to the King of Spain, who gave him the money. In 1519 he set out, with five ships, down the eastern coast of South America. He succeeded in getting three of his five ships through the treacherous strait at the bottom of the continent, which now bears his name.

Then he steered towards the East Indies, which he did not know, but whose position he had worked out, and after three months of terrible hardship, in which his crews were reduced to eating sawdust and leather, he reached the Philippine Islands, then known as the Spice Islands.

Magellan was slain a few days after landing, by unfriendly natives, but his crews brought his ships home across the Indian Ocean, round South Africa, up the Atlantic to Spain. This was the first voyage round the world.

Linacre, Thomas (c.1460–1524)
English scholar and doctor

Linacre was a scholar who in 1500 was appointed tutor to Henry VII's eldest son, Prince Arthur. He was also a physician who was court doctor to both Henry VII and Henry VIII, and in the latter's reign he founded the Royal College of Physicians. He was a promotor of the New Learning in England, and among his pupils had been Erasmus (*p. 122*) and Sir Thomas More (*p. 121*).

Vasco da Gama (c.1470–1524)
Portuguese explorer

Vasco da Gama probably made the greatest contribution to the prosperity of the little kingdom of Portugal of any man in her history. In 1497 he set out with four small ships from Lisbon on a long voyage round the bottom of South Africa (the Cape of Good Hope) and sailed up to East Africa. At Malindi he picked up some Arab pilots who guided his craft across to India. He reached Calicut in May 1498, thus completing the first voyage from Europe round Africa to the East. He filled up the ships' holds with all kinds of goods – spices, jewellery, ivory and so forth – and set out home again, reaching Lisbon in 1499. There he received a wonderful welcome from the King and his people.

Portugal could now trade directly with the East without having to pay expensive taxes to the various countries through which their goods-laden caravans had previously had to pass to get to Europe.

Ismail I (1486–1524)
Founder of the Safavid dynasty in Persia

Ismail came to the Persian throne in 1500. He found the country in a depressed state, with little order and no national pride. So he set out to build an empire, and in the first years he enlarged its boundaries enormously. He was much loved by his subjects, and was the first to call himself Shah, or emperor, taking the word as the Persian equivalent of Caesar.

Cabral, Pedro Alvares (c.1460–c.1526)
Portuguese explorer

No sooner had Vasco da Gama (*p. 118*) got back from his momentous voyage to India round Africa, than King Emanuel

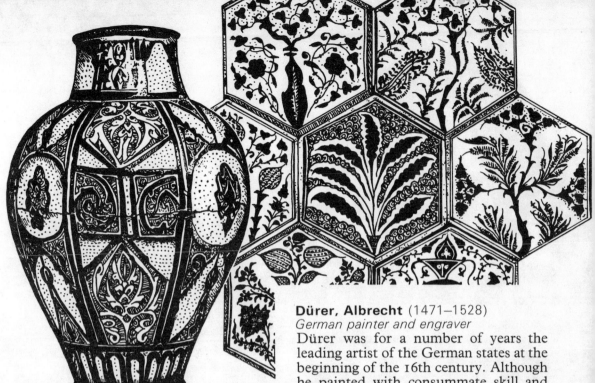

A large jar and wall tiles of the kind produced in Persia at the time of Ismail

I of Portugal sent Cabral, with 13 ships, to trade in the East. Cabral set out, but for some unexplained reason drifted westwards, and in April 1500 he landed at Brazil. Stepping ashore, he claimed it for Portugal. Then he embarked again, this time managing to get on course and go round the Cape of Good Hope to Calicut in India where he set up a Portuguese trading station.

Machiavelli, Niccolo (1469–1527)
Italian statesman

Machiavelli entered politics in Florence, and proved to be a skilful negotiator. He was employed on many diplomatic missions, and for a while he served Cesare Borgia (*p. 113*). His experiences of the various Italian states, which were warring constantly in the late fifteenth and early sixteenth centuries, led him to think a good deal about how government ought to work. Eventually, he retired and wrote books. One of these was *Il Principe* (the Prince), and it has become famous as a kind of handbook for statesmen, particularly those who have wide, even dictatorial powers.

Dürer, Albrecht (1471–1528)
German painter and engraver

Dürer was for a number of years the leading artist of the German states at the beginning of the 16th century. Although he painted with consummate skill and great feeling, and was court painter to the Emperor Charles V (*p. 127*), it is as an engraver on copper that much of his fame rests. It is said that he invented etching, that is, cutting a picture in wax on a metal plate with a fine needle, and then covering this wax with acid so that it etches the design into the metal only where the needle has cut the wax. His series of woodcuts demonstrate a masterly technique and a powerful expressiveness.

Niccolo Machiavelli

Hampton Court Palace which Cardinal Wolsey (inset) built during the reign of Henry VIII

Wolsey, Thomas (c.1473–1530)
English cardinal and statesman

Wolsey came from the humblest beginnings (he was the son of a prosperous Ipswich butcher) but was educated at Magdalen College, Oxford and by skilled and intelligent moves steadily raised himself to the highest post in the land, Lord Chancellor. From about 1511 to 1529 he ran the government of England, so that the King, Henry VIII, who was young and gay, could go on amusing himself. This freedom of action enabled Wolsey to make himself very rich, too, and his wealth and his ostentatious spending made him extremely unpopular. But he was a good servant to the King, and when he failed, in 1529, to obtain the divorce the King wanted from Catherine of Aragon to marry Ann Boleyn, nothing can forgive Henry his ingratitude in arresting the old cardinal and ordering him to be tried for treason. Wolsey set out from his estates in the north and travelled to London to sit for trial, but he was taken ill at Leicester and died.

Wolsey built Hampton Court Palace and the college at Oxford that came to be called Christ Church.

Babar (1483–1530)
First Moghul Emperor in India

Babar means Tiger, and this was the nickname of Zahir ud-din Mohammed, a descendant of Timurlaine (*p. 103*) and Genghis Khan (*p. 88*), who in 1525 invaded India and defeated a huge army of the Afghan Emperor of India. He captured the capital, Delhi, and also the city of Agra, and by 1527 was master of a large part of what is now India. He created the Moghul Empire, began to organize it, and also wrote his memoirs.

Turré, Mohammed (d. c.1530)
Moslem African ruler

In the early years of the 16th century there was a strong kingdom in the Nigeria region of Africa. It was called the Songhoi kingdom and it was ruled by Mohammed Turré, an African who was also a Moslem. This remarkable man, about whom one longs to learn more if only it could be discovered, had a (for those times) modern administration; taxation was organized fairly and effectively, a police force operated in the country and kept order, and a system of weights and measures was in general use

in markets and shops. Turré also encouraged the proper use of farming techniques, financed irrigation by sponsoring the cutting of canals, and is said even to have founded a college in the kingdom's capital, Timbuctoo.

Turré died in 1530 and for a while the Songhoi kingdom declined. It was never to rise to quite the same heights again.

Zwingli, Ulrich (1484–1531)
Swiss religious reformer

Zwingli was a Swiss pastor who, about the same time as Luther (*p. 123*), began to question the teachings and practices of the Roman Catholic Church. In 1523, a few years after he had settled down to teaching theology, he introduced the new ideas of the faith at Zurich. His work was accepted by the authorities, who admitted him to their councils. In the religious wars which followed, he accompanied the soldiers as a chaplain, and was killed in battle in 1531.

More, Sir Thomas (1478–1535)
English scholar and statesman

Thomas More was brought up by Cardinal Morton, one of Henry VII's principal advisers. He went to Oxford where he worked with Erasmus (*p. 122*) and then he entered Parliament. He was also a skilful barrister, and a political career of the highest order was opened to him. He succeeded Cardinal Wolsey (*p. 120*) as Lord Chancellor, and because he was not a cleric, the King, Henry VIII, thought he could get More to support him all the way in his break with Rome.

For a while More agreed to support his king, but when Henry decided to call himself Supreme Head of the Church, More refused to acknowledge the title. Henry retaliated by having him tried for high treason and More was sentenced to death. In 1534 the King had made it treasonable to deny his new title.

More was also a writer; among his best known works were *Utopia*, in which he comments upon this world by portraying an imaginary one, and *Richard III*, a woefully inaccurate portrait of that much maligned king.

A Moghul prince and his retinue of courtiers entering Agra

121

Erasmus, Desiderius (c.1466–1536)
Dutch scholar

Erasmus' real name was very different, Geert Geerts. He was a Dutch boy who went into a monastery. Gifted with exceptional brains, he got tired of the lack of ideas among the clerics in the monastery, and he left to go to Paris university to study. Soon he established himself as a brilliant teacher, sought by many throughout Europe.

But even Paris began to bore him, and he moved on, never staying anywhere for long. He used to visit all sorts of learned establishments, like Oxford, Cambridge, Basle, and certainly at Oxford and Cambridge he found much contentment and intellectual stimulus.

Erasmus wrote many works, and edited the New Testament in Greek. Much of his writing stimulated people into questioning the doctrines of the Church, as well as the accepted philosophical points of view about nature, creation and science. But he never gave any support to the reformers like Luther.

Tyndale, William (c.1495–1536)
English preacher

Tyndale studied theology at Oxford and at Cambridge. He was influenced by the thunderings of Luther (*p. 123*) against the Church at Rome, and wanted to play a part in bringing the Reformation to England. So he translated the New Testament into English and had it printed in Germany. Copies were then smuggled into England, but most were confiscated on their arrival.

In 1536 he was handed over to the authorities in Flanders who imprisoned him and then burned him at the stake.

Pizarro, Francisco (1470–1541)
Spanish conqueror of Peru

There had been great civilizations in Peru since nearly 2000 BC. The most recent was the Inca Empire, which dominated Peru from about 1100 AD. In 1530 Francisco Pizarro, a Spanish adventurer, did exactly the same thing in Peru as Cortes (*p. 124*) had in Mexico. He landed on the Peruvian coast, attacked the capital city and captured the ruler, Atahualpa.

Pizarro promised to release him if he would fill a room with gold and silver. A line was drawn half way up the wall, to mark the level of the gold required. But when Atahualpa's servants reached it, the Spaniards raised the line another foot or so, and on until the precious metal reached the ceiling. Pizarro then ordered the Inca ruler to be put to death. Immediately Peruvian resistance collapsed, because their system was such that all power and orders came from the ruler, down through nobles and on to regional governors. But none of these individuals had ever made decisions: they merely passed them on.

Another splendid civilization was destroyed for the sake of riches, and all in the name of Christianity.

Paracelsus, Philippus Aureolus (c.1493–1541)
Swiss doctor

This interesting medical man's real name had a splendid ring, Theophrastus Bombastus von Hohenheim. He taught himself medicine, very largely through observation of people of different walks of life and the kinds of complaint from which they suffered. One thing he noted was that diseases were not necessarily the result of the breakdown of the general condition, or humour, of the body. They had specific causes and so ought to be able to be cured by specific treatments. Paracelsus also believed in the curative value of hot baths with chemicals in the water.

Copernicus, Nicolas (1473–1543)
Polish astronomer

Nicolas Kopernik, or as history has come to know him, Nicolaus Copernicus, was an astronomer from Poland who suggested that the earth and the other planets moved around the sun, and not the other way around. This does not seem startling today, but in those times men were used to thinking that the earth was flat, and that if you walked far enough, you would eventually fall off it. Indeed, in many

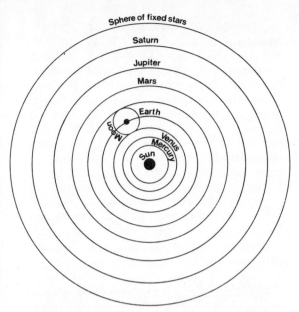

Nicolas Copernicus and a drawing showing his theory of the Universe

places it was a serious offence to say otherwise.

Copernicus studied at the Polish university of Cracow and then taught in Italy.

Holbein, Hans (c.1497–1543)
German born painter

Holbein was the son of Hans Holbein the Elder (c.1465–1524), a Bavarian painter of historical scenes. Young Hans also painted historical pictures, and later on took to portraits. He came to England towards the end of his life and was commissioned to paint Sir Thomas More (*p. 121*). Over the next few years Holbein carried out commissions to paint all kinds of people in England, including Henry VIII, his third wife Jane Seymour, and a little later, his fourth wife Ann of Cleves.

Luther, Martin (1483–1546)
German religious reformer

Martin Luther, the German monk and scholar who questioned the doctrines of the Roman Catholic Church in the first quarter of the 16th century, is the most famous name in the story of the Reformation. But there were others like Huss (*p. 104*) and Savonarola (*p. 111*) who had tried before Luther and paid with their lives.

What upset Luther particularly was the practice of selling indulgences, introduced by the Church on a wide scale. Agents of the Pope actually sold pieces of paper to humble peasants and lords alike forgiving them their sins in return for money to help build a new Cathedral of St. Peter at Rome. There was no justification for this in the Scriptures. Nor was there much guarantee that the Cathedral would get all the money.

In 1517, Luther wrote down all his complaints – more than 90 of them – and nailed the list to the doors of Wittenburg cathedral. A fearful storm of argument followed. Luther was in great danger, and when he was summoned to appear before the Diet of Worms where he was later condemned, he had to have a safe conduct guaranteed.

The argument developed out of all calculation. Peasants used it to rebel, states went to war. Followers of Luther's ideas ranged themselves against those who supported the orthodox church. Luther himself may not have realized what the result of his actions would be.

Luther's translation of the Bible from original sources was to have a profound influence on the German language and on European religion.

Cortés, Hernan (1485–1547)
Spanish Conqueror of Mexico

In some respects you could say Cortés was a great hero. He conquered Mexico, and opened up its vast mineral wealth to Spain. But in doing this he destroyed the ancient Mexican civilization, which in his time was dominated by the Aztecs. His men behaved with the most frightful cruelty to these marvellous Indian peoples, doing so in the name of Christianity.

Cortés was the son of a Spanish noble who set off for the West Indies in search of adventure. In 1518, the Spanish governor of Cuba sent him to explore the Mexican mainland, with a small force armed with muskets and equipped with horses. He came upon the Aztecs, bargained with them, and then treacherously turned on them. He destroyed their capital city of Mexico, and captured their king, Montezuma. Then he dismantled the whole apparatus of government and turned them, nobles and common people alike, into slaves.

Henry VIII (1491–1547)
King of England (1509–1547)

This monster of ingratitude was perhaps one of the worst monarchs England ever had the misfortune to endure. He came to the throne in 1509, aged 18, handsome, gifted, able to speak several languages, compose music, and play all manner of games better than most men. He was popular and his people looked forward to a reign of progress and splendour, for the 16th century was a splendid age. Thirty-eight years, six wives, hundreds of friends, and many millions of pounds later, he died – fat, unable to walk, legs ulcerated to a revolting degree, consumed with self-pity, greed and vengeance, the most hated man in the British Isles, for whose end the whole nation had been waiting with baited breath.

In the interval, Henry had squandered the fortune left by his father Henry VII (*p. 114*), raised vast new sums through taxation, divorced and humiliated his first wife Catherine of Aragon, broken with the Church of Rome, and declared himself Supreme Head of the Church, making it treasonable not to accept this. He executed Sir Thomas More and Thomas Cromwell, two able – though different – men who ran his affairs, and drove a third, the brilliant Cardinal Wolsey, to his death. He had smashed down the monasteries to get at their riches to fill his empty treasury, debased the coinage, got England involved in expensive and fruitless wars, and made himself the laughing stock of Europe by his many adventures in marriage. He had two of his wives executed, and he might have done the same to the last one, Catherine Parr, if his own death had not intervened.

Xavier, Francisco (1506–1552)
Spanish missionary

Xavier was one of Ignatius Loyola's original collaborators in the foundation of the Society of Jesus. He devoted his career to carrying the work of the new order to the Spanish and Portuguese colonies in the East, and between 1540 and 1552 he preached and worked at Goa where he greatly influenced the corrupt Europeans; in the Moluccas, Ceylon, Japan and Macao he founded missionaries and converted thousands of natives. He was canonized in 1622.

Rabelais, François (c.1494–1553)
French author

Rabelais became a monk for a while, but did not feel he could take that life very seriously, for there were so many inconsistent things about the church, its doctrines and its practices. He studied medicine and then practised as a doctor in Lyons. But he grew tired of that, too, and travelled about western Europe.

During his days as a doctor he wrote two novels, *Gargantua*, and *Pantagruel*. These were written under a pseudonym and were very successful. They are full of humour and depth and in parts are very coarse. Gargantua was a giant whose development as a child was quite grotesque.

Rabalais wrote other works, some no less amusing, and these were also filled with both wisdom and common sense.

Henry VIII, Ann Boleyn and courtiers

Servetus, Michael (1511–1553)
Spanish religious reformer

Miguel Serveto, as his name was in his native Spain, became a doctor. He practised in several places in Europe and also carried out research. Some say that he anticipated William Harvey (*p. 153*) by a century in discovering the circulation of the blood.

But Servetus is better known as a martyr. He studied theology as well as medicine, and found he could not accept the doctrine of the Trinity (Father, Son and Holy Ghost in one person), nor could he favour infants being baptized. So he published works expressing his views, but these got him into trouble with the Inquisition, which arrested him and tried him. He escaped but was caught again in Geneva and burned as a heretic.

Cranmer, Thomas (1489–1556)
Archbishop of Canterbury

'This hand hath offended'; so saying, Archbishop Cranmer plunged it into the flames licking around his body, at the stake in an Oxford street one March day in 1556. It was a brave, defiant act by a man who for most of his life had been too pliant, too ready to sail with the wind.

Cranmer, the author of the *Book of Common Prayer* (the language of most of which is among the most beautiful in English), was appointed Archbishop of Canterbury by Henry VIII in 1533. In this post he granted Henry VIII the divorce he wanted from Catherine of Aragon, though as a good Christian he must have known it was not justified. For the next fifteen years he served his king well, and the king's son, Edward VI, well, too. Then followed Mary I, bent on restoring England to the Roman Faith, if necessary by faggot and stake. One of her victims was Cranmer. He, after all, had pronounced her mother's marriage to Henry VIII annulled. That made her illegitimate, and Cranmer could not expect to be forgiven for that.

So she had him burned. During the trial he tried to recant and say he would accept the restoration of the old faith, but it was no use. Mary wanted his blood. So he plunged his hand into the fire. It was the one with which he had written offering to recant.

125

Jacques Cartier and the Indians he encountered when he discovered the Gulf of St. Lawrence in Canada.

Loyola, Ignatius (1491–1556)
Spanish soldier and religious leader

Ignatius Loyola began his career as a soldier, but while recuperating from a wound he studied theology, and decided to give up fighting. Instead he set out to create a new religious order, to be called the Society of Jesus, which was to bring Christianity to people who did not accept it, and to win Protestant Christians back to the orthodox Roman Faith. The Pope approved, and Loyola became general of the new order. The Society of Jesus (made up of 'Jesuits') still exists, and it has had a fascinating history of devotion to its aims, of success, and of struggle often against overwhelming odds. Loyola was canonized in 1622.

Cabot, Sebastian (1476–1557)
Venetian explorer

Sebastian Cabot came to England with his father, John, in 1484. They were en-

couraged by Henry VII (*p. 114*) to look for a route to Asia by sailing West across the Atlantic. Leaving Bristol in 1497 they reached Cape Breton Island, off what is now Canada, two months later. A year later they set out again and this time reached Newfoundland. John died in 1498, but Sebastian spent the next fifty years in the service of several European kings as navigator or pilot. He made maps for Henry VIII of England and was senior pilot to Charles V, Emperor of the Holy Roman Empire. He drew a map of the world, and in 1551 he founded the Merchant Adventurers' Company in London, which organized exploration voyages to search for new trade routes, especially to the Spice Islands.

Cartier, Jacques (1491–1557)
French explorer

John and Sebastian Cabot (*p. 126*) had landed at Cape Breton Island, off Canada, in 1498, but they did not appreciate they had touched the tip of a huge continent. In 1534, Cartier, a navigator, took an expedition westwards from St. Malo to find a sea route to India. He discovered the Gulf of St. Lawrence in Canada, and on a second voyage there he sailed as far as Montreal. It was another sixty or more years before a settlement was made in Canada, by Champlain (*p. 147*).

Charles V (1500–1558)
Holy Roman Emperor (1519–1556) and King of Spain (1517–1555)

Charles V was one of the most splendid rulers of the sixteenth century. His lands, when his empire was at its height, were more extensive than any previous ruler's, and they included Spain and all her territories overseas (S. America, Mexico, the East), Holland, Burgundy, Germany, Naples. His career was a full one, and his wars were often successful. He defeated and captured the King of France at Pavia in 1525. In 1527 he invaded Rome, sacked it, and took the Pope prisoner. He defeated the Turks in 1532 when they were led by their great Sultan, Suleiman the Magnificent (*p. 128*).

Then towards the end of his life, Charles abdicated his realms, one by one: some he gave to his son, Philip of Spain, and some to his brother Ferdinand. Finally in 1558 he retired to a monastery.

Mary I (1516–1558)
Queen of England (1553–1558)

Mary Tudor was Henry VIII's daughter by his first wife, Catherine of Aragon. To begin with she had all the advantages of being brought up as a princess, and heir to the throne. Then, in the late 1520s, when the king had begun to admire another woman, Ann Boleyn, Catherine and Mary were banished from court. The succeeding saga of getting his marriage annulled meant more humiliations for the Queen and Mary, and not surprisingly she grew up bitter and vengeful.

In 1553, she succeeded her half brother Edward VI (1547–1553) as monarch, after a vain attempt by John Dudley, Duke of Northumberland, to put his daughter-in-law Lady Jane Grey on the throne. At once, bishops, prelates and scholars were ordered to accept her programme of restoring the Roman Faith, and when they refused they were arrested, tried and burned at the stake.

Mary then married Philip II of Spain, a man considerably younger than her, and not a bit interested in her charms, such as they were. She longed for an heir, even believed for a while she was carrying one, but eventually the realization that she was too old dawned on her, and she gave way to self-pity.

In the last year of her short reign she lost the port of Calais to France. It was England's last possession on the French mainland.

Gustavus Vasa I (1496–1560)
King of Sweden (1523–1560)

During the 15th and first part of the 16th century Sweden had been under the dominion of Denmark. The country had declined and the people had suffered. Gustavus, a Swedish noble, led the revolt against Danish rule, and by 1523 had driven out the Danes. He was elected king, the first of a dynasty of four kings. In 37 years he transformed his kingdom into a prosperous and happy nation. The Protestant faith was the accepted religion, trade flourished, schools were built, roads and canals were constructed, and the peasantry protected.

Melanchthon (1497–1560)
German religious reformer

Melanchthon, the Greek name for Philip Schwartzert, was an ardent supporter of Martin Luther (*p. 123*) and in the early years of the Reformation, he worked with Luther on the setting up of their reformed Church organization. He was professor of Greek at Wittenburg, and in 1521 published a book on the doctrines which the reformers were questioning. But Melanchthon was also anxious to see if the Reformed faith and the Roman Catholic faith could be reconciled, and Christianity thus united. He worked to this end, but it was not possible. Even today Christendom is divided on issues.

Michelangelo (1475–1564)
Italian artistic genius

Michelangelo and Leonardo da Vinci (*p. 116*) were the two greatest figures of the Renaissance, towering over a host of other very skilled men. Michelangelo was not as gifted scientifically, so far as we have been able to find out, but as a sculptor and painter he was the equal of Leonardo. Indeed, there are many who would put his statue of David or his painting of the ceiling of the Sistine Chapel in the Vatican on a level higher than anything Leonardo produced. And Michelangelo was also the author of some of the loveliest sonnets in the Italian language.

Michelangelo was also an architect, and perhaps his most celebrated achievement was the design of many principal features of St. Peter's Cathedral in Rome, especially the wonderful dome.

This sad, temperamental genius, although he was highly paid for many of his commissions, continually grumbled about being short of money. He lived for nearly 90 years, but never seemed to find peace.

Calvin, John (1509–1564)
French religious reformer

Calvin really was something of a pessimist. Not content with Luther's Protestant Reformation, he sought to make all men believe that their destinies were already arranged for them. Whether they would be received into the Kingdom of Heaven or not at their death was determined at birth. All they could do was pray and hope that things would not be too bad.

In 1541 he set up a sort of state in Switzerland, at Geneva, in which he ruled as if he was the appointed prime minister of God. He argued and quarrelled with many thinkers. He also set up a sort of college for theological studies. But in an age when Protestantism had not yet become the dominant belief in western Europe, his state provided a refuge for Protestants and a centre for them to prepare their campaigns to get their doctrines accepted.

Vesalius, Andreas (1514–1564)
Belgian anatomist

Vesalius is famous for having dissected a human body and named many of the principal organs, blood vessels, muscles and glands. He also showed that the personality was not regulated by the heart but by the brain and the nervous system.

To produce his drawings, Vesalius had to find bodies, and it is possible the ones he used for cutting up were obtained under doubtful circumstances. The Inquisition caught him, tried him for stealing bodies from churchyards and sentenced him to death. This was commuted to a pilgrimage to the Holy Land.

Suleiman I (c.1496–1566)
Sultan of Turkish Ottoman Empire (1520–1566)

Suleiman was known as 'the Magnificent', and no wonder, for his reign as Sultan was the most colourful, successful and interesting of all the long line of Ottoman rulers. He hated warfare, and yet much of his reign was spent in aggressive conquering campaigns in Europe and Asia. He overcame Hungary and smashed an Austrian army at the battle of Mohacz in 1526. Three years later he was at the gates of Vienna. He also conquered parts of North Africa, the Near East as far as Baghdad, and his fleets dominated the Mediterranean.

At home he reformed the government administration and brought it up to date. He loved pageantry and ceremonial and found as many opportunities as he could for state occasions when he could dress up and entertain foreign heads of state and ambassadors. His reform of the law of land holding earned him the title 'the law-giver'.

In 1551 Suleiman conquered Persia, making his dominions stretch from Morocco to the Tigris, from the Black Sea to the Nile.

Nostradamus (1503–1566)
French doctor

Nostradamus was born Michel de Notredame. He qualified as a doctor, but during

Michelangelo's bas-relief,
Pitti Madonna, which is in the
Bargello Gallery in Florence

his earlier years of work he also became interested in astrology. This put him in a difficult position, for he found he could often predict how an illness would progress. In 1547 he established himself as a medical prophet, and perhaps cast gloom far and wide among his patients. He wrote predictions of a general kind in verse and published them. When he correctly predicted the way in which Henry II of France would die, he was appointed court physician to the next king, Charles IX. His work has remained a fascinating text.

Ascham, Roger (1515–1568)
English scholar

Roger Ascham was tutor to Elizabeth I when she was Princess Elizabeth. He was a fine scholar and he did a very good job of teaching her, for though she was not the strong-minded and dictatorial queen some historians would have us all believe, she was an extremely well-educated woman.

Ascham had also been tutor to Mary Tudor, who was queen from 1553 to 1558. In 1559 he was appointed prebendary of York.

The Brueghels (16th century)
Three eminent painters of the late Flemish school

Pieter Brueghel (c.1520–1569), known as the Elder, worked in Brussels and Antwerp. A master of landscapes, he was famous for his pictures of peasant life, executed with great vitality and gay design. His son Pieter (c.1564–1638) the Younger, was nicknamed 'Hell Brueghel' because many of his pictures have portraits of devils, flames and so on. He, too, painted rural scenes, but also executed several pictures of biblical stories. The Younger's brother, Jan Brueghel (1568–1625), known as 'Velvet Brueghel', painted many beautiful landscapes.

Sansovino, Jacopo (1486–1570)
Italian sculptor

Sansovino's real name was Tatti, but he studied under the art tutor Sansovino and so admired him that he took his name. Interestingly, this Sansovino, too, had been born with a different name.

Jacopo was employed to work as sculptor in Florence and then in Venice. In 1529 he became Venetian state architect. His works were many, and the best include the Cornaro Palace, the Library of St. Mark, and the Zecca (the mint).

Floris, Franz (1517–1570)
Flemish designer

Floris, whose real name was de Vriendt, was a designer of buildings, furnishings and decoration. He was also a painter and engraver, and his books on design were beautifully illustrated. His original decorative schemes for palaces and houses were an important influence in European architecture and furnishing. They marked a form of transition between Renaissance ideas and Baroque, in northwest Europe and especially in France.

Moray, James Stuart, Earl of (1531–1570)
Scottish statesman

This half-brother of Mary, Queen of Scots (*p. 135*) was one of the most wonderful men ever to serve Scotland. Bold, scholarly, politically astute, generous, he acted as his half-sister's adviser in the first years after she came back to Scotland from France in 1560. But she would not always accept his counsel. What was worse, they clashed frequently over religion, for he was a Knox convert and she a devout Catholic.

Finally, he jøined the lords who expelled her in 1568, and took over the government as Regent, in the name of her baby son, James VI. As ruler, Moray was effective and popular, a rare combination, and in three years he did much to restore order in the kingdom. Then, suddenly in 1570, he was murdered, possibly by agents of Mary, and all Scotland mourned.

Cellini, Benvenuto (1500–1571)
Italian sculptor

Cellini's greatest contribution was probably his autobiography which tells so much about what Renaissance Italy of the 16th century was really like. But he was also a distinguished sculptor who specialized in bronze portrait busts. He studied under Michaelangelo, and he also learned the skill of goldsmithing. One of his best works was a model of the Crucifixion, which is now at the Palace of the Escorial in Spain.

Knox, John (c.1512–1572)
Scottish reformer

Knox was primarily responsible for the conversion of Scotland to the Protestant faith. Most of this was carried out while Mary, Queen of Scots (*p. 135*) was out of the country in France. When she returned he had to face a woman as determined to undo all his work as he was to maintain it.

Knox made himself extremely unpopular with the queen by his long, trenchant, stirring sermons, which he directed against women in general, especially women given any power. Once, Mary had him arrested and tried, but the Privy Council acquitted him. This made him extremely popular, and alienated her even more from her subjects.

Knox died in 1572, certain that Scotland was confirmed in the new faith.

Coligny, Gaspard de (1519–1572)
French Protestant leader
Coligny was the son of a noble. He served with distinction as a soldier, and then took command at sea, becoming an admiral in 1552. Sometime in 1557, at war with Spain, he was captured and spent two years in a Spanish gaol. His experience there converted him from being a supporter of the orthodox Catholic church into a Protestant, and when he was released he became one of the leaders of the French Protestant Group, the Huguenots. By 1572 he was their recognized chief, but this did not save his life when at the massacre of St. Bartholomew in Paris, Catherine dei Medici (*p. 135*) ordered the wholesale killing of thousands of Protestants visiting the city for a meeting.

Vasari, Giorgio (1511–1574)
Italian painter and art historian
Some of Vasari's pictures were quite good, and rank in what you could call the second division of 16th century Italian paintings. But he is much more important as the first man seriously to write detailed biographies of artists of the Renaissance. He had worked under the wonderful Michelangelo – and what a training that must have been! In 1550 Vasari produced his famous *Lives of the Artists*, as it is called for short, and it included life stories and criticisms of the work of every major Italian artist from Cimabue to Michelangelo.

Parker, Matthew (1504–1575)
Archbishop of Canterbury
Matthew Parker was the Archbishop of Canterbury appointed by Elizabeth I and William Cecil in 1559 to superintend the new religious settlement they wanted, a compromise between the extremes of Roman Catholicism and more austere Protestantism. He organized the publication of the Bishop's Bible, and re-drafted the articles of the English church to 39 in number.

That the settlement was a smooth one may be largely credited to Parker.

John Knox preaching at a cathedral in Scotland

Don John of Austria at the Battle of Lepanto

Titian (?1477–1576)
Italian (Venetian) painter

Tiziano Vecelli was the head of the Venetian school of painting. He was patronized by several leading Italian nobles and was for some years court painter to Emperor Charles V (*p. 127*).

Titian, in a life of nearly 100 years, produced many works. He was very adept at the use of colour, and one shade of red which he used, sometimes for people's hair, is known as Titian Red to this day. One of his pictures, the *Death of Actaeon*, fetched more than £2,000,000 in a London sale room in 1971.

Don John of Austria (1547–1578)
Spanish general

'Don John of Austria is going to the war!' is the refrain of one of G. K. Chesterton's most wonderful poems, *Lepanto*. This poem about the great battle in which the hitherto invincible Turkish fleet was defeated in 1571 by the fleet of the Holy League, commanded by Don John, celebrates the greatest success in the spectacular career of this illegitimate son of the Emperor Charles V (*p. 127*). Others included the capture of Tunis in North Africa from the Turks in 1573, and the defeat of the Dutch at the battle of Gembloux in 1578.

It is thought he was poisoned in 1578, possibly at the connivance of his half-brother Philip II of Spain (*p. 139*) who was jealous of his success.

Palladio, Andrea (1518–1580)
Italian architect
Palladio designed buildings in the classical style, following principles of architecture laid down by the Romans. But he disliked unnecessary ornament, and his buildings are conspicuous for the sparing use of it. He also introduced the colonnaded loggia as a feature of design, and the 'motif of a bay with a round-headed opening flanked by two square headed openings'.

His style was taken up and developed in England by Inigo Jones (*p. 152*).

Camoens, Luiz Vaz de (1524–1580)
Portuguese poet
Camoens was a great patriotic poet, who wrote about pioneering exploits and exploration in Portuguese history. He was also an adventurer, joined several expeditions, lost an eye, spent some time in prison, and finally found favour at the court of King Sebastian.

His best known work was *Lusiads*, a long verse history of Portugal, which dramatized among other things the great voyages of Vasco da Gama (*p. 118*).

Alva, Duke of (1508–1582)
Spanish military commander
Fernando Alvarez de Toledo, Duke of Alva, was a well-tried Spanish general whom Philip II of Spain (*p. 139*) sent to the Netherlands (Holland and Belgium) to put down the rising led by William the Silent, Prince of Orange (*p. 134*). In a six year struggle, during which he practised awful cruelties, Alva caught and executed many leaders, but could not break the revolt, for he was unable to find William.

In 1580, Alva was appointed commander in chief of the Spanish army which invaded and eventually conquered Portugal and brought it, with its huge overseas empire, into the Spanish Empire.

St. Theresa of Avila (1515–1582)
Spanish religious reformer
Theresa was a Carmelite nun, the daughter of a Spanish noble living in Avila. When she joined the order in 1535 she was shocked to find that an order once famous for strictness and austerity had become lax and undisciplined. She experienced visions, about which she wrote and these indicated that it was her duty to reform the order.

Armed with this, she gathered round her a number of workers who were glad to live the old life of austerity, straw beds, short rations, hard work, hours of silent prayer. Her reputation began to spread to all the Carmelite houses, and also outside. One of her helpers was a young Carmelite monk, Juan de Yepes, and he was encouraged to found a community of Carmelite monks. He later changed his name to John of the Cross. Between them, Theresa and John transformed more than 30 establishments.

Gilbert, Sir Humphrey (c.1540–1583)
English explorer
Gilbert was Raleigh's half-brother (*p. 144*), and in 1583 led an expedition to North America to found an English colony. He landed in Newfoundland and set up a colony at St. John's. On his return journey his ship, the *Squirrel*, was sunk and all on board were drowned.

Ivan IV (the Terrible) (1530–1584)
Czar of Russia (1533–1584)
Ivan became ruler of the kingdom of Muscovy when he was only three. His first years were taken care of by a council of nobles, but in 1544 he assumed the authority himself, and three years later had himself crowned Czar. This word came from Caesar, and it was the first time it was used by a ruler of Russia.

Ivan was called the Terrible because he dealt so severely with revolts against his authority. It would be quite wrong to regard him as a savage Asiatic chief. He was in fact more of a cultivated European, who encouraged the arts, fostered trade (he had a commercial treaty with Elizabeth I of England), and began to beautify the city of Moscow.

Ivan also conducted wars of expansion, and he added huge tracts of Siberia to his domains.

William I (the Silent) (1533–1584)
Chief Stadholder of Holland (1579–1584)

In the second half of the 16th century what is now Holland and Belgium were part of the Spanish Empire. They were ruled by a succession of tough and harsh governors (except for Don John of Austria, *p. 132*) and forced to accept Roman Catholicism. In about 1568, the people rose against their masters, and for the rest of the century there was continued revolt against Spanish dominion.

William, who was Prince of the state of Orange and Count of the state of Nassau, was invited to lead the opposition. Over the next years, the Dutch suffered several defeats but never gave in, for from time to time they won victories. In 1579 the northern Dutch states declared their independence of Spanish rule, and elected William their chief *stadholder*, which means chief head of state.

William, known as the Silent because he knew how to keep a secret, was assassinated in 1584.

Mary, Queen of Scots, attempting to protect Rizzio who was subsequently murdered by her husband, Lord Darnley

Ronsard, Pierre de (1524–1585)
French poet

Ronsard was a most brilliant and sensitive lyric poet. He went deaf while still in his teens, and so he was never able to hear his verse read. Together with Joachim du Bellay and some friends he founded *La Pléiade*, a literary movement that rejected the conventions of mediaeval verse, and tried to emulate classical literature.

The French monarchy has always liked artists and writers, and Ronsard was much favoured by Charles IX who made him court poet.

Batory, Stephen (1533–1586)
King of Poland (1575–1586)

The history of Poland has been a chequered one. Periods of greatness were followed by sad eras of low ebb, and occasionally even eras when the nation was divided between its neighbours. But the later part of the 16th century was a good one for Poland. One of its best kings was Stephen Batory, who was elected by

the nobility to rule the land. He governed well, put down a serious rising in Danzig, and in a three year war with the Russian Czar, Ivan IV he defeated him.

Batory also aimed to liberate Hungary from the Turks, but died before he could despatch an army down through the Transylvanian mountains.

Mary, Queen of Scots (1542–1587)
Queen of Scotland (1561–1567)

This tallish, dark, striking-looking woman, who could speak several languages, was quick tempered, un-reliable, obstinate and arrogant. She had, in fact, all the wrong qualities with which to rule any kingdom: for Scotland they were disastrous.

Born a few days before her father's death in 1542, she was married off at 18 to the French Dauphin, who became king the next year and died the year after. In her childhood, the government had been badly run for much of the time. And most important of all, Scotland had turned Protestant. When she came back to rule her Kingdom in 1560, she was a devout Catholic. Who would give way?

This was where her bad qualities let her down. She quarrelled with all her advisers, and she led a private life un-becoming in a queen of those days.

She married her cousin, Lord Darnley, a drunken, cruel and boorish brute. So she took up with her Italian secretary, Rizzio. Darnley promptly murdered him. A short while later Darnley himself was killed when a house he was staying in was blown up by gunpowder. Though not proved guilty, she was always suspected.

In 1568 her nobles drove her out of Scotland. She fled to England, to seek refuge with Elizabeth I, her cousin, but the English queen imprisoned her. Over the next seventeen years a series of plots were hatched against Elizabeth, most of which had among their aims her replacement on the throne by Mary, who was the heir apparent. The last one, in 1586, was unmasked by Sir Francis Walsingham (p. 136). Mary was tried for her part in it, and found guilty. She was executed at Fotheringay Castle.

Catherine Dei Medici

Dei Medici, Catherine (1519–1589)
Queen of France

Catherine was great granddaughter of Lorenzo the Magnificent, and in 1533 she married Henry, second son of Francis I of France. He became King Henry II in 1547. Her enormous strength of will and ambition were now directed into making her husband, her first, her second and then her third son, successively kings as Henry II, Francis II, Charles IX and Henry III, into powerful monarchs. She also determined to guide the religious policies of France.

At first Catherine was in favour of the Catholics and Protestants agreeing to differ and trying to live side by side. But after a while, she turned on the Protestants. In August 1572, on the night of the 24th, St. Bartholomew's Day, several thousand leading Protestants were in Paris, going to bed before a big meeting the next day. Suddenly, royal guards and troops clattered down the streets and broke into inns and lodging houses and slaughtered all the visiting Protestants they could find. It is said some 8,000 perished, including their leader, Admiral Coligny.

135

Paré, Ambroise (c.1517–1590)
French surgeon

Paré became a surgeon, and his early experiences were as a field surgeon in the French army. This brought him in touch with a multitude of possibilities for operation, and he developed a variety of new techniques. Perhaps his most famous innovation was the idea of using ligatures (or stitches) to sew up arteries while attending to wounds. Up to then, it was customary to apply hot rods to them to seal off the torn ends, a process called cauterizing. Paré left the army and was quickly offered a job as royal physician; he served four French kings.

Walsingham, Sir Francis (1530–1590)
English statesman

Francis Walsingham was one of the most remarkable men of the Elizabethan Age (1558–1603). He devoted his prodigious talents to one end, looking after the state affairs of his queen and protecting her from plots and dangers. He formed an intricate and extremely effective secret service force of people who detected numerous conspiracies against the queen or the government. Many times he was able to strike the conspirators down before they were fully ready. He actually saved Elizabeth's life on several occasions. The most sensational plot he broke was the Babington conspiracy, which, in 1586, aimed to murder the queen and put Mary, Queen of Scots, on the throne, and to restore Roman Catholicism in England.

Walsingham also found out all the details of the great Armada invasion planned against England for 1588 but the queen would not spend the money to defend her country. It was fortunate the Spanish fleet was led by the useless Medina Sidonia (*p. 141*).

Walsingham died in 1590.

Montaigne, Michel de (1533–1592)
French writer

Montaigne is famous for his Essays which were published in three volumes. He had studied a lot of ancient Greek and Roman literature, and had wanted important men of his day to consider modelling their lives on some of the heroes of Greece and Rome. He was a courtier to Charles IX for some time.

Marlowe, Christopher (1564–1593)
English poet and playwright

Marlowe was a humble shoemaker's son, who won a scholarship to King's School, Canterbury and another, a few years later, to Corpus Christi College at Cambridge. It was at the university that he started to write poetry and plays. By the age of 20 he had several major poems and plays finished. Among the best of his works are the plays *The Massacre of Paris*, *Tamberlaine*, *Edward II* and *Dr. Faustus*. His genius was hardly less brilliant than that of William Shakespeare (*p. 142*).

Marlowe is said to have been employed as a secret agent by Sir Francis Walsingham (*p. 136*). Many of his friends were brilliant men, who held very advanced views on religion – at least for that time. The precise way he died is uncertain. It is believed that he was stabbed in a brawl at a tavern in Deptford.

Palestrina, Giovanni (c.1526–1594)
Italian composer

Quite a lot of the late mediaeval type of church music you can hear in a church or chapel in Italy today will probably have been composed by Palestrina. A distinguished composer, Palestrina's works include over 90 masses; he also composed a large number of motets, hymns and other liturgical pieces, as well as some excellent madrigals. His *Stabat Mater* heralded the oratorios of people like Purcell and Handel.

Frobisher, Sir Martin (c.1536–1594)
English sea captain

Frobisher took an expedition across the Atlantic in 1576 to look for a north-west passage across Canada to the East. He discovered the bay named after him. In 1578 he returned to Canada to look for gold, but was not successful. He commanded a squadron at the defeat of the Spanish Armada.

Hawkins, Sir John (1532–1595)
English sea captain

Hawkins was a cousin of Sir Francis Drake (*p. 137*) and was Devonshire born. He spent many years in the regrettable slave trade, cruelly transporting Negroes from West Africa to the Americas in return for cash. Then he engaged in the same sort of raids on Spanish fleets and ports as Drake. In 1573 he was appointed treasurer of the English navy, which enabled him to do something about improving the fleet, but the Queen was ever reluctant to spend money, and quite often Hawkins had to find funds himself.

He was one of the principal commanders, along with Drake, against the great Spanish Armada which entered the Channel in 1588. Elizabeth knighted him for his services.

Drake, Sir Francis (c.1540–1596)
English sea captain

Sir Francis Drake is a great English hero, and rightly, for he not only sailed round the whole world and brought back a ship filled with Spanish treasure, he helped to destroy the Spanish fleet in Cadiz harbour, and then to destroy their rebuilt fleet as it came up the channel to invade England in 1588. He caused the Spanish government millions of pounds worth of losses in ships, treasure and supplies. 'El Draco' was feared by sailors from Spain almost as much as the Devil himself.

Drake was Devonshire born, like many of the Elizabethan sea-captains, and he started out on his raiding expeditions in the 1560s. Not only did he attack Spanish squadrons in the West Indies, he also terrorized the ports on the west coast of Spain itself. Queen Elizabeth turned a blind eye to his activities for most of the time, occasionally administering an official reprimand for the sake of the Spanish ambassador's feelings, but Drake knew it was not heartfelt.

This splendid sea captain died on yet another raiding expedition in the West Indies in 1596.

From top to bottom: Walsingham, Marlowe, Palestrina and Drake

Burghley, William Cecil, Lord (1520–1598)

English statesman

It is difficult to think of a more able, cunning and utterly loyal servant of the crown and England than William Cecil.

He had entered government service in the time of Henry VIII, and despite the differing religious leanings of the monarchs, Henry, Edward VI, Mary I and Elizabeth, he had kept his head – and his job – by skilful adjustment of his views! He learned to dissimulate and to practise statecraft in all its artifice. When Elizabeth came to the throne in 1558 she did not hesitate to pick him as her principal secretary of state, certain, as she put it, that he would serve her faithfully without yielding to temptations of bribery and favour.

For nearly forty years this marvellous man ran the government of England. He served the queen and her country through many difficult and dangerous times. He supported all kinds of schemes for the betterment of the people, in education, trade, building and the settlement of the Protestant Church.

Philip and his advisors making strategic plans for his great Armada

Philip II (1527–1598)
King of Spain (1556–1598)
This extraordinary man was endowed with a variety of characteristics. He was morose, slow-witted, interfering, not always just, but he was also extremely patient, very hard working, conscious of his royal dignity and of the great role Spain was to play in European politics and development.

Philip was the son of Charles V (*p. 127*) and of Isabella of Portugal. In 1554 he married Mary I of England (*p. 127*), who was a good many years his senior, and very plain as well. When she died in 1558, he tried to marry her half-sister and heir, Elizabeth I, but the fiery English queen would not have it. So he married the daughter of Henry II of France.

In 1556 his father abdicated huge parts of his great Empire in favour of Philip, including the vast territories in the East and in the New World. With the almost limitless wealth which this Empire provided, Philip devoted his life to maintaining the Catholic faith supreme in Europe: but in the effort he lost many wars, and spent a huge fortune. The Netherlands finally managed to break free from Spanish dominion in the 1590s: his great Armada (invasion fleet) sent against England in 1588 was routed and most of it sent to the bottom of the sea. He did conquer Portugal, but found it very costly to subdue.

In all these years he failed to encourage trade or industry, although he did patronize the arts.

Spenser, Edmund (1552–1599)
English poet
Edmund Spenser is best remembered for his long allegorical poem, called *The Faerie Queen*, which, among other things, presented a justification for Protestantism. It also heralded a defence of the Puritan attitude towards the church, something increasingly of concern to all thinking people.

But while many people recall this poem, only a few know that his output, even in an age of prodigious output by poets, was enormous. The publication

and success of *The Faerie Queen* led to a demand by many to read his other works.

Spenser was secretary to the Lord Deputy in Ireland for some years, and lived in Kilcolman Castle. This building was burned down by Irish rebels in 1598 and he lost a son in the flames. So he came to England, acutely depressed, and he died shortly afterwards. He was buried in Westminster Abbey.

Brahe, Tycho de (1546–1601)
Danish astronomer
Brahe upset the theories of Copernicus (*p. 122*) when he attempted to show that the planets moved round the sun, which in turn moved round the earth. He discovered new astronomical bodies, including a star which was named after him.

In 1576 Frederick II of Denmark set him up in an observatory on the island of Hveen, which came to be called Uraniborg, or the Castle of the Heavens. There Brahe worked for twenty years, until he fell out with the government on the death of Frederick. He left Denmark to head the observatory at Prague.

Elizabeth I (1533–1603)
Queen of England (1558–1603)
Elizabeth I has always appealed to historians and historical novelists alike. Possibly this is because, although they know a lot about her, they are still not really sure what motivated her. She had brains, good looks in her younger days at least; she was artistic, sensitive and brave. And yet they do not understand her. Why did she never marry? Did she make the momentous decisions of her reign or were they the work of her brilliant ministers Cecil, Walsingham and Bacon? Why did she hesitate over matters where instant resolution was so clearly needed, such as signing the death warrant of Mary, Queen of Scots (*p. 135*) or paying out money to the navy to equip ships to fight the Spanish Armada? She is a constant enigma, and as long as she is will continue to fascinate everyone interested in the 16th century.

Elizabeth was the daughter of Ann

Elizabeth I in council with her Ministers

Boleyn and Henry VIII. When she was born her mother was in the ascendant, but a few years later Ann was executed for alleged adultery with other men. Elizabeth was regarded as illegitimate and banished from court. She grew up in a fairly hostile atmosphere, where the only care taken of her concerned her education. Because she was a Protestant she was in some danger when her half-sister Mary I was queen from 1553 to 1558. But in 1558 Elizabeth's chance came.

Her first act was to appoint William Cecil (*p. 138*) her chief minister, and it was the best decision she ever made, for he was the most brilliant statesman in England, possibly in Europe. Between them, with splendid help from other important men like Walsingham (*p. 136*) and Bacon, they pursued the middle course in religion and created the Church of England in a form not unlike what we know to-day. They avoided war with Spain by secretly allowing privateers like Drake to smash up Spanish ports and fleets carrying treasure in the New World, but openly apologizing and reprimanding Drake and his colleagues for their dastardly behaviour. They encouraged trade, industry, building and legal reform. The East India Company was formed. Settlements were made in North America. They kept peace with France, too.

At the end of her reign the country had a strong position among European nations and her own prestige was undimmed.

Gilbert, William (1540–1603)
English physicist

Gilbert is generally said to have been the discoverer of electricity. He was fascinated by magnetism, and he carried out numerous experiments involving magnetic forces. When he wrote about them in his book on magnetism in 1600, he discussed electric forces. This book is said to be the first English scientific book of any importance.

Akbar the Great (1542–1605)
Moghul Emperor (1556–1605)
Akbar had nearly 50 years as ruler of the Moghul Empire in India, and in that time he introduced many new ideas of government, fostered trade and kept his neighbours in order. He was faced with a country with many religions, but instead of making everybody accept Islam, his own faith, he allowed them to practise whatever they liked, provided it did not threaten the security of the state. He even welcomed Christian missionaries from Portugal.

Fawkes, Guido, or Guy (1570–1606)
English conspirator
Guy Fawkes was a Roman Catholic convert who agreed to help blow up the Houses of Parliament when James I, lords and commons were sitting. He organized the depositing of barrels of gunpowder in the cellars, and actually undertook to ignite the fuse himself. But he was caught, taken to the authorities and questioned. Under torture he revealed many details, and Robert Catesby and others were arrested and executed.

Fawkes died on the gibbet in January 1606. His plot is celebrated every year on 5th November by exploding fireworks, but it seems this celebration is not a very old custom. The event went unmarked for generations.

Henry IV of Navarre (1553–1610)
King of France (1589–1610)
One of the best kings France ever had, Henry IV tried very hard to reconcile Catholics and Protestants in the civil war-torn kingdom to which he succeeded in 1589. He was himself a Protestant, but in 1593 he adopted the Catholic faith in order to try to heal the breach. It was one way to end the civil war because while the

Protestants would have been content for him to be a Catholic, as they knew he would allow them to follow their own worship, the Catholics would not have felt they could trust him. In 1598 he issued the Edict of Nantes which granted rights to the Protestants, or Huguenots, as they were called.

The last twelve years of his successful rule were devoted to restoring the financial and economic position of France, stimulating trade and industry, early colonial exploration and settlement, and to building.

It was a tragedy for France that Henry was assassinated by a mad monk, in 1610.

Hudson, Henry (c.1550–1611)
English explorer
The huge inland sea in Canada called Hudson's Bay, was named after the English navigator Henry Hudson who discovered it in 1609. He had been looking for a north-west passage through Canada to the Far East, in an expedition financed by the Dutch East India Company. When Hudson was returning, some members of his crew mutinied and turned him out into a small row boat. He was never seen again.

El Greco (1546–1614)
Spanish painter
El Greco's real name was Domenikos Theotocopoulos, a Greek-born painter who studied under Titian and then went to live in Toledo, in Spain. Greco settled in the small town – you can see his house today, for it is a national monument – and over the next years he produced many fine pictures. One of these was the *Burial of the Count of Orgaz*, which is particularly fine, rendered sombre by his method of using contrasting colours to dramatic effect. Throughout his work there is startling evidence of profound mystical insight.

Medina Sidonia, Duke of (1550–1615)
Spanish nobleman
Alonso Perez de Guzman, 7th Duke of Medina Sidonia, was, inexplicably, picked by Philip II (*p. 139*) to head the

great Spanish Armada, which sailed up the English Channel to invade England in 1588. Medina Sidonia had never been to sea, and did not know a mast from an anchor. And it is therefore hardly surprising that so splendid a fleet, whose second line of command included some of the best sea captains in Spanish history, was completely defeated. These men were under this fool who was himself obliged to accept detailed orders sent in long letters written by Philip II from his palace outside Madrid and delivered by fast horse and packet boat to Sidonia's flagship.

Astonishing to relate, Sidonia was not sacked for his abysmal failure; on the contrary, he was given fresh command, and lost Cadiz, in 1596.

Tyrone, Hugh O'Neill, Earl of (1540–1616)
Irish patriot

Hugh O'Neill, second Earl of Tyrone, a descendant of the ancient O'Neills, Kings of Ulster, was leader of the Irish resistance to English dominion in the last years of the 16th century. He was a brilliant general and defeated several armies sent against him by the English, notably one under the command of the Earl of Essex, Queen Elizabeth I's favourite.

When James VI of Scotland became King of England in 1603, Tyrone made his peace with him, and was guaranteed his estates. But the King continued the policy of settling English people in Ireland at the expense of the native Irish, and Tyrone objected. After a while, he was driven out of Ireland and went to the Spanish Netherlands.

Cervantes Saavedra, Miguel de (1547–1616)
Spanish writer

Cervantes wrote *Don Quixote de la Mancha*, a delightful novel about a chivalrous knight who went round championing all sorts of romantic causes which were for the most part ridiculous. This knight even charged with lance at full tilt at a windmill!

But it was not his only book. Cervantes wrote short stories, plays and some poetry. He also had a varied career apart from his writing. He lost his left hand in the great battle of Lepanto (1571), was captured by pirates and imprisoned for five years, and collected taxes in Granada.

Hakluyt, Richard (c.1550–1616)
English geographer

Hakluyt is said to have introduced globe maps of the world into English schools. He entered the church and was archdeacon of Westminster. But his principal fame lies in a long book, called in full *Principal Navigations, Voyages and Discoveries of the English Nation*, but better known simply as *Hakluyt's Voyages*.

Shakespeare, William (1564–1616)
English playwright and poet

So very little is known about this very great man that many people have doubted whether he ever wrote any of the works attributed to him. Many alternative names have been put forward as the author or authors of his works – to name a few: Bacon (*p. 145*), the Earl of Oxford, Beaumont and Fletcher, and Christopher Marlowe (*p. 136*). The last would be most easy to understand, if one accepted that Marlowe was not killed in a tavern brawl in 1593.

Whoever did write the works, however, produced the most marvellous literature of all time. Shakespeare was born at Stratford-upon-Avon in 1564 and lived there until he was grown up. He had business connections, and he also became an actor, performing in London. His first work as a writer did not appear until 1593, at the age of 29, and it was a long poem called *Venus and Adonis*. But thereafter until his death, he turned out an astonishing quantity and range of plays and verse. Among the most celebrated plays are *Hamlet, Macbeth, Richard III, Julius Caesar, The Merchant of Venice, Twelfth Night, Midsummer Night's Dream*. They and the others are all remarkable for their 'unique powers of characterization and mastery of dramatic speech in both verse and prose'.

Lady Macbeth in a scene from Shakespeare's famous play

Napier, John (1550–1617)
Scottish mathematician

If you have had to learn about logarithms in arithmetic and have not liked them, you should blame John Napier who, in about 1614, invented them. He was a Scottish mathematician who studied many other subjects as well, including agriculture and astrology. Napier also introduced calculating apparatus that was a forerunner of the computer type machine devised by Babbage in the 1830s.

Raleigh, Sir Walter (c.1554–1618)
English sailor and poet

Sir Walter Raleigh was one of the most colourful of English figures in the later years of the time of Elizabeth I (*p. 139*). He was a scholar who became a sailor and found favour with the Queen. In 1585 Elizabeth granted him a charter to sail to America to found colonies in her name. His followers settled near the Potomac river, and he called the settlement Virginia, which is today one of the States of the U.S.A. There, he is said to have discovered the potato and the tobacco plant, both of which were being used by the native Indians.

When James VI of Scotland became James I of England and Scotland, in 1603, Raleigh's position at court changed. The new king was jealous of anyone whose abilities and courage were higher than his. Raleigh ended up in the Tower where, with his family, he stayed for several years. In that time he wrote a history of the world and some marvellous verse. In 1616 he persuaded James to let him out to lead an expedition to find gold up the Orinoco river, but the voyage was a catastrophe. On the return journey, Raleigh clashed with Spanish ships. The King was anxious to keep peace with Spain, and so as a sop to the Spanish king, he had Raleigh tried and executed in 1618.

Sir Walter Raleigh and in the background American Indians picking tobacco leaves, a crop he discovered when colonizing Virginia

Hilliard, Nicholas (1537–1619)
English goldsmith and miniaturist
Hilliard was the first Englishman to paint miniature pictures, a delicate and painstaking skill which was popular for portraiture. He was appointed goldsmith to Elizabeth I and also held royal appointments from James I. His miniature of Elizabeth is very well known.

Bacon, Francis, Viscount St. Albans (1561–1625)
English statesman and lawyer
Francis Bacon had one of the best brains of the 16th or early 17th century in England. He was a scholar, lawyer, essayist, statesman, scientist and philosopher. He held various offices under Elizabeth I and under her successor James I, whose Lord Chancellor he became in 1618.

But it was as Lord Chancellor that Bacon betrayed not only the trust put in him by his king, but also the high intellectual calling to which he aspired.

In 1621 he was accused of accepting bribes before making judgments on cases brought to him in his official capacity, and to the horror of the whole court he confessed. A huge fine of £40,000 and a short sentence in the Tower followed.

Apart from his career, so well begun and so dramatically closed, he wrote a set of brilliant essays, and applied himself to wide-ranging philosophical studies. In the scientific field he originated the idea of experimental research.

Maurice of Orange Nassau (1567–1625)
Stadholder of Dutch Republic (1587–1625)
Maurice was son of William the Silent (*p. 134*) and he continued the struggle for independence from Spanish dominion. He was a brilliant leader of men, and won two vital victories over the Spaniards, at Turnhout in 1597 and at Nieuport in 1600. These marked the beginning of the end of the Spanish dominion. His great nephew was William III (*p. 166*) who became King of England, Scotland and Ireland in 1688.

Abbas I (the Great) (c.1557–1628)
Shah of Persia (1586–1628)
Abbas seems to have spent the best part of a long reign fighting against his neighbours or against tribes and nations anxious to appropriate sectors of his dominion. On the whole he was successful against all comers. He beat the Uzbeks in 1597, the Turks at Basra in 1605 and at Sultanieh in 1618, and in 1623 he invaded and captured Baghdad.

In the intervals, Abbas introduced many reforms into Persian government and local administration, and he encouraged arts and science, especially Persian medicine.

Donne, John (1573–1631)
English poet
John Donne was one of the leading poets of the 17th century, a startlingly brilliant writer, whose love sonnets and wry meditations on life are of enduring interest. He was also a priest whose sermons have been described as the best sermons of the century. They are certainly full of wisdom and practical advice, appealing to the heart as well as to the head.

Donne's career was an interesting one. He was brought up as a Roman Catholic but converted to the Church of England. He accompanied the Earl of Essex on his ineffective raid on Cadiz in 1596. He entered the Church at the suggestion of James I, in 1614, and in 1621 he was appointed Dean of St. Paul's. It was in this great church (burnt down in the Fire of London in 1666) that the greatest of his sermons were delivered.

Tilly, Johan, Count of (1559–1632)
Flemish general
Tilly was a brilliant, artful general on the Imperial side in the Thirty Years War. He took over the command of the Imperial armies when Wallenstein (*p. 146*) was first dismissed in 1630. He successfully besieged Magdeburg but was crushed at Breitenfeld in 1631, by Gustavus Adolphus. A year later he was again defeated, this time at Lech, where he was wounded and died.

Gustavus Adolphus at the Battle of Lützen

Gustavus Adolphus (1594–1632)
King of Sweden (1611–1632)
This was the greatest king Sweden ever had, and he was also the leading military figure to emerge from the first half of the Thirty Years War (1618–1648). Known as the Lion of the North, Gustavus championed the Protestant powers in that hideous war and beat nearly every army the Catholic Imperial powers could send against him. One of his most brilliant successes, however, was in diplomacy. He persuaded the French to come in on the side of the Protestants.

At Lutzen in 1632 he defeated the Imperial general Wallenstein (*p. 146*) but was killed by a stray bullet after the battle. At home, Gustavus had instituted many reforms in the government, and he was sorely missed when the news reached Sweden of his untimely death.

Wallenstein, Albrecht von, Prince (1583–1634)
Bohemian war general
The Thirty Years War threw up several first rate generals, but few were as brilliant as Wallenstein.

Wallenstein came to the notice of the Holy Roman Emperor, Ferdinand II, who was virtual leader of the Catholic powers against the Protestant powers in the war. Ferdinand made him a duke and appointed him commander of the Imperial armies. For some time he was successful, but he got involved in intrigues among the heads of royal families and he was dismissed. When he was re-instated in 1632 he fought Gustavus Adolphus at Lutzen and was defeated, though Gustavus was killed.

The Emperor dismissed him again, and as he tramped round Europe looking for a fresh command, he was assassinated by some Irish and Scots soldiers of fortune who were on his staff.

Lope de Vega (1562–1635)
Spanish playwright
Lope Felix de Vega Carpio was born in Madrid. He fought a duel in 1588 and was banished, so he went with the Spanish forces in the Armada against England. He returned to Madrid in 1596, became a priest in 1614 and a doctor of theology in 1627.

This busy man founded the Spanish national drama, and in his time wrote nearly 2,000 plays, interludes and sketches. Many of these were swashbuckling cloak and dagger romances; some were very fine pieces of literature.

Champlain, Samuel (c.1567–1635)
French explorer
Jacques Cartier (*p. 126*) discovered the St. Lawrence river in Canada and reached Montreal, but it was Champlain who founded the first colony in Canada. He went up the St. Lawrence in 1603 in search of furs, and with him were some French families anxious to make a new life. In 1608, with the authority of a governorship, he founded Quebec and some of his followers made a settlement.

Champlain made several expeditions further into Canadian waters, and discovered the Great Lakes in 1615.

Jansen, Cornelius (1585–1638)
Dutch theologian
Jansen disliked the Jesuit Order, which had been founded by Ignatius Loyola (*p. 126*). His opposition was summed up in his book *Augustines*, which was published shortly after his death. It re-stated the doctrines of St. Augustine, in particular those on grace and free will. The book provoked enormous argument throughout the Christian Church.

Those who believed in Jansen's views were later to be known as Jansenists. Many of them gathered at the abbey of Port Royal in France, and lived there according to the great theologian's principles, but they were persecuted by Louis XIV.

Rubens, Sir Peter Paul (1577–1640)
Flemish painter
Rubens was another foreign painter who received a knighthood from Charles I of England. He travelled widely and visited Italy, France, Spain and England. In 1608 he settled in Antwerp, and began to paint a variety of pictures, landscapes, portraits and religious subjects. One, *The Descent from the Cross*, a triptych now in Antwerp Cathedral, is considered one of his greatest pictures.

When he was in England in 1629, on a mission on behalf of the Spanish royal family, he painted Charles I and his wife, Henrietta Maria, and it was then that he was knighted. Rubens' pictures are remarkable for their vigour and spirit, their exuberance and their detail. His women were often on the plump side.

Strafford, Thomas Wentworth, 1st Earl of (1593–1641)
English statesman
Black Tom Tyrant, as he was often called because of his dark clothes and appearance and his stern manner, was one of the better products of the early 17th century. It is a tragedy that he started off as a member of Parliament ready to attack the King for his abuses of royal power, and then switched sides to do the King's 'dirty work'.

Wentworth came from a family that was famous for sticking up for Parliament's rights. So when, after the Petition of Right, in 1628, of which he was a major champion, he changed sides and offered his services to Charles I who had decided to rule without Parliament, his colleagues were shattered. They might well be, for his abilities were of the highest order. After good service in the North of England and in Ireland, he came back to be the King's chief minister in London. He was responsible for many of the King's ill advised actions, for he was out of touch with what the country wanted.

Finally, Parliament insisted that Wentworth should be tried for his actions, and he was sentenced to death. The King had promised to save him, but when it came to it, deserted him. Wentworth's last words were – 'Put not your trust in princes!'

Van Dyck, Sir Anthony (1599–1641)
Flemish painter
This fine artist studied under the great Rubens (*p. 147*). In about 1631 he came to London and was favoured by Charles I, of whom he painted several pictures, the best known of which portrays the king on horseback. Charles gave van Dyck a knighthood, which was an unusual honour for a foreigner.

Galileo Galilei observing the swing of a candelabrum in Pisa Cathedral

Galilei, Galileo, (1564–1642)
Italian astronomer and physicist

In about 1580 Galileo Galilei, a student in Pisa, sat watching a candelabrum in Pisa Cathedral swing on a rope from side to side. After a time he noticed that the swing took the same time, from left to right, although the distance was getting shorter – this is the theory of specific gravity. He had discovered that pendulum movement produces a regular time measurement. From this discovery Huygens (*p. 165*) eventually developed the pendulum clock.

Galileo became professor of mathematics at Padua, and in his time he put forward many revolutionary ideas. He showed that in vacuum bodies of different weights fall to the ground at the same speed. He invented the astronomical telescope and with it proved that Copernicus' theory (*p. 122*) was correct.

Like many scientists of the time, Galileo had many problems because of his ideas. Several times the church authorities, which had enormous powers in those days, compelled him to withdraw statements, which he did in the interests of science, so that he could go on working. He was a kind and considerate man, but his last years were unhappy, largely because he lost his sight and could no longer observe the sky at night through his telescopes.

Richelieu, Armand Jean du Plessis de (1585–1642)
French cardinal and statesman

Richelieu was in some respects the greatest man ever to emerge from France. He dominated French politics from about 1610 up to his death, and it is generally accepted that his influence and ideas were very good for the country indeed. He was adviser to the widow of Henry IV, and then to her son Louis XIII. He had one aim – to make France the greatest power in Europe – and through his will-power and his outstanding political gifts he achieved it.

At home he destroyed the power of the nobility by blowing up their castles and banning private armies. He brought in a revolutionary system of government through superintendents of regions, who had extensive local powers but who were directly responsible to the central government, that is, Richelieu. He encouraged road and canal construction, and stimulated trade and industry. Abroad he supported Protestant countries in the Thirty Years War, even though France was a Catholic country, because he did not like the power of the Catholic league of states. The result was that France emerged from the war by far the most powerful nation in Europe. To stop Spain endangering the peace, he supported the Portuguese in their successful strike for independence in 1640. He also encouraged French colonial expansion in the Far East, India and the West Indies.

Cardinal Richelieu

Pym, John (1584–1643)
English statesman

John Pym was one of the leaders of the Parliamentarians during the struggle between Parliament and the King, Charles I, which ended in civil war and the King's execution. He had been one of the main signatories of the Petition of Right (1628). After the death of Sir John Eliot in 1632, he became the virtual head of the Parliamentarians. As such he took the lead in a number of moves against the King. In 1642 Charles tried to arrest five members of Parliament at the House of Commons for their opposition to his will, of whom Pym was one.

When Parliament finally went to war, Pym organized the party in London, and arranged the transfer of the power of raising taxes from the King. In 1643 he was given a commission in the Parliamentarian army as Lieutenant of the Ordnance, but died almost at once.

Hampden, John (1594–1643)
English statesman

John Hampden was the splendid Parliamentarian M.P. for Wendover in Buckinghamshire, who in 1636 refused to pay the Ship Money Tax raised by Charles I. He did so because he said that the tax, first raised by Aethelred II (the Unready) in the early 1000s to build ships to beat off the Danes, was meant to be paid only by people living in coastal counties. Buckinghamshire was inland. He was tried for his refusal and lost, but he became the hero of the hour, at a time when the king had made himself extremely unpopular through his dictatorial behaviour. Charles had been governing without Parliament since 1629.

When the Civil War finally began in 1642 John Hampden was one of the Parliamentarian leaders. He raised a regiment of troops to join the Parliamentarian army, but was wounded in battle at Chalgrove Field and died soon afterwards.

Hampden was one of the most respected of the Parliamentarian leaders.

Laud, William (1573–1645)
Archbishop of Canterbury

Archbishop Laud made himself hated in England in the reign of Charles I for several reasons. He imposed new high church doctrines and practices on the Church of England at a time when people were trying to get away from memories of Roman Catholicism. He was high-handed and intolerant with all opposition to his views. He also interfered in state matters, and as one of the King's chief ministers when Charles was ruling without Parliament, gave him a lot of bad advice.

When Parliament was winning the Civil War, Laud, who had been arrested by the Long Parliament in 1640, was put on trial and sentenced to death. In 1645 he was executed.

Grotius, Hugo (1583–1645)
Dutch legal expert

Nowadays, international law is one of the most important subjects in any syllabus of legal studies. But in the time of Grotius few people bothered about it. Then he wrote a large work, *De Jure Belli et Pacis*, which was in effect a manual of principles of international law, that is, rules of how nations and states should behave towards each other.

Van Diemen, Anton (1593–1645)
Dutch governor

Van Diemen was governor-general of the Dutch East Indies from 1636 to his death in 1645. He had worked for the Dutch East India company in Holland and in the Indies for several years, becoming the company's general manager.

The execution of Charles I

Torricelli, Evangelista (1608–1647)
Italian physicist

Torricelli was secretary and friend to Galileo (*p. 148*). When that amazing genius went blind in the closing years of his life, Torricelli succeeded him as professor at the Florentine Academy. During his work in Florence he worked out the theory of barometric pressure as a guide to weather forecasting and invented the barometer. His instrument did not have a dial and hands as modern barometers do – it consisted of a glass tube and a quantity of mercury.

Charles I (1600–1649)
King of England, Scotland and Ireland (1625–1649)

Charles I started off his reign badly. He kept the odious Duke of Buckingham on as his favourite, although the duke was the most hated man in England. Then he quarrelled with Parliament. In 1628 they got him to agree to the Petition of Right, which restated many of the terms of Magna Carta, but he went back on his word, dissolved Parliament and ruled as a dictator for the next eleven years. In 1640 he had to call a Parliament again to raise money – all his illegal efforts to do this, like Ship Money (Hampden, *p. 149*), having failed to provide enough. Parliament would not grant him taxes unless he agreed to curb his powers. No agreement was possible and the two sides drew up for war (1642).

At the end of three years, Charles and his Royalists were beaten, and negotiations took place to restore him to the throne with limited powers. But all the while he plotted with foreign countries to bring troops over to help him get back his old position. Parliament found out, put him on trial for treason against the state and sentenced him to death. He was executed in January 1649.

Charles was slim, short, with fine features. He had excellent taste in art, patronized artists and loved animals. But he was stubborn, arrogant, politically untrustworthy, at times incredibly stupid, and he never learned from his mistakes. That cost him his head.

Descartes, René (1596–1650)
French philosopher

Descartes is one of the greatest names in western philosophy. He was essentially a mathematician, and he applied the techniques of mathematical reasoning to his philosophical thinking.

His philosophy could be summed up in his celebrated statement *Cogito ergo sum* (I think, therefore I am). He also argued that an infinitely perfect being (God) exists in the mind. As man is finite, the idea must have been implanted there by an infinite being, who must therefore exist. This was his argument for the existence of God.

Montrose, James Graham, 1st Marquess of (1612–1650)
Scottish Royalist leader

Montrose is one of the most romantic people in Scotland's history. Bold, handsome, generous, a brilliant leader of men, loyal and hardworking, he took command of Scottish forces in the Civil War, on the King's side, in Scotland, and won several successes. But in 1645 he was badly defeated and had to leave the country. In his absence he heard of the defeat of the King's cause and his final trial and execution. So Montrose raised an army, came back to Scotland and invaded, hoping to drive the Parliamentarians out. But they were waiting for him. He was taken by surprise, tried and executed.

Marquess of Montrose

Torstenson, Lennart, Count of Ortala (1603–1651)
Swedish general

Torstenson learned the military arts the best possible way. He served under his king, Gustavus Adolphus (*p. 146*), the foremost soldier of the Thirty Years War (1618–1648). He was made commander-in-chief of the Swedish forces in Germany in 1641, at a time when the Swedish star was flagging, as Gustavus had been killed nine years earlier. He won the battles of Schweidnitz, Breitenfeld (second battle), Juterbog and Jankau, in three years, and actually invaded Austria itself in 1645. He was a worthy successor to the great Gustavus, but like his king his career was cut short, too, for he had to retire because of ill health.

Jones, Inigo (1573–1652)
British architect

Inigo Jones studied art in Italy and learned all about the new architectural work of the great Palladio (*p. 133*). He came back to England and spent some time designing stage sets for plays in London, introducing for the first time movable scenery.

In 1615 he was appointed surveyor general of works, which gave him responsibility for royal buildings. He designed the Queen's House at Greenwich, laid out Covent Garden and rebuilt the Banqueting Hall in Whitehall. In his work he showed very clearly the influence of Palladio, but he himself became a major influence in British architecture.

Van Tromp, Maarten (1597–1653)
Dutch admiral

Van Tromp is said to have sailed up the English Channel, in 1652, with a broom tied to the masthead of his flagship to show that he had swept the seas of English ships. Certainly he did defeat Robert Blake, the great English sailor, in November, but he was himself defeated by Blake the next year, and died in the heat of battle with a bullet through his heart.

Before the Dutch War with England, van Tromp had had a splendid career against the Spanish fleet in the 1630s, and had become one of Holland's most popular admirals.

Oxenstierna, Count Axel (1583–1654)
Swedish statesman

The great Gustavus Adolphus of Sweden (*p. 146*) appointed Oxenstierna as prime minister of the Swedish nation in 1612. It was a wise and very successful choice. This astute diplomat and politician handled Sweden's affairs for the next forty years. He tried to stop Gustavus from taking Sweden on to the Protestant side in the Thirty Years War (1618–1648), but when he failed, he backed his king right to the end. Gustavus took care of the military side, and proved himself the best general of the first half of the war.

When Gustavus was killed at Lutzen in 1632, and the Swedish throne passed to his daughter Christina (*p. 152*), Oxenstierna looked after the government and acted as her confidential adviser.

Christina (1626–1689)
Queen of Sweden (1632–1654)

Queen Christina was only six when she succeeded her brilliant and dashing father, Gustavus Adolphus (*p. 146*) as monarch of Sweden. For several years her kingdom was managed by the very able minister, Count Oxenstierna (*p. 152*) but in 1644 she started to rule herself.

Christina devoted the rest of her time on the throne in bringing art and culture to Sweden, but in so doing she neglected more earthly things like economics and diplomacy, and she let Sweden run down.

Suddenly, in 1654, she abdicated. She had had enough, she said, though it was thought she had had a broken love affair and could not concentrate any longer. She retired to Italy and set up a small court there to which she invited all kinds of artists and writers.

Bergerac, Savinien Cyrano de (1619–1655)
French poet

Cyrano de Bergerac was famous in France as a swashbuckling adventurer, who served in the army, fought duels all

The swashbuckling adventurer and poet, Cyrano de Bergerac, duelling

over the place, pursued attractive women, and wrote romantic poetry. He was badly wounded in one battle, and had to give up the more martial aspects of life. Then he turned to writing, and produced a number of plays.

His fame was exaggerated in a play about him written by the 19th century French playwright Rostand.

Harvey, William (1578–1657)
English physician

In about 1628 William Harvey discovered how the blood circulated in the human body. He had been a doctor at St. Bartholomew's Hospital in London. His work brought him great fame. He was physician to both James I and Charles I and attended the latter at the Battle of Edgehill in 1642. As a young man he studied medicine in Italy, where one of his teachers was the great Galileo.

Blake, Robert (1599–1657)
English admiral

One of the finest commanders ever to wear an admiral's uniform, Robert Blake was an M.P. for his home town of Bridgwater in the Short Parliament. On the outbreak of civil war in 1642 he joined the Parliamentarian cause, and raised a force to defend Bristol against the Royalist army.

When Parliament had won and the king had forfeited his head on the scaffold, in 1649, Blake was given command of the Commonwealth fleet to pursue Prince Rupert's Royalist fleet. He caught him and destroyed the fleet. Three years later, Blake defeated four Dutch squadrons in four engagements. It was a splendid success for Cromwell's government. Cromwell buried him in Westminster Abbey, but his body was removed at the Restoration.

Cromwell, Oliver (1599–1658)
English statesman, soldier and Lord Protector

Without doubt Cromwell was one of the most remarkable and brilliant men ever to walk across the pages of British history. As a statesman he raised Britain to a point where nations in Europe sought her opinion over disputes, where her strength was regarded as almost unchallengeable. As a soldier, although he never fought a battle till he was over forty, he won a series of the most amazing victories, generally with numbers less than those of his opponents. As Lord Protector he tried to give Britain good government, re-structured the tax laws, reorganized the legal system, and granted a wide measure of religious toleration in an age which demanded it but was at the same time slow to accord it.

Oliver was born in Huntingdonshire, the son of a relatively prosperous squire who was something of an acquaintance of the royal family. It is said that young Oliver may have met young Charles Stuart (later Charles I) when the king, James I, came to stay with the Cromwells early in the king's reign. He was a good local squire himself, and he entered Parliament in 1628, right in the middle of the days when Parliament was challenging the king's powers. Cromwell, coming from East Anglia, an area with a pronounced leaning towards independence of will and interest in reform, found himself lined up against the king, Charles I (1625–1649) in the matter of the Petition of Right. The next year Charles dissolved Parliament and ruled for eleven years alone – and did so very badly.

Oliver retired to Huntingdon to look after his estates. In 1640 he was elected to Parliament when the king finally agreed to call one again. By this time many members were angry men, and in 1642 Parliament went to war with the king.

To begin with Cromwell played a secondary role as a cavalry commander, but in 1644, at Marston Moor in Yorkshire, where Fairfax (*p. 158*) was in command, he used his cavalry arm to crushing and decisive effect, and drove the Royalists off the field. It was a great victory. Then he and Fairfax created the New Model Army, a force of troops raised not from local and untried men conscripted just for one engagement but a regular body of men who volunteered to serve more permanently. It was the beginning of the regular army. In 1645 this new army was put to the test at the battle of Naseby, and it covered itself with glory. The result was decisive. Charles was defeated and fled to the Scots. Cromwell's reputation, meanwhile, rose to a high pitch, and he was regarded as England's foremost general.

In 1648, when the king was in Parliament's hands and was discovered trying to get foreign troops to rescue him, Parliament decided to try him for treason. The trial result was inevitable, and he was executed. Cromwell played a leading though probably reluctant part in this. He is said to have regarded the death as 'cruel necessity'.

The death of the king did not solve the problems of what to do with the government and the country, and for a few years no one person was really in charge, although most people recognized Cromwell as the strongest man in the land. He went to Ireland to crush Royalist resistance there, and then to Scotland on a similar expedition, where he defeated Royalist Scots at Dunbar. A year later he defeated Prince Charles (later Charles II) at Worcester. This was his last battle, and in some ways it was his greatest, for he achieved the maximum results with the minimum losses.

Still there was no solution to the government problems, and in 1653 Cromwell, now exasperated, marched with a detachment of troops to the House of Commons, dissolved the Parliament sitting there and threw out the Speaker and his paraphernalia of office, the mace and sceptre. He had himself declared Lord Protector and ruled the country with a firm but kind hand for the next five years.

They were not easy years. Britain, having killed one ruler for his absolutism,

Oliver Cromwell addressing his troops

was now faced with another of the same stamp. But Cromwell was greatly respected both at home and abroad. When he died in 1658 he was not missed by some, but there were many who admired him and what he tried to do. He was essentially too far ahead of his time. Many of his ideas have since been realized, and today his place in British history is assured.

Tasman, Abel Janszoon (1603–1659)
Dutch explorer

Van Diemen, who was the Dutch governor of the Dutch East Indies (Sumatra, Jara, etc.), sent Tasman, in 1642, to voyage and chart round the bottom of the Australian continent. Tasman discovered the island now called Tasmania, which he christened Diemen's Land. He also discovered New Zealand and some of the Friendly Islands group.

Velasquez, Diego Rodriguez de Silvay (1599–1660)
Spanish painter

Velasquez was one of the greatest of all Spanish painters, and there were many of these in the front rank of European artists. He was made court painter when he was only 23, and in his time he produced some splendid masterpieces. He was particularly good at portraits, but his range of work was much wider. His work is notable for its sharp realism, and some of his finest portraits are hardly flattering to the sitters.

Mazarin, Jules (1602–1661)
Italian born cardinal

Mazarin was Italian born, and went into the diplomatic service in Italy. He attracted the attention of the great cardinal Richelieu (*p. 149*) when he was nuncio for the Pope, and Richelieu offered him high office in France. Mazarin became Richelieu's star pupil and right hand man. He adopted French nationality, and when the cardinal died in 1642, the King, Louis XIII, was only too glad to let Mazarin take over his job as head of the government.

Mazarin, who had been made a cardinal in 1641, proved to be nearly as able as his master, though he was not always so successful. When the parliament opposed his financial measures, Mazarin

Cardinal Mazarin with Queen Anne and the young Louis XIV

arrested the leaders of the opposition. This led directly to the outbreak of a series of riots and virtual civil war in France, known as the Fronde. Mazarin was kept in office largely through the good offices of the Queen regent, Anne, the child Louis XIV's mother, with whom he was believed to have had a long love affair.

He was instrumental in bringing the terrible Thirty Years War to an end, and also in discovering and raising to high military command two first class soldiers, the Prince of Conde and Vicomte Turenne (*p. 159*). He also broke the last remaining powers of the feudal nobles. His work made the task of Louis XIV, who in 1661 decided to govern for himself, that much lighter. He also accumulated a huge fortune, some of it undoubtedly dishonestly.

Pascal, Blaise (1623–1662)
French philosopher
Pascal is best remembered for a collection of wise, sometimes ironical, sayings, gathered in a book called *Pensées* (Thoughts). But he was in fact a brilliant mathematician who spent years studying complex arithmetical problems. He was also a physicist and worked on barometric pressures, fluids and so forth. It is said he was an infant prodigy, and before he was sixteen had drafted an original treatise on conic sections.

Hals, Frans (1580–1666)
Dutch painter
Frans Hals would probably be surprised to know he is remembered mainly for his painting of the *Laughing Cavalier*. For he was in fact one of the leading painters of the 17th century and is considered by many to rank alongside Rembrandt and Rubens. He painted many important works, including a canvas of *The Banquet of the Officers of St. George's Shooting Company*.

Shah Jehan (1592–1666)
Moghul emperor (1627–1666)
Shah Jehan is famous for his great love of his wife, Mumtaz Mahali, who died when young. To commemorate her he built the fabulous Taj Mahal, at Agra, one of the most wonderful monuments in the world. He also built the Peacock Throne, founded the City of Delhi and constructed a splendid mosque there.

His reign was not uneventful and he expanded Moghul territory by conquering some of the Deccan.

Prynne, William (1600–1669)
English agitator
Prynne was a 17th century trouble maker, the kind of fiercely independent-minded thinker which every age should be glad to have, once in a while. Trained as a lawyer, Prynne got into all kinds of trouble by his outspoken views on topical matters, many of which he produced in pamphlets. He attacked Charles I's Queen, Henrietta Maria, and this cost him a £5,000 fine, both ears lopped off, and a spell in prison. Then he attacked Archbishop Laud (*p. 150*) and the established Church, and this cost another £5,000, more imprisonment and his cheek branded.

His fortunes improved during the Civil War when he was made recorder for Bath. But he could not accept the execution of Charles I as right and was imprisoned again for his views. When Charles II was restored in 1660, Prynne received a post in the Tower.

Rembrandt (1606–1669)
Dutch painter
One of the most famous painters of all time, Rembrandt Harmensz van Rijn – for that was his name – had a full and often unhappy life. He came to Amsterdam to paint, and to teach art to enable him to develop his skill. Although he married a rich woman, he was always very short of cash, and in 1656 he went bankrupt. When he died 13 years later he was still in poverty.

Rembrandt's great quality was his use of light, especially in his landscapes. He turned out an enormous amount of work, some 650 oil paintings, 2,000 drawings and studies and 300 etchings. His art was founded on the direct study of nature.

'Bring out your dead', this man used to chant as he walked the streets of London during the Great Plague of 1665

Comenius, John Amos (1592–1670)
Czech theologian and teacher

John Amos Comenius was a Czech scholar who specialized in developing new ways of teaching adults and children. His fame in Poland attracted the attention of the Swedish government, who invited him to reconstruct the Swedish education system. Then he returned to Poland where he was appointed a bishop, but in 1656, in an uprising, his palace was burnt down and he left to settle in Holland. One of his last works was a new kind of children's book, which could be used as a visual aid in teaching.

Albemarle, George Monck, 1st Duke of (1608–1670)
British soldier

George Monck supported the Royalist cause in the Civil War, to begin with, but he was captured after a battle and was persuaded to change sides. Cromwell employed him in Scotland and in Ireland, and in 1653 he was appointed to command the English fleet in the first war with the Dutch, and twice defeated Admiral Van Tromp (*p. 152*).

When Cromwell died in 1658 and Britain nearly fell into anarchy, it was Monck who determined to invite the exiled Prince Charles to come home to be Charles II. This earned him a dukedom. He took control of the city of London during the Great Plague of 1665 and did much to reduce the loss of life.

Fairfax, Thomas, 3rd baron (1612–1671)
English general

Fairfax was for some years commander-in-chief of the Parliamentary armies in the Civil War. He was in this position at Marston Moor (1644) and Naseby (1645) which were two brilliant victories won by the genius of Cromwell.

Fairfax had agreed about the need to fight the Civil War, but when it was over, he could not bring himself to sit in judgment on the King, and he opposed the eventual death sentence which inevitably followed. Thereafter, though he did nothing of consequence to oppose the rule of the Commonwealth government (1649–1653) or that of Cromwell (1653–1658), he did not support it, either, and was quick to join Albemarle (*p. 158*) in inviting Charles II to take up his throne in 1660.

Molière (1622–1673)
French playwright

Molière's real name was Jean Baptiste Poquelin. Born in Paris, he was an actor who took a company of players round the city and in the provinces. In about 1658 he came to the notice of Louis XIV who patronized his theatrical company. This gave Molière time to sit down and write a number of comedies that were turning over in his mind. They were to become some of the best comedies in the French language, the best known being *Tartuffe*, *Le Misanthrope*, and *Le Médecin Malgré Lui* – masterpieces of situational comedy and social satire.

Milton, John (1608–1674)
English poet and scholar

Milton was one of England's greatest poets. His *Paradise Lost*, *Samson Agonistes*, and *Il Penseroso* are among the best verse in the language.

This brilliant scholar became a secretary to Oliver Cromwell (*p. 154*) throughout the Lord Protector's rule. He had endeared himself to the Parliamentarians by his excellent pamphlets on many subjects; for example on whether there ought to be bishops in the Church of England, and why the press should be free to say what it liked. Milton's last years were clouded because he went blind, and because Charles II could find no use for his wonderful talents.

Turenne, Henri de la Tour d'Auvergne, Vicomte de (1611–1675)
French general

Napoleon always said that Turenne was France's greatest general (though he probably expected his listeners not to include himself). Certainly this handsome, brilliant, aristocratic and bold man left his mark upon European military history.

Turenne was brought up a Protestant, and entered the French army when he was 19. Over the next 18 years he covered himself with glory on many battlefields of the Thirty Years War, winning great victories for France. Among these were Roussillon (1642) and Nordlingen (1645). He had found favour with Richelieu, who knew how to pick the best man for the job, and the great cardinal helped to advance his career.

When Louis XIV took over the government of France in 1661, he appointed Turenne marshal-general of the country. Seven years later, Turenne became a Catholic, and led the French army against the Spanish Netherlands. Turenne was killed in a skirmish in Baden in Germany.

De Ruyter, Michael Adrianzoon (1607–1676)
Dutch admiral

De Ruyter served under van Tromp (*p. 152*). His first victory against the English fleet was in 1666 when he attacked and destroyed the ships of the Duke of Albemarle off Dunkirk, and chased the fleeing remainder up the Thames Estuary. A year later, de Ruyter sailed up the Medway, in north Kent, and burnt the dockyard at Chatham.

In 1672 he took on a combined French-English fleet in Southwold Bay and nearly inflicted a decisive victory. As it was, the other side withdrew in disorder. Four years later he commanded the combined Dutch-Spanish fleet against the French in the Mediterranean, but was killed in an engagement off Sicily.

Spinoza, Benedict (1632–1677)
Portuguese-Jewish philosopher

Spinoza was one of the most profound Jewish thinkers of all time. Although he came of Portuguese stock, he was born in Holland, whither his family had fled persecution. From an early age he showed genius, and he also showed an independence of mind, which was to get him into a lot of trouble.

He was particularly taken with the philosophical work of Descartes (*p. 151*) and developed that great Frenchman's theories. But he was also an original thinker, who would turn down jobs because of the danger of interference with his independence of mind.

Marvell, Andrew (1621–1678)
English poet

'He nothing common did or mean
Upon that memorable scene.'

So wrote Marvell, on the execution of Charles I, a poet who supported the Parliamentarian cause and admired Cromwell (*p. 154*). He was obviously impressed with the brave dignity with which the King met his end on the execution block in Whitehall in January 1649.

Marvell was favoured by Cromwell, who made him one of his Latin secretaries, a post he shared with Milton (*p. 159*). He was a busy writer of verse on many subjects, from gardens to specific achievements of Cromwell, and of satirical prose. He attacked Charles II, defended Milton, and supported the Dutch War, in some splendidly biting pamphlets.

Hobbes, Thomas (1588–1679)
English philosopher

This brilliant scholar was born at Malmesbury in Wiltshire. His young life was one of great academic distinction, at Magdalen Hall at Oxford. When the Parliamentarians went to war with the King, Hobbes fled from England as he was a supporter of the Royalist cause. While he was abroad he met many of the leading thinkers and scholars of Western Europe, including Galileo, and he corresponded with the French philosopher Descartes.

Hobbes wrote several works, the best known being *Leviathan*, or the *Matter, Form and Power of a Commonwealth*. This is regarded as the greatest masterpiece of political philosophy in English, but it got him into trouble with the exiled Prince Charles (later Charles II) and his family in France. So Hobbes came back to England and made peace with Cromwell.

Bernini, Giovanni Lorenzo (1598–1680)
Italian sculptor

Bernini was one of the finest of the 17th century Italian sculptors and designers. He was highly original in his work and influenced Italian, indeed European sculpture, for over a century. He was master of the Baroque style. Among his most remarkable designs were the famous colonnade at St. Peter's in Rome, and the fountains in the Piazza Navona, also in Rome.

Louis XIV invited him to France to suggest improvements to the Louvre, but the envy of the Paris architects forced the King to reject them, though he did commission some superficial changes.

Lely, Sir Peter (1618–1680)
Dutch painter

Lely was born Pieter van der Faes. He came to London in 1640, set up as a portrait painter, and soon attracted the attention of King Charles I whose favourite painter Van Dyck (*p. 147*) had just died. Lely undertook many commissions for Charles and for his son, Charles II, who made him court painter and gave him a knighthood.

There are many portraits by Lely in Britain. Possibly some are not genuine. But among those that are, his range of studies of the leading admirals in the second war against the Dutch are remarkable for their characterization.

Calderón, Pedro (1600–1681)
Spanish playwright

Calderón was a leading 17th century Spanish playwright who devoted much of his work to court plays and masques. In a long life he produced over 100, but not more than a handful are now still widely known. He specialized in swashbuckling romance plays about bold knights with cloak and sword rescuing fair ladies in danger, and in classical and passion stories. His work was consistently good, and sometimes wonderful, all the while remaining essentially Spanish.

Rupert of the Rhine, Prince (1619–1682)
Austrian born general and admiral

Prince Rupert was the most heroic figure on the Royalist side in England's great Civil War, 1642–1647. He was the

Prince Rupert of the Rhine

nephew of Charles I and for a while his principal field commander.

Rupert was a dashing, if headstrong, cavalry expert who often spoiled a victory in the field by failing to pursue the remnants of a defeated force and cut them down. The battle of Edgehill in 1642 was an illustration of this: the Parliamentarian forces, though beaten, were allowed to escape to fight again.

When the king lost at Naseby, at which Rupert distinguished himself by his courage, he surrendered to Parliament and was dismissed. He left England, tried to lead naval forces against the Commonwealth, but was unsuccessful.

When his cousin Charles II was restored in 1660, Rupert received high office in the navy. He was made admiral of the fleet in 1673, and was first lord of the admiralty from 1673 to 1679.

Walton, Izaak (1593–1683)
English author

Walton made money in the ironmongery business. Then he retired and began to write pen portraits of famous contemporaries. One was a life of John Donne (*p. 145*) the celebrated poet and preacher. But by far his greatest work was his *Compleat Angler*, or to give it its full title, *The Compleat Angler, or the Contemplative Man's Recreation*. This was a veritable mine of information about fishing, hunting and falconry, with details about fish, animals and birds, the countryside, indeed everything to do with these recreations.

Colbert, Jean Baptiste (1619–1683)
French statesman

Colbert was a fascinating character of French political history. He adored hard work, like England's Richard Nevill, Earl of Warwick (*p. 109*) and he was a brilliant financier and general manager of men. He began his career as a junior to Mazarin (*p. 156*), and doubtless the Italian born cardinal marked him out as a potential successor to himself and Richelieu.

In 1665 Louis XIV, who shared Mazarin's confidence in him, appointed Colbert controller-general of finance. This was much the same as head of the government, and in his time he reorganized the finances of France and made them prosper; he encouraged trade and exploration abroad, and industry at home. He built up the French navy, commissioned road and canal works, revised the civil code of law, and set up the famous furniture workshops in the Gobelins, in Paris, in which were to be produced, over the next century, the very finest pieces of furniture ever made.

Shaftesbury, Anthony Ashley Cooper, 1st Earl of (1621–1683)
English statesman

Shaftesbury was one of the more interesting statesman of the reign of Charles II. He had been a member of Cromwell's government during the Lord Protectorate (1653–1658) but had joined Albemarle (*p. 158*) in fetching Charles II back to the throne in 1660. He was rewarded by being appointed chancellor of the exchequer in 1661 and Lord Chancellor in 1672.

Shaftesbury was a staunch Protestant with an exaggerated fear of Roman Catholicism. He brought in bills to outlaw catholicism but incurred the wrath of the King. But in 1679 he introduced an important piece of reform: he steered the Habeas Corpus Bill through Parliament, which said no man should be held for questioning or pending a trial for any crime until he had actually been formally charged.

For some time he dominated British politics, taking the side of Parliament against the King. His fears of the Roman Catholics, especially of James, Duke of York, who was to become James II, were to find some political justification after his death.

Corneille, Pierre (1606–1684)
French playwright

France had a wonderful era of art and literature, lasting for nearly two hundred years, from about 1600 to about 1790. Paris was the centre of the art world of all Europe, and Frenchmen were leaders in every field of art. Three writers dominated 17th century French literature, Molière, Racine and Corneille.

Pierre Corneille began as a law student, but soon took to writing verse and comedy plays. Then after some years he found he preferred more dramatic tragedies, and a succession of these came from his pen between 1635 and 1665, notably *Le Cid*, *Oedipe* and *Andromède*. These and others established him as the leading dramatic playwright of his age, though towards the end of his days, his work was overshadowed by that of Racine (*p. 166*).

Monmouth, James Scott, Duke of (1649–1685)
Illegitimate son of Charles II of England

The Duke of Monmouth was the son of Charles II by an attractive young girl friend from Wales, Lucy Walter. He was brought up by a kind noble family, and in 1663 he was acknowledged by his father, who began to make a special favourite of him, granting him privileges.

In 1670 he was appointed to command the King's forces which went to the aid of the French in the Third Dutch War, and he distinguished himself. But he was a staunch Protestant, and this began to detach him from his father who was drifting towards Catholicism.

When Charles died in 1685 and was succeeded by his brother James II, Monmouth invaded England and organized a rebellion in the West Country to get himself on the throne. The rebellion collapsed and Monmouth was executed.

Condé, Louis de Bourbon, Prince de (1621–1686)
French general

As the young Duc d'Enghien, this great soldier crushed a Spanish army at the battle of Rocroi, in 1643, towards the end of the Thirty Years War. In 1646 at Nordlingen he defeated the army of the Emperor of the Holy Roman Empire, with the aid of Turenne (*p. 159*), and by the end of the war he and Turenne were Europe's most distinguished soldiers, with the exception of Oliver Cromwell.

After the war, Condé, as he became when his father died in 1646, got into trouble with Mazarin (*p. 156*) and was disgraced. But he was later pardoned, and retired to study literature and philosophy.

Gwynne, Nell (Eleanor) (c.1650–1687)
Welsh born mistress of Charles II of England

Nell Gwynne was born of Welsh parents and came to London in the 1660s. She had red hair, flashing eyes, a trim figure (to begin with) and was extremely attractive. She got a job as an orange girl at the King's Theatre in Drury Lane,

Nell Gwynne, the mistress of Charles II and in the background the King's Theatre, Drury Lane, where she once worked as an orange girl

which was patronized by Charles II.

Nell Gwynne became the mistress of Lord Buckhurst but before she was 20 she caught the eye of Charles II who made her his mistress and installed her in Whitehall, with all the luxury of a queen. The king had many mistresses in his life, but it was always said Nell Gwynne was the only one who never interfered in politics. She bore him two illegitimate sons, one of whom was created Duke of St. Albans and is the ancestor of the present Duke.

When Charles lay dying in 1685 one of his last requests was to his heir, James, not to let Nell come to any harm. James, for once in his life, kept his promise and Nell received a pension.

Bunyan, John (1628–1688)
English preacher and writer
Bunyan is famous as the author of *Pilgrim's Progress*, a book about a religious journey through life, the places being named in many cases after virtues and vices. In his time he was a formidable preacher for the non-conformists, that is, those who did not like the established religion. His sermons were often fierce and hard hitting, and he landed up in prison for 12 years (1660–1672), during which time he wrote several books, including *Pilgrim's Progress*.

Morgan, Sir Henry (c.1635–1688)
Welsh adventurer and colonial governor
Morgan was believed to have been sold as a boy slave to a plantation in the West Indies. He soon got himself into the buccaneer crews, and by 1660 had become captain of a pirate ship. He attacked many Spanish fleets and coastal towns in the West Indies and in South America. These adventures interested Charles II, who made him lieutenant governor of Jamaica.

The Palace of Versailles which Le Brun decorated

Jeffreys, George, 1st Baron (1644–1689)

English judge

Famous (or notorious) as the Hanging Judge, who sent hundreds of people to the gallows for their part in Monmouth's rebellion, Jeffreys was in other respects an able and conscientious lawyer. Charles II made him Lord Chief Justice in 1683 and Lord Chancellor in 1685, and he remained in that office until the abdication of James II in 1688. By that time, Jeffreys knew he had many enemies who would get even with him once James was deposed, and he attempted to leave England disguised as a woman. He was detected, however, when a sailor tried to make a pass at him. Jeffreys was put in the Tower of London where a few weeks later he drank himself to death.

Le Brun, Charles (1619–1690)

French painter and designer

Le Brun was director of the Gobelins furnishing and interior design organization set up by Louis XIV and Colbert (*p. 161*). In this position he dominated French art for a generation. All the designs and pictures that came out of the Gobelins workshops bore the stamp of his ideas. He was court painter to Louis XIV. Among his design works was the gallery at the Louvre. He also supervised the decoration of the palace of Versailles, the splendid royal residence being built by Louis XIV out of a hunting lodge there, which had been enjoyed by his father Louis XIII.

Fox, George (1624–1691)

English founder of the Quaker movement

Few men have got into so much trouble for their views as George Fox. This remarkable man violently disagreed with the established church and its doctrines in England, and he spent years of his life preaching and writing about his objections. He used to interrupt sermons in church, lectures in universities, classes in school, questioning all manner of statements. He formed a Society of Friends and the members went about the land in the same way as he did. They got themselves called Quakers by a particular judge who was called upon to try Fox for trouble making. Fox warned the judge to tremble at the word of God, whereupon the judge made a joke about 'quaking' at this, and they have been called this ever since.

Boyle, The Hon. Robert (1627–1691)
Irish chemist
Boyle is still called the 'Father of Modern Chemistry'. Among his many discoveries and innovations was the theory that all substances in the universe were made up of atoms of one kind or another. This was a forerunner to the Atomic Theory of John Dalton (*p. 215*) which was later proved at the end of the 19th century.

Boyle introduced the famous law, known as Boyle's Law, which states that the volume of a given amount of gas at a constant temperature varies inversely with the pressure. Boyle also showed that air was very important in the distribution of sound.

Malpighi, Marcello (1628–1694)
Italian anatomist
Malpighi was the first anatomist to use a microscope to study anatomical structure. He made many discoveries, some bearing his name, including the Malpighian layer, under the skin, the Malpighian corpuscles in the spleen, and the structure of the brain.

La Fontaine, Jean de (1621–1695)
French writer of fables
La Fontaine's fables are nearly as famous as those of the Greek writer, Aesop. They came out in several volumes over about 25 years, and they were dedicated to well known French figures. He was an exceptionally talented man. He disguised his criticism of society by referring to animals and nature in general in his verse and prose, rather than to individuals themselves. La Fontaine moved in the best literary circles and was an intimate friend of people like Molière (*p. 159*) and Racine (*p. 166*).

Huygens, Christiaan (1629–1695)
Dutch physicist and astronomer
Huygens was the first person to make a pendulum clock. The principle of pendulum movement had been demonstrated by Galileo (*p. 148*) in the 1580s, but Huygens gave practical application to it in 1657.

Huygens was also a distinguished astronomer, and he discovered the ring and fourth satellite of the planet Saturn. He also discovered polarization and developed the micrometer. He spent many years in France, engaged in research at the invitation of Louis XIV.

Purcell, Henry (1659–1695)
English composer
Purcell was one of the greatest of all English composers, and deserves to be compared with the best of the European composers of the time. He became organist at Westminster Abbey when he was only twenty, and was noticed by Charles II who made him royal composer.

Purcell's output was considerable and covered a wide area. He wrote the score for operas, such as *Dido and Aeneas*, and *The Fairy Queen*. He also composed oratorios like *King Arthur*, and Te Deums, Chorales, and so forth. He also composed anthems for public events, thus heralding the job of the Master of the King's Musick.

Sobieski, John (1624–1696)
King John III of Poland (1674–1696)
'There was a man sent from God, and his name was John'. This text from the New Testament was read by many bishops and clergy from pulpits throughout Austria in 1683 when John Sobieski, King of Poland, drove the Turks away from the city of Vienna, which they had been besieging. He had in fact saved the Empire from collapsing before the Turks.

John was the son of the Governor of Cracow in Poland. In 1674, after he had formed an army which beat the Turks in battle at Choczin, he was elected King of Poland. His rescue of the Austrians in Vienna did not help Poland, though it made him the hero of Christian Europe.

Racine, Jean Baptiste (1639–1699)
French poet and playwright

Racine was a major playwright in French literary history. He wrote during the brilliant days of Louis XIV, the Sun King (*p. 168*), and was a contemporary of Molière and Boileau. At first Molière, who was an actor-producer as well as a playwright, put on Racine's plays, but they fell out and Racine went to a rival company. He was a court poet from 1663. Among his most famous works are *Bérénice*, *Iphigénie*, *Phèdre*, and *Esther*, tragedies of strict classical form and simple dramatic power.

Dryden, John (1631–1700)
English poet

Dryden was one of England's most celebrated poets, and his output was very large. Many of his works were political in their content and message. For example, his poetry play, *Amboyna* (1673), was an attack on the Dutch with whom England had been at war on and off for a generation. He also attacked the Duke of Monmouth, the favourite illegitimate son of King Charles II, in his work *Absalom and Achitophel*, and he wrote a justification of his conversion to Roman Catholicism in *The Hind and the Panther*.

He was made poet laureate in 1670, but fell out of favour when William III, the Protestant champion of Western Europe, succeeded as King in 1688.

William III (1650–1702)
King of England, Scotland and Ireland (1688–1702)

Dutch William, as he was called, because he was the prince of the state of Orange in Holland and the chief *Stadholder* (or head of state) of the Dutch provinces, never got to understand the English, Scots or Irish whom he was called upon to rule in 1688 when his father-in-law James II (1685–1688) was driven into exile. Small wonder, though, for the English politicians who had invited him over to take the throne were utterly unreliable, and some downright treacherous. Many spent the best part of his reign plotting to restore James II.

William III

In his time, William was responsible for many improvements in English government and institutions. The Bank of England was founded. The coinage was reformed. The press was freed from censorship. But he was best in diplomacy and war, always trying the former before resorting to the latter.

When in 1701, the War of the Spanish Succession broke out, William managed to negotiate an alliance of powers to take on France and Spain. These included Britain, Holland and the Empire. One of his last acts was to see that the supreme command of the allied armies should go to Marlborough (*p. 170*).

Pepys, Samuel (1633–1703)
English admiralty secretary and diarist

Pepys is remembered for his diary – ironically, because no one deciphered it until over a century after his death. But he was perhaps more valuable to England for the work he did in building up the Royal Navy when he was secretary to the Admiralty. Much of the brilliant success of the navy in the next century can be attributed to the care and skill with which he brought naval administration to the pitch needed to maintain the fleet in a permanent state of readiness, to deal with all threats to the country or its precious trade routes and interests.

His diary, however, is also very valuable as a social document of London life in the first years of Charles II's reign.

Hooke, Robert (1635–1703)
English philosopher and scientist
Hooke worked with the celebrated chemist, Robert Boyle (*p. 165*). Then he became professor of geometry at Oxford. In his time he carried out numerous experiments, worked out all manner of theories and thought up all kinds of inventions. He is said to have devised a steam-engine. He invented the quadrant. He experimented with a balance spring in a watch. He invented a microscope, a marine barometer, and a new type of telescope.

On top of all this, he also designed buildings, and after the Great Fire of London in 1666 he built a new hospital, Bethlehem Hospital (Moorfields), and also the Royal College of Physicians.

Hooke's microscope and reflector

Bossuet, Jacques Bénigne (1627–1704)
French churchman and demagogue
Bossuet earned a great reputation for making sermons and speeches. He was a very learned cleric who became tutor to Louis XIV's son and bishop of Meaux.

People all over France wanted to hear this man give a sermon, and when the king asked him to deliver one at court in 1661, Bossuet obliged with a long discourse which moved the whole congregation. Devout, learned, stingingly critical of all members of the church who did not follow the orthodox line, he minded not whom he attacked in the interests of the state religion.

Locke, John (1632–1704)
English philosopher
Locke studied at Christ Church, Oxford. He became a physician and attended the Earl of Shaftesbury as his adviser. Then he turned towards philosophy, and over a long period of time produced a brilliant work on the subject of what questions the human understanding was capable of dealing with.

Locke had a number of government appointments, but fell out of favour when Shaftesbury was exiled in 1683. He was welcomed back by William III who made him adviser to the government on coinage.

Coehoorn, Baron Menno van (1641–1704)
Dutch military engineer
Coehoorn was a fortifications expert. He was the equal of the great French engineer, Vauban (*p. 168*) and in the war between William III and Louis XIV, from 1691 to 1698, which was largely a war of sieges of forts and castles along the borders of France and the Netherlands, all Coehoorn's talents were called into play, as indeed were Vauban's. Coehoorn invented a small bronze mortar gun.

Aurangzeb (1618–1707)
Moghul Emperor of India
Aurangzeb was the last and one of the greatest of the Moghul Emperors of India. He was the third son of Shah Jehan (*p. 157*) and when his father was taken ill, in 1657, he skilfully removed two elder brothers and one younger one, so that he could rule in his father's name. Then he confined the old man and let him die, by which time he had become absolute ruler of India.

Aurangzeb's rule was marked by prosperity, but all the while his position was insecure because too many important people knew of his behaviour to his family. He was austere, morose and unsympathetic. Though happiest in camp with his troops, or in the field of battle, he never got very close to them. At the end of a long life, he was driven off his throne by a raiding tribe, the Mahrattas.

Louis XIV and his court, where extravagances seemed unlimited

Vauban, Sébastien le Prestre, Marquis de (1633–1707)
French military engineer

In some wars, towns and cities, castles and forts, had to be besieged. To do this effectively, it helped to employ army engineers who understood the technicalities of mining castles, constructing fortifications, dismantling buildings and so on. Louis XIV had one of the most brilliant military engineers of all time in Sebastien Vauban, who for a generation from about 1655 besieged scientifically, thoroughly, and often successfully, many famous castles and fortifications, particularly along the border between France and the Netherlands. Vauban was made a marshal of France in 1703.

Bérain, Jean (c.1640–1711)
French architect and designer

When Le Brun died in 1690 (*p. 164*) his influence on French art and interior design gave way to that of Bérain. This artist, who had, like Inigo Jones (*p. 152*), designed theatre sets and costumes, introduced a new style of decoration called the Rococo. This was a gay, bubbling, irresponsible style, based on shell motifs (rocaille is the French for a shell) but his designs were not liked immediately.

Louis XIV (1638–1715)
King of France (1643–1715)

'*Le Roi Soleil*' (the Sun King), so called because of the splendour of his court and the glories of the earlier part of his long reign, Louis XIV was certainly the most colourful monarch of French history. The first years of his reign were managed by Cardinal Mazarin (*p. 156*). Then, when he died in 1661, Louis decided to rule by himself. He appointed as chief minister Colbert (*p. 161*) who managed the country while he, Louis, devoted himself to making Paris the artistic and cultural centre of the world. He succeeded in doing so by attracting to the city the finest artists and craftsmen of Europe to work for him in beautifying the city's new buildings, palaces and other homes. At the same time Louis had an aggressive foreign policy based on establishing France as the strongest nation in Europe. This was in part successful, but it cost his country dear in men and money. He also developed the empire abroad in Canada, India, the Far East and the West Indies.

But despite a reign filled with successes in the field of battle, brilliant generals and statesmen, architects, designers, painters, inventors, scientists and writers, the law of diminishing returns gradually wore

168

his resources down. Early in his reign he had had a lot of furniture made in silver, for example, but by the end of his reign it had nearly all to be sold.

When he died in 1715, soon after the crippling war in which Marlborough won so many splendid victories, his son, grandson and eldest great grandson had all died before him, and he was succeeded by his second great grandson who became Louis XV.

Dampier, William (1652–1715)
English explorer
William Dampier began his career as a buccaneer, raiding the coast of Peru, then in Spanish hands, and also Mexico and Chile. In 1699 he was sent out by the British admiralty to explore Australia, and the various groups of islands in the area. He made many discoveries, including the Straits named after him, and he charted and recorded the details of his voyage which ended when he brought his ship home to England the other way round, thus circumnavigating the globe. It was he who found Alexander Selkirk, the Scottish explorer who had been marooned on an uninhabited island in the Pacific, on whose adventures Daniel Defoe based his famous book *Robinson Crusoe*.

Leibnitz, Gottfried Wilhelm (1646–1716)
German mathematician and philosopher
Leibnitz invented the differential calculus, a systematic analytical method of dealing with particular classes of mathematical problems, generally, though not necessarily, to do with motion. He also invented a calculating machine. His work on the calculus coincided with similar studies being pursued by England's Sir Isaac Newton (*p. 173*) and for some time there was a heated controversy as to who arrived there first.

Leibnitz persuaded Frederick I of Prussia to found the university of Berlin, in 1700, and in return he was made its president. He became influential as a philosopher, whose optimism was to be bitterly satirized by Voltaire (*p. 183*).

Charles XII (1682–1718)
King of Sweden (1697–1718)
Charles XII was a military genius of a kind, but the good that he did was more than cancelled out by many campaigns of reckless ambition. His whole adult life was given over to war. In 1700 he smashed a Russian army of 50,000 men at Narva. Then he beat them again at Grodno. In 1709, he laid siege to Pultowa in the Ukraine, but was severely beaten by Czar Peter the Great of Russia (*p. 172*).

Charles took refuge in Turkey, an ancient enemy of Russia, and after a stay returned to Scandinavia where, in 1716, he set out to invade Norway. In the siege of Halden he was shot dead by a musketeer. His campaigns bled his country white, and after his death, Sweden ceased to be reckoned an important European power.

Maintenon, Françoise, Marquise de (1635–1719)
French courtesan and wife of Louis XIV
Mme de Maintenon's real name was Françoise d'Aubigne. She spent much of her childhood in a convent. She was brought to the notice of the King, Louis XIV, who fell in love with her. He enabled her to buy the estate at Maintenon and he elevated it to a marquisate. His wife died in 1683 and two years later he married Françoise secretly. They remained together for the rest of his life.

It was said she had a strong influence over him in political matters, but there is very little evidence of her having interfered to the detriment of France.

Addison, Joseph (1672–1719)
English writer
Addison entered government service as an under secretary of state. He was also a gifted writer, and in 1710 he started a paper, the *Whig Examiner*, while writing for other papers, such as Sir Richard Steel's *Tatler*. He and Steele joined together to produce *The Spectator*, which was filled with good literary criticism and much satirical comment on society. He continued in the meanwhile in government service, and reached high rank.

Bottger

Bottger, Johann Friedrich (1682–1719)
German ceramicist

In 1708, Bottger, a chemist working in Meissen, in Saxony, discovered that by using kaolin it was possible to make porcelain. The secret had been known by the Chinese for many centuries, but no one in Europe had discovered it. Two years later, the Elector of Saxony, fascinated by some of Bottger's early pieces, established a factory at Meissen, and under the direction of Bottger, some exquisite pieces were made, which became the envy of craftsman and men of taste all over Europe. Bottger kept the secret for several years.

Watteau, Jean Antoine (1684–1721)
French painter

Watteau was known for his pastoral scenes. He decorated interiors of grand houses, often using shepherds' and shepherdesses' scenes. He decorated the ceiling in the famous Hôtel de Poulpry in Paris. He is most famous for his melancholy and wistful pictures of *Fêtes Galantes*.

His style of work was sometimes imitated by bronze makers making mounts for furniture items, in the Régence Period of French 18th century furniture.

Marlborough, John Churchill, 1st Duke of (1650–1722)
English soldier and statesman

Marlborough was an outstanding military genius, a gifted statesman, a skilful diplomatist, a kind friend and a generous enemy. But there was also another side to this catalogue of virtues. He was shifty, untrustworthy, greedy where money was concerned, occasionally unreliable, and ambitious. Perhaps it was the mixture of these qualities that made him so fascinating both in his own time and since.

John Churchill was the son of a poor Devonshire knight. James II liked him, and entered him for the army when he was old enough. In the field of battle Churchill proved courageous and enterprising, saving the life of the Duke of Monmouth at a siege in Belgium in 1673.

By 1688, Churchill, who had become Baron Marlborough, was high up in the counsels of the king, but he was secretly plotting with others to depose James and replace him with William, Prince of Orange. When William was invited to come over, Marlborough came to join him, along with the others. But although William rewarded him, advancing him to an earldom, he watched him carefully, for Marlborough had betrayed James who had for so long favoured him. He could do it again – and indeed in 1692 he did, when he plotted to get James back to England again. For this Marlborough spent some time in the Tower.

William released him but never trusted him again. In 1701, when the War of the Spanish Succession broke out, William made Marlborough commander-in-chief of the allied armies against France. The appointment was wonderfully justified and he covered his name with honour and glory.

In four splendid victories, that rank along the greatest in all military history, Marlborough dealt severe blows against the French and their allies. They were Blenheim (1704), Ramillies (1706), Oudenarde (1708) and Malplaquet (1709), the last being very costly in men to the British. A grateful nation gave an estate at Woodstock near Oxford to Marlborough, who had been made a Duke in 1702. This estate then had a huge palace built on it, designed by Sir John Vanbrugh (*p. 173*).

Marlborough's career was ended somewhat sharply when his wife Sarah was displaced in the queen's favour by Mrs Masham, and before long Marlborough himself was dismissed from all his commands. It was said he was trying to get himself made Captain-General of the British Army. Then he was charged with having taken large sums of money by helping himself to a percentage of the gold and coinage sent out by the government to Europe to help finance the allies in their support of the British in the war. It was probably true, for Marlborough could not resist money, especially easy money, and he had expenses to pay of all

The Duke of Marlborough at the battle of Malplaquet

kinds. He was disgraced and retired to live abroad for a while.

He was invited to return when George I came to the throne in 1714, and restored to some of his positions. Then in 1716 he was struck by a severe attack of apoplexy and rendered partly incapable of movement or coherent thought. Slowly he sank into stupor and died in 1722, a shadow of his former greatness.

K'ang Hsi (1654–1722)
Chinese emperor (1662–1722)

This splendid Chinese ruler gave China years of peace and encouraged internal development. He arranged for a collection of classical Chinese texts to be prepared, patronized artists, scholars and craftsmen, and gave great assistance to the King Tetchen porcelain works. His wars of annexation of neighbouring territory were quick and successful. One province he secured was Tibet. Although he curbed the missionary activities of many Christians, he remained friendly with some of them and even employed them at his court.

Leeuwenhoek, Anton van (1632–1723)
Dutch scientist

Leeuwenhoek lived for nearly 91 years, and was born and died in the same years as Sir Christopher Wren (*p. 172*).

He was a medical scientist who had started his career as a humble clerk in an Amsterdam warehouse. His discoveries, mostly associated with the human body, were made through his skilled use of the microscope and his intricate observations. He described red blood corpuscles; he showed how the capillaries work; he detailed the structure of muscle fibres; and he pointed to the composition of the hair.

Sir Christopher Wren and a monument to his skill – St. Paul's Cathedral, London

Wren, Sir Christopher (1632–1723)
English architect

'*Si monumentum requiris, circumspice*'. 'If you seek a monument to me, look around you'. This is inscribed on the tomb of Sir Christopher Wren in St. Paul's Cathedral in London, which he built on the ashes of the old cathedral destroyed in the Great Fire of London of 1666. This remarkable designer also rebuilt over 50 other damaged and destroyed churches. He drew up a plan for a new London which, unfortunately, the City Fathers rejected as it would have demolished a lot of their buildings in order to provide the wider streets he wanted.

Wren was an architect in the tradition of Palladio (*p. 133*) and Inigo Jones (*p. 152*) but he had decidedly individual ideas of his own. His later work is much like the Baroque architecture of Western Europe. He had begun his career as an astronomer, and had even been a professor of astronomy at Oxford. Other buildings by Wren include quarters at Hampton Court, the Sheldonian Theatre at Oxford and the Library at Trinity College, Cambridge.

Kneller, Sir Godfrey (1646–1723)
German born painter

Kneller was born in Lübeck in Germany, but once he had achieved celebrity as a portrait painter, he came to live in England, in 1675. Over in England his brilliant portraiture got him commissions to paint members of the royal family, including Charles II, and William III made him his principal painter.

During William's reign Peter the Great, Czar of Russia, visited England, and Kneller painted his portrait. He also undertook pictures of celebrated statesmen and writers of the time.

Peter I (the Great) (1672–1725)
Czar of Russia (1689–1725)

Peter the Great was a man of contrasts. He was violent, cruel, impatient, revengeful. But he was also courageous, far-seeing, intelligent and sensitive. He destroyed many established institutions but introduced his country to many more good influences from the west.

As a young man he had visited England and Holland, some of the time in disguise, and had worked in dockyards. When he got home, he ordered his bodyguard and advisers who wore beards to remove them. They were reluctant as beards were sacred, so Peter sent for a pair of clippers and began to cut them off himself.

Peter went to war with Sweden, in which he ultimately triumphed. Determined for Russia to play an influential part in European affairs he decided to build a new, strategically placed capital, St. Petersburg (now called Leningrad), to bring his essentially Asiatic empire into the orbit of Europe. He also introduced much Western art and architecture to the new city.

Vanbrugh, Sir John (1664–1726)
English architect and playwright
This versatile Englishman had four careers in his lifetime, one after the other. First he was a soldier and distinguished himself by his bravery. Then in the 1690s he started to write witty plays. The first was *The Relapse*, and this was followed by *The Provoked Wife* and *The Confederacy*. They were all very funny and very bawdy, in an age when this was not frowned upon.

When the next century came, we find Vanbrugh has become a celebrated architect, designing grand palaces and huge private houses. One was Castle Howard, in Yorkshire, one of the grandest stately homes in the north of England. His most famous structure, however, was Blenheim Palace, built for the Duke of Marlborough, where Winston Churchill was to be born.

Vanbrugh built the Haymarket Theatre (since rebuilt) and this led him to his fourth career, manager of a theatre; but he was not a success in this field.

Newton, Sir Isaac (1642–1727)
English physicist and mathematician
Isaac Newton was born in the year in which Galileo (*p. 148*) died. He grew up to become perhaps the finest and most respected scientist Britain has ever produced. He was educated at Grantham Grammar School and took a BA at Trinity College, Cambridge.

Sir Isaac Newton

One day, as a young physicist, Newton observed that when apples fell off trees they went down at a speed that varied according to the distance they had to travel to the ground. He believed that this meant the earth had a gravitational force pulling them down, and thus his theory of gravity was born. He applied this principle to the movement of the planets and stars in the Solar System. He then began to study the nature of light and the construction of telescopes and he built a reflecting telescope with which to study the heavens closely. This led to the discovery of the composition of light.

There were many other original ideas evolved and developed by Newton, including the differential calculus and his famous Laws of Motion which are the foundation of the science of mechanics today.

In his lifetime, Newton was greatly respected everywhere, not only for his astonishing gifts as a scientist and thinker, but also for the modesty with which he demonstrated them, and the kindliness he showed to everyone who came his way. Nothing was too much trouble. He never displayed impatience with those less intelligent than himself.

Robinson Crusoe with 'Man Friday' in an illustration from Daniel Defoe's book

Congreve, William (1670–1729)
English playwright
In his time Congreve was regarded as the wittiest of all English playwrights, though perhaps today not so many people would laugh at his lines. He had been educated in Ireland, working with Jonathan Swift (*p. 176*).

He began to write comedy plays in 1692, when he produced the *Old Bachelor*, which was a great success. There followed *Double Dealer*, *Love for Love*, and *The Way of the World* (the one for which he is best remembered). Ironically, this last play is quite often staged these days, but in his time it was not a great success.

Law, John (1671–1729)
Scottish financier
Law was a gambler who in 1716 opened a bank in France which issued paper notes. It was a mixed success, but with the profits he acquired an interest in the district of Louisiana in the southern part of the United States, an area which was ultimately sold by Napoleon (*p. 202*) to the Americans.

Then he got too bold. He bought up the East India and China companies and merged everything under the Mississippi Scheme. This collapsed in 1720 and he disappeared, to die in poverty in Italy.

Steele, Sir Richard (1672–1729)
Irish born writer
Steele was an accomplished essayist and playwright who flourished in the reigns of Queen Anne and George I. He started the magazine *The Tatler*, which catered for high society and included articles on behaviour, customs and fashion. He was careful, however, not to offend the reigning house in his works, which other writers were doing regularly, and he was duly rewarded. He was knighted in 1715.

Defoe, Daniel (1660–1731)
English author
Daniel Defoe was an author of immense energy and skill. In his time he produced hundreds of works, books, pamphlets and articles. Some were commissioned

by the governments of his day. Others were his own opinions, expressed sharply and often satirically, and he got into trouble on several occasions, more than once spending periods in gaol. His journalism, published in his *Review* was a precursor to today's publications.

Towards the end of his active life Defoe started to write novels, a new form of literature in England at the time. He produced *Moll Flanders*, and others, but the most famous by far was *Robinson Crusoe*, a story based on the experiences of the Scottish explorer Alexander Selkirk, who was marooned for years on an uninhabited Pacific island.

Peterborough, Charles Mordaunt, 3rd Earl of (1658–1735)
British soldier and statesman
Peterborough had a flamboyant and busy career as a ship commander, a statesman, and a military commander in the field. His support of William III (*p. 166*) when coming to the English throne earned him high office. In Queen Anne's reign he commanded Allied armies fighting in Spain during the War of the Spanish Succession. He stormed Barcelona, captured several other cities and entered Valencia. Then he heard that a new French-Spanish army was besieging Barcelona again. He hurried back, took charge of a British squadron of ships, and sailed into Barcelona harbour where he scattered the French ships.

Then Peterborough, whose exploits were proving hardly less spectacular than Marlborough's (*p. 170*) was recalled. He had been hoping to get the job of supreme commander. For some years he stayed out of service, and interested himself in the arts. In the reign of George I he was appointed Commander-in-chief of British naval forces.

Eugène, Prince of Savoy (1663–1736)
Austrian general
Eugène was a French-born noble whose mother was banished from France. He went into the Austrian army, and began upon a military career that was to be hardly less distinguished than that of his contemporary and friend Marlborough (*p. 170*).

His first major experience was with John Sobieski, King of Poland (*p. 165*) who saved Vienna from the Turks in 1683. But it was in the War of the Spanish Succession (1701–1713) where Eugène's genius shone to its fullest. He was with Marlborough at Blenheim in 1704. Four years later he was with Marlborough again, in command of the Imperial army, at the victory of Oudenarde, and at Malplaquet in the following year.

When the Turks attacked the Austrian Empire again in 1716, Eugène, once more in command of the Imperial army, beat them in two great battles. To do this Eugène defeated an army of 150,000 men at Peterwardein, took Lemesuar, and in 1717 after a desperate siege, gained Belgrade.

Fahrenheit, Gabriel Daniel (1686–1736)
German physicist
Fahrenheit was born in Danzig, but spent most of his working life in Holland and England. He experimented with thermometers of various kinds, and in about 1714 struck upon the idea of using mercury (or quicksilver) as the fluid which should trickle up and down the glass tube to indicate the temperature of a liquid. Previously, alcohol had been used.

This led him to fix a scale of temperature which became famous all over the world under his name. The freezing point was $32°$ and the boiling point was $212°$, relating to pure water.

Fleury, André Hercule de (1653–1743)
French cardinal and statesman
Fleury had an ecclesiastical career. Then in 1715 he became tutor to the young Louis XV, who had just succeeded his great grandfather Louis XIV. In this position, he executed a very considerable influence over the king, on the whole quite a good one. In 1726 he was appointed chief minister of France, and for the next seventeen years strove to keep France out of European wars.

Churchill, Sarah, Duchess of Marlborough (1680–1744)

Sarah Jennings was in her youth the bosom friend of the Princess Anne, daughter of James, Duke of York, who became James II (1685–1688). When she was 18 she married John Churchill, then an army officer who was a favourite of James, and from that moment she set out to advance her husband's career. When Anne became Queen in 1702, Sarah and her husband, who was now Duke of Marlborough, were relied upon practically, to run the country. He fought the battles in Europe during the War of the Spanish Succession while she dominated the Queen and the statesmen at home.

Then in 1711, certain people who had grown tired of her imperious ways, prevailed on Queen Anne, who had become equally tired, to dismiss her and Marlborough, and they fell from power.

Sarah spent the last years of her life in arguments with the government about the financing of the construction of Blenheim Palace, awarded to the Duke in recognition of his victory, and with the builders.

Pope, Alexander (1688–1744)
English poet

Pope produced some very fine poetry in his younger days, after a youth in which he was bedevilled with ill-health and deformity, and intervening years of hard study. An early work was *The Rape of the Lock*, and in 1720 he published a translation of Homer's *Iliad* which was extremely well received.

Pope's infirmities had a severe effect on his mind and temperament. He became increasingly moody and given to fits of temper. Quite often he burst into print with scurrilous remarks or tales about people who were, or had been, friends. Hardly anybody who earned his displeasure escaped the withering fire of his pen.

Swift, Jonathan (1667–1745)
Irish writer

Jonathan Swift was a clergyman who eventually became Dean of St. Patrick's in Dublin. But he was very much more famous as a satirical writer whose wit, humour and criticism were eagerly read by many. Swift attacked all kinds of causes and all sorts of people, especially prominent statesmen. He particularly satirized the great Duke of Marlborough.

Swift wrote several books and papers, but none was so well received as his brilliant satire on politics, *Gulliver's Travels*, enjoyed by children and adults alike. He spent many years in London where he was lionized much of the time as the most amusing writer of his day.

Walpole, Sir Robert, First Earl of Orford (1676–1745)
English statesman

Not only was Walpole the first prime minister of Britain, he also held the position without a break for longer than anyone since. He was a kind man and a good financier, but like most of the men of his day he was open to bribery.

In 1701 Walpole entered parliament as Whig M.P. for the small Norfolk village of Castle Rising. Later he became secretary of state for war and in 1715 was made chancellor of the exchequer. It was here that his financial genius proved invaluable, and when the South Sea Bubble crisis occurred in 1720 he was the only man who seemed able to clear up the mess. George I was delighted with the way he sorted out the trouble and showed his confidence in him by making him head of the government.

Walpole was a strict man, and ruled his cabinet strongly. This was a good thing for England at the time, when it had been weakened by war and financial crises. He reformed the tariff system and put aside £1 million a year to pay off government debts.

In foreign policy he steered clear of war, which he knew was expensive and wasteful. So it was with reluctance that he eventually took Britain into war with Spain, in 1739. At first the war did not go well and because it was known that he opposed it, this was blamed on him. He was forced to retire and created Earl of Orford.

Johann Sebastian Bach, one of the greatest musicians of the world. Four of his sons also became musicians

Bach, Johann Sebastian (1685–1750)
German composer

Bach, a composer supreme in the history of music, had his first lessons from his father and brother. Most of his life was spent in the royal courts of Germany, first as an organist, later as a teacher, and finally as a composer. This unique musician, who died blind at the age of 65, in his lifetime composed much of the world's best known and most loved music.

While much of his work was for the organ, Bach also wrote concertos, suites, and many choral works like the *Mass in B Minor* and the *St. Matthew Passion*. Among his most famous compositions are the six *Brandenburg Concertos*. This wonderful man was the father of several sons who composed as well.

Bolingbroke, Henry St. John, Viscount (1678–1751)
English statesman

Bolingbroke was an amazing individual. Some thought of him as the greatest man in the world; his father thought he should be put to death. Queen Anne, George I and George II all had trouble with him, while his political colleagues, most of whose brains were not at the same level, found it impossible to keep up with him.

Bolingbroke was foreign secretary in 1710. He was anxious to bring the War of the Spanish Succession to an end and to break the power of Marlborough. He negotiated the Treaty of Utrecht, and left England for France, where he espoused the cause of James Edward Stuart (*p. 181*), becoming his secretary. But he could not agree that Britain should be brought back to Roman Catholicism, and he came to England again to offer his services to George I, in 1723. These were refused, but he was allowed to live in Middlesex, where for some years he enjoyed a wonderful existence among poets and writers. He wrote himself, and among other things produced attacks on Walpole (*p. 176*) the then prime minister.

Walpole steadfastly refused to give Bolingbroke any job, and finally he left for France where he lived from 1736 to 1742. Then he came back again and lived in London. He wrote several political works, one of which was on how a monarchy should be run in Britain, and this had a profound and lasting influence on George III.

Fielding, Henry (1707–1754)
English novelist

Fielding is often called the Father of the English Novel, though he was by no means the first author to write a novel in English. He was by profession a lawyer, and he began his writing career with a few plays, as many people did; these were moderately popular. But after about 1740 he started on his realistic novels, which were powerful and fascinating books, creating the vogue for tales of adventure in which the hero is often a likeable rogue. The first was *Joseph Andrews* in 1742, *Jonathan Wild* followed in 1743 and the most celebrated of them all, *Tom Jones*, was published in 1749.

Montesquieu, Charles de Secondat and Baron de la Brède (1689–1755)
French writer and philosopher

Montesquieu gave up a career as a lawyer to devote his time to writing. In *Lettres Persanes* he cleverly criticized French society of his time by showing it as seen through the eyes of two Persians travelling through the country.

His works in general had a very profound effect on the development of democracy in Europe and America. *Causes de la grandeur des Romains et de leur décadence* was his greatest work.

Surajah-Dowlah (c.1728–1757)
Nawab of Bengal

Surajah-Dowlah was a cruel and violent ruler of Bengal, in India, who in 1756 tried to break the power of the European merchants and banking houses in Calcutta. He took the city by storm, and then locked up over 100 Europeans in a dungeon for a night in the heat of the summer. Nearly all the occupants died of thirst during the night. One who did survive was a Mr. Holwell, who wrote an account of it. The place became known amongst English propagandists as the Black Hole of Calcutta.

A year later, Robert Clive (*p. 182*) avenged this by crushing Surajah-Dowlah's forces at the famous Battle of Plassey, and the tyrant was murdered shortly afterwards.

Handel, George Frederick (1685–1759)
German (later English) composer

Although Handel was a Briton by naturalization he must rate as the country's greatest composer.

After settling in England in 1712 he worked as director of the Royal Academy and as director of the Covent Garden opera house. His works include the *Messiah*, an oratorio, and the *Water Music* and the *Fireworks Music*, which were written especially for the king. He also composed numerous concertos and suites, and works of many kinds for the organ. In his time his music was extremely popular. People waited to hear his latest tunes with the same sort of enthusiasm that greets the popular music of today.

Montcalm, Louis Joseph de, Marquise (1712–1759)
French general

Every British child is told how General James Wolfe (*p. 178*) fought and won the battle of the Heights of Abraham, outside Quebec in Canada, in 1759, securing Canada for the British empire. They know that Wolfe was killed in the hour of victory. The French commander opposing him was Montcalm. This distinguished French soldier, whose gifts were hardly less than those of Wolfe, was also killed at the same battle, which may have had something to do with its outcome.

Wolfe, General James (1727–1759)
English soldier

Wolfe's daring was once described as madness, to which the king George II, replied that he wished some of his other generals were a little insane too. Wolfe was fighting in Europe before he was 16, in the War of the Austrian Succession, and was present at most of the great battles of that decade, including Dettingen and Fontenoy. He was also at Culloden, in Scotland, in 1746.

In 1759 he was made commander of a force in Canada sent up the St. Lawrence river to Quebec. It was a daring raid planned to help Britain in its bid to win Canada from France.

The English General Wolfe and the French General Montcalm whose forces engaged in the battle of the Heights of Abraham, which resulted in victory for Britain and the death of both men

To attack Quebec it was necessary to scale the Heights of Abraham, which were heavily guarded. This he did and then led the British against the French with complete success. During it he was mortally wounded and died within earshot of his guns. But the British force had won the day and thus won Canada.

Montagu, Lady Mary Wortley (1689–1762)
English poet

Mary Pierrepont, daughter of the Duke of Kingston, was a child prodigy. She taught herself Latin, wrote excellent verse, and entertained her father's guests at dinner by her witty conversation, while still a child.

She married Edward Wortley Montagu, and travelled with him to the Levant in 1716 where he was ambassador at Constantinople. She kept a fascinating diary of events there and wrote many letters about the country of the Turks. After a while, she and her husband parted, and she went to live in Italy. From there she wrote many more letters, which were published.

Oeben, Jean-Françoise (c.1720–1763)
French cabinet maker

Oeben was probably the finest of all the many splendid cabinet makers employed in Paris during the 18th century. His work was quite exquisite. It was often extremely intricate. Pieces took years to make, and some had very complex locking and secret compartment mechanisms all made by hand. His triumphal piece, not finished by himself, was the *Bureau du Roi Louis XV*, a cylinder desk made between 1760 and 1769 for the King. Oeben designed it and started to construct it. This astonishing craftsman died bankrupt, owing to bad debts.

Hogarth, William (1697–1764)
English engraver and caricaturist

Hogarth engraved many pictures in his time. Each of which was done on a block or a sheet of metal, and thousands of copies could be taken from them. This means that Hogarth prints are not as rare as may be thought. But they are on the whole very fine engravings.

Hogarth drew scenes from London life, not always attractive scenes at that, for in some parts where there was poverty and disease, women lay about the streets sobering up from the effects of too much gin, which could be bought for a few pence. Some of his drawings are very frightening.

To make his point, sometimes, Hogarth over-drew his pictures, exaggerated the features of the villains and making the more innocent characters look positively angelic. This was called caricature, and it certainly brought home to many the sharp social contrasts of city life.

Madame de Pompadour who was the mistress of Louis XV

Kay, John (c.1700–1764)
English inventor

In 1728, Kay, who came from Bury in Lancashire, inherited a woollen factory in Essex. He experimented with ways of making a loom work faster, and in about 1733 produced the 'flying shuttle'. This doubled the rate of working a loom. Up to then one man could only work cloth as wide as he could stretch his arms to throw and catch the shuttle. Kay fastened a string to two levers fixed on the loom so that when, with one hand the operator jerked the string to left or right, he flicked the shuttle across one way or other. This left him free to work the comb as well, and so he could work twice as fast. It enabled the loom operator to produce broad cloth, too, the advantages of which are obvious.

Pompadour, Jeanne Antoinette Poisson, Marquise de (1721–1764)
Mistress of Louis XV

Madame de Pompadour first met Louis XV in 1744, and such was this woman's charm over him that the following year she was installed at the palace of Versailles as his mistress.

Between 1745 and 1764, sometimes to the detriment of France, she completely controlled the policies adopted by Louis. Although she was particularly influential in internal affairs, she also recommended the alliance with Austria which was largely responsible for France's disastrous involvement in the Seven Years War (1756–1763).

Cumberland, Prince William Augustus, Duke of (1721–1765)
English general

'Bloody' Cumberland, as he became known because of the frightful cruelty he ordered after the battle of Culloden, in Scotland, in 1746, was the third son of George II. He was appointed to command the government's forces in Scotland which were trying to put down the Second Jacobite Rebellion, led by Bonnie Prince Charlie, the Younger Pretender (*p. 186*).

Prince Charles had had much success to begin with, and even advanced far into England. But having retreated and fought his way through Scotland, the last engagement was at Culloden, near Inverness. The day went against the prince who fled from the field. It was then that Cumberland, when asked whether the defeated should be spared, replied 'No quarter.' These were the most frightful two words uttered in Scotland for many a day. The bulk of the Scots who were ready to surrender were cut down and killed where they stood or sat.

James Edward Stuart (1688–1766)
Scottish Pretender to the British Throne

James Edward Stuart was the son of King James II (1685–1688) and his second wife. When James II was forced to abdicate, he took his family to France, for the English government elected William, Prince of Orange, to rule as William III (*p. 166*). When James II died in 1701, the French king Louis XIV encouraged James Edward to make a claim for the throne, but the conditions were not favourable until 1715. In that year, the Highland Scots rebelled against George I, a German King of England, Scotland and Ireland, and invited James Edward over to take his father's old throne. James however proved a poor leader. Although there were one or two successes, the British government forces triumphed and the revolt was crushed. James left Scotland never to return. He lived for almost fifty years in Italy, mainly in Rome. He married Princess Clementina Sobieski in 1719 and had two sons.

Boucher, François (1703–1770)
French painter

Boucher was favoured by Madame le Pompadour, one of the mistresses of Louis XV, and thus rose to become one of the greatest painters in France. He was appointed court painter in 1765. His work influenced a whole generation of painters, especially in the fields of historical and pastoral subjects. Boucher had a wonderful sense of interpretation of the human body.

Brindley, James (1716–1772)
English canal builder

Imagine being absolutely illiterate and yet being responsible for constructing over 300 miles of canals, with their locks. This was the achievement of Derbyshire-born James Brindley who had been an apprentice millwright. In 1760, the Duke of Bridgewater, who owned coal mines in Lancashire and was finding road charges high for moving his coal about, commissioned Brindley to build a waterway from the mine at Worsley to Manchester.

He did it in about twelve years, and all without paper calculations. He worked it out in his head, and his obvious skill inspired such confidence that men were willing to carry out his instructions without drawings.

Louis XV (1710–1774)
King of France (1715–1774)

Louis XV, great grandson of Louis XIV, succeeded to the throne when only five years old. So for the first part of his reign France was governed by a regent, Philippe, Duke of Orleans.

It was not until the death of Cardinal Fleury in 1743 that Louis started to take more personal control of the administration of the country. But disordered finances gave him a bad start, and he never really recovered. Long affairs with many mistresses, notably Madame de Pompadour, led to his administration growing weaker and more inefficient, while the national economy ran down. He was hated more and more by the discontented masses.

He allowed himself to involve France in the Seven Years War which saw France and Austria fighting Prussia and Britain and as a result of that, through the Treaty of Versailles, he lost the French holds in Canada and India.

But he was the patron of an unique school of artists, interior decorators, cabinet makers, jewellers, potters and builders. The furniture made in Paris in his time, in which he took an enormous personal interest, was the most wonderful furniture ever made.

Scene from the Battle of Plassey in which Robert Clive defeated the Nabob of Bengal to make Bengal a British province

Clive, Robert, 1st Baron Clive of Plassey (1725–1774)
English soldier and governor of Bengal

Clive had been a very rebellious child. When he first went to India as a clerk with the East India Company, aged 18, he became so unhappy that he tried to commit suicide; the gun did not go off, and this marked a change in him. Soon after war broke out in India between England and France; he joined the army and distinguished himself by his bravery. He really made his name, in 1751, when with a small band of men he captured Arcot, the capital of the Carnatic province.

In 1757, as a lieutenant colonel, he was sent to Calcutta to avenge the tragic Black Hole of Calcutta disaster. On the field of Plassey, outside Calcutta, with a much smaller force, he utterly defeated the Nabob of Bengal and then made Bengal a British province.

In 1765 he took over as governor of Bengal and during his term tried to end the corruption which was rife among officials of the East India Company. In doing so he made many enemies, and when he returned to Britain two years later, he found they had engineered a committee to be set up to investigate allegations of his corruption. Although the charges were found groundless, he was embittered, and in 1774 once more turned to suicide. This time he succeeded.

Goldsmith, Oliver (1728–1774)
Irish playwright and poet

Goldsmith dabbled in many things – and failed, except in literature. He began to write seriously in the 1750's and his first success came in 1762 with *Citizen of the World*. The two works which gave him a lasting place in English literature were

The Vicar of Wakefield (a novel) and *She Stoops to Conquer*, a very witty play.

Pugachev, Emil (c.1744–1775)
Russian revolutionary

Pugachev, a Cossack cavalryman, led a rebellion of discontented peasants in south Russia against the Empress Catherine. He made his cause more popular when he claimed to be the Empress's dead husband, Czar Peter III, who was said to have been murdered in 1762. At first he had great success, and took several towns, giving the Russian government cause for concern. But in 1775 he was defeated in a great battle and captured. The government's commander put Pugachev in an iron cage, to humiliate him, and had him dragged to Moscow where he was executed before a huge crowd.

Hume, David (1711–1776)
Scottish historian

Hume was a brilliant Scottish philosopher and historical scholar who also studied law and pursued a career in the diplomatic service. His place in 18th century philosophy was a high one, and he influenced metaphysical thinking for a long time after his years. He wrote important works, among which were a *History of England*, and *a Treatise on Human Nature*.

Voltaire, François Marie Arouet de (1694–1778)
French writer and philosopher

Voltaire was a master of satire as well as being an astute historian and philosopher. But the satirical ability demonstrated in masterpieces such as *Candide* did little to endear him to the French authorities; twice as a young man he found himself imprisoned in the Bastille, the huge fortress prison in Paris, and the latter years of his life were spent in Swiss exile.

For three years of his life he lived in England, and for three years in Prussia where he wrote his epic, *The Age of Louis XIV*. He became an intimate friend of Frederick the Great of Prussia, and whilst he was never enamoured of that country, he did greatly influence the monarch in his advanced ideas of government. Voltaire also made a significant impact on the ideas which led to the outbreak of the French Revolution, in 1789.

Linnaeus, Carolus (1707–1778)
Swedish botanist

Linnaeus is very famous for having spent years studying the flowers, trees and plants of the fields and woods, classifying them according to their types, and giving them all Latin names in families. But he was extremely busy in many other fields as well, such as studying medicine, travelling throughout the remotest parts of Europe, occupying professorial chairs lecturing, and writing about botanical subjects of many kinds.

Pitt, William, Earl of Chatham (1708–1778)
English statesman and war leader

Pitt established himself in Parliament with his oratory and his biting sarcasm, when Walpole (*p. 176*) was still prime minister. He proved his integrity as paymaster general, and this won him a good reputation. In 1756 the Seven Years War broke out between England and France, and during the first months everything went wrong for Britain until Pitt was called to office by the King. He took almost dictatorial powers from 1757–1761 and during that time Britain was victorious.

Pitt was, apart from Winston Churchill, the greatest war leader Britain has ever had. His confidence in his plans helped him succeed, and so did his astuteness in picking the right men for the right commands. His object was to break French dominance in Europe, and he believed he had to do this not just in the battle fields of the continent, but also in India and Canada, both of which were won by splendid victories.

In 1761 Pitt quarrelled with the new King George III, and resigned. From then on he attacked the government, particularly on the harsh measures used in America. He died in the House of Lords while opposing a new tax introduced in America by the government.

Rousseau

Rousseau, Jean Jacques (1712–1778)
French philosopher and writer

Rousseau led a varied life until he found fame with his essays on arts and science, in which he put forward the radical idea that the savage was nobler than the civilized man.

His greatest work was his *Social Contract* which he wrote in 1762. It advocated liberalism and in particular, democracy, alien philosophies to France at that time. In it he stated that men were born free but lived everywhere in chains.

Apart from his philosophical writings he wrote a number of operettas of little repute, and his *Confessions* which were published after his death. Rousseau's works had a direct influence on the political forces which brought about the French Revolution in 1789, and culturally provided an inspiration to the Romantic movement.

Garrick, David (1717–1779)
English actor

Garrick is by tradition regarded as one of the greatest men of the English theatre. Born in Hereford he came to London with Dr. Johnson (*p. 185*) and he made his name with a masterly performance in Shakespeare's *Richard III*. He continued to have great success in Shakespearian plays and amassed a considerable amount of money. He also made a multitude of friends in the literary world.

Chippendale, Thomas (1718–1779)
English furniture designer

Chippendale designed and made some of the finest furniture ever to come out of 18th century England. He began as a woodcraft apprentice in Yorkshire, and sometime about 1748 he wandered to London to set up a small furniture business in St. Martin's Lane. He made furniture to order for many famous houses, like Woburn (the home of the Dukes of Bedford) and Harewood in Yorkshire. Sometimes he made pieces suggested, or actually designed, by the great Scottish architect Robert Adam (*p. 190*).

Chippendale became famous when in

Furniture designed by Thomas Chippendale

1754 he published *The Gentleman and Cabinet Maker's Director*, a sort of catalogue of furniture designs. This was enormously successful. His influence has been far reaching, but many experts prefer the ideas of Hepplewhite and Sheraton (*pp. 186, 198*).

Cook, James (1728–1779)
English navigator and explorer

Cook was one of the most accomplished navigators in history. As a young sea captain he was sent on a survey of the St. Lawrence river in Canada. Then he went out to the Pacific ocean in the *Endeavour* to observe the transit of the planet Venus. He also charted New Zealand and much of the Australian coast, and came back via the Cape of Good Hope.

A short while afterwards, Cook went out to the Pacific again, this time to look for another continent that was believed to be somewhere to the south of Australia. He did not find it, as there is not one there, unless you include Antarctica, but he did find several interesting groups of islands like the New Hebrides and the Tahiti group.

In 1776 Cook went out to the Pacific once more, but this time it was a journey

with a sad ending. He was to look for a passage across the top of North America, from the Pacific side. His journey took him to Hawaii, and it was there that he was murdered by natives with whom he had wanted to be friendly, but who misunderstood his gestures.

Maria Theresa (1717–1780)
Empress of Austria (1740-1780)
Maria Theresa succeeded to the Austrian throne in 1740 and with it acquired the lands of the Hapsburgs. This was the main cause of the Austrian Succession War which lasted for the first eight years of her reign. She lost Silesia to Frederick the Great of Prussia and Austrian lands in Italy to Naples.

She carried out reforms internally which strengthened the resources of Austria, but she was again humiliated when an alliance with France led to war with England and Prussia in which Austria was badly defeated. One of her territories, Hungary, always fought magnificently on her behalf.

Blackstone, Sir William (1723–1780)
English legal expert
Blackstone was a legal scholar who made little progress in a legal career. So he turned to lecturing on law, and in 1758 became the first Vinerian Professor of English Law at Oxford University.

From 1765 to 1769 he published a series of *Commentaries on the Laws of England*. It soon became the most important statement on style and accuracy in English law, and it earned him a lot of money. The *Commentaries* are still referred to in English law courts.

Johnson, Samuel (1709–1784)
English writer, lexicographer and wit
Johnson, the son of a Lichfield bookseller, spent his whole childhood among books. He went to Pembroke College, Oxford, but never took his degree because of his extreme idleness.

After an unsuccessful attempt to start a school, Johnson went to London where he earned a meagre living as a freelance writer. In 1747 he began work on his famous dictionary which took him eight years to complete. But when it was published it brought him instant fame. He was inundated with people wishing to talk with him, and with offers from publishers. He received an honorary degree from Oxford University.

Because of his wit he was often called upon to entertain at dinner parties. He formed the Literary Club, a select gathering of London wits and intellectuals.

He spent most of the rest of his life in comparative luxury, living in the region of Fleet Street and the Law Courts, for nearly 50 years.

Diderot, Denis (1713–1784)
French philosopher
Diderot spent twenty years on a huge work, the *Encyclopedia*, or *Dictionnaire Raisonné des Sciences, des Arts et des Métiers*, in 28 volumes. This was in effect a manual of intellectual war, providing progressive thinkers with an armoury of information and opinion with which to counter the forces of reaction represented by the King, and the Paris aristocracy. He was also a novelist, poet, playwright and a shrewd, original and progressive literary critic.

Choiseul, Étienne François, Duc de (1719–1785)
French statesman

Choiseul both rose and fell through the whim of his King's mistresses. It was after serving with distinction as a soldier in the war of the Austrian Succession, that he caught the eye of Madame de Pompadour, the mistress of Louis XV, and soon afterwards he was promoted to lieutenant-general.

He was then appointed ambassador to Vienna and to Rome before returning to France to take control of the army ministry where he made vast improvements. He led the nation into the Seven Years War, and at the end of it negotiated for France the best terms possible, in the 1763 Treaty of Paris. Thereafter he was, for about 11 years, a close adviser and friend of the king.

Frederick II, The Great (1712–1786)
King of Prussia (1740–1786)

Frederick II was known as Frederick the Great for his major achievements in increasing Prussia's importance in Europe. As a young man he tried to get away from his father and his influence, but he was arrested, charged with being a deserter and led to believe he would be severely punished.

The year that he became King he tried to bring Silesia under Prussian control and began the War of the Austrian Succession, which lasted for several years. In alliance with France and Bavaria he won battles at Mollwitz, Cholusitz, and in 1744 he invaded Bohemia. At the peace of Dresden in 1745 he secured Silesia.

In 1756 he made an alliance with England and then began the Seven Years War against Austria, France, Russia, Sweden and Saxony. During this war his military genius shone out, and although he was beaten in several battles he continued to show great determination. After the peace Prussia emerged as a great military state.

Frederick was also a splendid king in time of peace. He instituted reforms and encouraged many fundamental changes in his country. He was also a writer and his works included *Memoirs of the House of Brandenburg* and a *History of the Seven Years War*.

Hepplewhite, George (d.1786)
English furniture designer

Hepplewhite was a mystery. Nothing is known of his beginnings, or even his date of birth. He seems to have learned cabinet making in Lancashire, and then come to London to set up in business designing and possibly making pieces, like Chippendale, for the houses of the wealthy. He died in 1786. Two years later, his widow published his own catalogue of designs called *The Cabinet Maker and Upholsterer's Guide*. This made his name famous. It had 300 pictures, many showing the influence of Robert Adam, and on the whole the designs are more delicate than those of Chippendale. There is no furniture anywhere known to have been made by Hepplewhite.

Charles Edward Stuart, Prince (1720–1788)
Pretender to the throne in Britain

Bonnie Prince Charlie, as he was called, is one of the most colourful characters in British folk history. It was he who in 1745 led a daring rebellion to reinstate the Stuarts on the British throne. His father James Edward (son of James II) was, they claimed, the rightful heir.

He landed in the Western Highlands and marched to Edinburgh which he captured. He then decisively beat the English army at Prestonpans. Six weeks later he arrived in England, marched down and took Derby where his troops rested.

When news reached London that Charles was just 125 miles away, the Hanoverian king, George II, prepared to quit the country, and many of his ministers considered joining the pretender. It is commonly supposed that had Charles pressed on he could have taken London. But he did not receive the support from the English he would have done 30 years earlier, and on the advice of his friends he turned back.

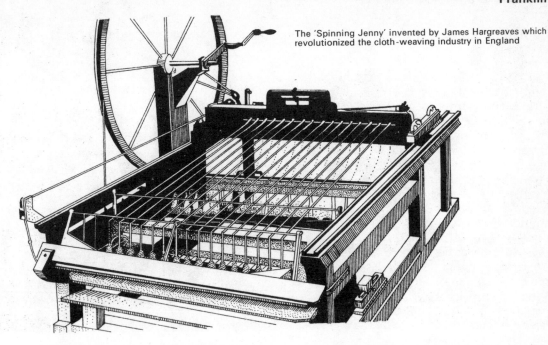

The 'Spinning Jenny' invented by James Hargreaves which revolutionized the cloth-weaving industry in England

Eventually he was beaten at Culloden by the Duke of Cumberland.

With a high price on his head Charles was helped across to the continent by Flora Macdonald. He spent the rest of his life a despondent drunkard, and was buried in Rome along with his father.

Hargreaves, James (1720–1788)
English inventor
Hargreaves invented the 'Spinning Jenny'. This was a spinning engine, whereby one man could work several spinning wheels at one time. First demonstrated in 1764, it led to a revolution in cloth weaving in England. It is a remarkable fact that Hargreaves was illiterate.

The machine could do the work of thirty men in the same period of time, but you will appreciate this frightened workers who saw themselves threatened with redundancy. Some smashed up his home and drove him out of Lancashire. He settled in Nottingham, but died very poor.

Gainsborough, Thomas (1727–1788)
English painter
As a young man in his native Suffolk Gainsborough showed a decided talent for painting, and at the age of 14 he was sent to London to study. Six years later he set up a studio in Ipswich where he painted portraits, and his success was such that he soon moved to the more prosperous city of Bath.

His skill brought him widespread fame and in turn a place in the Royal Academy when it was first created in 1768. Notable among his portrait subjects are *The Blue Boy*, *Mrs. Siddons* and *Garrick*.

Franklin, Benjamin (1706–1790)
American scientist and statesman
Franklin was one of the most distinguished Americans of the 18th century. He was born of poor parents and was largely self-taught. As a young man he printed and published his own newspaper, the *Pennsylvania Gazette*, and in time he became influential in Pennsylvanian state politics. Franklin was also very interested in physics, and he carried out many experiments, especially connected with electricity. It was he who invented the lightning conductor.

By 1775, his fame was such that the men who were building the new American republic invited his views about the Declaration of Independence, and later about the American Constitution.

John Wesley preaching Methodism to the American Indians

Smith, Adam (1723–1790)
Scottish economist

Smith was a member of the brilliant intellectual group which dominated Scottish – and indeed English-speaking scholarship – in the middle of the 18th century. In 1767 he went into the country to prepare a revolutionary work on economics. Called an *Inquiry into the Nature and Causes of the Wealth of Nations* (known for short as *Wealth of Nations*), it was a searching analysis of division of labour, money, prices, wages and means of distribution. It had a marked influence in political circles throughout the Western world. Smith was also a member of Dr. Johnson's famous Literary Club.

Joseph II (1741–1790)
Holy Roman Emperor (1765–1790)

Joseph was Maria Theresa's son (*p. 185*) and ruled Austria jointly with her from 1765 to 1780. When Poland was broken up and divided between her neighbours, for the first time in 1772, he acquired a large area for Austria. When his mother died in 1780, he assumed full power, and he ruled with a firm hand, curbing the power of the Church.

Wesley, John (1703–1791)
English founder of Methodism

Imagine preaching forty thousand sermons in a life time, travelling over 5,000 miles a year for forty years to do it, writing numerous hymn tunes, verses, books and pamphlets, visiting hundreds of homes, organizing many discussions and meetings, all in the interests of a new branch of Christianity called Methodism. All this was done by one man, John Wesley, who in the 1740's began to preach the new religion, which did not allow bishops, refuted all high church theology, ritual and dress, and actually allowed people who were not ordained priests to preach and even take services.

Eighteenth century England and Wales, and to a lesser extent Scotland, were easily receptive to this new faith, largely because of the miseries of the Industrial Revolution. By the last decades of the century there were sharp class differences which had not been there fifty or more years earlier. Working men associated the orthodox Church of England with their oppressors, and so took to Methodism as a political gesture as much as a religious one.

Wesley certainly worked well. When

he died his new religion was extremely secure, and it has remained so ever since.

Potemkin, Gregor Alexandrovich (1731–1791)
Russian statesman

Potemkin was an extraordinary man who became the lover – and possibly the secret husband – of the Empress Catherine of Russia, and then when she tired of him, found her a succession of replacement men friends.

His career began in the army, and in 1771 he came to the notice of the Empress who fell in love with his handsomeness. For the next twenty years Potemkin guided Russian politics with her, and on the whole he did this well, to the considerable advantage of the country. Among his achievements were the building of the Black Sea Fleet, the annexation of the Crimea, the defeat of the Turks in several campaigns, and the founding of the city, fortress and port of Sebastopol.

Mirabeau, Honoré Gabriel Victor Riquetti, Comte de (1749–1791)
French orator and revolutionary leader

Mirabeau, an aristocrat by birth, was always a revolutionary. When in the army in early life, he was imprisoned on several occasions for wild behaviour and intrigue.

In 1789 he was a member of the States General and during the first two years of the French Revolution he played a leading part, chiefly in trying to moderate the more extreme elements.

He was against the total abolition of monarchy, for he believed in it, but with restricted powers. In 1791 he was elected president of the National Assembly, but died soon afterwards.

Mozart, Wolfgang Amadeus (1756–1791)
Austrian composer

Mozart came from a well known family of musicians. He showed talent from a very early age, especially on the harpsichord. But although he was later to become well respected and to have appointments to Austrian royalty, he died in poverty.

He wrote over 600 works, including many lively operas such as *The Marriage of Figaro*, *Don Giovanni* and *Cosi Fan Tutte*, many symphonies and a lot of chamber music as well as religious music. He feared he was being poisoned, and while writing his last *Requiem Mass*, he fancied he was composing his funeral song.

Rodney, George Brydges, 1st Baron (1719–1792)
English admiral

Rodney began his career as an administrator. He was Governor of Newfoundland from 1748 to 1752. In 1751 he got himself elected M.P. at Westminster – in his absence, and then after leaving Newfoundland, he pursued a career in the navy.

As an admiral during the Seven Years War (1756–1763) Rodney made himself widely famous for several exploits. He captured St. Vincent and Grenada, and then took Martinique. In 1778 he was made admiral. In 1780 he seized a whole Spanish convoy off Cape Finisterre, and near Cape St. Vincent seized seven more ships out of eleven in another convoy.

The crowning victory of his career was off Dominica in 1782 when he smashed a French fleet under Admiral de Grasse and captured de Grasse himself.

Reynolds, Sir Joshua (1723–1792)
English painter

Perhaps the most celebrated art institution in this country is the Royal Academy of Art. Its first president was Sir Joshua Reynolds, who was elected in 1768, a year before being knighted by George III.

At this time portrait painting was fashionable, and although Reynolds preferred landscape works he dedicated himself to portraiture and became the leading artist in this field. The subjects of his pictures include *Dr. Johnson*, *Oliver Goldsmith* and *Edmund Burke*. He was a member of Dr. Johnson's famous Literary Club.

Adam, Robert (1728–1792)
Scottish architect

Adam introduced a whole new range of architectural ideas into 18th century British building design and decoration. They were based on ancient classical principles which he had studied closely on a long visit to excavations near Pompeii in Italy. His new ideas were much more graceful and light than the heavy Baroque style which was beginning to wear thin in Britain in the middle of the 18th century.

Adam designed many famous homes, including Osterley Park, Middlesex, Harewood House, Yorkshire, and the Adelphi Buildings in London's Strand. He also designed furniture and commissioned well known cabinet makers like Chippendale (*p. 184*) to carry out his decorative designs. It is sad to relate that Adam was seldom paid by his customers, and he was bankrupted.

Arkwright, Sir Richard (1732–1792)
English inventor

Arkwright was a barber in Bolton in Lancashire. In the 1760s he got interested in the 'Spinning Jenny' of Hargreaves (*p. 187*) which revolutionized the weaving industry. He and his colleague, John Kay (*p. 180*), developed a machine that would do the 'Jenny's' job by water power. It was called a Spinning frame, and it was capable of producing a fine yarn of great strength.

Kay and Hargreaves never made much money from their ideas, but Arkwright was more lucky. He became rich, attracted the attention of George III, who loved inventions, and received a knighthood.

Du Barri, Madame (c.1743–1793)
French courtesan

Madame du Barri, who was born Marie Jeanne Becu, became mistress of Louis XV in 1768. She was already someone else's mistress, and seems to have carried on both liaisons for some time. She patronized arts and crafts, especially furniture makers, and commissioned many elaborate pieces of furniture for her palace at Valenciennes. Robespierre (*p. 192*) arrested her in 1793 and she was tried and executed by guillotine.

Louis XVI (1754–1793)
King of France (1774–1793)

When Louis XVI came to the throne of France in 1774 the people were already discontented. In the early years of his reign, however, many of their grievances about taxation and finance were alleviated by some good measures.

But Louis' extravagant wife, Marie Antoinette, (*p. 190*), overruled him on several occasions and many able ministers like Necker were dismissed. There was growing criticism of the spending at Court and this led to the calling of the States General in 1789. In July of the same year the Revolution broke out.

Louis' life was endangered by the death of Mirabeau (*p. 189*). Louis tried to escape from France, got as far as the border but was caught there and brought back to Paris. He was deposed by the national convention and a republic was declared. He was then tried for treason, found guilty and executed, in January 1793.

Marie Antoinette (1755–1793)
Queen of France (1774–1793)

This silly and extravagant woman made herself extremely unpopular in France, turned the French people against her husband, Louis XVI, and eventually drove him to be deposed and finally executed.

She was the daughter of Emperor Francis I of the Holy Roman Empire. She married Louis when he was heir to the French throne. Once she was in France she behaved badly, and was arrogant with her French courtiers. She spent the country's money wildly, so much that she came to be called 'Madame Deficit'.

When the Revolution broke out in 1789, she tried to get Louis, who was not personally very unpopular, to leave Paris and escape abroad. But they were caught and brought back in ignominy. She still learned nothing, and sent a

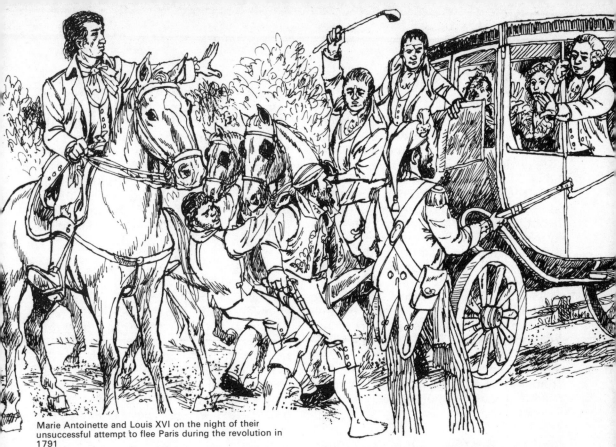

Marie Antoinette and Louis XVI on the night of their unsuccessful attempt to flee Paris during the revolution in 1791

message to foreign powers to bring forces against France to liberate her and Louis. These were intercepted, and in 1792 both were tried. Louis was executed in January 1793 and Marie Antoinette followed him to the guillotine in September.

Gibbon, Edward (1737–1794)
English historian

Gibbon's name rests almost entirely upon one work – but what a magnificent work it was, the *Decline and Fall of the Roman Empire*, in five large volumes. It took him years to complete this most detailed and accurate story of the days of ancient Rome; the first volume appeared in 1776. For generations it remained a standard work, and it was years before any of his fundamental propositions were shown to be at fault.

Gibbon was a member of parliament for several years. He was made commissioner of trade and plantations. He also moved in the best literary circles; towards the end of his life he moved away from England and settled in France.

Lavoisier, Antoine (1743–1794)
French chemist

Lavoisier was a brilliant scientist who demonstrated that matter is indestructible. He also showed that chemical reaction could be expressed in terms of a chemical equation. This interesting man worked as a government scientist for nearly 20 years, but when the Revolution came, the revolutionaries arrested him and eventually guillotined him on the grounds that the new France had no need for men of science.

Hébert, Jacques René (1755–1794)
French journalist and revolutionary

Hébert experienced poverty for several years in Paris in the 1780s. He also published subversive newspapers attacking the king and the government. When the Revolution broke out in 1789, Hébert readily joined the revolutionary ranks. He was an extreme radical who denied the existence of God. Robespierre, who was the dominant person in France in 1792–1794, had Hébert arrested and guillotined because of his extreme views.

Robespierre, Maximilien François (1758–1794)
French revolutionary

Robespierre was known to his contempories as the 'Incorruptible'. He was an extremist, a very sincere man, and completely dedicated to his cause. He had been a member of the States General since the start of the French Revolution in 1789, but it was not until 1792 that he became leader of the radical left, when he successfully called for the removal of the other leaders, Danton and Hébert. He was one of those who insisted on the execution of the king, Louis XVI.

As chairman of the Second Committee of Public Safety he virtually became prime minister, and was largely responsible for the Reign of Terror which followed. Many people, some quite innocent, were sent to the guillotine. Ironically he was himself overthrown by revolutionaries and guillotined very soon afterwards.

Danton, Georges Jacques (1759–1794)
French revolutionary

Before the Parliament of Paris in 1791 Danton, like many of his revolutionary comrades, was a lawyer. At about this time he became an extreme radical and it was he who helped stir up the Tuileries riots. He rose to become leader of the revolutionaries.

The following year he was elected to the National Convention and was among those that voted for the execution of the deposed king, Louis XVI. He was president of The Jacobin Club whose members formed the backbone of the Revolutionary party, and who took power. But he was in turn thrown out and eventually executed by Robespierre.

Wedgwood, Josiah (1730–1795)
English potter

Wedgwood brought a new dimension to pottery in the country. He opened a factory in Staffordshire which he called the Etruria works, and in it he modelled all sorts of vases, bowls, jugs and so forth, in ancient classical styles. This rendered pottery a very beautiful thing to look at. Previously the beauty of these things had been confined to porcelain, a material invented and made by the Chinese for centuries, but whose secret had only been discovered fairly recently, in Europe, by Bottger (*p. 170*).

Wedgwood became extremely rich. He commissioned the best artists of the day like Reynolds and Gainsborough to produce designs for his workmen to make in pottery.

Boswell, James (1740–1795)
Scottish author

Boswell is best remembered for his friendship with Dr. Samuel Johnson (*p. 185*) and for the biography that he wrote of the great man. His tremendous admiration for Johnson can be measured by the length of time he spent with him, very frequently as a butt for his jokes.

Boswell associated with many of the great British and European writers of the day, and was also a lawyer.

Robespierre and the revolutionary instrument of execution, the guillotine

Catherine the Great

Catherine the Great (1729–1796)
Czarina of Russia (1762–1796)
Catherine the Great was not even Russian, though she ruled and loved the country as if her roots had been embedded there for generations. She was a German princess who married Czar Peter III. He was almost moronic, spending his time playing with tin soldiers when important matters of state required urgent attention. In 1762 he was deposed, probably with her connivance, and the nobles elected her to rule. She had already shown she was a woman of spirit. Now she showed she had intellect, political skill and courage.

Catherine wanted to introduce many new ideas of government. At first, she had the support of the nobles, but when she said it was time that serfdom, on which their estates thrived, was abolished, they said it was excessive, and she had to abandon her scheme. This was unfortunate, because in doing so she went back on promises, and this made her much more unpopular than she need have been.

In the 1770s, Russia was faced with a dangerous revolt, led by Emil Pugachev (*p. 183*) who claimed to be her dead husband. For some years he was successful, largely because many Russians wanted him to succeed as he would be better than Catherine. But government forces wore Pugachev down and he was caught and put to death. Catherine introduced many western European ideas into Russia, and had buildings and furniture designed and constructed by western architects and craftsmen.

Burns, Robert (1759–1796)
Scottish poet
Robbie Burns is Scotland's national poet. Some of his verse is perhaps second rate, but much of his work is very fine indeed, such as the *Cotter's Saturday Night*, and *Tam O'Shanter*.

Burns was a farmer by inheritance and not by choice. He let the farm run down because he did not know how to run it, nor did he care much. Instead he was composing verses, and in the 1780s he began to publish. He was a great success in Edinburgh literary and social circles, and he became very famous. At the same time, he could not live on the money he earned, and he worked in the Customs Department. Burn's health gave out before he was 40.

Walpole, Horace, 4th Earl of Orford (1717–1797)
English man of letters
Walpole was the youngest son of the first prime minister of England, Robert Walpole (*p. 176*) and inherited his title after the deaths of two elder brothers. He devoted his life to writing, making friendships with literary and artistic men, and to cultural activity. He bought a house, called Strawberry Hill, near Twickenham, and altered it to look like a Gothic mansion, in an age when Baroque and Palladian architecture were still the rage.

He had a printing press on which he published his own works, and some of those of famous friends, like Gray. He also wrote hundreds of amusing and informative letters which are a splendid insight into 18th century literary manners.

Wilkes, John (1727–1797)
English political agitator and reformer

Wilkes' early life was a rather unconventional one. He belonged to a depraved set of people who indulged in orgies at Medmenham Abbey, the home of the Dashwood family, in Buckinghamshire. But after a while, he began to take some notice of the society of his day, and started a newspaper called the *North Briton* with which he attacked the king, ministers and all kinds of people on various grounds. Then he stood for Parliament, won a seat, but was arrested when he went to the Commons to take it. So he stood again and was elected again, and expelled again. The London mob was furious, carried him round London shoulder high and clamoured for justice for Wilkes.

He kept up his campaigns for parliamentary reform, and got himself elected lord mayor of London in 1774. In that year the Commons felt it had to admit him, and he took his seat, keeping it for sixteen years. Wilkes was a reformer, and one of his achievements was ensuring that newspapermen had uninterrupted freedom to report parliamentary debates.

Burke, Edmund (1729–1797)
Irish politician, orator and writer

Although a notable politician, it is as a writer that Burke is best remembered. A fiery Irishman, his ideas were very advanced for his day. He supported Fox in his opposition to George III, Wilberforce in his opposition to slavery, and the Americans in their fight for independence from Britain.

He was, however, opposed to the French Revolution because he feared it aimed to overthrow both organized government and Christianity. Macaulay said of him that the time would never come when men would not be wiser for reading his books. Among these was *Reflections on the French Revolution* (1790).

Galvani, Luigi (1737–1798)
Italian physicist

If you connect a very mild electric current to the pair of legs of a frog, the frog will jump. So, of course, would you if you put the current on your legs and increased it! This action is called galvanization, and was named after the distinguished Italian physicist, Galvani, who demonstrated the effects of electricity on animals and said that the twitching was the result of electricity being present in the body.

Tone, Wolfe (1763–1798)
Irish rebel leader

Tone was an Ulsterman who gave his life to the cause of Irish independence. He wrote pamphlets attacking English government methods in Ireland, and he organized rebel groups, finally welding them in a body called the Society of United Irishmen who sought no less than complete independence.

He then went to France to enlist support for a revolutionary uprising to be backed by a landing of French troops in Ireland. This was obtained, but the force was scattered at sea before it could land. He was captured, tried and executed in public.

Ch'ien Lung (1711–1799)
Chinese Emperor (1736–1796)

Ch'ien Lung was one of the most remarkable of a long succession of emperors in China. He increased the territory of his country, patronized the arts, encouraged porcelain manufacture, and organized a catalogue of the imperial library. Ch'ien was particularly anxious to maintain good relations with European countries, and he encouraged traders who wanted to set up enterprises in Chinese ports.

Howe, Richard, 1st Earl (1726–1799)
English admiral

Howe won a great victory at sea against the French, in June 1794. It was long remembered as the Glorious First of June. It was a particularly distinguished achievement on his part, for at the time he was nearly 70, far older than sea captains of the age were wont to sail out into battle. He was made an earl and promoted to admiral of the fleet.

George Washington

Washington, George (1732–1799)
First President of the United States (1789–1797)

Washington was commander of the armies of the colonists in North America who in 1774 rebelled against the British government. They were protesting about having to pay huge taxes to the British government whilst they had no representation in the Westminster Parliament which imposed the taxes.

In a nine-year war he succeeded in overwhelming the British government forces, and forced Britain to recognize the independence of the United States, which had already been declared on 4 July 1776.

Washington's career was unblemished, and his success so decisive, that when the Americans came to elect their first president it was not hard to guess who it would be. He held office for two terms.

Suvorov, Count Alexander Vasilievich (1729–1800)
Russian general

Suvorov was a Russian general, but he had been born a Finnish national of Swedish descent. He fought in the Seven Years War, and held high command in the Russian War with Turkey of 1773–1774. When the two antagonists went to war again in 1787, Suvorov was appointed commander in chief and he beat the Turks in a great battle where the day was carried by a spectacular bayonet charge by Suvorov's troops. He succeeded also in beating French armies in Italy in 1799.

Kant, Immanuel (1724–1804)
German philosopher

Kant was a very distinguished and original philosopher. In three important works, *The Critique of Pure Reason*, *The Critique of Practical Reason*, and *The Critique of Judgment*, he tried to harmonize materialism with idealism. Up to then, believers in each had claimed that their system was the only one. He said that experience alone provides us with knowledge, but that from the beginning in men's minds there exist certain ideas quite independent of experience which can be applied to the material which experience provides.

His own life was uneventful. He was not married, he never wandered very far from the place where he was born and died, Königsberg, where he was professor of logic and metaphysics from 1770 to 1797. His influence on western philosophy has been enormous.

Necker, Jacques (1732–1804)
French financier and statesman

Necker was one of the few men in the 18th century capable of introducing some order to the French finances. During the Seven Years War (1756–1763) he made his fortune. He became minister of finances on the removal of Turgot. He introduced reforms, improved the efficiency of the state's finances and made the taxation system fairer.

He was dismissed in 1781 by Louis XVI for his support for Protestantism, but was recalled in 1788. He was again dismissed, the following year, when he advised the king to call a meeting of the States General, (the French Parliament). This proved to be a prelude to the outbreak of the French Revolution.

Priestley, Joseph (1733–1804)
English chemist

The human body cannot survive long without oxygen. This vitally important gas, which has many other uses as well, was discovered by Dr. Priestley, a chemist who in the 18th century made many important discoveries. He was also a minister of the church.

Priestly is credited with having first made hydrochloric acid, which is sometimes called Spirits of Salt; sulphur dioxide, a pungent gas which has good disinfecting qualities; and ammonia, a very astringent gas which also has disinfecting properties.

Cornwallis, Charles, 1st Marquis (1738–1805)
English general

Cornwallis had a long and distinguished career as a military leader, though he was not always successful in battle. He first came to prominence in the American War of Independence when he was made a major-general. In 1781 he was defeated at Yorktown by the Americans, with French help. The loss of the American states was hailed with anger by many in Britain, and Cornwallis, whose defeat was one of the final events of the war, might have been disgraced.

As it was, he was made commander-in-chief in India, in 1786, and went on to cover himself with glory there. He smashed the rebel Tippoo Sahib at Seringapatam in 1791. For this he was made a marquis. Then he went to Ireland as viceroy, in 1798, and won distinction for his firm but moderate methods.

Nelson, Horatio, Viscount (1758–1805)
British admiral

Nelson is, unquestionably, the greatest admiral in the history of the world. He was not only a wonderful leader of men, he also had the courage to try daring new tactics, which invariably succeeded.

He was the sixth child in a Norfolk parson's family of 11 and first went to sea on board his uncle Captain Maurice Suckling's ship. When he was just 17 years old he lost his eye in the siege of Corsica.

But it was in 1797, as rear admiral, that he first rose to fame as a naval commander. He was then serving under Admiral Sir John Jervis and played a vital part in winning the Battle of Cape St. Vincent for Britain. Soon after he lost an arm in a siege on the Canary Isles.

At this time sailors suffered tremendous hardships; frequent flogging and terrible food were normal. Nelson was a man of great humanity and sympathized with the lot of the ordinary seaman.

In 1798 Nelson was searching for Napoleon and the French fleet in the Mediterranean. He caught up with them at Aboukir Bay at the mouth of the Nile and attacking after dark succeeded in destroying all but two frigates. It was a brilliant victory. Nelson was wounded in the head. He went to Naples to recuperate, and it was there that he met Emma Hamilton, wife of Sir William Hamilton. She nursed him back to health and they fell in love. Her husband did not seem to mind. Nelson returned to action, serving under Admiral Sir Hyde Parker in the North Sea.

At the battle of Copenhagen in 1801 Nelson was about to make a typically daring strike when Hyde Parker signalled him to retreat. Nelson lifted his telescope to his blind eye and told his captains 'I really do not see the signal' – and ordered the advance. The French and Danish fleets were routed.

In 1803 he was made Commander in Chief of the Mediterranean fleet which was blockading the French at Toulon. They were allowed to leave the harbour, and Nelson pursued them in his flagship *Victory*. He caught up with them near Cape Trafalgar in October 1805.

On the 21st the two fleets drew up in broadside lines ready for action. Nelson signalled his famous command 'England expects that every man will do his duty' and then took an unusual step by attacking the French at a right angle. But as *Victory* broke through their lines a French sharp shooter spotted him walking on the deck, and shot him.

The death of Nelson at the moment of victory

Nelson died soon after hearing the news that the battle had been won, thanking God that he had done his duty.

Schiller, Johann Christoph Friedrich von (1759–1805)
German poet, playwright and philosopher

Schiller was the son of an army surgeon, who received a strict military education before he turned to writing. He began by writing a stirring romantic drama called *die Räuber*. Then he took to writing historical works, and obtained the post of professor of history at Jena University. He became very friendly with Goethe (*p. 210*), and this led him to produce poetry, some of it extremely fine and regarded among the best of all German poetry.

From 1799 to his death he lived at Weimar, chiefly to concentrate on writing, but also to be near Goethe whom he revered. He produced many plays, including *Wallenstein*, *Maria Stuart*, and *William Tell*. From his early days to his maturity, the theme of his plays was always the idealist, an interest reflected in his philosophical writings, which were inspired by Kant (*p. 195*).

Fragonard, Jean Honoré (1732–1806)
French painter and engraver

Fragonard studied art under the great Boucher (*p. 181*). He was commissioned to produce a set of paintings by Madame du Barri for her home at Versailles. He also produced a number of engravings that are considered among the greatest to have come out of France.

Fox, Charles James (1749–1806)
English politician and orator

Fox came into the House of Commons at the age of 19, after being educated at Eton and Oxford. He joined the Tories and was soon appointed to office. But when the War of American Independence broke out in 1774 he found his sympathies lay with the colonists, and he crossed over to join the Whigs. It was then that he first revealed his gifts of oratory.

He was a champion of liberty and he opposed the expansion of the powers of the king, George III. He campaigned for parliamentary reform. In 1782 he was made foreign secretary, but his friendship with the extravagant Prince of Wales, whom the King detested, led to his dismissal.

He led the opposition to the young William Pitt when that 24-year-old genius became prime minister. After Pitt's death he became foreign secretary in a coalition government, but died later the same year.

Pitt, William 'the Younger' (1759–1806)
English statesman

Pitt, the Younger, son of the Earl of Chatham (*p. 183*), was a child prodigy. He graduated from Cambridge at the age of seventeen and was an M.P. at twenty.

He showed extraordinary talent as an orator and politician and at twenty-three was made Chancellor of the Exchequer. When the Government fell, in December 1783, George III took the unprecedented step of asking Pitt to form a ministry. It was labelled the 'mince-pie' ministry, since it was considered unlikely to last beyond Christmas. However it lasted till April when Pitt called a general election and was overwhelmingly returned to power. He headed the government for seventeen years.

His domestic policies cut back the national debt and he cut duties to bring about a greater freedom of trade. He introduced an India Act which reframed the constitution of the East India Company.

In 1801 he disagreed with George III over the question of admitting Roman Catholics to Parliament and resigned. In 1804 he was returned to power and tried to form another coalition of powers against Napoleon. The next year saw Nelson's magnificent victory at Trafalgar, but six weeks later Napoleon's crushing success at Austerlitz marked the death of the newly formed coalition. The next year Pitt, the strong, determined and courageous leader died, exhausted, after a short but incredibly active life.

Sheraton, Thomas (1751–1806)
English furniture designer

Sheraton was a brash north country craftsman and designer who came from Stockton-on-Tees. He had a hard youth, made little money, and finally came to London to try to do better. But we know nothing of any workshop or business. Nor is there any furniture actually made by him surviving anywhere.

He published a book of designs, in which among other things he criticized other cabinet makers and designers, like Hepplewhite and Chippendale. He advocated the use of light colour woods, like satinwood, and he favoured painting chairs, tables, etc. There is no doubt about the beauty of his ideas, and they strongly influenced English and European design for some time.

Haydn, Franz Joseph (1732–1809)
Austrian composer

Haydn's musical career began in the choir of St. Stephen's, Vienna, with which he sang for nine years. After that, he wrote under patronage, many operas, masses, sonatas, symphonies and oratorios – demonstrating his versatility.

A friendship with Mozart helped him develop his ideas on the orchestra, and later he became recognized as the first true master of the symphony. He wrote the Austrian national anthem, over 100 symphonies, some of which are often played today in concert halls around the world, and oratorios like *The Creation*.

Paine, Thomas (1737–1809)
English political thinker

Tom Paine was the author of a remarkable work called *The Rights of Man*. This was a defence of the French Revolution, which also consisted of a call to the British to throw out their monarchy and set up a revolutionary government. He had to leave England, and he went to France to assist the revolutionary government, of which he had been elected a member.

Paine had emigrated to America in the year of the outbreak of the War of Independence. He published a pamphlet called *Common Sense* on independence for the American colonists, and this influenced the famous Declaration of Independence of 1776.

Montgolfier Brothers, The, Joseph (1740–1810) and Jacques (1745–1799)
French aviators

Many attempts of one kind and another were made to fly in the 18th century. One of the more successful was the hot air balloon experiment of the Montgolfier brothers. The balloon had a cage suspended below it, and a brazier of burning coal heated the air above it, pushing a jet of hot air into the balloon, causing it to lift off the ground. Its travels through the air were dependent on natural winds. The Montgolfier balloon got off the ground and remained airborne, for the first time, for about ten minutes, at Annonay in France, in June 1783.

Hofer, Andreas (1767–1810)
Tyrolean patriot

Hofer was a romantic hero of Tyrolean birth. His people, who for the most part occupied mountain villages, objected to the Bavarian government's rule over them, and in 1809, led by him, they rebelled. In the first engagement Hofer defeated the Bavarian government forces, and the shock ran round central Europe. The next year, Hofer was himself beaten in battle, but not by the Bavarian government alone, who were assisted by France. Hofer was captured and shot.

Ney, Michel (1769–1815)
French marshal in Napoleonic armies

Ney was engaged in many of Napoleon's battles and was granted several honours by him. He was one of Napoleon's most trusted marshals.

After Napoleon abdicated in 1814, Ney was made peer by Louis XVIII, but he rallied to Napoleon when he returned from Elba, and commanded the Old Guard of his army at Waterloo. When Napoleon had been defeated there, Ney was executed for treason.

Fulton, Robert (1765–1815)
American engineer and inventor

Fulton, who was born in Lancaster County, U.S.A., started life as an artist, travelling to Britain to study painting. But in 1793 he gave it up to concentrate on mechanics and engineering.

He held patents for various machines for spinning flax and rope. His greatest achievement, although he could not interest anyone in it at the time, was a submarine which he built in France. If he could have produced a fleet of submarines, they would have been in a position to sink most of Nelson's fleet.

He also built one of the first steamships to be produced at a reasonable cost.

Sheridan, Richard Brinsley (1751–1816)
Irish playwright and politician

Sheridan's work was in the great tradition of the Irish playwrights, and his wit won him prominence in the latter part of the 18th century. Before he was 24 he wrote *The Rivals*, which was a great success and which remains a standard work of English literature. His other great triumphs were *The School for Scandal* and *The Critic*

He entered parliament in 1780 and won a considerable following with his skilled oratory. He became a friend of the Prince of Wales who introduced him to gambling. This was the beginning of his downfall. Sheridan lost a lot of money; this, with a disastrous theatrical project, landed him deeply in debt, and he died with the bailiffs in his house.

Kosciusko, Tadeusz Andrzej (1746–1817)
Polish patriot

Kosciusko was educated at Warsaw university and then went into the French army to study artillery. He served in the Colonist's army in the American War of Independence (1774–1783) rising to major-general, and supervised the fortifications being built at West Point.

In 1784, he went home to Poland and almost at once obtained high rank in the Polish army. In 1794 he organized a national rebellion, was elected Dictator by the revolutionary council, but a few weeks later was seized by the Russian army and imprisoned, from which he was released in 1796, and told to leave that part of Europe. He went to live in France, where he worked in exile for Polish independence.

Bligh, Vice-Admiral William (1754–1817)
English admiral and discoverer

Bligh is famous all over the world for his brutality and stern discipline when captain of the ship, HMS *Bounty*, on its voyage of exploration in the South Sea Islands to get breadfruit plants (1787–1789). There was a mutiny, led by one of his officers, the Manxman Fletcher Christian, who cast Bligh and some loyal officers into an open boat with no weapons or instruments.

With astonishing fortitude and technical skill, Bligh brought the row boat more than 5,750 kilometres across the Pacific to Timor, with no lives lost. At Copenhagen (1801), Bligh commanded a ship with great bravery and dash, and was praised by Nelson.

In 1805, Bligh became governor of New South Wales, in Australia. In 1808 he was deposed by some of his soldiers, but restored by officials sent out from England. In 1814 he was promoted to vice-admiral.

Austen, Jane (1775–1817)
English novelist

Jane Austen was the daughter of a Hampshire clergyman and lived at home for all of her short life. She began to write novels in her early 20s but it was not for years that she even thought about getting them published.

Pride and Prejudice is probably her most famous work. She had completed it by the time she was 22 but it was not published until she was 38. Her other major works were *Sense and Sensibility*, *Mansfield Park*, *Emma*, *Northanger Abbey* and *Persuasion*. They are all marvellous documents of English middle class country life in the early 19th century and masterpieces of observation.

Hastings, Warren (1732–1818)
English administrator, first Governor General of India

Warren Hastings, orphaned as a child, started his career as a clerk in the East India Company. He stayed there for 15 years, in which time he worked his way up to being appointed President of the Council of Bengal. In 1773 he was given the new title of governor general. In the next 13 years he laid down the foundations of the Indian civil service. He also had to fight many skirmishes with rebel tribesmen. He increased Britain's stake in India considerably, and when he returned to England he expected praise.

But instead he faced impeachment for corruption and oppression. He was tried in a trial which lasted for seven years, in the House of Lords, and eventually was cleared on all charges. But by the end he was a broken man and he retired to the country, to Daylesford in Oxfordshire.

Revere, Paul (1735–1818)
American adventurer

Revere is remembered most of all in American history as an adventurer in the War of Independence. Appointed carrier for the Massachusetts Assembly he rode all the way from Boston to Lexington to warn his countrymen that the British were on the march, in 1774, the starting point of the war.

But he was by trade a silversmith and an engraver. Much of the best silver pieces of the last years of the 18th

Paul Revere on his famous ride to warn his countrymen that the British were on the march

century in the U.S. were designed and made by him. He also invented a process for rolling sheet copper.

Watt, James (1736–1819)
Scottish engineer

James Watt gave the world one of the most significant machines of all time – the condensing steam engine. In 1757 he was made scientific instrument maker at the University of Glasgow, where he studied the mechanical potential of steam. While working on the repair of a steam engine in 1764 he was to hit on the idea which made him world famous, namely how to condense the steam separately.

He went into partnership with Matthew Boulton, an English engineer, and together they set up a manufacturing business to make Watt's inventions. His other discoveries include the hydrometer, the marine screw propeller and the centrifugal governor for regulating engine speed.

George III (1738–1820)
King of Great Britain (1760–1820)

George III was the first of the Hanoverian Kings really to take pride in being British. At the outset of his reign he tried to govern and to endear himself to the people. He failed in the first but succeeded in the second.

His reign spans the industrial revolution, the War of Independence in the United States of America, and the great war with Napoleon. And among his subjects were some of the greatest men in British history – William Pitt, Earl of Chatham, his brilliant son, also William, Nelson, Wellington and writers such as Johnson, Burns, Byron, Coleridge, Shelley and Keats.

During the last years of his reign he became ill with a disease which made him behave as if he was slightly mad. In 1811 he had a bad fit from which he never recovered, and his eldest son took over as Regent.

Young, Arthur (1741–1820)
English agriculturalist

Arthur Young toured England and Ireland, making observations on the state of agriculture, and his *Annals of Agriculture* is a standard work on the subject. It played a part in the agricultural revolution of the late 18th century.

He also made political observations, and in his *Travels in France* reported on the condition of that country's politics before the revolution. It had a considerable influence on French political leaders of the radical party.

Schwarzenberg, Karl Philipp, Prince of (1771–1820)
Austrian general

This great soldier was an ambassador for Austria at the Imperial Russian Court in 1808. His diplomatic skill was put to use in the negotiations between Napoleon and the Austrian Emperor for the hand in marriage of the emperor's daughter, Maria Louisa. Napoleon was impressed with Schwarzenberg and invited him to take command of an army in the great invasion of Russia in 1812. But when Napoleon's Grand Army had been compelled to retreat in disorder, Schwarzenberg was appointed to command the combined Prussian and Austrian army which in 1813 defeated the great Frenchman at Leipzig.

Napoleon Bonaparte (1769–1821)
French Emperor (1804–1815) and military genius

Napoleon is one of the most outstanding soldiers of modern history and is among the greatest commanders of all time. At the height of his career he ruled nearly all Europe. Born in Corsica, and receiving his military education in France, he rose to prominence during the turbulent years that followed the French Revolution. In 1795, at the request of the government, he defeated counter-revolutionaries with a 'whiff of grapeshot'.

After this he defeated the Austrian army in Italy, and as he advanced on Vienna they sued for peace. His popularity in France made the Directory (as the government was called) afraid of his power, and he was sent to Egypt where he hoped to damage British trade with India. But his campaign was foiled by Nelson's victory at the battle of the Nile.

In 1799 he returned to Paris and was made part of a three man consulate. He then declared himself first consul for ten years and later assumed the title Emperor. His sense of discipline brought an end to the years of turmoil that had gone before. He made plans for a Bank of France, he stabilized the franc and improved the taxation system as well as making government and judicial reforms.

By 1805 he was at war again, with three of the great powers of the time – Britain, Austria and Russia. He succeeded in defeating Austria and Russia at Austerlitz in 1805 and then defeated Prussia at Jena in 1806. This gave him command over Europe, and he tried to bring about Britain's surrender by implementing a plan to damage their trade by means of a Continental Alliance.

In 1810 he divorced his wife Josephine, the woman he loved, whom he had married in 1796, because she failed to give him any children. He then married Marie Louise, the Emperor of Austria's daughter.

Russia defied Napoleon's Continental System and so he invaded that vast land in 1812, defeating the Russian army at Borodino. But when he entered Moscow the Russians were burning it to the ground. His army was hungry, tired and suffering from the cold Russian winter. Retreat was inevitable: only a fraction of them reached France again, where Napoleon tried to raise money and troops for a new army.

The nations of Europe gained hope from this defeat, and gradually started arming themselves against Napoleon. Although he was able to defeat them at first, they gradually wore down his depleted resources. He was eventually beaten in 1813 at the battle of Leipzig; the allies marched on France and he was forced to abdicate. But the next year he returned from Elba, his island of exile, and soon gained support in France.

A sick man, he was finally defeated at Waterloo in 1815 by the combined forces of Wellington and Blücher. He was banished to St. Helena where in 1821 he died of a stomach cancer.

His idea of a united Europe was a good – even noble – one, but he did not see that such a union had to be a voluntary one if it was to work effectively.

Keats, John (1795–1821)
English poet

'A thing of beauty is a joy forever'. This line from Keats' *Endymion* sums up what he felt and tried to express in his work. When he died he had managed to put much of this feeling into his poetry and left an important legacy to English literature.

The son of a London livery stable keeper he had for a time studied medicine at St. Thomas's Hospital, but he never practised. When he was 21 he had his first book of verse published. After that came some of the most beautiful poems in the English language, including *La Belle Dame Sans Merci*, *The Eve of St. Agnes*, *Ode to a Nightingale*, and *Ode on a Grecian Urn*. Keats died, tragically, aged 26, in Rome, crippled with consumption.

Napoleon inspecting chasseurs of the Guard

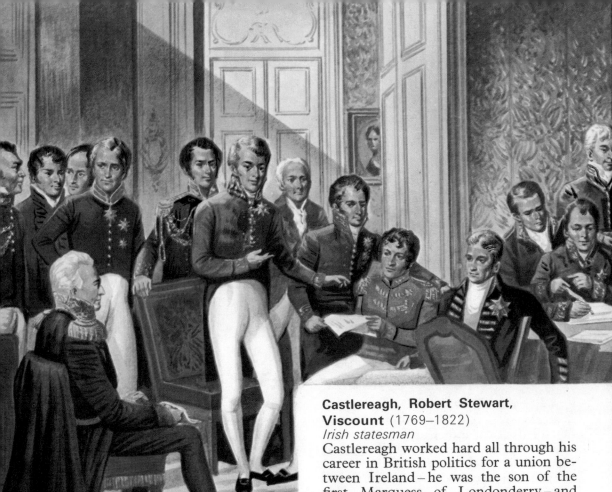

The Congress of Vienna with Prince von Hardenberg seated on the right

Hardenberg, Karl August, Prince von
(1750–1822)
Prussian statesman

After an early career in minor government posts Hardenberg came into his own when serving in the war between Prussia and France (1792–1795). When the war was over he was one of the principal architects of the peace treaty. He served in the Prussian cabinet until 1806.

Hardenberg played a large part in reorganizing Prussia after the war of liberation for which his services were rewarded by being made a Prince. He improved the army system, abolished serfdom and reformed education. As chancellor of Prussia he took part in the Congress of Vienna.

Castlereagh, Robert Stewart, Viscount (1769–1822)
Irish statesman

Castlereagh worked hard all through his career in British politics for a union between Ireland – he was the son of the first Marquess of Londonderry – and England.

In 1805 he became secretary for war and held office for four years. Towards the end of his term he fought a duel with Canning (*p. 207*) who accused him of fighting the war with Napoleon half-heartedly, and he had to retire from politics for a while.

In 1812 he was made foreign secretary and held this office until his death in 1822. His principal ambition was to see Napoleon defeated and then to ensure that a balance of power was maintained in Europe. He succeeded in stopping both Russia and Austria from becoming as powerful on the continent as Napoleon had been.

Castlereagh became a target of hatred by the people, on account of the strict measures the government introduced to stop the working class from agitating for reforms. When in 1822 he committed suicide crowds cheered as his coffin was carried to Westminster Abbey.

Shelley, Percy Bysshe (1792–1822)
English poet
Shelley, one of the greatest poets in the English language, was born with riches, and given a good education. He developed an independent spirit which troubled him for most of his life.

He was expelled from Oxford for publishing a pamphlet defending atheism. At nineteen he married a girl younger than him, but who left him after three years because of his moodiness and cruelty. After this misfortune he began writing poetry and produced *Queen Mab*.

In 1818, he married again. Ill health persuaded him to leave England and move to Italy with Byron (*p. 205*) and Keats (*p. 203*). While there he wrote most of his best poetry, including *Prometheus Unbound*, *Ode to the West Wind* and *Adonaïs*. He was drowned during a storm at sea.

Pusey, Edward Bouverie (1800–1882)
English theologist
Pusey, who studied at Oxford and later taught there, became a leader of the church movement known as the Oxford Movement. He was against the rationalism of the lower churches and the ideas of the non-conformists, and although also against the idea of restoring Catholicism in England, he tried to bring their high church attitudes back into the Church of England.

St. Vincent, John Jervis, 1st Earl (1735–1823)
English admiral
St. Vincent was commander of the British Mediterranean fleet from 1795 to 1798, when Britain and France were at war. In 1797, off Cape St. Vincent, he attacked a huge French fleet of 27 ships, with about half the number of his own. In a great victory he destroyed the French. This wonderful exploit earned him an earldom.

In 1801, St. Vincent was appointed first lord of the admiralty, and he did much to improve conditions in the navy, in particular by cutting down corruption among suppliers and commissariat officers in the dockyards.

Jenner, Edward (1749–1823)
English physician and surgeon
Jenner was one of the most eminent of Britain's many medical researchers, contributing to the world a method of inoculation against smallpox.

It was while practising as a doctor in the country that he noticed that dairy maids who had contracted the mild disease of cow pox were not affected when smallpox epidemics were in the area. He injected a young lad named Phipps with cow pox serum, and when the inflammation had subsided injected him with smallpox serum – which would normally have meant certain death for the boy. But weeks went by and there was no sign of the disease. It was an answer to smallpox, which was then still one of the most dangerous scourges.

In gratitude parliament voted him gifts of £10,000 and then £20,000.

Byron, George Gordon Noel, Lord (1788–1824)
English poet
Byron grew up something of a bitter person, who was quick to become angry, partly because of a deformed foot. He became Lord Byron when he was ten, on the death of his great uncle, and he was educated at Harrow and Cambridge where he first started writing poetry.

When in 1812 the first two Cantos of *Childe Harold's Pilgrimage* were published, he leapt to fame. The immediate success of this poem made his subsequent work admired throughout Europe, where Romanticism was flowering. He went on to write *Don Juan*, *Prisoner of Chillon* and *Giaour*, and many poems which became widely loved and which had a marked influence on English literature.

He had an unsuccessful marriage and his unconventional behaviour was thought so bad that he decided to leave England. In 1823 he fought with the Greek army to help them in their struggle for independence from the Turks. He died of a fever at Missolonghi.

President Thomas Jefferson at his desk

Jefferson, Thomas (1743–1826)
American president (1801–1809)

'All men are created equal . . .' This famous excerpt from the American Constitution is often quoted today by all manner of people. The constitution, perhaps the clearest statement of true democracy set down since the days of ancient Greece, was largely drafted by Thomas Jefferson, who had been governor of Virginia.

Jefferson was probably one of the cleverest men ever to emerge from the United States. He was elected president in 1801 and served for two terms, during which he did much for his country, including the encouragement of westward expansion.

Raffles, Sir Thomas Stamford (1781–1826)
English colonial administrator

Raffles founded Singapore as a British colony in 1819. He had had a distinguished career in the Malay States, and had become lieutenant governor of Java, in the Celebes Islands. In Java he had introduced reforms in the internal administration.

Blake, William (1757–1827)
English painter, engraver and poet

Blake began life as an engraver. He also wrote some beautiful poetry, and he began to produce this with illustrations engraved by himself. He is said to have introduced a more efficient means of etching on copper plate, and printing therefrom. It was not long before he was in demand as an illustrator of other people's books, and he favoured engravings of religious subjects.

A profound mystic throughout his life, Blake was an individual at odds with the society in which he lived; in his *Songs of Innocence and Experience*, prophetic books and in his powerful paintings and engravings he displays a brilliant originality.

Beethoven, Ludwig van (1770–1827)
German composer

This German composer of wonderful music, who wrote some of the world's greatest symphonies, spent his last eight years in the isolated world of total deafness.

His first musical education was from his father. After more formal training he began to move in the high circles of Bonn society where he built up many friendships with the aristocracy, notably with Count Von Waldstein. Later Beethoven moved to Vienna where he worked under the patronage of the upper classes.

His final years were not only marred by the deafness which prevented him from hearing his finished compositions, but also by further ill health and by personal worries.

Beethoven's work includes nine symphonies as well as sonatas, operas, and concertos. The symphonies are his most famous works, especially the fifth and ninth (choral). He was a leader of the romantic movement in music, which coincided with the romantic age in poetry and painting in the early years of the 19th century.

Canning, George (1770–1827)
English statesman

As Foreign Secretary Canning was both bold and wise in his policies. He believed in the greatness of Britain but also worked for the rights of smaller states.

Educated at Eton and Oxford, he soon became well known for his oratory and wit. He was elected M.P. for Newport in the Isle of Wight at the age of 23 and within three years had won the confidence of William Pitt, the prime minister, and was appointed Under Secretary for Foreign Affairs. In many ways he was a most attractive personality – clever, and extremely sympathetic to any who suffered hardship.

He became Foreign Secretary in 1807. England at that time was at war with Napoleon Bonaparte, and because Canning felt that the war minister, Castlereagh, was not sufficiently committed, he challenged him to a duel. Neither man was seriously hurt, but both were forced to retire, in temporary disgrace.

He served in a number of minor posts until Castlereagh committed suicide in 1822. Then it was his turn to become Foreign Secretary once more, and during this term of office achieved his most notable deeds. He supported the Greeks in their rebellion against Turkey, aided the Italians in their fight against Austria, and, surprisingly for a minister of a country with such a large empire of its own, gave support to the Spanish Colonies in South America in their campaigns for independence.

In 1827 he succeeded Lord Liverpool as Prime Minister, but tragically died within four months.

Goya, Francisco de (1746–1828)
Spanish painter

Goya first became famous in Spain for his remarkable frescoes. Later he became portrait painter at the court of Charles IV.

The war of independence inspired a series of powerful etchings of which the *Disasters of War* stands out as one of the most famous expressions of the horrors of war. As a painter Goya expressed a strong feeling for drama. He was also a great experimentalist in methods.

Schubert, Franz (1797–1828)
Austrian composer

Like many great musicians, Franz Schubert was a child prodigy. By the age of 17 he could play several instruments well, was a very fine pianist, and had composed a wide range of music, including his *Symphony in D*. He was greatly influenced by Beethoven's music, dedicating in 1827 a set of piano variations to him as he was dying.

Tragically, there was only a year of life left to Schubert, who had contracted a dangerous disease in 1822. When he did die in 1828, aged only 30, Schubert had written an enormous amount of music, including 600 songs, some of which, like *Who is Sylvia?*, the *Erlkönig* and *Hark! Hark! the Lark!* are among the most famous in the history of music.

Lamarck, Jean Baptiste Pierre Antoine de Monet (1744–1829)
French naturalist

After an early career in the army Lamarck dedicated his time to studying botany and zoology. He was ahead of Darwin in his first ideas on evolution, and suggested that changes in surroundings bring about changes in the structure of plants and animals.

As professor of zoology at *Le Jardin des Plantes* in Paris he was engaged in much theoretical work, and devised the grouping of animals into vertebrates and invertebrates.

Davy, Sir Humphrey (1778–1829)
English chemist and inventor

Sir Humphrey Davy was born in Penzance and studied chemistry as a youth. By the time he was 24 he had been appointed professor of chemistry at the Royal Institution in London. He held this post for ten years, when he left England with his wife and a young assistant Michael Faraday (*p. 228*) on a three-year European tour.

In 1820 he received one of the greatest honours of the scientific world when he was elected president of the Royal Society. He had been knighted at the age of 34.

He invented the Davy safety lamp for miners, which is still used. He discovered the anaethestic properties of nitrous oxide (laughing gas), the fact that chlorine is an element, and that diamonds are a form of carbon.

George IV (1762–1830)
King of Great Britain (1820–1830)

George IV earned a bad reputation as a young man. He associated with women not considered suitable for an heir apparent, gambled wildly, hunted and danced. As Prince of Wales he was leader of the young set, and he led many of them into very bad ways.

He also had deep artistic interests and patronized many artists. He surrounded himself with friends from the theatre, literature and the world of arts. Among these were the playwright Sheridan, and the architect Holland. His interest in architecture led to his commissioning Holland to building the Royal Pavilion at Brighton, an extravaganza of oriental and other tastes.

He was unpopular with the people as king because of his apparent support for government action against the working classes after the Napoleonic Wars. He was not mourned at his death, but the world of art at least had good cause to be thankful to him.

Bolivar, Simon (1783–1830)
South American patriot

In the early 19th century, the countries of South America which had been under Spanish dominion since the 16th century, decided to rebel in an effort to seek independence. There were several leaders, and the most celebrated was Simon Bolivar. He had been born in Venezuela. Bolivar had splendid gifts as a general and a leader of men. In 1811 he began to drive the Spanish government out of Venezuela. Then when he had done this he carried the war across into other states, and by 1824 much of South America was free. There were new states of Venezuela, Peru and Equador.

Bolivar became known as the Liberator, and was adored by the ordinary people, but his last years were clouded by severe opposition to his aims to unite all South America under him. The state of Bolivia is named after him.

Siddons, Sarah (1755–1831)
English actress

Sarah Siddons was the most amazing actress of her day, and people who saw her, even only once, talked about it ever afterwards. She was the daughter of the celebrated actor manager, Roger Kemble, who was ancestor of a whole family of people who made careers on the stage.

In 1773, Sarah married a member of her father's company, William Siddons. Her career as a leading actress began in 1775 when she was badly received in a London play. So she went into the provinces for several years to improve her technique, and in 1783 returned to the

George IV who was a patron of the arts, here admires the beautiful and talented actress, Sarah Siddons

London stage where she scored an immediate success in such roles as Lady Macbeth, Queen Katherine in *Henry VIII* and Constance in *King John*.

Stein, Baron Heinrich (1757–1831)
Prussian statesman

Stein was an early German nationalist. As a high ranking minister in the Prussian government between 1801 and 1808 he made many reforms in taxation, the civil service, and the administration. He also abolished serfdom which was still rife in some German states.

A man with a great sense of national pride, he was keen to aid Scharnhorst and Gneisenau re-organize the army, but in 1808 Napoleon forced him to retire.

After the wars with Napoleon were over Stein's plans for Germany, which he put forward at the Congress of Vienna, were thwarted by Metternich (*p. 222*), an anti-progressive Austrian who engineered the Congress the way he wanted.

Monroe, James (1758–1831)
American president (1817–1825)

The Monroe Doctrine was long a fundamental feature of United States foreign policy. In simple terms it states that the United States will not interfere in the affairs of states outside her sphere of influence, the two American continents. In return she expects not to have interference inside her sphere. This was stated by James Monroe, the fifth president of the U.S.A., 1817–1825.

Monroe was a local statesman in Virginia. He was its governor twice, and also helped to negotiate the purchase of the territory called Louisiana from Napoleon of France. He was also secretary of state for six years, from 1811–17. Among his most popular acts was the recognition of the Spanish American republics.

Gneisenau, Count August (1760–1831)
Prussian field marshal

Gneisenau started his military career fighting in America, and he also had early experience in Poland.

With Napoleon's rise to prominence in Europe Gneisenau joined the Prussian Army. After the Prussians were defeated at Jena, in 1806, Gneisenau, with Scharnhorst and Stein, worked on the reorganization of the army to make it capable of withstanding Napoleon.

At the battle of Waterloo, which finally destroyed Napoleon's ambitions in Europe, Gneisenau was on Blücher's staff.

Bentham, Jeremy (1748–1832)
English legal expert

Bentham, a legal scholar, spent much of his life trying to get the law of the country up to date, to bring it into line not only with practice elsewhere but also to make it more reasonable. He claimed that legislation, like all other forms of conduct, should be to ensure the greatest happiness of the greatest number. He also believed that the morality of actions is judged by their utility, or their capacity for rendering pleasure or preventing pain.

Bentham geared his work to the growing misery of the industrial working classes and to the increasing efforts of many kind people to redress their wrongs.

Goethe, Johann Wolfgang von (1749–1832)
German poet, playwright, philosopher, scientist

Goethe is the most celebrated German poet of all time. A formidable genius, he excelled at every form of literary expression, and mastered in his lifetime an enormous variety of knowledge from natural history and science to classical study.

His interest in folk song initiated in European verse a new spontaneity that was to characterize the Romantic movement. This vitality is demonstrated in his plays *Egmont* and *Götz*. Having studied law at Leipzig and Strasbourg, he was

Johann Wolfgang von Goethe

finally invited to settle at the Weimar court, the intellectual centre of Germany. A journey to Italy inspired him to write in a more classical form, as in his *Iphigenie auf Tauris*. His masterpiece, *Faust*, was completed, and until his death he poured forth an abundance of poetry, novels, dramas and essays. Admired throughout Germany and Europe, his personal life included many turbulent love-affairs, and passionate relationships.

Scott, Sir Walter (1771–1832)
Scottish novelist, poet and biographer

Walter Scott was the son of an Edinburgh lawyer. From early childhood he developed a keen interest in nature and in what went on about him. In 1792 he qualified as an advocate in Edinburgh and later was made sheriff depute of Selkirkshire. But soon after this he began to write seriously as a profession.

He started by writing poetry, and eventually made a name for himself. He did not begin work on his novels until 1814, but then, over the next 18 years, he produced a wide range of historical and adventure books under the title the *Waverley Novels*, of which the best known were *Rob Roy, Ivanhoe, The Bride of Lammermoor, Quentin Durward*.

His output was enormous, but although he earned a great deal of money he ran up large debts, many of them on a huge house which he improved. He continued to write and acquired many honours, including a baronetcy in 1820.

Wilberforce, William (1759–1833)
English politician and reformer

William Wilberforce, the son of a Hull merchant, devoted almost his entire life to the abolition of Negro slavery.

At 17 he went to Cambridge, but soon tired of academic life and left when he inherited a large fortune from his uncle. In 1780 he entered parliament as M.P. for Hull, and began campaigning for the abolition of slave trading. He campaigned for many years, winning the support of the church, writing letters and pamphlets, making speeches and visiting foreign countries.

Slowly his campaign began to find support in high places and by the start of the 19th century he felt he had enough support to put it to parliament. In 1801 his Abolition Bill was passed, thus ending the British slave trade.

He went on to fight for the freedom of slaves already transported to the West Indies. They won this freedom in 1833, the year he died.

Trevithick, Richard (1771–1833)
Cornish engineer and inventor

As an engineer in a Cornish mine, Trevithick first proved his ability as an inventor when he introduced a water pressure engine. He continued working with engines, but his attention was turned to steam power. He was the first man to have a steam locomotive tried out on a railway. His engine carried ten tonnes of iron, seventy men and five wagons, for just over fourteen kilometres at about 8 kilometres an hour.

Trevithick was disappointed, however, that no one took his invention very seriously. So he went abroad to South America to help revolutionaries fight for their independence from Spain. When he came back, no one remembered him or his ideas.

Kean, Edmund (1787–1833)
English actor

In his generation, Kean was probably the most celebrated actor in London. He had spent several years learning to act in the provinces, and in 1814 he appeared as Shylock in Shakespeare's *Merchant of Venice* at the Drury Lane Theatre. He was an overnight sensation, and for several years was the most popular actor of the time. He specialized in Shakesperian roles, particularly the stronger, more tragic parts, like Othello, Richard III, Macbeth and King Lear.

In his private life, however, Kean was an unhappy man. He got involved in all kinds of disputes, which damaged his reputation. By 1830 he was seriously disturbed mentally, and he broke down completely in 1833.

Telford, Thomas (1757–1834)
Scottish surveyor and engineer

Telford was the son of a Dumfriesshire shepherd. He was apprenticed to a stonemason when he was 13 and worked in Scotland for some time. Eventually he moved south to London where he was employed on the building of Somerset House. He studied architecture and civil engineering at the same time.

Experience in all kinds of construction led to an appointment in charge of a road building programme in Scotland. In 25 years he gave that country a complete road network, and built more than a hundred bridges, as well as improving docks and harbours. He also constructed the Caledonian Canal. One of his greatest engineering achievements was the Menai Suspension Bridge over the Menai Straits, between Caernarvonshire and Anglesey, in North Wales.

Malthus, Thomas Robert (1766–1834)
English economist
The Malthusian theory, published in 1798, said that populations, if they are not regulated, increase at a rate much faster than the means of supporting them in food and materials. The alternative to regulating was disease, war and poverty. It caused a stir, for in those days it was not considered acceptable to take measures to prevent conception.

The theory was put forward by this Surrey vicar, supported by brilliant mathematics and logic; he was deeply hurt when his work met with so much controversy.

Pedro I, Dom (1798–1834)
Emperor of Brazil (1822–1831)
Dom Pedro was the second son of King John VI of Portugal. In 1821 his father made him Regent of Brazil, Portugal's Principal colony in South America, but Dom Pedro disliked the way the Portuguese were governing Brazil – as did many Brazilians – and when a revolt broke out, Dom Pedro joined the rebels. He declared Brazil independent and was elected Emperor, in 1822. He was popular to begin with, but when he tried to rule like a dictator he was forced to abdicate, in 1831. He then returned to Portugal and finally became King.

Nash, John (1752–1835)
English architect
Among the greatest architects in the English tradition was John Nash, who designed many grand houses in London and elsewhere. In his long life, Nash made improvements to the streets of London and he laid out Regents Park and its terraces. He designed the famous Regent Street, but perhaps the best known example of his work is Buckingham Palace, which he completely redesigned, and which was later embellished by Sir Aston Webb.

Cobbett, William (1763–1835)
English journalist
William Cobbett led a most interesting life. He spent his youth on his father's farm. Then he joined the army, in 1783, taught himself English grammar and began to write pamphlets criticizing what he found in the army. One of these was very severe and he had to leave the country to avoid prosecution. He went to America where he wrote more pamphlets, this time criticizing the new American government system. He had to leave and he came back to England, in 1800.

Cobbett then became a serious political commentator, campaigning for social reform. He also took up farming again. He stood up for all sorts of causes, usually supporting the humbler folk, and in 1810 was jailed for attacking the use of foreigners to flog British troops accused of discipline offences.

In his time he wrote many books. The best known is his *Rural Rides*, a detailed account of many parts of England as seen by him on a long series of travels around the country.

Macadam, John Loudon (1756–1836)
Scottish road engineer
With another road engineer, Thomas Telford, Macadam set about inventing a new road surface which would be more suited to the heavy traffic that was building up on British roads.

His method was to break up large stones and mix these with fine gravel. The composition would harden as traffic went over it. This was the origin of the Macadam surface road.

Constable, John (1776–1837)
English landscape painter
In an age when most artists spent their time depicting great battle scenes or heroes, Constable, the son of a Suffolk miller, concentrated on the beauties of the countryside around him – the trees, clouds, skies and rivers.

Constable revolutionized English landscape painting, but was never given the acclaim in Britain that he was in France, until after his death. One of his best known works, *The Hay Wain*, is a study of an everyday scene in the beautiful countryside of his native Suffolk. It is a masterpiece of clarity and depth.

The Russian poet Alexander Pushkin

Pushkin, Alexander Sergevitch (1799–1837)
Russian poet

Pushkin wrote a great deal of fine poetry in a relatively short life, and was long regarded as Russia's greatest poet. He modelled his work on several western European poets, like Byron. Among his works were *Eugene Onegin*, a novel in verse form which has been set to music, and *Boris Godunov*.

As well as writing verse, Pushkin worked in a government office for some years, but his advanced political views got him into trouble, and he was banished to southern Russia.

Paganini, Niccolo (1782–1840)
Italian violinist and composer

Paganini was the greatest violinist of his day. He could make his instrument almost sing with notes, and his handling of difficult pieces of music was unparalleled. Whilst it is not really fair to compare his virtuosity with that of a later or contemporary master, few people have attempted seriously to argue that he was the greatest violinist of all time.

Mehemet Ali (1769–1841)
Viceroy of Egypt

Mehemet Ali gave Egypt a regular army, made improvements to her irrigation system and introduced elements of Western civilization. Ali had proclaimed himself Viceroy in 1805, an office which all, including the Turkish Sultan, approved of. In 1811 he defeated the Mamelukes in Cairo.

In 1820 he annexed parts of the Sudan to Egypt, and from 1821 to 1828 his troops occupied parts of the Morea and Crete to help the Turks – but the European powers deprived him of the spoils of war. He retired to Egypt, and during the last years of his life went mad.

Wellesley, Richard Colley, 1st Marquis (1760–1842)
Irish administrator

Wellesley was the elder brother of the great Duke of Wellington (*p. 220*). While his career was eclipsed by that magnificent man's amazing life, it was nonetheless a very distinguished one.

He was appointed governor-general of India in 1797 and in eight years he consolidated British rule there by removing princes and officials who were sympathetic to the French. Then he became British ambassador in Spain, foreign secretary (1809–1812) and even attempted in 1812 to form a government when Spencer Perceval, the prime minister, was shot dead in the House of Commons.

Wellesley was also lord lieutenant in Ireland twice, and did much to bring peace to that strife-torn land, largely by championing the rights of catholics.

O'Higgins, Bernardo (1778–1842)
Irish-Chilean patriot

Bernardo O'Higgins was the son of Ambrose Higgins, an Irish administrator in South America who did much to modernize the Spanish dominion of Chile. Bernardo led a band of Chilean nationalists who in 1810 broke into rebellion against Spanish rule. He was made commander of the Chilean national forces in 1813 and broke the Spanish at a great battle at Chacabuco in 1817. The triumphant Chileans elected him head of state, and he ruled for six years as a virtual dictator. In his time many reforms were carried out, for the Spanish had done little to make government work in the country, having used methods more relevant to the 16th century.

Stendhal, pen name of Marie Henri Boyle (1783–1842)
French writer

Stendhal was a diplomat who had served in Napoleon's army in the invasion of Russia in 1812. After the Napoleonic Wars he took to writing biographies and art histories, and his books on Haydn and Rossini, the composers, were very well received.

Later, Stendhal turned to novels, and produced *Le Rouge et le Noir* in 1831, which was a great success. His works were not however appreciated properly by literary critics in his time, but a generation later they were re-discovered, having a strong influence on the realist school of writers.

Bernardo O'Higgins leading a band of Chilean nationalists in the rebellion of 1810. In the foreground is a statue of the patriot

Arnold, Thomas (1795–1842)
English educator

After being ordained in the Church of England, Thomas Arnold became headmaster of one of England's best known public schools, Rugby, when he was only 33.

While headmaster, between 1828 and 1842, he introduced mathematics, history and languages into the school curriculum. He also stopped the bullying of little boys by their elders. His work had an important effect on the development of Britain's public schools, and consequently upon the ideals of the British and the Indian Civil Service. He was the author of several historical works. His son was Matthew Arnold, the famous essayist, critic, and poet.

Dalton, John (1766–1844)
English chemist

Dalton enunciated the atomic theory. This was that all matter was made up of atoms, in different orders, and that atoms were the smallest particles in the universe. This theory held good for many years.

Dalton, who was a Cumberland man, and a lecturer at Manchester College, made many contributions to scientific knowledge. Among these were establishing that the Northern Lights are an electrical phenomenon, describing colour blindness, stating the law of partial pressures, and investigating the expansion of gases by heat. He arranged a table of atomic weights for all the elements then known.

Bernadotte, Jean Baptiste (1763–1845)
King of Sweden (1818–1845)

Bernadotte served as a general under Napoleon, distinguishing himself in the battles of Austerlitz and Jena. But Napoleon did not trust him, and to get him out of the way he had him elected heir to the throne of Sweden, in 1810.

Bernadotte changed his religion and his name, and while the king of Sweden still lived, he assumed almost total control of the country. He refused to comply with the wishes of Napoleon and in the end went to war with him. He became King of Sweden in 1818.

As Charles XIV he won the reputation of being both a good and wise king. This man of humble background who made his way as an ardent revolutionary in the struggles against the French monarchy founded the present Swedish royal line.

Jackson, Andrew (1767–1845)
American general and president (1829–1837)

'Andy' Jackson created a legend around his name as a daring and brilliant field commander in the war between Britain and America in 1812–1814. He defended New Orleans against enormous odds and became a public hero.

In 1821 he was made Governor of Florida, elected to the Senate in 1823 and became the seventh president of the U.S.A. in 1828. As head of the State he was a sound administrator, and his government was relatively free from corruption.

Fry, Elizabeth (1780–1845)
English prison reformer

Elizabeth Gurney came from a Norfolk family of Quakers. She had quite a rich background, and she decided to devote much of her life to making things easier for people less fortunate. She made a good marriage, to Joseph Fry, a London merchant, and they had several children. As these grew up, she found time to devote to her good works. One day she visited a prison, and was appalled. Conditions were terrible. Wives and children had to stay in jail because their husbands were inside and could earn no money to keep them. So Elizabeth Fry used her money to campaign for prison reform. She worked hard, with John Howard, and she also helped the wives and children with money, presents and other services. In time, things were improved, but insufficiently.

She also got interested in nursing, and probably started the first nursing service in England. She later became friendly with Florence Nightingale (*p. 256*).

O'Connell, Daniel (1775–1847)
Irish patriot

O'Connell qualified in law and spent 20 years in practice. But what he saw in court opened his eyes to the condition of the Irish peasantry – especially the injustices inflicted upon the Catholics. In 1823 he formed the Catholic Association which attempted to remove the laws stopping Catholics from sitting in Parliament and holding government offices.

He was a splendid orator, but as he was also a kindly man who hated violence, he hoped to conduct his campaign peacefully. In 1828 he was elected to Parliament, but could not take his seat. A year later the Catholic Emancipation Act was passed and this allowed Catholics to sit at Westminster.

In parliament he agitated for the repeal of the Act of Union of 1800 which had shut down the Irish Parliament in Ireland and merged it with Westminster. It was the beginning of the Home Rule for Ireland movement. In 1843 he was arrested for sedition and conspiracy against the government, and was tried, found guilty, and fined £2,000. The sentence, however, was quashed on appeal to the House of Lords.

Stephenson, George (1781–1848)
English railway inventor

The son of a poor colliery fireman from Wylam near Newcastle upon Tyne, Stephenson at the age of 15 was helping his father at the colliery for long hours during the day and studying by candlelight at home during the evening.

He conceived the idea of an engine to take over the burden of taking trucks of mined coal to the distribution point at the pit head, instead of men pulling them.

So in 1814 he built a locomotive, tried it out and found it successful. He then took his idea to another colliery.

It was not long before the idea of passengers travelling in cars pulled by engines occurred to him and in 1823 he set up a locomotive works in Newcastle. He was then appointed construction engineer for a new railway being planned between Stockton and Darlington. And it was here that in 1825 the first successful passenger locomotive drew a line of carriages at 25 kilometres per hour.

In 1830 the Liverpool to Manchester line was constructed and the train was driven by his new tubular boiler engine, called the *Rocket.*

Poe, Edgar Allan (1809–1849)
American poet and novelist

Poe is remembered best for his horror stories like *The Pit and the Pendulum, The Murders on the Rue Morgue* and *The Fall of the House of Usher,* which have been acted on stage and filmed. But he would much rather have been remembered for his enormous output of poetry, much of it of the highest quality. He was a leading American poet of the 1800s.

Poe's life was as dramatic as the most exciting of his stories. He took jobs, lost them, went through bouts of madness, took to drink, sobered up, enjoyed riches and suffered extreme poverty, and finally died during an attack of insanity aggravated by drink.

Chopin, Frédéric (1810–1849)
Polish-born composer and pianist

Chopin was born in a village near Warsaw. By the age of eight he had become a very accomplished pianist and was performing in public. He studied at the Warsaw Conservatoire and then went for further teaching to Vienna and Paris. In France he became famous, and his concerts were packed. The demand for his services as a piano teacher was enormous.

By this time Chopin had begun to compose and he was now producing some of the loveliest pieces for the piano ever written. His 24 *studies* and 24 *preludes* are hardly eclipsed by his *nocturnes* and *ballades*. His two piano concertos are vigorous, romantic and stirring.

Chopin contracted chest complications. He went to live with the French writer Georges Sand, but it was a stormy love affair. She demanded a great deal of his attention and he began to neglect his composing and later, his health. He visited England in 1848 and was rapturously welcomed, but the next year his lungs collapsed and he died.

Wordsworth, William (1770–1850)
English poet

This son of a Lakeland lawyer became one of England's greatest poets, and one of the leaders of the romantic movement in literature.

Wordsworth was born in Cockermouth and lost both his parents at an early age. He was brought up by his aunt and uncle. After being educated at Cambridge, he travelled extensively on the Continent where he became inspired by the liberal ideas flourishing at the time. As time went on, however, the military interpretation of the French Revolution by Napoleon upset him, and he lost his faith in liberalism. This, coupled with a number of personal problems, led him into a state of depression.

Wordsworth returned to his favourite area, the Lake District, to live with his wife, Mary Hutchinson, and his sister Dorothy.

His work about his early life, *The Prelude*, gives a good insight into the development of Wordsworth, and is full of colourful memories of his childhood. His other great works included *Intimations on Immortality*, *The Recluse*, *The Solitary Reaper*, and of course many sonnets, including *On Westminster Bridge*.

He succeeded Robert Southey as poet laureate, a title he would have despised in early life.

George Stephenson's steam locomotive drawing a line of carriages

Sir Robert Peel who introduced (top) 'Peelers' or
'Bobbies' as we still sometimes call them, today

Louis Philippe (1773–1850)
King of France (1830–1848)

Charles X (1824–1830) of France tried to make himself absolute, but instead provoked a revolution in 1830 which resulted in his having to abdicate. The leaders of the revolution then elected a cousin, Louis Philippe, who had been in exile throughout the time of Napoleon Bonaparte. Louis was a democratic man, and at first governed well. But there were great pressures on him from all sides. The socialists said he was not radical enough. The monarchists said he was not autocratic enough. The middle classes liked him but were powerless to save him when in 1848, the year of revolutions in Europe, he was driven off his throne. He escaped to live in England.

Peel, Sir Robert (1788–1850)
English statesman

Peel's father was a wealthy Lancashire cotton manufacturer and not a member of the aristocracy like so many Tories of the time. Peel, however, followed a similar education to many of his colleagues, first at Harrow, and then at Oxford where he obtained a double first in Mathematics and Classics. When he was 21 he entered parliament as M.P. for Cashel in County Tipperary. In 1812 he was made secretary for Ireland and while in office introduced a police force known as Bobbies, or Peelers, after him. As Home Secretary, which he became in 1822, he set out to cut down the severe penalties then imposed for minor offences (one could be hanged for stealing a sheep) and in six years he succeeded in reducing the number of crimes punishable by death from 200 to four, namely murder, high treason, forgery of a Bank of England note and arson in a Royal dockyard. Transportation sentences were greatly reduced as well.

Peel had the ability of seeing when it was time to change his mind on an issue. Although previously opposed to any reforms for Ireland, he realized that Catholics should be allowed to stand for office in Parliament and threw his vote in with the government, helping to pass the

Catholic Emancipation Bill in 1829.

He was prime minister for a few months in 1834 but was outvoted and resigned. Seven years later he again became head of a Tory administration and this time his talents were given full reign.

His financial reforms were memorable. Amidst a storm of protest he introduced a sevenpence in the pound income tax, but at the same time abolished duties on about 600 goods and reduced them on more than 1,000, thereby lowering the cost of living.

It was the repealing of the Corn Laws that ended this great man's administration. These had been passed in 1815, banning the import of foreign wheat when home grown wheat was below four pounds a quarter, thus protecting English farmers. But as the population grew there was not enough grain and the price rose. Added to this there was a frightful potato famine in Ireland from 1845 to 1848. In 1846 Peel repealed the Corn Laws, reducing the price of grain. But to do this he had to win the support of the Liberals, while many of his own party, including Disraeli, were against him. On another issue connected with Ireland many of Peel's party deserted him, and he was forced into resignation. He remained an M.P. right up to his death.

Balzac, Honoré de (1799–1850)
French novelist
Balzac is regarded as founder of the realist school in modern literature. He studied law and then became a journalist. His first book was an historical novel in the style of Walter Scott, which he wrote with a group of others.

Among his friends were Hugo, Vigny and Lamartine, other great French writers of the time. There were more than 2,000 characters in his books through whom he tried to show that surroundings played an important part in the way people think and behave. His industry was exceptional, he worked regularly for fifteen hours a day and wrote eighty-five novels in twenty years.

Honoré de Balzac

Turner, Joseph Mallord William (1775–1851)
English painter
Turner grew up in London, the illiterate son of a barber. But he always enjoyed sketching, and at the age of 14 he won a place at one of the Royal Academy Schools.

He exhibited his first work – a drawing of Lambeth Palace – in the following year. But the painting which brought him real acclaim was the *Battle of the Nile* in 1799. Although he had not been there, it captured wonderfully the real mood of a sea battle.

His paintings can be seen as falling into three periods. The first he devoted to historical subjects such as *The Garden of Hesperides* and *Dido Building Carthage*. Between 1820 and 1835 he studied the effects of light and colour and made great advances in this field. For the rest of his life he worked on seascapes, on which *The Fighting Temeraire* is perhaps the best known. You can see a permanent exhibition of his works in London's Tate Gallery.

Cooper, James Fenimore (1789–1851)
American novelist
This American novelist began his career by chance. He wrote his first book after his wife had challenged him to make good a boast that he could write a better book than the one he was reading.

He had spent his early career at sea and then retired to live the life of a country gentleman. His books included *The Pilot*, *The Last of the Mohicans*, *The Prairie* and *The Red Rover*.

Wellington, Arthur Wellesley, 1st Duke of (1769–1852)
Irish field marshal and statesman

Wellington holds the distinction of having been both head of the army and head of the government. But it is as a soldier that he excelled and is better known.

Born in Dublin, he was educated at Eton, and ironically, at military school in France. At 18 he joined the army and two years later he entered parliament as an Irish M.P. In 1794 he was promoted colonel, and soon after had his first experience of action, in Holland. He then went out to India where he fought against Tippoo Sahib, the rebel Indian leader, winning a great reputation for courage and generalship. In 1805 he returned to England and in 1807 was made Secretary for Ireland.

Wellington was then given command of a special force to land in Portugal and try, where others had failed, to drive Napoleon from the peninsular. In the following years he won several notable victories, including Salamanca (1812), Vittoria (1813) and Toulouse (1814). As a result of these he was offered a dukedom and became Duke of Wellington. He was now the foremost soldier in Europe.

Defeats for Napoleon throughout Europe had led, by this time, to his abdication and he was in exile in Elba. But his retirement was not to last and he returned to the mainland where he soon marshalled a fresh army.

On 18 June 1815 Wellington and Napoleon met in battle for the first time, near Waterloo, on the French border with Belgium. It was by no means an easy victory for Wellington, and one which he might have lost, had it not been for the timely arrival of Blücher and the Prussian army. But Wellington had stood up to Napoleon and proved to be more than his match.

Wellington became prime minister in 1828. He was a Tory and strongly resisted progressive moves like Catholic Emancipation and parliamentary reform. He resigned over these issues in 1830, but still fought them in the House of Lords. He organized the military in the Chartists riots.

In the last decade of his life he was head of the army once more and again served in the cabinet. After his death Wellington was given a state funeral in St. Paul's Cathedral. His reputation had stood so high that he was probably the most respected man in Europe. Certainly, in Britain, he was approached by all manner of people, who consulted him on every conceivable subject.

Braille, Louis (1809–1852)
French blind alphabet creator

Louis Braille was a three-year-old boy when he went blind. At ten he was put in an institution where he taught himself music. In his young adulthood he became an organist in Paris. This led him to devise his now famous system of raised point lettering to enable the blind to read. He became a teacher at the institution, in 1828.

Today, Braille is still widely used, although there are also several more modern electronic systems to help the blind to read.

O'Connor, Feargus Edward (1794–1855)
Irish political agitator

O'Connor was a fiery Irish lawyer who was elected an M.P. in 1832. But he was expelled from Parliament because he did not satisfy the qualifications needed. He joined the radical Chartist movement and soon emerged as one of its leaders.

The Chartists were campaigning for parliamentary reforms, including votes for all men. In 1848, the year of revolutions in Europe, the Chartists under O'Connor marched through London to Westminster with a huge petition of demands. The Duke of Wellington called on the demonstrators to disperse (he had troops behind him) and agreed to take the petition to parliament. When it was read, they found fictitious names on it, and Parliament therefore chose to ignore it. Four years later O'Connor was declared insane, but when he died in 1855 more than 50,000 attended his funeral.

The talented Brontë family – Branwell, Charlotte, Emily Jane and Anne

Kierkegaard, Soren Aabye (1813–1855)
Danish philosopher

Kierkegaard introduced a new feature of philosophy based on the belief that truth existed for the particular individual only as he himself produces it in action. For example, religion is an individual matter and the relationship of the individual to God involves suffering or experiencing something, in order to believe in God. In this respect he was a forerunner of the influential school of philosophy which was called the Existentialist School. Existentialism taught the active fulfilment of individual personality, the right of choice, and the inevitability of suffering.

The Brontë Sisters (19th century)
English novelists

Three daughters of Patrick Brontë, an eccentric Irish-born Yorkshire curate, came to be included among the most celebrated novelists of the 19th century. The daughters were Charlotte (1816–1855), Emily Jane (1818–1848) and Anne (1820–1849). The girls went to an oppressive boarding school, and each, after spells as school mistresses themselves, turned their hand to literature.

Their novels all reflect the unhappiness and poverty that they had known at home. They also reveal hidden passions of great depth which seem surprising in girls who were not thought to have had love affairs. Charlotte produced *Jane Eyre*, Emily produced *Wuthering Heights* and Anne who died aged 29 wrote the *Tenant of Wildfell Hall*. Their brother Branwell, an artist, was a drunkard and drug addict when he died, aged 31.

Heine, Heinrich (1797–1856)
German poet

Heine was Jewish born, and went, like most boys in his family, into banking. He did not like it, and instead studied law at Berlin and Gottingen. There he began to write poetry, and over the next few years produced some of the most beautiful lyric verse in the German language. An admirer of the French spirit of liberty, his work as a satirist and publicist ran foul of the authorities in his homeland, and he was compelled to write about Germany from a Parisian exile.

In 1840 he married his long-time girlfriend. Seven years later he was struck down with paralysis of the spine and languished in bed for several years, in increasing pain and discomfort, continuing to write some of his finest poetry.

221

Owen, Robert (1771–1858)
Welsh social reformer

Owen was a social reformer who was appalled by conditions in the factories which had sprung up all over Britain in the Industrial Revolution. In 1814 he set up a factory in Manchester and introduced an entirely new idea of how it should be run. Benefits were to be paid for sickness and on retirement. No children were to be employed at all. Workers' spare time was to be made better by organized recreation activities. Workers were also to have some form of partnership in the factory, whereby they received discounts on the goods they bought and shared in the profits made. This was the beginning of the cooperative movement, which has grown not only in Britain but in many other lands throughout the world.

Owen's ideas seem normal enough, but they were very revolutionary in 1814. He also fought to get conditions in other factories improved, but it was a struggle because so many members of parliament were either owners themselves or had reasons for resisting change.

Perry, Matthew Galbraith (1794–1858)
American naval officer

Perry was commander of the USS *Fulton*, one of the first U.S. steam-driven naval warships, in 1837. He had an exciting career, suppressing the slave trade and fighting against Mexico. Then, in 1853, he commanded a squadron which sailed to Japan to negotiate a commercial treaty with the government. It was the first such negotiation with a Western power and it brought Japan into contact with the Western World. From then on, the Japanese did not look back, and have brought their nation into the front rank of world economic and industrial countries.

Metternich, Prince Klemens (1773–1859)
Austrian statesman

Metternich was brought up in the courts of pre-revolutionary Europe. It is thought that it was the atrocities he witnessed as a young man in the French Revolution that caused him to grow up to be conservative, and totally afraid of liberalism and progress.

One of the first features of his career as a statesman was his arrangement of the marriage of Marie Louise (the Austrian emperor's daughter) to Napoleon, which he thought was advantageous to Austria.

But perhaps his greatest personal triumph was the way he engineered the Congress of Vienna which re-settled Europe after the Napoleonic war. He secured the stability of the old order and made sure of the suppression of liberal and revolutionary ideas for the next twelve years or so. This was largely done through the maintenance of the conservative Holy Alliance. He held on to power in Austria until a revolt in 1848 when he fled and spent his remaining years in England and Holland.

Macaulay, Thomas Babington, 1st Baron Macaulay (1800–1859)
Scottish writer and statesman

Although he was a distinguished statesman, Macaulay is best remembered for his historical writings. He was born in Leicestershire and educated at Cambridge. After obtaining his degree he was called to the bar.

Between 1830 and 1856 he was an M.P. for three periods of varying length, and while in parliament became paymaster of the forces, Secretary for War, and a member of the Supreme Council of India. His books included a *History of England* which covered the reigns of James II, and William III. In 1842 he published *Lays of Ancient Rome*, a long narrative poem of ancient Roman history, as well as many essays and sketches.

Macaulay was an infant prodigy, and remained brilliant all his life. When asked, at the age of three, how his toothache was, he said 'The agony has abated!'.

Stephenson, Robert (1803–1859)
English engineer

Robert assisted his father, George Stephenson (*p. 216*), in Newcastle upon

Tyne for some years, developing bigger and better locomotives. Then he was appointed chief engineer for the London and Birmingham Railway at about the same time that I. K. Brunel (*p. 223*) was made head of the Great Western. The two men became firm friends and often helped each other on knotty problems. In later years, Stephenson branched out into bridge building and constructed, among others, the Victoria Bridge at Berwick, one of the Tyne bridges at Newcastle, and his masterpiece, the tubular railway bridge across the straits between Caervarvon and Anglesey in North Wales.

Brunel, Isambard Kingdom (1806–1859)
British engineer

This brilliant, bustling, cigar-smoking little man left a remarkable legacy to mankind, with an unparalleled range of scientific and engineering achievements. He was engineer-in-chief of the Great Western Railway, which ran from London to Bristol, Bath and the West Country. He built Paddington Station, Maidenhead Bridge, Box Tunnel, Temple Meads Station in Bristol and the Saltash Bridge across the Tamar. Before that he had constructed the first tunnel under the Thames, under the supervision of his father.

Brunel also built three famous ships, all of which were unique in their classes, the *Great Western*, the *Great Britain* and the *Great Eastern*, the last destined to be the biggest ship afloat for 40 years. He invented railway telegraph, designed a tank, built a prefabricated hospital for British troops injured in the Crimean War, and designed the beautiful Clifton Suspension Bridge over the river Avon, erected after his death as a memorial. He designed the two end towers for the Crystal Palace building which housed the 1851 Great Exhibition.

This astonishingly versatile engineer and designer was extremely popular. He loved the men who worked for him. The last thing he did a few hours before he died of Bright's Disease was to send the railway yard men at Swindon, where he had built them a charming housing estate (that is still there), to go and see the *Great Eastern* sail past Portland Bill, near Weymouth, on its maiden voyage.

Isambard Kingdom Brunel and the Clifton Suspension Bridge he designed for the river Avon at Bristol

Dundonald, Thomas Cochrane, 10th Earl of (1775–1860)
Scottish admiral

Born into an old Scottish noble family, Dundonald entered the navy in 1793 and as commander of the sloop *Speedy* took over 50 prizes in just a few years. They included a 32-gun Spanish frigate.

But later he was accused of a Stock Exchange swindle, and expelled from the navy. He then became a mercenary, and with some success led the Chilean navy in its war for freedom from Spanish domination.

Dundonald then went to Greece to help the Greek navy against Turkey. In this struggle he introduced a steam propelled warship. Britain eventually granted him a pardon and he was reinstated in the Royal Navy, as a rear admiral. He was commander of the North American stations from 1848 to 1857, when he became a full admiral.

Cavour, Count Camillo (1810–1861)
Italian statesman

Cavour was the greatest statesman Italy has produced, probably since the days of ancient Rome. He succeeded in doing what no other man in Italy had done for centuries, that is, he united the different states into a nation. When he died in 1861, Victor Emmanuel, King of Sardinia, had been declared King of Italy, and an Italian parliament had been assembled, in which all states except Rome and Venice were represented. These two States joined during the next ten years.

Cavour began his career as a soldier. Then he retired to manage his family estates. In the year of revolutions in 1848, he entered politics. Four years later his skill as a negotiator, his toughness, and his political astuteness led to his being appointed prime minister of the Kingdom of Sardinia. Once in this high post, Cavour devoted his energies not only to reforming the administration of the kingdom but more especially realizing the great dream of uniting the Italian states. He worked tirelessly and without cease for nine years, bargaining, threatening where necessary, dissimulating, and in the end triumphing. But it broke his health, and he died in 1861, scarcely more than 50 years old.

Hsien Feng (1831–1861)
Chinese Emperor (1851–1860)

Hsien Feng, whose real name was I Chu, was the seventh emperor of the Manchu dynasty. He was not very effective as a ruler, and in his time (1851–1861) there occurred the serious and long-drawn-out rebellion called the Taiping rebellion. He also went to war with Britain in 1860, but was compelled to abdicate, dying a year later.

Campbell, Sir Colin, Baron Clyde (1792–1863)
Scottish soldier

Colin Campbell assumed his surname. His father was a carpenter named McLiver but Colin called himself after his uncle who had sent him to school. He fought his way through the whole Peninsular War and was promoted captain.

Count Cavour with the King of Italy, Victor Emmanuel

After that he was mostly involved in home duties, and became Lieutenant Colonel of the 98th Regiment of foot, in 1837.

As commander of the Highland Brigade in the Crimean War he was largely responsible for the victory at Alma and the 'thin red line' which held out against the Russians.

When the Indian mutiny broke out in 1857 he was made commander of the British forces and as such played a very large part in the relief of Lucknow. In 1858 he was created Baron Clyde, and on his return from India became a field marshal.

Thackeray, William Makepeace (1811–1863)
English novelist

This humorous and satirical journalist who had been a law student, kept the British public entertained for years with articles, reviews, books and drawings. He used a variety of hilarious pen names like Michelangelo Titmarsh, George Savage Fitzboodle, Theophilus Wagstaff and Charles James Yellowplush. He contributed regularly to *Punch*, the leading humorous magazine of the time.

But behind this was a serious writer who was extremely observant, with wonderful descriptive powers. In 1848 he produced his novel *Vanity Fair* which was an immediate success. There followed a spate of good books putting him in the front rank of English writers: *Pendennis, Henry Esmond, the Newcomes* and *The Virginians*.

Jackson, 'Stonewall' (Thomas Jonathan) (1824–1863)
American general

'Stonewall' Jackson got his name from his iron stand as a Confederate general against the Unionist forces, at the famous battle of Bull Run, in the Civil War. After that great triumph, he went on to defeat several more Northern (Unionist) armies, particularly at Fredericksburg and Chancellorsville, in what is called the Shenandoah Valley Campaign. It was really the first and only run of military successes the Conferederates enjoyed in the whole war.

Tragically, returning one evening from the victory at Chancellorsville, he was sniped at by his own men in error, and he died from the wounds.

General 'Stonewall' Jackson

Speke, John Hanning (1827–1864)
English explorer

There were several distinguished British explorers making discoveries in the unknown parts of the African continent in the mid-19th century. One of these was Speke, who had been a soldier in India. In 1854 he joined Sir Richard Burton on a dangerous expedition to Somaliland, and three years later the two men went in search of the source of the great river Nile.

Speke then went off on his own, and at Lake Victoria was convinced he had found it. The river, he said, began in the lake. Back in England Burton and others doubted his findings, and he determined to defend them at a meeting of the British Association, to be held at Bath. But a few hours before he was due to appear, Speke was killed in a partridge shooting accident.

Palmerston, Henry John Temple, Viscount (1784–1865)
Irish statesman

Palmerston inherited his title when he was 18, but because it was an Irish one he was still able to enter the House of Commons. He stayed in Parliament for 58 years and for nearly 40 of them was at cabinet level. His whole career was devoted to upholding the honour of Great Britain, the country he loved so much.

Palmerston started out as a Tory and was secretary of war from 1809 to 1828. By then, however, he had become disillusioned with their backward ideas. They would not move with the times. In 1830 he changed sides and became foreign secretary under Lord Grey.

It was as foreign secretary that Palmerston is best known. He championed the smaller European states in their struggles for independence, and he enhanced Britain's influence in European affairs very greatly by his polite but firm tone, his astute letters and speeches, and his skilful negotiations.

As prime minister in 1855 he joined with France to bring the Crimean War to an early close. He was defeated and resigned, but he returned to office in 1859 and stayed there until his death in 1865.

In his last years, Palmerston personified the growingly aggressive attitude of Victorians towards the rest of the world. He and his contemporaries knew that Britain was the most powerful nation on the globe, and he became increasingly tactless in his utterances. One of the last things the Prince Consort, Albert, did before he died in 1861 was to moderate the tone of a letter of Palmerston's to the United States of America, thereby undoubtedly averting a war situation.

Lincoln, Abraham (1809–1865)
President of the U.S.A. (1861–1865)

Lincoln was probably the greatest American president since the creation of the Republic of the United States in the 1780s. Certainly his rugged but kindly features helped to give him a father-figure image which no other president has had since. He was wise, tough, patient, and understanding, and sympathetic to people less well off than himself. Basically educated, he began work as a store clerk, became a village postmaster and then put himself through law school.

Lincoln became president in 1861 at a critical time in U.S. history. The country was bitterly divided over slavery. The whites of the northern states did not approve of it, the whites of the southern states said it was necessary for their sugar and cotton plantations. The northerners objected to the way the south treated these unfortunate coloured men. So the south broke away from the Union and formed a Confederation of their own, and civil war followed.

Lincoln determined to keep the Union intact and to abolish slavery. So he backed the north with every means in his and the government's power. The north won and the Confederation was broken up. In the meantime, Lincoln had abolished slavery in 1863. This splendid American was assassinated in a theatre only a few days after the end of the war, by an insane actor.

President Abraham Lincoln was assassinated while at the theatre, by an insane actor

Proudhon, Pierre Joseph (1809–1865)
French anarchist

'Property is theft'. This seemingly contradictory remark by this French journalist and political writer sums up the essence of his revolutionary writings.

Proudhon, a critic of all political organizations of his time, saw no future in organized government. He did not believe in private ownership of property, and his comment meant that the ownership of property necessitated injustice and exploitation by its very nature. Proudhon, bitterly opposed by Karl Marx (*p. 238*), was the founder of the anarchistic tradition of European socialism, evident in the Paris Commune and the Spanish Civil War.

Gaskell, Mrs. (Elizabeth Cleghorn Stevenson) (1810–1865)
English novelist

Elizabeth Stevenson was born in London, but she was sent to the country in Cheshire to be brought up by an aunt. In the 1830s she became friendly with the well-known non-conformist preacher, William Gaskell, and married him. Then she began to write novels which portrayed urban and rural life as it was in her time. Her book, *Cranford*, based on the small town of Knutsford where she lived, was a sensation. Not only did it give a picture of life in humble as well as wealthy homes, it also exposed many evils of Victorian society. She seemed much admired for her beauty and gentle disposition.

227

Faraday, Michael (1791–1867)
English chemist and physicist

Until he was 13 it looked as though Faraday would have to become a blacksmith like his father. His family, from Newington Butts, London, was poor, and could not afford to have him educated.

But when he was 13 he secured an apprenticeship with a bookseller, and devoted his evenings to studying chemistry and physics. He also went to lectures at the Royal Institution and heard the great chemist of the day, Sir Humphrey Davy.

Faraday's chance came when Davy asked him if he would like to become his laboratory assistant. He found Davy a hard master and a man who took great delight in being rude about him. But he was undeterred, and in 1825 was in a position to succeed Davy as Director of the Royal Institution Laboratory.

In 1833 he was made professor of chemistry, and in 1852 Queen Victoria gave him a house at Hampton Court.

He discovered benzene, liquefied several gases, and made new kinds of optical glass. But his greatest work was in the field of electricity and magnetism. In 1841 he discovered the induction of electric currents which led to the invention of the electric motor. His work in this field opened the way to such discoveries as wireless waves, television, X-rays and even atomic physics.

Baudelaire, Charles Pierre (1821–1867)
French poet

The poems of Baudelaire seem in many ways modern. Many of the conventions of verse were disposed of and he wrote with symbolistic references.

Born in Paris he frequently quarrelled with his military step-father, who dispatched him to India. But Baudelaire stopped at Mauritius on the way where he met a half-caste girl, Jeane Duval, who became his lover and his inspiration.

When he returned to Paris he spent a lot of time in the studios of great artists like Delacroix and Manet writing great art criticisms.

His greatest work was a collection of poems, *Les Fleurs du Mal*. Many people disapproved of Baudelaire's fascination with the macabre and his decadence, but his poetry has had a profound influence on other poets well into the twentieth century. Other works such as *Les Paradis artificiels* and *Petits Poèmes en prose* delved further still into the effects of drugs and alcohol as Baudelaire desperately searched for the good in a world overcome with evil.

Maximilien, Ferdinand Maximilien Joseph of Hapsburg (1832–1867)
Austrian prince and emperor of Mexico (1863–1867)

Maximilien was the brother of Francis Joseph, Emperor of Austria. When Mexico had been largely overrun by the French, by 1863, he was offered the throne of a new empire there. He entered the capital, Mexico City, and his armies expelled the Mexican national army. His position was safe so long as he had French support, but in 1866, Napoleon III withdrew French forces, whereupon the national army, led by Juarez, returned, overran the country and deposed Maximilien, who was then tried by court martial and executed.

Rossini, Gioacchimo Antonio (1792–1868)
Italian composer

Rossini was a composer who specialized in opera of all kinds. He was director of two Italian opera theatres and also of the Théâtre Italien in Paris. Among his many famous musical scores were *Il Barbieri di Siviglia* (*The Barber of Seville*), *Otello* (*Othello*) and *Guillaume Tell* (*William Tell*). Many arias and overtures from these and others are often played to-day. Rossini also composed religious music.

Morton, William Thomas Green (1819–1868)
American pioneer of anaesthetics

One of the great tragedies of medical history is that the man who first showed how you could anaesthetize a patient in hospital, and so perform an operation on him which would not hurt, died in great poverty and unhappiness. He was the dentist, William Morton, who in 1846 demonstrated before an audience of medical students and doctors at the Massachusetts General Hospital in Boston how to administer the gas ether, to a patient with a large lump in his neck. After a few deep breaths, the patient went unconscious, and the surgeon, with swift sure strokes, cut through the flesh and removed the lump. A few minutes later, the man woke up – and said he had felt nothing. It was a landmark in medical history.

Sadly, many people tried to belittle Morton's discovery, some even claiming they had thought of it first. While the arguments raged, Morton was shunned, as he had been accused of stealing other people's secrets. He could get no patients. In the end, he died in poverty. It was too late that he heard he had been called a benefactor of mankind by several academic societies.

Lamartine, Alphonse Marie Louis de Prat de (1790–1869)
French poet

Lamartine was a fine, sensitive French poet whose work, *Méditations Poétiques*, published in 1820, had a significant influence on the romantic movement in French literature.

He was also a politician who made spell-binding speeches. He supported the radical party and was in constant demand to speak from platforms, especially in the last years of the reign of Louis Philippe (1830–1848). When Louis was deposed in 1848, and a provisional government set up, Lamartine was made foreign secretary.

Dumas, Alexandre (1802–1870)
French novelist

Few cannot have heard of the novel, *The Three Musketeers*. This tremendous historical tale was the work of this French novelist, and it demonstrated his great ability as a story-teller. Although the stories of this one-time clerical worker were all his own work, many of his historical novels had the background researched for him. His other novels include *The Count of Monte Cristo* and *The Man in the Iron Mask*.

The three musketeers – the famous characters of Alexander Dumas's historical novel of the same name

General Robert E. Lee

Simpson, Sir James Young (1811–1870)
Scottish physician

Simpson discovered that if one gave a patient a whiff or two of chloroform gas, by pouring a few drops of the heavy sweet smelling liquid on to a gauze mask over his nose, he would pass out. One could then operate on him and he would feel nothing. When he tried it out on expectant mothers, so that they could have babies without pain, it caused a sensation. It also stirred up a lot of arguments, for some elements of the Scottish Church regarded it as part of God's will that women should have their children in pain. But in 1850, when Queen Victoria was given chloroform while she was giving birth to the Duke of Connaught, the argument died down.

Simpson received many honours for his discovery, but his last years were marred by an increasingly bad temper which made him quarrel unjustifiably with his colleagues in the medical world, amongst them Lister (*p. 259*).

Lee, Robert Edward (1807–1870)
American general, commander-in-chief of Confederate armies

Robert E. Lee, was the leading Confederate general in the American Civil War. He was extremely popular, brilliant, gentle mannered, and generous to his enemies; even his opponents hardly liked to go to war with him.

His career had begun in the American army, and he had been superintendent of the famous military academy at West Point. But on the outbreak of Civil War he resigned and took command of the Confederate Army in Virginia. Although he was defeated several times, especially at Gettysburg in 1863, he fought a number of amazing defensive campaigns and at least saved the Confederate armies from total collapse.

Lee surrendered to General Grant of the Unionist forces at Appomattox in April 1865, but his reputation and his popularity were untarnished. In his last years he was president of Washington College, which later became a university.

Dickens, Charles John Huffam (1812–1870)
English novelist

One of the greatest of English novelists, Dickens produced a long series of books which are remarkable for many things. They have humour, marvellous plots and descriptive passages, and wonderful pictures of a great variety of people, many of whom had delightful names like Mr. Bumble or Wackford Squeers, and the liveliest dialogue. These books were also vital social documents about life in the mid-Victorian era, not only among aristocratic and wealthy people but more especially among poorer and humbler folk. Indeed, his sharp and often very sad portrayals of pitiful people or tragic circumstances did a lot to stir the consciences of better-off people who had preferred to hide in their palatial homes and pretend that social injustices did not exist.

Dickens had lived for some of his childhood in abject poverty, so he knew what he was writing about. Among his books, the better known are *Pickwick Papers*, *Oliver Twist*, *Great Expectations*, *Nicholas Nickleby* and *David Copperfield*.

Morse, Samuel (1791–1872)
American artist and inventor
Born in Massachusetts in the U.S.A., Morse travelled to England in 1810 to study art. On his return to America he helped found the National Academy of Design at New York.

But it was an invention of his that won him a place in history. He patented the Morse Code, a telegraph system in which letters are represented by short and long taps in various sequences. It took him time to get his idea accepted, but in 1843 the U.S. government offered a large sum of money for a telegraph system from Washington to Baltimore, and his was chosen.

Mazzini, Giuseppe (1805–1872)
Italian politician
A great Italian patriot, Mazzini rose from being a lawyer to become one of the most important men in the movement towards unification of Italy. In 1830 he had joined the liberal thinking secret society, the Carbonari. But he was found out and imprisoned. He was later released on the condition that he left Italy.

He returned to Italy to take part in the revolution of 1848. Then he became a member of a three-man government. To his death, however, he remained an undeterred republican and would not be a part of a government under a king. He was again exiled from Italy and made further contributions to the unification movement from abroad by aiding Garibaldi in his expeditions.

Juarez, Benito Pablo (1806–1872)
Mexican patriot
Juarez was a Mexican national politician and administrator who was of Indian descent. His career was extremely stormy, but he rose to be president of the Mexican republic more than once. He introduced many necessary reforms in his somewhat backward country. His first term of office as president was from 1857 to 1861, and this was followed by a second four-year term. During the latter period Mexico was invaded by Maximilien (*p. 228*) and Juarez had to retire to a small area in the north to sustain resistance to French dominion.

When Maximilien was captured and executed in 1867, Juarez returned in triumph; he was elected president again, and governed Mexico from 1867 to his death.

Napoleon III (1808–1873)
Emperor of the French (1852–1870)
Napoleon III (Charles Louis Napoleon Bonaparte) was a poor imitation of his famous uncle, Napoleon Bonaparte (*p. 202*), on whom he attempted to model himself.

He was swept into power in France in the 1848 revolution by the magic of his uncle's name, in which there had been a revival of interest and enthusiasm. He was made president of the country which became a republic after the King, Louis Philippe (*p. 218*), had been forced to abdicate. A few years later, Napoleon had himself made Emperor of the French.

A somewhat foolish man, Napoleon did have some good ideas. But he was never able to back them up. He lacked the inspiration and the judgment that had taken his uncle to the pinnacle of fame. For one thing, he was repressive: the press was gagged, political parties were abolished. He involved France in the inglorious Crimean War (1854–1856) and this was a heavy drain on French resources. It was done largely for national glory, which did not result, and to take people's minds off problems at home, which it did not do.

Towards the end of his rule several unfortunate acts gave Bismarck (*p. 248*) the opportunity to attack and begin what was for France the disastrous Franco-Prussian War of 1870–1871. Napoleon was captured by the Prussians and held prisoner until peace was signed. He was then deposed, the empire abolished, and the Third Republic created. He fled to England to exile and died in Kent soon after.

Livingstone, David (1813–1873)
Scottish missionary and explorer

Dr. Livingstone is perhaps the best known of the many explorers and missionaries who during the 19th century went into unknown parts of Africa and the Americas to spread the Christian faith.

Born in Blantyre, Lanarkshire, he worked for 14 years from the age of ten in a cotton mill, going to night school in the evening where he learned Greek, science and medicine. He saved enough money to go to Glasgow University and then on to Charing Cross Hospital where he qualified as a doctor.

From 1840 he spent almost his whole life in Africa. Sent there by the Missionary Society, he discovered Lake Ngami and most of the Zambesi river, and found the Victoria Falls in 1855, naming them after the Queen. He left the Missionary Society and became British consul at Quelemine.

During this term he found time to carry out much geographical work, discovering among other places Lake Nyasa (now Lake Malawi).

He set himself the task of tracing the source of the Nile. But it proved too much for him and he arrived at Ujiji worn out and almost starving. It was there that he was found by the *New York Herald* journalist H. M. Stanley (*p. 252*).

He was begged to return to Europe, but he refused. Once more he set out to find the source of the Nile, but he died at Ilala.

Lyell, Sir Charles (1797–1875)
Scottish geologist

Lyell was called the father of modern geology, the science of the structure of the earth. As a young scholar he travelled all over Europe on geological expeditions. His work led him to dispute the theory that the geological changes in the history of the earth were due to violent alterations, and he believed they were for the most part gradual evolutions.

Lyell was also very interested in Darwin's theory of natural selection and he used his influence to support Darwin through years of controversy.

Andersen, Hans Christian (1805–1875)
Danish author

When Hans Andersen was only eleven, his father, a poor shoemaker, died, and there was no more money for the boy to go on at school. So he set out for Copenhagen where he decided to become a singer. But he had no real voice and no one wanted to hear him. When he was almost dying from starvation he was rescued by an agent of the King of Denmark, and the royal master arranged for Hans to complete his education.

In his adulthood, Andersen wrote children's stories, and many of these are among the loveliest and the saddest ever penned. *The Ugly Duckling* revealed that he never forgot his humble upbringing or the hardships of his youth.

Fox-Talbot, William Henry (1800–1877)
English pioneer of photography

In 1839 Fox-Talbot made a major advance in the development of photography when he invented and described 'photogenic drawing'. His idea was improved

The meeting of Henry Stanley and David Livingstone in Central Africa

and two years later the Talbotype Process was patented. Ten years after that he discovered a method of instant photography.

Russell, Lord John (1792–1878)
British statesman
A great liberal, Russell was one of the first advocates of parliamentary reform. In 1832 he became leader of the Whigs in opposition, and in 1846 was Prime Minister when the Tories were defeated.

As foreign secretary he was in favour of the 'Italy for the Italians' movement and helped keep Britain neutral in the American Civil War. He was prime minister again in 1865, but retired when the Whigs were defeated.

Victor Emmanuel (1820–1878) II of Sardinia (1849–1861) and I of Italy (1861–1878)
King of Sardinia and Italy
Victor Emmanuel has two claims to distinction in Italian history. First, he was an enlightened King of Sardinia, who very wisely appointed Count Cavour (*p. 224*) as his prime minister. Secondly, when that matchless Italian statesman had got all the states of Italy, except Rome and Venice, to unite in one nation, Victor Emmanuel was by far the most

suitable man to be proclaimed King of the new Italy, in 1861. And Cavour's faith was not misplaced. Victor Emmanuel governed extremely well for 17 years, strictly within his constitutional powers. In 1870 Rome joined the union.

Hill, Sir Rowland (1795–1879)
English pioneer of postal reform
Born in Kidderminster, Hill became a schoolmaster, and in the course of teaching geography he became very interested in Southern Australia and its colonization.

From this interest he became involved with the idea of organized mail, on a rate depending not on how far the letter travelled, but on how much it weighed.

In 1837 he issued a pamphlet on Post Office reform and advocated the issue of adhesive stamps for letters and parcels carrying different denominational values with the penny as the basic unit – which would be the charge for a letter. At first the idea was opposed, but the government of 1839 introduced it in their budget and the penny postage system came into being the following year.

From then on Hill worked for the Post Office department, was made secretary to the Post Office in 1854, and was knighted in 1860.

Clerk Maxwell, James (1831–1879)
Scottish physicist
James Clerk Maxwell became professor of physics at London in 1860, and in 1871 was appointed the first professor of physics at Cambridge. In this later post he supervised the erection and outfitting of the Cavendish Laboratory, now probably the most famous physics laboratory in the world.

His whole academic life, which was not very long, compared with that of, say, Lord Kelvin (*p. 254*) or Sir William Crookes was nonetheless filled with brilliant achievements. The most remarkable of these was his theory that light and electricity are the same in their eventual nature. This led to a much clearer understanding of the properties of electricity.

St. Bernadette (1844–1879)
French visionary
Bernadette Soubirous was the daughter of poor peasants in the district around the French village of Lourdes. She was not healthy and as she could not play games, spent a lot of time day-dreaming and watching the sky.

One day she claimed to have had a vision of the Virgin Mary, as the Immaculate Conception, speaking to her in a grotto outside Lourdes. The Virgin Mary is said to have told her that the waters in the grotto had healing powers. At first Bernadette was not believed, but when one or two people actually did get some sort of cure, it seemed obvious to many that some kind of miracle had happened. Her claim was debated fiercely all round France, especially among medical circles which, as you would expect, did not believe her.

She spent the rest of her life in a convent, doing good works for other people, getting slowly more and more sick, until she could no longer get out of bed. She died in 1879. Meanwhile, every year, people still go to the shrine at Lourdes and, miraculously, some get cured.

Eliot, George (1819–1880)
English authoress
George Eliot was the pen name of Mary Ann Evans, a prosperous Midlands farmer's daughter who showed, even at an early age, an amazing facility for writing prose. In the 1850s she began to write articles in periodical magazines and these attracted a great deal of attention. To get them accepted she had at first to use a pen name, and one of a man at that, such was the average prejudice against women doing anything creative. She became popular, however, among literary people who knew her secret, and she moved in these circles for the rest of her life.

George Eliot's novels included *Adam Bede*, the story of a carpenter who married a simple-minded village girl, *Silas Marner*, a very sad and emotional tale, and *Middlemarch*, a novel about a typical 19th century provincial town.

Flaubert, Gustave (1821–1880)
French novelist
Flaubert, against his own will, studied law in Paris. While he was there he became friendly with Victor Hugo, among other literary figures. It was not long after he left that he put his talent for writing into practice.

Two factors seem to have influenced his work. One was a dislike of the middle classes, and the other was a nervous disease which gave him a very morbid outlook on life.

As a novelist his masterpiece was *Madame Bovary*. It is an impressive tragedy of a woman who is unhappily married and turns to an immoral life. Flaubert was also a master of the short story, and is considered to have influenced Guy de Maupassant, regarded as one of the best short story writers of all time.

Carlyle, Thomas (1795–1881)
Scottish essayist and historian
Carlyle spent his young adult years writing in many fields – literary criticism, autobiography, magazine articles, essays and biography. Then in 1834 he moved from Edinburgh to London to live in Chelsea, where he remained until his death. He soon became known as the 'Sage of Chelsea'.

In 1837 Carlyle produced his masterly account of the French Revolution and this established him as a leading figure in literature. Eight years later he brought about a considerable change in Victorian man's opinion about Cromwell, by means of his brilliant study and his editing of the great statesman's letters and speeches. He then devoted a large part of the years 1852 to 1865 to a very detailed and penetrating biography of Frederick the Great (*p. 186*).

Disraeli, Benjamin, 1st Earl of Beaconsfield (1804–1881)
English statesman
This brilliant Jewish dandy was laughed at when he made his first speech in Parliament, aged 32. But as he sat down he said, 'I will sit down now, but the time will

Benjamin Disraeli

it was here he really showed his brilliance. He sent a British fleet to check the Russian threat to Turkish interests in the Balkans; he stopped Russia from trying to take over Turkish territories at the Congress of Berlin in 1878, and he sent an expeditionary force to Afghanistan to stop Russian advances towards India.

When the ruler of Egypt, the Khedive, put his Suez Canal shares up for sale, Disraeli bought them on behalf of the British government. This was a great personal gamble as he had to borrow more than £4 million from Lord Rothschild to complete the deal, for Parliament was not sitting at the time. But it gave Britain control of the Suez Canal, the short route to India and the East.

Disraeli was made Earl of Beaconsfield, but stayed head of the administration until its defeat at an election in 1880. He retired and died the following year.

Disraeli was very popular with Queen Victoria. When she shut herself off from the people after her husband, Prince Albert, died in 1861, it was he, more than anyone, who got her to take up her public duties again.

Dostoevsky, Fyodor Mikhailovich (1821–1881)
Russian novelist

Since his death, Dostoevsky has become known as one of the greatest of the Russian novelists. His life was full of interest and danger. He spent some time in the army, then he took up writing. He got involved in a plot against the government, was caught and sentenced to death. Luckily for him this was commuted to imprisonment in Siberia. When he got back to European Russia he started up a magazine called *The Times*. It was, apart from anything else, very critical of the government, and it was closed down. He tried again but was unsuccessful. Then he got into debt and had to leave the country.

Although his earliest novels were written in the 1840s, it was some of his later ones that made him famous. Among these were *Crime and Punishment*, *The Idiot* and *The Brothers Karamazov*.

come when you will hear me.' And hear him they did, for he twice became prime minister. Although a Conservative, Disraeli had spent his first years in parliament as an independent, while assessing how things were developing. In 1846 he attacked Peel (*p. 218*) over the Corn Laws and split the Conservatives.

In 1868 Disraeli took over from Derby as prime minister. But he was swept out of office with the Conservatives soon afterwards, when a general election chose a Liberal government under Gladstone. Disraeli returned as prime minister in 1874. His work at home included the Public Health Act, a Combination Act making strikes legal, and a Merchant Shipping Act which prevented the overloading of ships.

He then turned to foreign policy, and

Giuseppe Garibaldi and his redshirts invading Sicily

Emerson, Ralph Waldo (1803–1882)
American essayist
Ordained as a minister in a non-conformist church, Emerson travelled to Europe where he met Coleridge, Wordsworth and Carlyle, with whom he maintained correspondence for over 40 years.

Emerson's essays and lectures were drawn from his own experiences and observations over the years and they expressed his philosophy. With the approach of the American Civil War he became outspoken as an anti-slavery campaigner and he was pleased to see the war begin. He originated wise adages. One was: 'We boil at different degrees.'

Garibaldi, Giuseppe (1807–1882)
Italian patriot
Garibaldi was a leader of the movement to make a nation out of the various states in Italy. An officer in the Piedmontese army, he was a man of widely recognized bravery and leadership, and in 1860 he created a loyal force of 1,000 tough, patriotic men who were ready to follow him anywhere. He dressed them in red shirts, and with them invaded Sicily, one of the states that did not want unity. In a swift campaign he conquered the island and then prepared to cross to the mainland of Italy to take Naples. Equally swiftly he expelled the king of Naples.

The fight for unity went on until 1870, and in the first all-Italian Parliament, which was elected soon afterwards, Garibaldi had a seat representing Rome.

Longfellow, Henry Wadsworth (1807–1882)
American poet
One of the most famous narrative poems in the English language is *The Song of Hiawatha*. It is about a Red Indian chieftain who tries to get his people to give up continual fighting and think more about peace.

It was written by Longfellow, the professor of literature at Harvard university from 1836 to 1854, who contributed other long poems to American literature which have become celebrated, which include *Paul Revere's Ride* and *The Village Blacksmith*.

Darwin, Charles Robert (1809–1882)
English naturalist
Darwin, along with Karl Marx and Sigmund Freud, radically altered man's way of thinking. He upset centuries of beliefs, and he was to have a profound effect on the nineteenth century.

Darwin showed that man was descended from an ancestor common to man and the anthropoid apes; he put forward a theory of evolution which contradicted the long accepted view of the origins of man as deriving from Adam and Eve.

Darwin was educated at Shrewsbury, Edinburgh and Cambridge. While he was at Cambridge he became seriously interested in natural history and geology, and, in 1831, he went on an expedition to the South Seas in HMS *Beagle*. Over five years he collected numerous details about flowers, animals, rocks and fossils.

His first book, *On the Origin of Species*, published in 1859, explained his theory of evolution. This was that individual animals of any species are slightly different from one another, in that some are better equipped to tackle the conditions of nature than others. Because these are the ones who survive long enough to reproduce themselves and thrive, their own characteristics are passed on to their offspring, and all living things are continually adapting to fit their surroundings.

The *Descent of Man*, which he published 12 years later, was another sensational book. It showed that Man, like other animals, was derived over millions of years from more primitive ancestors.

Blanc, Louis (1811–1882)
French socialist
Louis Blanc, who was a journalist, began to write reviews for socialist papers. But he rose to real prominence through two books he wrote in 1840, *Organisation de Travail* and *Histoire de Dix Ans*.

He was bitterly critical of Louis Philippe, the French king (1830–1848), and he became a member of the revolutionary government which turned him out in 1848. Blanc persuaded the new government to give a guarantee of employment to all workers, but the politicians failed to implement this promise, and this discredited his idea. He came to live in England, returned to France in 1871 and after the abdication of Napoleon III, took a seat in the National Assembly. He wrote a 12-volume study on the French Revolution, which is a standard work on the subject.

Trollope, Anthony (1815–1882)
English novelist
Born in London, Trollope came from a background of misfortune. His mother was a hard-working novelist herself, and but for that the family would have been in poverty because of his father's inability to manage his affairs.

Trollope is best remembered for his *Barsetshire* series of novels which began in 1855 with *The Warden*. The books draw in great depth some very colourful characters, and sensitively depict life in a cathedral town.

After this series Trollope turned to writing a number of political novels which included the *Prime Minister* and the *Duke's Children*. He was for some time a fully employed civil servant, and wrote his books in his spare time.

Rossetti, Dante Gabriel (1828–1882)
English painter and poet
At the age of 20, Rossetti, a gifted poet, was one of the founder members of the Pre-Raphaelite Brotherhood, a school of Victorian painters who endeavoured to recapture a purity of painting that they considered to have been lost since Raphael (*p. 117*). With him were Holman Hunt and John Millais. He turned his attention to water colours, mostly of legendary or romantic subjects. Then he tried his hand at stained glass windows, as well as painting a number of great pictures for churches.

Only two years after marrying Elizabeth Siddal, whom he and his associates painted many times, she died of narcotics, and in grief he buried all his manuscript poems with her.

Wagner, Richard (1813–1883)
German composer

This German composer started his career as a conductor and gradually became involved in opera. He had achieved some limited success before he was accused of taking part in an uprising in 1848.

He was forced to leave Germany and went to Zurich where he stayed for the next decade, having an affair for much of the time with the wife of one of his best friends. In 1870, after he had returned to Germany, he married Franz Liszt's daughter Cosima.

One of his most famous operas is *The Flying Dutchman*; his greatest achievement was the epic *Ring* cycle.

His music had strong patriotic tones, and much of it dealt with Germanic mythical heroes.

Karl Marx expounding his politics

Marx, Karl (1818–1883)
German political philosopher

The political works of Marx have had a more profound effect on the governments of the twentieth century than perhaps any other single factor. Marx, a Jew born in Trier, which was then in Rhenish Prussia, also lived in Paris and London.

In London he dedicated himself to his work, developing his theory of socialism and the need for radical reform. In his works *Das Kapital* and *The Communist Manifesto* (which he worked on with Engels), he gave an impetus to much of the radical thinking of the time.

Marx was among the first to see history as being a process determined by economic and materialistic factors. He saw Communism as a natural development from Feudalism and Capitalism. Marx thought therefore that his version of socialism would come first to industrialized countries like Britain and Germany. As it turned out he was mistaken. Communism has been looked to as a solution to poverty rather than as an extension of industrialization. And the first communist state was set up in Russia, in 1918, then nearly a century behind Western Europe in development. Marx's theories are believed in by millions of people all over the world.

Turgenev, Ivan Sergevitch (1818–1883)
Russian novelist and playwright

Turgenev was one of Russia's greatest writers. He had started his career as a government servant, but in his free time he began to write. In about 1850 he came into a huge fortune and this enabled him to forget about a job and devote his time exclusively to writing and to do so in comfort.

There followed a series of great novels and short stories, of which *Helene*, *Fathers and Sons* and *Virgin Soil* are among the best.

Smetana, Bedrich (1824–1884)
Czech composer

Smetana has come into his own a great deal in recent years, as a European composer of high quality. While audiences have enjoyed his opera, *The Bartered Bride*, for a century, his symphonies and some of his chamber music have emerged as great works only in the last generation or so.

Cetewayo (d.1884)
Zulu ruler

Cetewayo ruled Zululand from 1873–1879 and defeated the British at the battle of Isandhlwana, only to be defeated himself at Ulundi. He was restored as ruler of his kingdom in 1883 but was rejected by his people and he died in exile the following year. He had been a great Zulu chief who earned the respect of friends and enemies alike.

Shaftesbury, Anthony Ashley Cooper, 7th Earl of (1801–1885)
English politician and social reformer

As a young man Shaftesbury seemed to have life set for him. He was born into a rich family, found safe seats in parliament and was lord of the admiralty by 1834. However, he decided to devote his time and money to the cause of improving the lot of those less fortunate than himself.

In 1828 he began to agitate for better treatment of lunatics, then for a ten-hour day for adults working in factories, and also for the abolition of child labour. Next he turned his attention to the institutions for children and to improving lodging houses for the poor. When he died in 1885 there was no comparison between their condition and the squalor in which he had once found them.

London's Shaftesbury Avenue is named after him, and the statue of Eros in Piccadilly Circus was erected in his memory.

Hugo, Victor (1802–1885)
French writer

Hugo, one of the great figures in French literature, established himself as a leader of the Romantic movement in his country with his novels and verse. But he was not always popular with the establishment,

and the Emperor Louis Napoleon banished him.

Born into the aristocracy, Hugo made a name for himself at the age of 17 when he won three prizes in a Toulouse poetry competition. As well as novels Hugo wrote plays, among which was one on the English Lord Protector, Cromwell. His full length books included *Les Misérables* a masterpiece of social history.

Grant, Ulysses Simpson (1822–1885)
18th President of the U.S.A. (1868–1876)

After serving in the American army during the Mexican war, like his great opponent Robert E. Lee, Grant left the army. But with the outbreak of the Civil War in 1861 he re-enlisted, on the Union side.

During the war he broke the confederate control of Mississippi by taking Vicksburg where he captured 30,000 confederate troops. After further successes at Lockout Mountain and Missionary he was given command of the Union Troops. He organized the army in an all-out attack and gradually wore down the confederate resistance. He received their surrender at the Appomattox court house in 1865.

In 1868 he became president of the U.S.A. and was re-elected in 1872. While he was himself perfectly honest, his administration was marred by scandal.

Gordon, Charles George (1833–1885)
British general

Gordon first saw action at Sebastapol in 1855 during the Crimean War. Five years later he was sent to China where he took part in the capture of Peking.

He then moved to the Sudan as an engineer, and later became its governor. He retired, but the British government asked him to relieve the British garrison there which had fallen into rebel hands. Soon after his arrival he was besieged by the Mahdi, and it was five months before a British relief expedition was organized in England. It arrived two days too late. Khartoum had been taken and Gordon had been murdered on the palace steps.

Ranke, Leopold Von (1795–1886)
German historian

Ranke's books on history changed the whole approach of historians to their subject. He promoted the idea of objective writing, instead of relying on legend and tradition, and in doing so criticized many of his contemporaries.

Liszt, Franz (1811–1886)
Hungarian composer and pianist

This Hungarian musician was not only an exceptionally fine pianist but also a very accomplished composer. After studying music throughout Europe he became a concert pianist, but withdrew from the stage in 1835 and lived in semi-retirement. He had three children, one of whom was to marry the composer Richard Wagner.

The works he is best remembered for are his lively and much loved *Hungarian Rhapsodies*, but he composed many more lengthy concertos and symphonies.

Lind, Jenny (1820–1887)
Swedish singer

The Swedish Nightingale, as she was called, had one of the most marvellous voices ever heard in a concert hall. It was pure, natural, seemingly untrained but still perfectly harmonious, and its range was enormous.

She appeared in London in 1847 in opera, but she did not like the rather free and easy atmosphere and behaviour of London theatrical people. So she gave up the stage and concentrated on recitals. She married her accompanist, Otto Goldschmidt, and they lived in Dresden for a while. Then they came to England and he founded the London Bach Choir, in which Jenny led the sopranos. Her voice was such that she attracted attention from the greatest people in many walks of life.

Lear, Edward (1812–1888)
English nonsense poet

As well as writing some of the best nonsense in the English language, Edward Lear was also a very serious and talented landscape painter. He was employed by the Earl of Derby to paint the animals in his private zoo, and while he was there wrote his *Book of Nonsense* for his son. In Lear's *Nonsense Songs* we find famous comic characters such as *The Owl and the Pussycat* and *The Dong with the Luminous Nose*.

In 1836 he left the Earl's home and set up a studio as a landscape painter near Rome, telling of his travels in Mediterranean countries in his *Illustrated Journals of a Landscape Painter*.

Alcott, Louisa M. (1832–1888)
American writer of children's books

Louisa May Alcott had to earn a living at at an early age because her father had no sense of responsibility, and would not go out to work. She started to make dresses. Then she began to write stories for magazines. During the American Civil War she was a nurse in a Unionist hospital. This affected her health and she went home again.

Once back home she decided to write books, and her first children's story was *Little Women*, which was immediately successful. This earned enough money for the whole family. Then she followed it up with other books like *Good Wives* and *Little Men*.

Browning, Robert (1812–1889)
English poet

Browning was a gifted poet who, from time to time, produced some extremely fine verse. Early in the 1840s he met Elizabeth Moulton Barrett, who was also a poet, and who lived with her family in London's Wimpole Street. They were all dominated by her stern father. Elizabeth was confined largely to bed, believed to be an invalid, but Browning was not convinced that she was as ill as that. He gave her enormous encouragement, reading her verses, writing and reading his to her, and in 1846 he asked her to marry him. Because of her father, they had to elope, fleeing to Italy where they lived happily for fifteen years before she died. One of Brownings more popular works is *Bells and Pomegranates* which includes *The Pied Piper of Hamelin*.

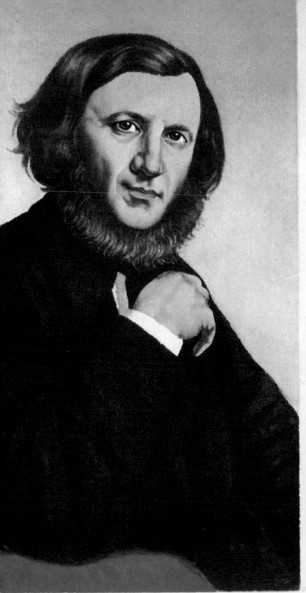

English poets, Robert Browning and his wife, Elizabeth Barrett

Newman, John Henry (1801–1890)
English cardinal

Newman entered the Church and rose to be the leader of the Church of England reform movement, known as the Oxford Movement. This was also called the Tractarian movement on account of the large number of religious pamphlets (or tracts) it published.

His work led him to try to bring the Church of England closer to the Roman Catholic Church, but this brought him violent criticism. So he left the English Church and became a Roman Catholic. Soon afterwards, he became a priest and set up a ministry in Birmingham which gathered a huge following. Newman's great work was rewarded when in 1879 the Pope created him a cardinal.

Nasmyth, James (1808–1890)
Scottish engineer

Nasmyth invented the steam hammer. He did so for I. K. Brunel (*p. 223*) to use in forging a huge wrought iron paddle-shaft for his ship, the *Great Britain*. It was but one of numerous inventions produced by this ingenious engineer who also wrote a delightful autobiography. His inventions brought him great wealth.

241

Napier, Robert Cornelius, 1st Baron (1810–1890)
British field marshal

Lord Napier is famous for a celebrated march across Abyssinia in 1869 to relieve the town of Magdala, then in the hands of native rebels. For this he was made a baron. Before that he had had a distinguished career as army engineer building bridges, roads and canals in India, often under conditions of warfare and violence.

In 1870 he was appointed commander-in-chief of the British Army in India, and became a field marshal in 1883. In later life Napier was Governor of Gibraltar, then Constable of the Tower of London. There is a statue to commemorate him at one end of Queen's Gate in London's South Kensington.

Schliemann, Heinrich (1822–1890)
German archaeologist

This German archaeologist remained an amateur, retiring from business early to try and prove that what the Greek poet Homer wrote about Troy was not myth – as many were saying – but fact.

With this object in mind he set about excavating the remains of the ancient city of Troy, and in the face of considerable public criticism he unearthed the sites of nine cities, one of them the city of King Priam, that had been overthrown after a ten-year struggle with Greece. One of the clues which led to his excavating at the right spot was the appearance of ancient coins of the period in local markets, which had been scavenged by urchins and sold to traders.

Van Gogh, Vincent (1853–1890)
Dutch painter

A tense, emotional person, Van Gogh left a highly individual mark on the development of painting. While he is now regarded as a master of art, few had any time for his paintings during his lifetime. It was a troubled life. Having lived in England and performed missionary work amongst the miners of Belgium, he moved to Paris, where he became influenced by the Impressionists. When he moved to Arles the provencial landscape

Vincent Van Gogh

inspired him to a brilliant explosion of light and colour. He thought he had found satisfaction when he started living with the artist Gauguin. But they ended up quarrelling, and Van Gogh cut off the lobe of one of his ears in remorse.

He was committed to an insane asylum, and not long after leaving it, shot himself on the scene of his last painting, the *Corn Field*.

Moltke, Count Helmuth Von (1800–1891)
Prussian soldier

Moltke played an important part in making Bismarck's early wars successful. With the support of Bismarck and Von Roon he re-organized the Prussian army. Moltke directed the strategy of the wars against Denmark (1864), Austria (1866) and France (1870–1871) in which Prussia was successful. The war with Austria lasted only a few weeks and ended when the Prussians inflicted a crushing defeat at Königsgratz, for which Moltke was responsible.

Whitman, Walt (1819–1891)
American poet

Whitman was without doubt one of the greatest of all American poets. But in his own lifetime he found few admirers in his own country. He was not an easily

Walt Whitman

satisfied man. In his early career he worked in a doctor's office, solicitor's office, as a teacher and as a printer. He finally settled in journalism, but did not hold any one post for very long.

In 1855 he had his first book of poems *Leaves of Grass* published, and then a book of prose *Specimen Days and Collect*. These major works of his life are full of exuberance, vitality and stylistic innovation.

In the 1870s he became paralysed, and but for the help from some trans-Atlantic admirers, would probably have died in poverty.

Sherman, William Tecumseh (1820–1891)
American army commander

Sherman was brigadier-general of the Union reserves during the American Civil War. He fought at the battle of Bull Run, served under Grant at Shiloh and Corinth, and took part in the capture of Vicksburg. He is best known, however, for leading the famous march through Georgia, from Chattanooga to Atlanta, after a series of fights.

In 1865 he received the surrender of the confederate army under Johnson. Four years later he succeeded General Grant (*p. 239*) as commander-in-chief of the U.S. army.

Blavatsky, Helena Petrovna (1831–1891)
Russian spiritualist

Madame Blavatsky was the grand-daughter of a Russian princess. She married a Russian general, then left him, and spent several years travelling about Tibet and India. There she became fascinated with spiritualism, occult sciences and psychic powers. After much study she claimed to be able to perform miracles. She returned to Europe, and then went to the United States, where she founded the Theosophical Society to promote her psychic work.

Many people believed in her powers, and joined the Society, but when its activities and beliefs were investigated some flaws were found. But this did not affect her popularity, which lasted up to her death.

Manning, Henry Edward (1808–1892)
English cardinal

Manning started his career as a member of the Church of England and was archdeacon of Chichester Cathedral for eleven years, from 1840. He then became a Roman catholic, and rose to be archbishop of Westminster in 1865. Ten years later he was made a cardinal. He took a great interest in temperance and benevolent movements.

Tennyson, Alfred, 1st Baron Tennyson (1809–1892)
English poet

Lord Tennyson is regarded by many as one of the greatest of Britain's poets. Brought up in Lincolnshire, where he went to grammar school, he was the son of a clergyman.

He started writing poetry at Cambridge but his first attempts were far from successful, and it was not until he was 33 that he became famous with his poems, *Le Morte d'Arthur*, *Ulysses* and *Locksley Hall*. In 1850 he wrote *In Memoriam*, thought to be his greatest poem. His other works included *The Charge of the Light Brigade*, *The Idylls of a King* and *The Revenge*. Tennyson was made Poet Laureate in 1850, and created a baron in 1884.

A scene from Tchaikovsky's *Swan Lake*

Tchaikovsky, Peter Ilyich (1840–1893)
Russian composer

Tchaikovsky, the son of a Russian mines inspector, showed musical talent at an early age. Although he was encouraged to study music, when his family moved to St. Petersburg, he went to the university to study law.

He worked for some time as a civil servant after qualifying, but when he was 22 he went back to the university to study music. He never completed his course, but instead moved to Moscow to help his former teacher Nicholas Rubinstein. His operas and first symphonies brought him to fame in Moscow.

He did not have a happy life. Supposed to be a homosexual, Tchaikovsky had a most unsuccessful marriage which broke up only weeks after the wedding. It left him in a state of nervous exhaustion, and he retired to the country to try to compose in peace. He made very few trips away from his retreat. But it was soon after he had made a journey to England that he contracted cholera and died. Shortly before his death his last work, the *Pathétique* Symphony, had its first performance. He was one of the best loved of all Russian composers. His works include six symphonies and several concerti.

Maupassant, Henri René Albert Guy de (1850–1893)
French writer

Maupassant is regarded by some as the greatest short story writer of all time. He certainly influenced many other writers, notably Britain's Somerset Maugham. Among the many collections of short stories by Maupassant were *Boule de Suif*, *La Maison Tellier* and *Contes et Nouvelles*. His supremacy has not been challenged. His style, dramatic, sometimes cynical, always rivetting, was so well constructed in French that it has lent itself to translation in several other languages without any loss of the sense or drama.

Kossuth, Lajos (1802–1894)
Hungarian patriot and statesman

Kossuth was a tremendous patriot for the cause of his native Hungary. In 1848, the year of revolutions throughout Europe, he led the rising in Hungary.

He persuaded the National Assembly to declare Hungary an independent state, and took control of it with the absolute power of a dictator. But soon afterwards the revolution was crushed, and Kossuth was forced to flee, taking up exile in Turkey.

Lesseps, Ferdinand, Vicomte de (1805–1894)
French diplomat and promoter of the Suez Canal

While Minister for France at Madrid between 1848–1849, de Lesseps had the brilliant idea of constructing a canal across Suez. He received the concession for its construction from Said Pasha of Egypt in 1854, and was a principal founder of the fund-raising company which won public subscriptions to carry out the work. This was carried out between 1859 and 1869.

He was also president of the French company that worked on the Panama Canal, but gave up because of financial and political difficulties.

Rossetti, Christina (1830–1894)
English poet

Christina Georgina Rossetti was the sister of Dante Gabriel Rossetti (*p. 237*), and they had been refugees from the state of Naples in Italy. Their father was professor of Italian at London University, and they grew up in an academic atmosphere.

Christina developed an intense devotion to religion very early in her life, and it never left her. For this reason she declined offers of marriage, thinking that she could not reconcile happiness with a man with spiritual love for God. So her poetry was in many respects sad and wistful. In 1862 she produced a collection of verse called *Goblin Market and Other Poems*, illustrated by her brother, Dante. She went on writing verse for some years, and it was simple, pure and flowing. In her everyday life she was the soul of kindness and helpfulness. Many people thought her a saint.

Hertz, Heinrich Rudolf (1857–1894)
German physicist

Like James Clerk Maxwell (*p. 233*) Hertz did not live long, but in his time packed in an enormous amount of research in physics and produced important discoveries. Hertz discovered electric or electro-magnetic waves, measured their length and speed, and showed how you could treat them in the same manner as light waves, that is, bend, reflect or polarize them. His work was a great help towards the search for ways of bouncing waves from one place to another without the need for cables and wires, and enabled people like Marconi to make progress with their wireless experiments.

Engels, Friedrich (1820–1895)
German socialist
Engels worked with Karl Marx on the famous *Communist Manifesto* which was published in 1847. He also agitated for reform in the state of Baden in Germany, but had to leave the country because of his activities. He came to England on business, but became horrified by the poverty and conditions created by the Industrial Revolution, writing several studies upon the subject. He joined up with Marx once more in spreading socialism. Engels had some private funds of his own and for years he kept Marx in pocket money, but Marx was never particularly grateful.

Pasteur, Louis (1822–1895)
French chemist
Pasteur is France's most famous scientist. He discovered that germs existed, and caused infection. He also showed that you could destroy many of them by applying heat, and his technique of 'pasteurizing' fluids like milk to free them from germs is still practised everywhere. Pasteur discovered an inoculation against the dread disease of anthrax, and he found a cure for hydrophobia, or rabies, which you could catch if you were bitten by a mad dog.

Pasteur's work on germs encouraged Britain's Lord Lister (*p. 259*) to introduce his revolutionary antiseptic system.

Huxley, Thomas Henry (1825–1895)
English biologist
A friend and contemporary of Darwin, Huxley was born in Ealing. He studied medicine and practised as a surgeon in the Royal Navy and in civilian life.

He was diligent in research and experimental work and undertook many studies in biology. His theories went a long way to corroborate those of Charles Darwin (*p. 237*).

He became president of the Royal Society in 1883 and was in constant demand as a speaker and a member of Royal Commissions. He was made a privy councillor in 1892 but turned down both a baronetcy and a knighthood.

Stambuloff, Stefan (1855–1895)
Bulgarian statesman
Stambuloff was a leading figure in the Bulgarian national revolt against the Ottoman Empire in 1875. When the state of Bulgaria was recognized he was elected to the board of regency which was to rule it in 1886, and a year later he became prime minister. His policy was to steer a middle course between Russia and Turkey, and not to offend either, though he was pro-Russian. He governed well, but was eventually forced to retire, and was assassinated in 1895.

Stowe, Harriet Beecher (1811–1896)
American novelist
Harriet Beecher Stowe produced a novel, *Uncle Tom's Cabin*, in serial parts in a magazine in 1852. It was a sensation, for it revealed a lot of the uglier side of life endured by American negro slaves, something the white people in the northern states had been aware of for years, but which the whites in the southern states had been conveniently overlooking. Slaves provided them with their livelihood – for they worked the plantations in the hot, sultry weather that white men did not like.

Harriet was attacked, but unrepentant she produced another novel, *Dred*, further underlining the miseries. When the Civil War broke out in 1861, over the question of slavery, her campaigning was vindicated, particularly when Lincoln abolished slavery in 1863.

Millais, Sir John Everett (1829–1896)
English painter
This Southampton-born son of an old Norman family was, with Rossetti and Holman Hunt, a principal member of the Pre-Raphaelite Brotherhood (*p. 237*) of the Victorian age. In the precise detail which marks the work of the Pre-Raphaelites, Millais painted pictures of religious and mythological subjects such as *Christ in the House of his Parents*, a banquet scene from Keats' *Isabella*, the *Return of the Dove to the Ark* and *Mariana of the Moated Grange*.

Later, he broke away from the style

and developed his own, turning his brushes to portraits and landscapes. He became a baronet and president of the Royal Academy.

Nobel, Alfred (1833–1896)
Swedish inventor
Nobel invented dynamite – by accident. He was making some nitroglycerine, a highly explosive fluid that goes up at the smallest jolt, when some fell out of a flask down towards the floor. But it fell into a box of fine earth powder, called *Kieselguhr* (infusorial earth), and it did not go off. Nobel noticed that the fluid soaked into the powder and formed a sort of paste. With great care he lifted some of the paste out and kneaded it into a pellet. Then he took it outside the laboratory and set it off. It exploded with great force. He had found a safe way of handling nitroglycerine, and he called it dynamite.

Nobel's invention made him millions of pounds. But it also made warfare much more destructive, and in his later years his conscience was troubled. When he died, he left the bulk of his great fortune invested to provide large prizes to be awarded to brilliant people every year. There were to be five, for scientists, authors and workers for peace.

Morris, William (1834–1896)
English craftsman and poet
Morris was going to become a clergyman until his friends in the pre-Raphaelite movement made him realize his interest in the church was limited to a keen love of Gothic architecture.

From then on he became a painter, under their guidance, and later found his own medium when he turned his attention to house furniture and decorations. His work was to prove lastingly popular, and today it has great antique value. In the later part of his life Morris spent a lot of time writing about idealistic socialism. He and his friends looked back to the golden age of the craftsman, foreseeing the debasing effect of mass-production in both social and aesthetic areas.

A William Morris chair

Brahms, Johannes (1833–1897)
German composer and painter
In November 1973 Pablo Casals (*p. 312*), the greatest cellist in the world, died, aged 97. He had known Brahms who had known Liszt (*p. 240*) who had known Chopin (*p. 217*). Brahms was a wonderful pianist who gave concerts to packed houses all over Europe. He had begun by playing 'honky-tonk' pianos in scruffy pubs in Hamburg docklands, to supplement the income of his father, a musician who earned very little money.

He turned to composition in the 1850s, and over the next 40 or more years produced an enormous number of symphonies, piano concertos, songs, piano pieces, and so forth. The best known of his works are probably the piano concertos No. 1 and 2, which are wonderfully romantic.

Brahms was not a happy man. He never married, for he was said to be too frightened of women.

William Ewart Gladstone

Gladstone, Rt. Hon. William Ewart
(1809–1898)
British statesman

Gladstone had one of the most distinguished political careers of the 19th century. He was prime minister for a record number of four times.

The son of a Lanarkshire baronet, he was born in Liverpool and educated at Eton and Christ Church, Oxford. After the 1st Reform Bill was passed in 1832 he won the Newark seat in Parliament.

A year after Gladstone had made his powerful maiden speech on slavery Peel included him as a junior minister in his government, and in 1843 made him president of the board of trade. Gladstone left the Conservatives and joined the Liberal party, for whom he was chancellor of the exchequer before succeeding Lord John Russell as leader of the party in 1867. When they returned to office the following year he became prime minister for the first time. During his term of office he disestablished the Irish Church, and passed the Irish Land Bill and Education Act (1870).

Disraeli took over as prime minister in 1874 but in 1880 Gladstone became the first leading statesman to go to the electorate and woo them. The Liberals were returned to power. But it was not a successful administration and apart from passing the Third Reform Bill Gladstone was thwarted. When his Irish Home Rule Bill was defeated twice he had to resign.

The Conservatives were defeated within a year and Gladstone came back to power. Again he was defeated on the Irish Home Rule Bill and this time spent six years in opposition.

In 1892 the 83-year-old Gladstone, now known as the Grand Old Man of British politics, once more became prime minister. His first action was to bring in the Irish Home Rule Bill yet again, but once more it was defeated and he retired.

This splendidly handsome figure, whose whole life was one of high moral rectitude, was for much of his life very popular. He refused all titles and honours and died, as he had lived, just Mr. Gladstone. But he was never popular with Queen Victoria who, when Gladstone retired after sixty years of service to the state, did not even bother to thank him.

Bessemer, Sir Henry (1813–1898)
British inventor

This Hertfordshire-born engineer revolutionized iron production when he discovered that by pumping a current of air into pig iron, he could make steel. His name is still used in the Bessemer Converter, where the process is completed. As a result of his work, Britain was for some time the leading producer of steel in the world.

Bismarck, Prince Otto Von (1815–1898)
Prussian statesman

Bismarck was a tough and realistic man with a vision of a united Germany to which he devoted his life. He won his reputation as the 'Iron Chancellor' for his policy of solving problems by 'blood and iron', rather than by discussion.

Bismarck studied law and then followed a varied career in Prussian politics until he became President of the Cabinet in 1862. It was then that his policy of blood and iron came into practice when he waged war against first Denmark (1864) and then Austria (1866), over the Schleswig-Holstein question. In both wars Prussia was victorious.

It is not only at war but also at peace that he is remembered. His most lasting achievement was his success in moving Germany towards true unification. At this time what we now know as Germany was a mass of small states around the mighty Prussia and Austria. Bismarck brought first the Northern States together in the North German Confederation and later got the Southern states to join. He was made first chancellor of the new German empire.

While in office he brought in many social and economic reforms. A new emperor succeeded in 1888, the Kaiser Wilhelm II, and Bismarck quarrelled with him. He resigned in 1890.

Carroll, Lewis (Charles Lutwidge Dodgson) (1832–1898)
English author

Lewis Carroll was the man whose imagination gave birth to the tales of *Alice in Wonderland* and *Alice Through the Looking Glass*, its sequel.

He was in fact a mathematics tutor at Oxford, but he is remembered best as a writer. He published several other stories, but none have achieved anything like the reputation of the Alice stories.

Strauss, Johann (1825–1899)
Austrian composer

Although his father was a musician, Strauss was made to study law. But he flouted this imposition, and soon emerged as a young composer and conductor of promise.

He toured Europe and America with his own orchestra, playing his very popular music which included *Blue Danube Waltz*, *Tales from the Vienna Wood*, *Wine, Women and Song* and *Die Fledermaus*.

Prince Otto von Bismarck

Ruskin, John (1819–1900)
Art critic and writer

After excelling at Oxford, Ruskin met the great landscape painter Turner. This meeting inspired him to begin a study of art to prove that the modern painters were greater than the old masters.

It expanded into a major work, and his *Modern Painters* is a brilliantly written treatise, not only on artists, but also on his own views on true art.

In similar prose he went on to write the *Seven Pillars of Architecture*, an appraisal of the contemporary Gothic revival. His *Stones of Venice* is also a major literary work. In the last years of his life, in which he lived in the Lake District, he went out of his mind.

Daimler, Gottlieb (1834–1900)
German engineer

Daimler made one of the earliest cars with gas-driven engines ever to take to the road. In 1885, together with two other engineers, he built his own car, which was driven successfully at about 8 m.p.h. In 1890 he founded the Daimler Motor Company which built the first Mercedes cars.

Nietzsche, Friedrich Wilhelm (1844–1900)
German philosopher

Nietzsche, the son of a Lutheran minister, was a brilliant young man, and after graduating was offered a professorship. He has been said to be the thinker behind the Nazi movement of the 20th century. While he would probably not have agreed with the ideas of men like Hitler, he did believe that an élite should lead the masses away from conventional morality and superstitions. He showed a great contempt for the ordinary man throughout his work. His best known work, *Also Sprach Zarathustra*, promoted his idea of the super man. Zarathustra was himself one of the great leaders in early Aryan mythology. Nietzsche's importance lay in his challenge to reconsider the most deeply rooted tenets of our morality.

Wilde, Oscar Fingall O'Flahertie Wills (1856–1900)
Irish playwright, poet and wit

One thing that made Oscar Wilde one of the most famous names in literature was his incomparable wit and humour. He had an epigram, a funny reply or a wise observation for anything you cared to say to him. Many of these he remembered and used in his four most brilliant comedy plays, *Lady Windermere's Fan*, *A Woman of No Importance*, *An Ideal Husband* and *The Importance of Being Earnest*. This last play has been considered the finest comedy in the English language.

Wilde had a brilliant academic career, winning a double first class honours degree at Oxford and carrying off the Newdigate Prize for Poetry. He spent some years in journalism, literary criticism and lecturing. Then he started on his famous plays which earned him a lot of money.

Wilde was a homosexual in the later part of his life. He dissipated nearly all his wealth by becoming legally involved with the Scottish family of Queensberry; he sued Lord Queensberry for calling him a homosexual, and losing the case because Queensberry proved it was true, he ended up in the criminal court where he received a two-year sentence.

In Reading gaol he wrote a long narrative poem, the *Ballad of Reading Gaol*, one of the most beautiful in the language. When he came out, he went to France and died there in poverty and disgrace in 1900.

Verdi, Guiseppe (1813–1901)
Italian composer

After a humble start – his father was a grocer, and he was not accepted for a place at music school – Verdi rose to be one of the greatest Italians of his day. He eventually had the opportunity to study music at La Scala, the great opera house. Soon after this, misfortune struck him when his wife and both children died.

Then *Nabucco*, his second opera, was produced at La Scala. It was a tremendous success and Verdi was accepted as a composer. After this his way was paved with success, and his great output of work, which lasted into old age, included *Aida*, *Rigoletto* and *La Traviata*. Qualities which helped him in his career were a feeling for the theatre and a tremendous memory for tunes.

Victoria (1819–1901)
Queen of the United Kingdom of Great Britain and Ireland (1837–1901)

Victoria reigned for longer than any other British monarch. Her long life spanned one of the most exciting periods in British history and at the end of it many things had been radically changed.

When she came to the throne on the death of her uncle William IV she was an attractive and intelligent 18-year-old. In 1840 she married Prince Albert of Saxe-Coburg. It was a devoted relationship which was only ended by his early death in 1861. They had had nine children, one of whom was Prince Edward, who became Edward VII on his mother's death.

Victoria and Albert, although limited by parliament in power, were determined to exert some influence over the workings of parliament. They carefully studied all the documents brought to them and sometimes had a calming influence on their ministers.

After Albert died Victoria cut herself off from people and some M.P.s began to suggest compelling her to perform her duties, or even to declare Britain a republic. Disraeli however persuaded her to come out of mourning.

Drawing on the experience of her life with Prince Albert she helped transform Britain and extend its empire. At the end of her life the empire covered a quarter of the world's land surface.

Queen Victoria

McKinley, William (1843–1901)
American president (1897–1901)
McKinley was an Ohio born lawyer who served many years as a member of the House of Representatives. In 1896 he was elected Republican President of the United States and served until 1900 when he was re-elected. The next year, however, an anarchist assassinated him.

Zola, Émile (1840–1902)
French novelist
It was once said that while Ibsen went down to the gutter to cleanse it, Zola went down to bathe in it. What the author of this comment was trying to say about Zola was that while writers like Ibsen were writing powerful plays aimed at social change, Zola was revelling in portraying low life.

In fact he was merely writing about the conditions of men in exploited circumstances. It is true that there is little romantic about his work, but he has achieved immortality through the powerful social observations of novels like *Nana, Germinal, La Terre* and *La Bête Humaine.*

He began his career as a journalist, but had little success and turned to short story writing. He championed the cause of Alfred Dreyfus (*p. 280*) and became unpopular with Frenchmen as a result.

Rhodes, Cecil (1853–1902)
British colonist and financier
Cecil Rhodes, the son of a country clergyman, first went to Africa because it

was felt it would be better for his health. He became a diamond digger there, returning to England to study at Oxford University. He amassed a considerable fortune, and in 1881 Rhodes was elected a member of the Cape Parliament representing Kimberley, the site of his diamond mines.

At this time South Africa was split between areas ruled by Britain and areas ruled by the Boers – descendants of the Dutch settlers. Rhodes' aim was to unite these and bring them into the British Empire.

He helped Britain acquire land in Africa, including the huge area later known as Rhodesia. He became prime minister of the Cape Colony in 1890 and stayed in office for six years, but was forced to resign when his part in the Jameson Raid was discovered.

Rhodes had little to do with the Boer War, and he was dead by the time peace was signed. He left £6 million in his will, most of which was to be used for scholarships to Oxford.

Mommsen, Theodor (1817–1903)
German historian

The 19th century produced many brilliant German historians, some of whom devoted their time to the study of Roman history. None was as painstaking, thorough or in the end produced as lasting a result as Mommsen, to whom even today historians specializing in ancient Rome owe an immeasurable debt. Mommsen was a professor of law and of history. He was also a member of the Prussian Parliament, and at the end of his life he won a Nobel Prize for Literature.

His greatest achievement was a huge catalogue of Roman inscriptions, of which he was editor. This enabled historians to date numerous events, terms of office, reigns, etc., in Roman history. He also wrote a long and detailed history of Rome, in which he demonstrates the greatness of Julius Caesar (*p. 35*).

Salisbury, Robert Arthur Talbot Gascoyne Cecil, 3rd Marquess of (1830–1903)
English statesman

Salisbury was the leading Conservative statesman in the last years of the 19th century and was prime minister three times between 1885 and 1902.

He entered parliament as M.P. for Stamford in 1853 and in 1878 was foreign secretary under Disraeli. When Disraeli died in 1881 he became the new leader of the Conservative party, then in opposition, and he became prime minister briefly in 1885. For most of the last decade of the century he combined the offices of foreign secretary and prime minister. It was an almost unique situation, but one in which he could deal with foreign affairs without consulting his colleagues. In many ways this proved good for Britain.

Salisbury advocated the expansion of the British Empire, but advised conciliation where possible. At home his ministries brought in a local government act, while abroad British territories in Africa were expanded under his government's encouragement.

Kruger, Stephanus Johannes Paulus (1825–1904)
South African statesman

Kruger was born in the Cape Colony in South Africa, but emigrated to the Orange River area in the Great Trek (1836). He helped to found the state of the Transvaal and this was recognized as independent in 1852.

In 1877, the Transvaal was annexed by Britain following difficulties between the Boers and the British. A Boer rebellion followed, led by Kruger. When it was over he was made president. It was a difficult time: the Boers and the British were unable to bury their differences. And in 1899 the Second Boer War broke out. But Kruger was too old to take part, though he did travel around Europe looking for support for the Boer cause.

Dvořàk, Antonin (1841–1904)
Czechoslovakian composer

Dvořàk, the son of a butcher, and one himself for a short while, started composing in secret while playing the viola in an orchestra.

He found recognition in 1873 with his strongly patriotic *Hymnus*. He was then commissioned to write his famed *Slavonic Dances*. The influence of Brahms was strong in Dvořàk, who by 1891 had won world wide recognition and the offer of the directorate of the New York conservatoire. It was there he wrote his ninth symphony, *From the New World*, which is perhaps his most popular work, and among the most beautiful pieces of music ever created.

Stanley, Sir Henry Morton (1841–1904)
Journalist and explorer

Stanley was born in Wales as John Rowlands, but he was adopted by a New

after being captured enlisted in the U.S. Navy.

He worked as a reporter in Asia Minor, Crete, Spain and Abyssinia, until 1869 when he was commissioned by the New York Herald to lead an expedition to find the British explorer Dr. Livingstone. This he did after many months' search, and greeted him with the famous words 'Dr. Livingstone, I presume'.

After this expedition he continued exploring in Africa, charting several regions and setting up trading posts for the Belgian government.

Chekhov, Anton Pavlovich (1860–1904)
Russian playwright

Chekhov became a doctor but gave up practice early on in order to write. Chekhov produced several brilliant plays which are frequently produced at theatres or on television in many countries every year. Among these are *The Cherry Orchard*, *Uncle Vanya* and *The Three Sisters*. The plays are tragic, with some flashes of humour, and they are realistic portraits of what was his social milieu.

Verne, Jules (1828–1905)
French writer

Verne was one of the earliest science fiction writers. After studying law and writing an opera libretto he began to write extraordinary tales, and often predicted what science would later produce. His work had a strong influence on that of H. G. Wells (*p. 292*).

His books, which are still as popular as ever, included *Journey to the Centre of the Earth*, *Around the World in Eighty Days* and *20,000 Leagues Under the Sea*.

Irving, Sir Henry (1838–1905)
English actor

Irving's real name was John Henry Brodribb; he changed his name upon deciding to go on the stage for a career. This amazing dramatic performer became the greatest actor of his generation, and the first to be given a knighthood, in 1895. His ashes are buried in Westminster Abbey.

Paulus Kruger

Orleans merchant who gave him his own name. He had a spirit of adventure throughout his life, which first showed when he ran away from a British workhouse in 1856 and found his way across the Atlantic from Liverpool to New Orleans.

When the American Civil War broke out he joined the Confederate Army, and

In his time he acted great dramatic parts as diverse as Macbeth, Othello, Shylock and Mephistopheles, some much better than others. But his striking presence endeared him to his public, who came year after year to see him. In 1878 he joined Ellen Terry (*p. 272*) at the Lyceum Theatre, as manager, and this partnership lasted 24 years.

Barnardo, Dr. Thomas John (1845–1905)
Irish born philanthropist

Dr. Barnardo's Homes for orphaned children have long been famous in Britain and other parts of the world. They were founded by Dr. Barnardo, an Irish born clerk who gave up his job to study medicine. He came to London in 1867 and was deeply moved by the number and condition of children running or crawling about the streets, evidently without homes and in desperate need of care. So he founded the East End Mission for destitute children, and by talking and writing to famous people, and lobbying them, he persuaded them to help him open other homes. These came to be known as Barnardo Homes.

Ibsen, Henrik (1828–1906)
Norwegian playwright

The plays of Ibsen did much to pioneer the now popular trend of social drama. They are more than just entertainment – they convey a serious moral rooted in acute social and psychological observation.

Before 1879 he had written a number of works which had not been terribly successful, but in that year *The Doll's House*, which was the first of his great plays, caused a sensation. Among those that followed were *The Master Builder*, *An Enemy of the People*, *Ghosts* and *The Wild Duck*.

Ibsen had a strong influence on world dramatic writing, and he was particularly championed by George Bernard Shaw.

Cézanne, Paul (1839–1906)
French painter

This specialist in still-life and landscape

Henrik Ibsen

painting had a profound influence on 20th century painting. He based his intensely individual style on the way he treated his subject as a series of highly organized planes, giving the finished work a strong sense of weight and solidity. He was the leader of what came to be called by the art critic, Roger Fry, the post-impressionist school of painting, a school which had given up representing 'camera' vision in favour of a new perception of structural forms.

Among Cézanne's works were *La Maison du Pendu*, *Les Baigneurs*, *Scène Champêtre* and *Léda au Cygne*.

Kelvin, William Thomson, 1st Baron Kelvin of Largs (1824–1907)
British physicist, mathematician and inventor

This astonishingly brilliant scientist was just 22 years old when he was appointed professor of natural philosophy at the University of Glasgow. He held the post for another fifty-three years, during which time he made some of the most startling discoveries of the nineteenth century, patented a large number of mechanical and electrical devices, and put forward a number of theories which have since been proved correct.

Born in Belfast he moved to Glasgow as a young boy. From there he went to Cambridge where he studied at Peterhouse and obtained a first class honours degree by the time he was 21. Apart from the routine work of professor at Glasgow the rest of his life was marked by a number of discoveries and theories.

He put forward the idea of an absolute measurement of temperature, and the Kelvin scale is still in use today. He introduced the theory of the dissipation of energy. By mathematical analysis he laid the foundation of the theory of electric oscillations. He helped to lay the first Atlantic telegraph cable, and he also did a lot of work on magnetism, becoming one of the world's leading experts. He invented the household electricity meter, safety circuit fuses and dynamo electric machines.

He was knighted in 1866, was President of the Royal Society from 1890–1894, and was raised to the peerage in 1892.

Grieg, Edvard (1843–1907)
Norwegian composer

Grieg's most famous orchestral works are the two suites for *Peer Gynt* which form incidental music to Ibsen's (*p. 254*) play, *Peer Gynt*. They made his name as a composer, not only in his own Norway but all over Europe. Thereafter, he produced a quantity of fine music in the best romantic manner, including his piano concerto in A minor which is a favourite of concert-goers everywhere. While his music is in the main-stream of European composition, it is also expressive of Scandinavian sentiment. A careful taste, a strong visual sense and an intense awareness of folk heritage combined to produce a successful, individual style. His work influenced Sibelius (*p. 300*), the great Finnish composer, and also that of Delius (*p. 279*).

Campbell-Bannerman, Sir Henry (1836–1908)
Scottish statesman

C-B, as he was called, was prime minister from 1905 to 1908. He was a staunch liberal, and initiated many advanced policies. He granted the Boers self-government in South Africa; he tried to reform the House of Lords, which badly needed it; and he championed the efforts of people like Lloyd George who were working to bring relief to poor workers. Campbell-Bannerman also gave Winston Churchill his first government post.

Kuang Hsu (1871–1908)
Chinese Emperor (1875–1908)

Born in Peking, Kuang Hsu succeeded to the Manchu title when he was only four. Consequently, China was ruled by a regency until 1884. But even then he had very little power, and when he wanted to introduce reforms he was overruled by his reactionary aunt. From 1898 to the end of his life he was completely dominated by other people. His weakness led to the general deterioration of the Manchu empire which was overthrown altogether a few years later.

Swinburne, Algernon Charles (1837–1909)
English poet

Swinburne, who was a friend of D. G. Rossetti (*p. 237*) and William Morris (*p. 247*), first came to the notice of the literary world with the publication of *Atlanta in Calydon*, in 1865. This was a dramatic story in Greek form. He went on to develop ideas against religion and against conventional behaviour, and his *Poems and Ballads* of 1865 summed these up. But the book stirred up criticism.

Then he went on to write verse in support of republican ideas, for he hated the very existence of monarchy and absolutism. He was in a way at the tail-end of the Romantic movement in poetry, which rebelled against authoritarianism. He wrote a trilogy on Mary, Queen of Scots and a romance in rhyming couplets, called *Tristram of Lyonesse*.

Nightingale, Florence (1820–1910)
English nursing pioneer

Florence Nightingale was one of the most famous women of the 19th century. In some ways her fame was greater than her achievements merited, for, apart from her good work getting the British army hospital at Scutari in Turkey cleaned up during the Crimean War (1854–1856) and founding a nursing school at London's St. Thomas's Hospital, she did very little. For the last thirty years of her life, for example, she sat around at home most of the time receiving guests from all walks of life who came to pay their respects. Possibly

Florence Nightingale at the Turkish hospital in Scutari

her greatest achievement was the fact that she bullied the civil service, in the shape of the War Department, to get them to agree to her cleaning up the Turkish hospital; she did create respect for the nursing service, and did much to give nursing a foundation of efficiency and sound medical practice.

Eddy, Mary Baker (1821–1910)
American founder of Christian Science
Mary Baker Eddy was an amazing woman. An invalid for many years, she tried all sorts of remedies, but did not get any better. Then it came to her that she should try mental and spiritual healing, and, imitating the paralysed man in St. Matthew's Gospel (in the New Testament) who talked himself into walking again, she got herself up and out and claimed to have cured her own ills. She then devoted her life to spreading a new gospel, that sickness could be cured by prayer and meditation, and that disease was really the product of imagination. As a belief, Christian Science is still followed widely in many countries.

Tolstoy, Count Leo Nicholaievich (1828–1910)
Russian novelist
Tolstoy was a mystic who introduced a new form of Christianity in Russia. He rejected the Orthodox Church and preached a Christianity based on the acceptance of evil, through which good will eventually come. He acquired a large following, and his creed was greatly helped by his writings, including novels as well as works on religion. His best known novels are *Anna Karenina* and *War and Peace*. *War and Peace* is a long tale about Russia during the time of Napoleon's vain attempt to conquer it in 1812, and it gives a lucid insight as to how people in Russia reacted to Napoleon's invasion.

Mark Twain (Samuel Langhorne Clemens) (1835–1910)
American author
Clemens started his career as a printer and then became a pilot on the Mississippi river. It was from this work that he found his pen name, for 'Mark Twain' was the cry used when sounding the shallow stretches of the river to indicate a depth of two fathoms.

This American certainly led an interesting and varied career, forsaking the boats to work as a secretary for his brother, to try his hand at gold mining and editing a local newspaper – before settling down as an author. He launched himself in this field when he returned from some travels in Europe and published a book *Innocents Abroad* which won him a reputation as a humorist.

His varied background gave him great resources to draw upon when writing, and two of his books based on personal experiences are established as classics in the world of literature. They are *Huckleberry Finn* and *Tom Sawyer*. Others are *A Tramp Abroad* and *A Connecticut Yankee in King Arthur's Court*.

Edward VII (1841–1910)
King of Great Britain (1901–1910)
Albert Edward was the eldest son of Queen Victoria. As a young man he was a great disappointment to her, and so she never let him have anything to do with state affairs. The result was that he led a long, idle life of pleasure, mixing with the racing fraternity, actresses, and earning himself an undesirable reputation. Nonetheless he was very popular.

When he succeeded as Edward VII in 1901 he had had almost no experience in state craft. But all the same he showed himself to be a statesman of some skill. He was largely responsible for bringing Britain and France closer together after many years of hostility. He also helped to make Anglo-Russian and Anglo-Japanese relations better.

Edward's coronation in 1902 was postponed because he was struck by acute appendicitis. Lord Lister (*p. 259*) the world's leading surgeon, advised operating to remove it, a daring operation at that time. When he recovered Edward created the Order of Merit (OM). There were twelve original members, and Lister was one of them.

Sir William Gilbert and Sir Arthur Sullivan

Gilbert, Sir William Schwenck (1836–1911) and Sullivan, Sir Arthur Seymour (1842–1900)
Creators of the Savoy Operas

Gilbert and Sullivan are the most famous couple in the story of light musical opera. Gilbert wrote the books and Sullivan the music for a collection of thirteen comic operas which were extremely popular in Britain and North America in the last quarter of the 19th century and have remained so ever since.

Gilbert began as a barrister. In those days he also wrote much humorous verse and many funny stories for magazines. He was extremely witty in his conversation, though often at other people's expense. In 1871 he began to collaborate with Sullivan to produce comic operas, but their real success began when in 1875 the theatre manager Richard D'Oyly Carte put on *Trial By Jury*. It was an immediate sensation, and the two men went on to produce twelve more, including *HMS Pinafore*, *The Mikado* and *The Yeomen of the Guard*.

Gilbert was extremely quarrelsome, however, and the partnership broke up on one occasion for four years. After Sullivan's death he went on writing, and was knighted in 1907. He died trying to save someone's life in a pond near his house at Harrow.

Sullivan was the composer in the partnership. He had been an organist and choirmaster, and wrote some music which stands among the best produced by British composers of the late 19th century. Although he made his name and a lot of money out of the Savoy Operas, he always wished he could be better known as a more serious composer. His work was recognized, however, when Queen Victoria knighted him in 1883.

Cronje, Piet Arnoldus (1840–1911)
Boer general

Cronje was one of the most dashing – and at first most successful – of the Boer generals in the South African War of 1899–1902. It was he who had compelled the Jameson raiders to surrender in

1896, and so when the war broke out in 1899, the Boers gave him a high command. Their faith was justified: he trapped Lord Methuen's British force at Magersfontein, on its way to relieve Kimberley, and defeated it. In 1900 he was surrounded at Paardeburg by General Lord Kitchener (*p. 262*) and had to surrender.

Stolypin, Peter Arkadevich (1863–1911)
Russian statesman

Stolypin was a brilliant politician whom Nicholas II brought in as prime minister in 1906 to introduce long overdue reforms in the government, but it was felt that he was too late. The forces of revolution were growing stronger, and all Stolypin could do was stem the tide while at the same time grant more freedom to newspapers, political theorists, writers and so on. He was assassinated in 1911, which was a terrible tragedy for Russia, for Nicholas responded by re-introducing repressive measures.

Lister, Joseph, 1st Baron (1827–1912)
British surgeon and discoverer of the use of antiseptics

Before the 1860s, more than half the people who had operations died from wound infections. In 1867 Lister discovered the properties of antiseptics, and thereafter this kind of infection became increasingly rare.

Lister was born in Upton, Essex, the son of a strict Quaker family. He studied at the University of London for degrees in classics and medicine.

It was as professor of surgery at Glasgow that Lister first became aware of the high degree of infection which followed surgical operations. Analysing the infection, he realized that the only way to stop it was to prevent it reaching the patients in the first place.

Most ways of killing germs known to him were also harmful to human beings. But he found that a sufficiently dilute solution of carbolic acid would kill germs and not harm the patients.

After this he revolutionized the routine of surgery, cleaning everything that came into contact with the patient with carbolic acid solution. Gradually he noticed a decline in the number of cases of infection at the Glasgow infirmary.

This was by far his greatest achievement, but not his only one. He was the first man to repair a broken knee cap by wiring it together, and he also invented the drainage tube for large abdominal wounds. One of the first patients to experience his method was Queen Victoria.

He was made a baronet in 1883 and raised to the peerage in 1893. He was president of the Royal Society from 1895 to 1900 and was one of the first 12 members of the Order of Merit.

Booth, William (1829–1912)
English founder and general of the Salvation Army

Booth started as a methodist minister, but he formed his Salvation Army on military lines in 1865, when he embarked on missionary work in the East End of London.

As the name suggests, the Army existed then, as now, to help people, especially those who found themselves in difficult times, like alcoholics, the homeless, strays, orphans, the unemployed, etc.

Strindberg, Johann August (1849–1912)
Swedish playwright

Strindberg was one of the major influences in European literature of the late 19th century. He wrote plays, books, articles, essays, and his dramatic works were noted for their social and psychological realism, qualities long absent from the conventional theatre.

His own life was unhappy: he had three wives, all of whom he failed to understand, and he was fiercely opposed to the idea of emancipation for women. He was consumed with self criticism and bitterness, but this indeed served to heighten the intensity of his work, and his play, *The Father* is one of the most savagely dramatic plays ever penned.

Viscount Wolseley among his troops

Schlieffen, Count Alfred von (1833–1913)

German general

Schlieffen's life spanned that of Britain's Field Marshal Viscount Wolseley (*p. 260*) and in some ways their careers were alike. After a long and distinguished career, he became chief of the German general staff in 1891, and remained in office for 14 years. In that time he restructured the army, as Lord Wolseley was doing to the British army. One of Schlieffen's ideas was to prepare a foolproof plan, bearing his name, by which a prepared German army would, in the event of war on the Western front, break through into Belgium, swing down into France, and cut through to Holland at the same time. The army would then

swing down to cut Paris off from the sea. If carried out properly it should knock France out of war.

Schlieffen died in 1913, mercifully too early to see his plan mutilated by his successors, who in 1914 failed to carry it out correctly. It is thought that it really would have worked if it had not been watered down.

Wolseley, Garnet Joseph, 1st Viscount (1833–1913)

Irish field marshal

Wolseley was the man who modernized the British army and got it into the kind of shape in which it was really capable of competing in a European war.

His career was a fascinating one. He joined the army at 19 and saw action almost at once, in a war in Burma, where he was wounded. Two years later he lost the use of his eye in the Crimean War. Then in 1857–1858 he fought in the Indian Mutiny, in 1860 in China, and from 1861 to 1870 in the Red River War in Canada. He commanded the British forces in the Ashanti War, was high commissioner in Cyprus, 1878, and supreme commander in the Transvaal in 1879. He was commander in chief in Egypt in 1882 and defeated the rebel leader Arabi Pasha at the battle of Tel-el-Kebir. Three years later he tried to save General Gordon at Khartoum but got there too late. In 1895 he was commander-in-chief of the whole British army. He wrote several books including a life on Marlborough.

Diesel, Rudolf (1858–1913)
German engineer

Every time you get on a 'bus, spare a moment to think about the man who invented the type of engine by which buses are driven, the Diesel Engine. It was invented by Rudolf Diesel, who in 1893 produced a successful model of an engine that was fired by fuel injection and not by gas explosion. His engine was manufactured by the wealthy firm of Krupp.

Today, Diesel engines power 'buses, lorries, railway engines, motor torpedo boats and even some cars. They use about the same amount of fuel as a petrol engine, but the fuel costs less.

Roberts, Frederick Sleigh, 1st Earl (1832–1914)
Irish field marshal

'Bobs', as he was known to the British army, was one of the most beloved generals of British military history. Tiny in stature, gentle mannered, bold as a lion, he won the V.C. during the Indian Mutiny, in 1858. Thereafter his rise up the army ladder was spectacular. As a major-general he crushed the Afghans in the Afghan War, 1878–1880. In 1880 he made his fame by marching over 300 miles from Kabul to Kandahar to relieve a beleaguered British force there. The journey was beset with dangerous inci-

dents. Later, he became commander in chief of the British army in India, and was raised to the peerage as a baron.

Later in his life he was made an earl, finally becoming commander in chief of the whole British army, the highest post in the service.

Chamberlain, Joseph (1836–1914)
English politician

By the time he was forty this son of a London shopkeeper had entered a Birmingham factory, risen to become the head of it, and retired with a fortune.

As Lord Mayor of Birmingham he began a programme of slum clearance in the city and later became M.P. for West Birmingham. He started as a Liberal and was Gladstone's president of the board of trade. But he did not agree with the Irish policy and drifted away from the party. In 1895 he became colonial secretary in Lord Salisbury's Conservative Government, and in this position he worked hard for expansion in Africa and for stronger bonds between Canada, Australia and New Zealand.

In 1903 he retired from office and began a campaign for tariff reform. But it was unsuccessful. It divided the Conservatives and it led to them being badly defeated at the 1906 election. For many years Joe Chamberlain was one of the best known and most colourful statesmen in Britain. His last years were marred by the effects of a stroke.

Grace, William Gilbert (1848–1915)
English cricketer

W. G. Grace, huge, tall, with a long dark beard was – and perhaps still is – the most famous name in cricket. He was a doctor with a good practice in Bristol.

In the 1870s he began to play for England and made his name as a hard hitting batsman and an amusing character who often resorted to gamesmanship. He could be relied upon to knock up a good score every time, and indeed by 1895 had scored over 100 centuries. He captained England in test matches.

Grace is still affectionately recalled in cricketing circles as 'W.G.'.

Cavell, Edith Louisa (1865–1915)
English nurse

Nurse Cavell was shot by a German firing squad in Belgium during the First World War, allegedly for helping Allied prisoners of war to escape. The shock of this terrible act horrified the whole civilized world.

Nurse Cavell was matron of a hospital in Brussels which, on the outbreak of the war, became a Red Cross Hospital. She became involved in an underground group, formed to help English, French and Belgian soldiers reach the Dutch frontier. The Germans found out, arrested Edith Cavell and the Belgian, Philippe Baucq and court-martialled them, with a sentence of death. The American ambassador to Brussels tried to persuade the Germans to hold their hand, but they would not, and sentence was carried out on 12th October.

Kitchener, Horatio Herbert, 1st Earl (1850–1916)
Irish field marshal

Kitchener was Secretary of State for War in 1914, when Britain went to war with Germany. He was the only man to appreciate that the war would last three years at least, and that more than a million men would be needed to fight on the British side. So he called for volunteers, and in a publicity campaign, splendidly managed, he raised nearly 3,000,000 men in two years. Sadly, many of them were to lose their lives in France in useless fighting in the trenches.

At the height of the war, on 5 June 1916, he was drowned in HMS Hampshire, a cruiser which was taking him on an urgent visit to Russia, when it was sunk off the Orkney Islands. It was a critical blow to the British, and his death was regarded as a calamity of the first magnitude.

Kitchener's career had been leading up to the point where he was the foremost soldier-statesman in the British empire. He had avenged General Gordon's death at Khartoum (*p. 239*) by smashing the Mahdi's power at the battle of Omdurman in September 1898.

He cleaned up the Boer resistance in the South African War (1899–1902). He reorganized the Indian army when he was commander in chief in India from 1902 to 1909. He re-organized the Egyptian army, too, and he visited Australia and New Zealand where he advised on bringing their armies up to date.

On his death, he was an earl, a knight of the Garter, holder of nearly every form of knighthood in Britain, and many foreign ones as well. He was the idol of the public in his day. Tall, good-looking, shy, gruff at times, he was ruthlessly efficient, brave as a lion, impatient, but withal fond of children and animals.

Ramsay, Sir William (1852–1916)
Scottish chemist

William Ramsay discovered the inert gases of the atmosphere, neon, xenon, krypton, helium and, with Lord Rayleigh, argon. He was professor of Chemistry at Bristol from 1880–1887 and at London from 1887–1912. His discoveries were marked by a Nobel prize for Chemistry in 1904.

Thebaw (1858–1916)
Last King of Burma (1878–1885)

Thebaw resented the interference of Britain in his country, and to make his point negotiated with the French Government for them to sponsor a railway network in Burma. The British took exception and declared war, in which Thebaw was utterly defeated and deposed from his throne. He spent the last years of his life in India.

Connolly, James (1870–1916)
Irish leader

When the Irish nationalists rose against the British government in the Dublin Rising of 1916, James Connolly, a quiet, brave, serious minded socialist, was one of the leaders. If the rising had succeeded, he would have held high office in the government they created. As it was, the rising was crushed. In the fighting Connolly was badly wounded. When he was caught, he was ill treated. Then he was tried and sentenced to death. The sentence of shooting was carried out, and in his case he was tied to a chair as he could not stand.

Rasputin, Grigor (1871–1916)
Russian court favourite

Rasputin was one of the most extraordinary people in history. The son of a poor Siberian peasant, with no education, he became a holy man or prophet among the illiterate peasants of his neighbourhood. Then he ventured to St. Petersburg where, by some artifice, he managed to get into the royal palace and actually saved the eldest son of Czar Nicholas II from bleeding to death. The boy had haemophilia. This persuaded the Czar and his wife, the Czarina, that he was a saint, and for the next seven years Rasputin lived in or near the palace and acted as their adviser. His manners were unconventional: he was constantly drunk, and he insulted everyone at court, no matter who they were. Eventually a number of nobles, led by Prince Felix Youssoupoff, murdered him, in 1916.

Pearse, Padraig (1879–1916)
Irish leader

Padraig Pearse was an Irish poet who joined the republican movement in Ireland. In the 1916 Easter Rising he commanded a detachment. He also drafted the Irish Declaration of Independence, a noble document of some pathos which called all Irishmen to fight for their ancient freedom and rights. When it was clear the rising had failed, Pearse surrendered to save further loss of life. He was tried and executed.

Anderson, Elizabeth Garrett (1836–1917)
English doctor

Elizabeth Garrett Anderson was the first woman doctor to be allowed to practise medicine in London. She had passed the necessary exams, but prejudice against women using their brains was high in those days, and the British Medical Association refused to let her work. So she obtained a diploma from the Society of Apothecaries and this enabled her to open a dispensary in London. This in time became the New Hospital for Women.

She spent much of her time campaigning to get women accepted as doctors, and foreign countries recognized her efforts by awarding her all kinds of honours. She was also the first woman mayor of a local authority in England. Her home town of Aldeburgh in Suffolk elected her in 1908.

Zeppelin, Count Ferdinand von (1838–1917)
German airship designer

During the First World War, people in eastern Britain were occasionally startled by the appearance and roar of a thin, pencil-shaped flying machine, with a cage slung beneath it. Over the edge of the cage occupants would throw out hand bombs which damaged houses and other buildings below. These were Zeppelins, the name of a series of types of airship made by Ferdinand von Zeppelin in his factory.

Zeppelin had been a soldier in the Austro-Prussian War (1866) and the Franco-Prussian War (1870–1871) and had even served on the northern side in the American Civil War (1861–1865).

The Zeppelin airship

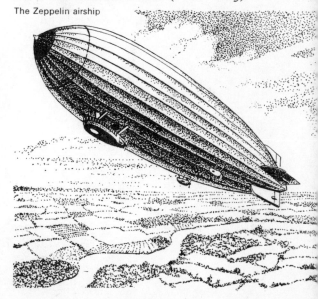

Rodin, François Auguste René (1840–1917)
French sculptor

This was one of the most distinguished sculptors in the last century. He had studied sculpture most carefully in Italy, and in the 1870s began to exhibit. One of his early pieces, *L'age d'Airain*, caused a storm of criticism.

Rodin spent many years working on some bronze doors for the *Musée des Arts Decoratifs*. He also executed superb portrait busts of people like Hugo, Bernard Shaw, Clemenceau and Balzac. His group, the *Burghers of Calais*, of which a copy stands outside the House of Lords in London, is a brilliant portrait of people pleading to be spared.

Jameson, Sir Leander Starr, 1st Baronet (1853–1917)
South African statesman

After studying medicine at Edinburgh, Jameson took up practice in Kimberley. But through Cecil Rhodes he became involved in pioneer work, and in 1891 was made an administrator of the South Africa Company at Salisbury, where he was very popular.

In the troubles between the Boers and Uitlanders Jameson and a force of 500 were defeated and taken prisoner. Later he was elected to the Cape Legislative Assembly, and in 1912 he retired from politics.

Debussy, Claude Achille (1862–1918)
French composer

Debussy had a sad life. He suffered for years from cancer which in the end killed him. But his music was in many respects light and gay, mellow and untroubled. One of his best known compositions was *La Mer*. Another memorable piece was *La Cathédrale Engloutie*, about a cathedral on the coast that subsides under the sea. He was a pioneer of modern music in France, and in his time he came to be known as one of the best composers of Europe.

The last Czar of Russia, Nicholas II, with the Czarina

Nicholas II (1868–1918)
Czar of Russia (1894–1917)

Nicholas was the last Czar of Russia. In succeeding his father in 1894, he found an empire that was largely still feudal; but he did very little to reform or improve his country. He got involved in a disastrous war with Japan in 1905 in which the Russian fleet was destroyed. This humiliation provoked a serious revolt, which was Communist inspired. Although it was crushed, Nicholas had to consider bringing in home reforms, and eventually agreed to the calling of the Duma, the Russian parliament.

In 1914 he took Russia into the First World War, although the country was not at all prepared for it, and he endured a series of defeats. Eventually, exasperated beyond control, the middle classes, agitated by several reforming groups, insisted on a change of government. Nicholas' absolute powers were stripped away. A year later amidst the turbulence of revolution he was exiled with his family to Eastern Russia and there, in 1918, they were all apparently murdered. No one knows who gave the order.

Laurier, Sir Wilfred (1841–1919)
Canadian statesman

Laurier was the son of French Canadian Catholic parents. He became a lawyer and then was elected to the Canadian House of Commons in 1874. He wanted very much to unite the French and British communities in Canada which then – as now – were sadly separated in many respects.

In 1896 he was appointed prime minister, and remained in office for 13 years. In that time he strengthened ties with the United States. He also worked for closeness with Britain, granting special trade terms between Canada and the British.

Renoir, Pierre Auguste (1841–1919)
French impressionist painter

Renoir, who became one of the most noted of the Impressionist painters, started his career as a painter of porcelain, and later of fans.

Exhibiting in their early exhibitions, he experimented, like his fellow artists, with the effects of light. His work became popular from about 1870 and he received a number of commissions for portraits. Some of his paintings of nudes are considered exquisite.

Rayleigh, John William Strutt, 3rd Baron (1842–1919)
English physicist

Rayleigh was a brilliant physicist who discovered, with Sir William Ramsay (*p. 262*), the inert gas argon. He held several important posts in the scientific field, including professor of experimental physics at Cambridge, 1879–1884, and of natural philosophy at the Royal Institution from 1887 to 1905. He was awarded a Nobel prize in 1904.

Roosevelt, Theodore (1858–1919)
American president (1901–1909)

America did not begin to play a dominant part in world affairs until the early years of the present century, although she had been for some time the most industrialized nation in the world. The man who brought America to the front rank among nations was 'Teddy' Roosevelt, a cheerful, boisterous, clever soldier-statesman who had a good record as governor of New York. He was vice president in 1901, when McKinley was assassinated, and this brought him into the White House.

Roosevelt set out to awaken the American people to their potential, and to move them to play a dominating international role. In 1905 he mediated between Russia and Japan in their war and brought it to an end. In 1908 he showed the major powers how strong America was by sending the U.S. Fleet on a world tour.

When the First World War did break out in 1914, all the major contestants waited to see which way America would move, and when she did come in on the British side, in 1917, the defeat of the German-Austrian powers was sealed. This was Roosevelt's achievement, although he was not himself in office.

Botha, Louis (1862–1919)
Boer general and statesman

Louis Botha was, apart from Smuts, the most remarkable of all the Boer soldier-statesmen. He was in command of the Boer force which confined the British in Ladysmith in the South African War (1899–1902) in 1899. The next year he became commander in chief of all the Boer forces, and it was he who finally surrendered to the British in 1902 when he saw that further resistance was a waste of time. He and Lord Kitchener got on well at the peace negotiations, and thereafter Botha gave his support to close ties with Britain.

In 1910 he was appointed the first prime minister of the new Union of South Africa, and remained in office for nine years. In 1914 he brought South Africa into the War on the British side.

Alcock, Sir John William (1892–1919) and Brown, Sir Arthur Whitten (1886–1948)
British aviators

Alcock and Brown were two British aviators who made the first non-stop trans-atlantic aeroplane flight, from Newfoundland, in Canada, to Ireland, a distance of nearly 2,000 miles. They covered it in 16 hours, 12 mins., landing in Ireland on 14 June 1919. The aircraft was a Vickers Vimy. Both men were knighted for their achievement.

Fisher, Sir John Arbuthnot, 1st Baron (1841–1920)
British admiral

Without doubt 'Jackie' Fisher was the greatest British sailor since Nelson. He was tough, rude, intolerant and often unsympathetic, but he was also bold, far-seeing, brilliant and quick to praise where praise was due.

With few advantages save of personal character he rose to the highest position in the navy, first sea lord, from 1904 to 1910. And in that time, he took hold of the Royal Navy, gave it battleships, cruisers, submarines, new disciplines and, above all, a new fighting spirit. In fact he made it a twentieth century navy, and the best in the world.

In 1914, when the First World War broke out, Winston Churchill, then first lord of the admiralty, called him back as first sea lord. They worked well for a while, but fell out over the Dardanelles Campaign. Fisher resigned, and never served again. Despite his bullying manner he was adored by the whole navy.

Bethmann-Hollweg, Theobald von (1856–1921)
German statesman

Bethmann-Hollweg followed Prince Bülow as chancellor of Imperial Germany in 1909. He was more aggressive than Bülow, and he backed his master, the Kaiser, in his belligerent attitude to other powers in Europe. When taxed with the fact that there was a treaty between Germany and Belgium protecting the rights of the smaller country, he said it was only 'a scrap of paper'. He continued as chancellor during the war until 1917, when Hindenburg persuaded the Kaiser to dismiss him.

Bell, Alexander Graham (1847–1922)
Scottish inventor

Graham Bell invented the telephone. It was an instrument he produced more or less by accident when trying to make apparatus with which to help deaf people hear, for both he and his father, Alexander Melville Bell, who had emigrated to America in the 1870s, had spent many years in research into ways of helping the deaf. Both men were naturalized and remained in the United States to pursue their work.

Alexander Graham Bell

De Wet, Christiaan Rudolph (1854–1922)
Boer general

De Wet was one of the most dashing Boer generals in the South African War. He took over as commander of the Boer forces in the Orange Free State after Cronje surrendered at Paardeburg. Thereafter he waged a guerrilla-type war against the British, and it took nearly two years to wear him down.

De Wet remained implacably anti-British, and when Britain went to war with Germany in 1914, and South Africa decided to support her, he rebelled. He wanted the German side to win. After giving promises not to interfere, he was released.

Rathenau, Walther (1867–1922)
German statesman

Rathenau was the son of a very rich Jewish businessman who made money from electrochemicals. He helped to run the family firm in the First World War, but became increasingly devoted to ideals of peace. He was engaged in many negotiations in Europe after the war, and in 1921 was appointed minister of reconstruction in the German cabinet. Then he became foreign secretary and tried to get a better deal for Germany in the matter of reparations, that is, payments to countries which the Germans had invaded and overrun during the war. His policies, though good, did not please all, and in 1922 he was assassinated.

Proust, Marcel (1871–1922)
French novelist

Proust was an invalid all his life. When his mother died, he shut himself up in a soundproof room in his house and worked with relentless concentration on a series of novels which were grouped under the title *A La Recherche Du Temps Perdu* (*Remembrance of Things Past*).

A solitary, introverted man, Proust analysed the aristocratic French society in which he had lived. Involuntary memory was at the basis of all his works: a smell, a taste or a touch was enough to evoke the clearest memory of past events and friends. It was the reappearance of these detailed images and sensations in his subconscious which convinced Proust of the sense of continuity of time.

Michael Collins

Collins, Michael (1890–1922)
Irish leader

Michael Collins is widely regarded in Ireland as the greatest Irishman since King Brian Boru (*p. 68*). He was born and educated at Cork, spent ten years in the English civil service in London, and then returned to Ireland to join the republican movement. In the Easter Rising of 1916 he captured the General Post Office, but had to give it up when the other leaders surrendered.

Collins narrowly escaped a death sentence. He was imprisoned and then released. He then rebuilt the resistance organization, and in three years (1918–1921) he and his trusted agents so completely disrupted the English administration that the English agreed to discuss terms. Some rebels, like de Valera, wanted a full republic. Collins wanted to settle for a Free State, similar to the agreement with Canada. This was agreed. But a bitter civil war broke out.

Collins was commander in chief of the Free State army and for a short while President, but on 22 August 1922 he was ambushed and shot dead by republicans. The funeral queue at Dublin was over three miles long, such was the love felt for him.

The remarkable and much loved actress, Sarah Bernhardt

Bernhardt, Sarah (1844–1923)
French actress

Sarah Bernhardt was among the greatest actresses of all time. Her career spanned half a century, and many said that at the end of it she was as fine, as word perfect and as sensitive as she was at the start.

She had been born in Paris, educated at the Conservatoire, the principal drama school in France, and gone on the stage. There was something about her, people remembered, that kept her apart from others, and this apparently made it hard for her to get parts. But when in the 1870s she did get her chance, with the Comédie Française, she was acclaimed as a brilliant new actress. She went for the hardest and most dramatic roles, such as Joan of Arc and Elizabeth I. She also played some male leads, like Hamlet.

Sarah Bernhardt was loved all over the world. In 1914 she had to have a leg partially amputated, but this did not deter her from continuing to take on more work.

Röntgen, Wilhelm Konrad von (1845–1923)
German physicist

Röntgen made a major contribution towards modern medical practice when in 1895 he discovered electro-magnetic waves which he named X-Rays. They are also known by his name. For this work he won both the Rumford Medal and the Nobel Prize for Physics.

Law, Andrew Bonar (1858–1923)
British statesman
Bonar Law was a Canadian who achieved the highest office of state in Britain, that of prime minister. He had been elected member of Parliament in 1900, and his gifts brought him quickly to the front, so that in 1911 he was leader of the opposition. In the War government in 1915 he was given a ministry, Secretary for the Colonies, and then he became chancellor of the exchequer.

When Lloyd George was defeated at the 1922 elections and the Conservatives won, Bonar Law was appointed prime minister, but by then his health had begun to break down. Scarcely a year later he had to resign, and he died soon afterwards.

Harding, Warren Gamaliel (1865–1923)
American president (1921–1923)
Warren Harding began as a newspaper man. He became a republican politician and entered the Senate in 1915, with a strong urge to see that the United States armed its merchant ships to prevent them being attacked by German naval ships. In 1921, Harding was elected president, but his administration was not a happy one. It was marred by tales of corruption among officials, many of which proved true. Added to this his own private life was not a healthy one. He died in office while out on a speaking tour.

Wilson, Thomas Woodrow (1856–1924)
American president (1912–1920)
Wilson had a splendid career as lawyer and politician, and in 1913 achieved the highest American ambition, the presidency of the United States. A great deal of useful legislation was initiated in his two terms of office, but he is best known for his strenuous efforts to ensure a lasting peace after the First World War (1914–1918) into which he led the United States on the British side in 1917.

Wilson's peace proposals were based on 14 points, which included independence for small states and no interference in their affairs by bigger states. Unfortunately, it was extremely difficult to get all the powers involved in the peace negotiations to see eye to eye. He worked extremely hard for weeks, interviewing, discussing, drafting papers, and in the end ruined his health. He tried to build up a League of Nations, similar to the present United Nations Organization, but could not get the American Senate to agree. During all this he was struck with paralysis, and was unable to do much for the rest of his life.

Conrad, Joseph (1857–1924)
Ukrainian born novelist in the English language
Conrad was born Theodor Josef Konrad Korzeniowski in the Ukraine in Russia. He went into the French merchant navy for a few years, and joined the British merchant navy in 1878. He loved the British and was naturalized in 1886, the year he qualified as a master. All the while stories of the sea, and of the islands and cities his ships visited, were forming themselves in his mind, and in 1894 he retired to write them down. Over the next years he established himself as a leading novelist, with wonderful powers of description, drama and characterization. Most famous of his books are *An Outcast of the Islands*, *Lord Jim*, *The Secret Agent*, *The Shadow-Line* and *The Nigger of the Narcissus*.

Puccini, Giacomo (1858–1924)
Italian composer
Although he had shown considerable talent as a child, Puccini was denied the opportunity of a proper musical education until he was 22, because he was poor. A royal patron then paid for him to attend and study at the Milan Conservatory.

Puccini succeeded Verdi as the master of Italian opera and must be considered as one of the greatest composers. His works include *Madame Butterfly*, *Tosca* and *La Bohème*.

Lenin addressing an intent crowd in industrial Russia

Lenin (1870–1924)
Russian communist leader

Vladimir Ilyitch Ulyanov was the son of a civil servant. He spent almost his entire young days in revolutionary activities of one kind or another. He grew up to be intolerant of other people's views, and with his dominating personality, enhanced by fierce eyes, heavy intellectual brow and dark beard, he would trample on anyone who tried to argue with him. But he had an uncanny ability to get men to listen to him, spellbound, for hours on end, and to get them to act.

He conceived the reconstruction of the Russian state and in 1917, after quite an exciting life including exile in Siberia, abroad, working underground, he had the chance. He managed to get Kerensky's more moderate government turned out and thereafter he ruled Russia with a strong but necessary discipline. Serfdom still existed here and there. The country was generations behind in development. Communications were woefully inadequate. And there was starvation, shortage, misery and corruption everywhere.

Lenin built a worker's republic. He had to use harsh methods, for only force could bring about social change of this magnitude. Religion was crushed. Private property was seized. Farms were taken over and run on a collective basis. Secret police watched everyone, kept the outside world from them and them from the outside world.

But to many millions of Russians the hardship proved to be worthwhile. Lenin died in 1924.

Monet, Claude (1840–1925)
French painter

Monet, a landscape painter of great skill and sensitivity, is regarded as one of the leading lights of the Impressionist school of painting. This was a movement towards the end of the 19th century, whose principal belief was that the artist's hand should record a single visual impression exactly as his eye received it, as at the first sight; that is, he should be concerned only with pure vision. Objects were subservient to the light and the atmosphere in which they were bathed and by which they were revealed.

Monet painted in this manner using bright colours laid on in separate tones. He executed numerous canvasses, and among the best were *Le Jardin de l'Infante, Gare Saint-Lazare, Camille ou la Dame en Vert*, and some landscapes along the Seine.

French, Sir John Denton Pinkstone, 1st Earl of Ypres (1852–1925)
Irish field marshal

French had a brilliant career as a cavalry commander in the British army, and especially distinguished himself in the South African War. When the First World War broke out in 1914, he was the natural choice for commander in chief of the British Expeditionary Force to be sent to France to help drive the Germans back out of Belgium and France. But, though he was bold and resolute, French's judgment had become faulty. When things went wrong he was quick to blame others, such as the government for not supplying enough shells. By the end of 1915, he had aged prematurely and was relieved of his duties.

In 1917 he was appointed Lord Lieutenant in Ireland and had to command British forces during a very trying time there. On one occasion, a gang attempted to murder him, but he escaped. He retired in 1921 and accepted a well-earned earldom.

Curzon, George Nathaniel, 1st Marquess (1859–1925)
British statesman

I am George Nathaniel Curzon.
I am a most superior person.

Some unkind person wrote that couplet about Curzon when he was still an undergraduate at Oxford, but it aptly summed up his whole attitude to life. He was brilliant, but he knew it, and he made himself heartily disliked by his arrogance.

He came to prominence when he was made viceroy of India in 1899, aged only 40. While his term was a good one, he quarrelled with most of the people with whom it would have helped to get on. He also moved about in unparalleled magnificence, which gave great offence.

After India he sought high office in the government at home. He was Lord Privy Seal in 1915, foreign secretary from 1919 to 1924, and hoped very much to be appointed prime minister in the new Conservative administration of 1924. But Stanley Baldwin was selected. The party did not want a peer (he had been made Earl in 1911 and Marquess in 1921).

Sun Yat-Sen (1866–1925)
Chinese revolutionary leader

In the later decades of the 19th century and the beginning of the 20th, the Chinese people groaned under the last years of the Manchu emperors, and there were several revolutionary movements. One was organized by Sun Yat-Sen, a doctor who had been educated in Hong Kong, a British colony. By 1911, the Manchu empire was falling down, and Sun Yat-Sen got himself elected president of the new provisional government. Thereafter his career became a chequered one as he served various governments and then had to resign for disagreements. He headed a splinter southern Chinese republic and became its president in 1921.

But when he died in 1925 all China was bereaved, for he had been a consistent opponent of the Manchus, had advocated sound reform policies and had not behaved with the kind of fierceness one might expect of revolutionaries.

Brussilov, Alexei Alexeivich (1853–1926)
Russian general

On the whole the Russian Imperial armies sustained a series of disasters on the Eastern Front in the First World War. But there were one or two redeeming successes, and these were won by the brilliant general, Brussilov. In 1916 he was made commander of the armies south of the Pripet marshes, facing the Austrian forces, and in a series of engagements he drove them back towards their frontiers. But it was too late. The Russian Imperial system was collapsing, and in 1917, a moderate democratic government took control, followed in 1918 by a more extreme socialist administration headed by Lenin. Brussilov was prepared to recognize the new government but would not serve it.

Hardy, Thomas (1840–1928)
English poet and novelist

Hardy was born in Dorset, a part of the world he loved all his life and eventually retired to. He trained as an architect, but for all his diagram drawings and planning of buildings, he had the creative urge of a poet and novelist, and in 1872 he published his first book, *Under the Greenwood Tree*. Two years later followed *Far from the Madding Crowd*. He also wrote the *Mayor of Casterbridge*, the story of a man who auctioned his wife at a market and lived to regret it, and many other tales of life in Wessex, which was his name for the Dorset region.

When he was nearly 60, Hardy began to write poems, and in the course of the next few years produced some of the most lovely verse in the English language.

Terry, Dame Ellen (1847–1928)
English acress and theatre manager

Ellen Terry was to actresses what Irving was to actors, the leading performer of the generation. She had an astonishing talent which never flagged, and people who had seen her once made a great deal of effort to come to see her again.

In 1878 she was Irving's leading lady at the Lyceum, and this was the start of a partnership that lasted until 1902, and in that generation they played a vast repertoire of parts.

Early in the present century Ellen Terry started to play for other managers and also formed her own company. She also had parts specially written for her by leading playwrights, a single honour, and these included Shaw and Barrie.

She was made GBE in 1925. Her life as an actress had been adorned with unparalleled success; as a private individual it had been sad and incomplete; none of her marriages worked.

Cadorna, Count Luigi (1850–1928)
Italian soldier

Cadorna was chief of the Italian general staff in 1914, and when Italy came into the First World War on the British side in 1915, he was appointed commander-in-chief of the Italian forces. He won several useful victories which helped the Allies. Then he retired to become a member of the War Council.

Asquith, Henry Herbert, 1st Earl of Oxford (1852–1928)
British statesman

Asquith became a Liberal M.P. after a legal career. He became home secretary in 1892 in Gladstone's last government. As Chancellor of the Exchequer in 1905–1908 he heralded some good reforms, and in 1908 he succeeded Campbell-Bannerman (*p. 255*) as prime minister. For the next eight years he guided the government through several crises, including the Parliament Act (1911), the Irish Home Rule Bill (1914), and entry into the First World War; he led the War Cabinet until the autumn of 1916 when he was ousted by Lloyd-George (*p. 288*).

Haldane, Richard Burdon, 1st Viscount (1856–1928)
British statesman

The Haldanes were a very distinguished family in many fields. R. B. Haldane had a brilliant career at the bar and ended up as Lord Chancellor twice (1912–1915 and 1924). He was also secretary for war from 1905–1912, and in that time did much to re-structure the army. It was a time when politicians did not want to spend too much money on regular forces, and Haldane introduced the idea of the Territorial army, made up of men who were civilians in ordinary life, but who spent a few weeks in military training every year, just in case the country went to war. Haldane eventually joined the Labour Party and was its Lord Chancellor in the first Labour Government, of 1924.

Pankhurst, Emmeline (1858–1928)
English political reformer

Did you know that less than fifty years ago, not all women in Britain were allowed to vote? It seems incredible, but in fact had it not been for the work of Emmeline Pankhurst, the date women got the vote might have been much later.

She was a lawyer's wife who, with her

Emmeline Pankhurst speaking to her followers

husband, began to campaign for votes for women in 1880. She was a member of the Labour Party, as it was the only political party interested in fighting for this elementary right. She organized her work well. Her supporters and she herself chained themselves to railings in Whitehall, interrupted meetings shouting 'Votes for Women', and generally made themselves a nuisance. Frequently they were arrested and imprisoned where, because they went on hunger strike, they were forcibly fed. Support ran higher and higher, but there was still a hard core of men who would not admit that women were just as capable of exercising a vote as they were.

When the 1914 War came, women worked like Trojans in the armament factories and in the fields, and afterwards, Parliament decided to give them the vote as a reward. But they made the present less acceptable when they limited it to those over thirty. Finally, in 1928 it was extended to all over 21. In that year Emmeline Pankhurst died.

Haig, Douglas, 1st Earl (1861–1928)
Scottish field marshal

Haig had been accused of throwing countless lives into several wasted battles on the Western Front in the First World War. While it may be true that the cost of gaining a few hundred yards of ground was indeed high, it was the type of warfare that was to blame and not the man, who in fact was devoted to his troops and was much loved by them.

This brave, quiet, scholarly Scot had had a fine army career, including brilliant service in the South African War (1899–1902). At the outbreak of the First World War in 1914 Haig was a full general, and he was made commander of the First Army. He handled his forces with great skill, and when in 1915 the government was looking for a replacement commander-in-chief of the British Expeditionary Force in France, Haig was given the job.

For the next three years Haig had to wage total war, using thousands of troops, against a determined enemy, but he finally wore them down. In October 1918 the Germans were exhausted and on the run from their lines. Victory for the Allied armies was assured. Haig, who was made field marshal and given an earldom, devoted the rest of his life to helping ex-servicemen.

Gjøa the ship that took Roald Amundsen to Antarctica

Amundsen, Roald (1872–1928)
Norwegian explorer

In 1911, two teams of explorers, one led by a Norwegian, Amundsen, and one by a Briton, Captain Scott, were racing separately across the icy wastes of Antarctica in order to get to the South Pole. Scott arrived to find that Amundsen had reached it first, about a month earlier.

Amundsen had already discovered a north-west passage to the Pacific Ocean north of the Canadian mainland. In 1928, Amundsen set out in a sea-plane to the north pole to search for the Italian explorer, General Nobile, who had failed to get an airship across the pole and come to grief. But Amundsen was lost on this journey.

Clemenceau, Georges (1841–1929)
French statesman

Clemenceau was known throughout France as 'The Tiger', partly because he looked like one when he was angry, and partly because of his grim determination. He had had a fascinating career, beginning as a news reporter in America during the Civil War (1861–1865). He entered French politics and was elected a deputy in 1876. Then in 1902 he was a senator, and in 1906 he was appointed prime minister of France. One of his important acts was to detach the church from the state. He also made himself unpopular with some sectors of the public for sending in troops to break a strike. But people did admire his courage.

In 1917 when France was at a low ebb in the First World War he was appointed prime minister again, and as such gave the people the lead they needed. He was largely responsible for selecting Marshal Foch to head the allied armies in the final drive against the Germans in 1918.

Rosebery, Archibald Philip Primrose, 5th Earl of (1847–1929)
British statesman

Rosebery succeeded Gladstone as leader of the Liberal party. He was educated at Eton and Christ Church, Oxford. Between 1892 and 1894 he was secretary for foreign affairs in Gladstone's last government, and when Gladstone resigned in 1894 he became prime minister.

The Liberals were defeated at the next election but he remained leader of the party until 1896, becoming an imperialist during the Boer War. He held office several times in Liberal administrations.

Before his death in 1929 he wrote a number of books, including works on Pitt and Peel. As a young man he had said his three ambitions were to win the Derby, marry an heiress and become prime minister. He achieved all three – his wife was a member of the Rothschild family.

Foch, Ferdinand (1851–1929)
French marshal
In the last year of the First World War, the situation on the Western Front had become stagnant. One vast battle, so costly in lives, was followed by another, but only a few yards, or at most miles, of ground were won. Something more dynamic was needed. The Allies agreed to put the whole war effort on the Western Front under one man, and Ferdinand Foch, who had been a teacher of military strategy at military school, was given the job. He fully justified the faith of all countries, and he carried the campaign to a splendid conclusion when the German lines broke in October 1918. They surrendered in November.

Nicholas, Grand Duke (1856–1929)
Russian general
Grand Duke Nicholas Romanoff was a nephew of the Czar Alexander II of Russia. When war broke out in Europe in 1914, involving Russia, he was made commander in chief of all Russian forces on the Russian front. But he sustained a series of reverses, and was eventually relieved by the Czar, Nicholas II, who took command himself. When the Revolution came in 1918, Nicholas fled to France where he lived in exile for the rest of his life.

Stresemann, Gustav (1878–1929)
German statesman
Stresemann was appointed chancellor of Germany in 1923 and minister of foreign affairs at the same time. He was deeply concerned that the hatred between the allied powers and his country, born out of the attitude of the Kaiser and nurtured in the First World War, should be replaced by understanding and mutual cooperation, and he was largely responsible for the Locarno Pact which guaranteed the frontiers of Belgium, France, Germany, Italy and the U.K., and accepted the demilitarization of the Rhineland. He received a Nobel Prize for Peace in 1926.

Balfour, Arthur James, 1st Earl (1848–1930)
British statesman
Balfour was one of the handful of British prime ministers who never married. He was the nephew of the Marquess of Salisbury, who was also prime minister, but though his uncle helped him along in his career, Balfour was brilliant in his own right. He became prime minister in 1902 when his uncle retired, and stayed in office for three years. He was the leader of the Conservatives in Parliament.

During the First World War Balfour held several ministries, including the foreign secretaryship from 1916 to 1919. It was his decision to grant the Jews a national home in Palestine, although other promises had been made to Arabs, thus beginning the Arab–Jewish rivalry in the Middle East that is a continual feature of world politics today. In his spare time, Balfour was also something of a philosopher, and wrote several important works on philosophy.

Tirpitz, Alfred Friedrich von (1849–1930)
German admiral
Tirpitz rose from the ranks to become the lord high admiral of the German Navy, in 1911. It was an astonishing career. From 1897 until 1916 he was also secretary for the navy, and in this key role he re-shaped the fleet, bringing it up to date, equipping it with many battleships and heavy armed cruisers, so that it could at last challenge the might of the hitherto unparalleled British navy. The submarine blockade inflicted on Britain in 1917 was largely Tirpitz's scheme and it was very nearly effective.

Doyle, Sir Arthur Conan (1859–1930)
Scottish novelist

Who has not heard of the most remarkable detective in fiction, Sherlock Holmes? This was the creation of Arthur Conan Doyle, a Scottish born doctor who practised for years in the South of England. He also accompanied the British forces in the South African War (1899–1902) and wrote a history of it.

Conan Doyle created Sherlock Holmes, the cold, logical, brilliant private detective who noticed so many tiny and seemingly unimportant things that his contemporaries missed. The first story, *A Study in Scarlet*, appeared as a serial in the *Strand Magazine*. Thereafter came *The Sign of Four* and *The Hound of the Baskervilles*, and five books of short stories of Sherlock Holmes. In one of them he killed Holmes off, but the public clamoured for his return. Three years later, Doyle resurrected him, but as one critic said: 'He was not the same man!'

Doyle took up all kinds of causes, including pressing for a hearing into the case of Oscar Slater who was later found to have been wrongly convicted of murder. He was also very interested in spiritualism.

Rivera y Orbaneja, Miguel Primo de, Marques de Estella (1870–1930)
Spanish statesman

Primo de Rivera was a tough, resolute and handsome Spanish soldier whose military career had been distinguished by bravery and leadership of a high order. In 1923, when many people were tired of the repressive and backward government of King Alfonso XIII, he organized a revolt that was carried out without bloodshed. After several months of internal disarray, he emerged as prime minister, and he restructured the government. He tried to introduce many 20th century ideas, and to bring the nation up to date. But after five years of absolute rule he was ousted.

Edison, Thomas Alva (1847–1931)
American inventor

As a reward for saving the life of a station master's son the 12-year-old Edison was given lessons in telegraph operation.

For several years he worked as a telegraph operator travelling all over the United States of America. But he saved enough from his earnings to leave the company and start his own workshop. There he began his amazing career as an inventor. Among his patents were vote recorders, the printing telegraph, the carbon telephone transmitter, the microphone and the phonograph (or gramophone).

In the later years of his life he produced his own talking motion pictures. During the First World War Edison worked for the American government.

Joffre, Joseph Jacques Césaire (1852–1931)
French marshal

Marshal Joffre was commander in chief of the French armies in the first part of the First World War. He stopped the German advance on Paris in September 1914 by a splendid victory on the river Marne, in which British troops under his command played a strong part. Joffre was tough, stubborn, blunt of speech, and he did not always get on with British generals with whom he had to work, but none of them doubted his fiery resolve.

Parsons, Sir Charles Algernon (1854–1931)
British inventor

Parsons was the fourth son of the 3rd Earl of Rosse. He was director of a large engineering works in Newcastle upon Tyne. In 1884 he invented a steam turbine, and in 1897 fitted it with a condenser to a vessel to produce the first steam turbine driven steamship.

Melba, Dame Nellie (1861–1931)
Australian singer

Nellie Mitchell was the daughter of a Scottish building engineer who emigrated to Australia. He heard her sing in the house and decided to spend some money having her taught properly.

She went eventually to Paris to study under Marchesi, and made her first

Dame Nellie Melba as 'Marguerite' in *Faust*

Pavlova, Anna (1885–1931)
Russian ballerina

Pavlova had to be seen to be believed. Ballet enthusiasts who remember the 1920s say that there was no one like her. She had been born in St. Petersburg, of humble parents, and had got herself to the Russian Imperial Ballet School. Almost at once it was seen she had star quality, and by the time she was twenty-one she was already being talked about as the coming principal ballerina.

She founded her own company with which she travelled all over the world, and everywhere she went she was enthusiastically received. Her most loved roles were the Dying Swan, Giselle and the Californian Poppy. Pavlova contracted pneumonia during an extremely exhausting series of performances, and died.

Grey of Fallodon, Edward Grey, 1st Viscount (1862–1933)
British statesman

Grey was Liberal foreign secretary from 1905 to 1916. He tried hard to get the powers of Europe to live at peace, but when he saw that France and Germany could not agree, he formed a Triple Entente (a treaty of friendship) between Britain, France and Russia, to keep some kind of check on German military ambitions which seemed very dangerous. It was his melancholy job to declare war on Germany in August 1914 for not withdrawing her troops from Belgium.

Galsworthy, John (1867–1933)
English playwright and novelist

Galsworthy is best known for his *Forsyte Saga,* a trilogy of works about a large prosperous middle class family, through three generations, which gives a wonderful insight into the way the British middle classes thought and acted in the years from the 1880s to the 1920s. But he wrote much more than that. Several excellent plays of his are often produced, including *The Skin Game, Strife, Escape* and *The Roof.* He was awarded the Nobel prize for literature in 1932. He wrote many other well-known novels.

appearance in Brussels in 1887, calling herself Melba, from Melbourne where she had lived in Australia. Then she came to England where she was a great success. She sang many parts, especially Lucia in the Donizetti opera, *Lucia di Lammermoor*, based on a novel by Walter Scott.

Melba, as she came to be known simply, was the leading singer for a whole generation, and everyone was delighted when she became a Dame of the British Empire in 1918.

Coolidge, Calvin (1872–1933)
American president (1923–1929)

Coolidge was a lawyer who got himself elected to the Senate of Massachusetts in 1911. He was popular, and succeeded in being elected governor of Massachusetts for the years 1918–1920 during which time he cracked a police strike and won a lot of public support.

Coolidge was a republican, and when Warren Harding was elected president in 1921 he was appointed vice president. Harding died in office which meant that Coolidge had to take over. He stood again in 1924 and was elected for a second term, serving to the end, in 1929.

Paul von Hindenburg

Hindenburg, Paul von (1847–1934)
German field marshal and president (1925–1934)

Hindenburg was one of the greatest of the German generals. He fought in the Austro-Prussian War of 1866 and the Franco-Prussian War of 1870–1871. Thereafter he rose up the military ladder to reach the rank of general in 1903. Then he retired in 1911. That might have been the end of his career, but in some ways it was only the start.

Three years later he was appointed to command German forces in East Prussia and he smashed the Russians at a great victory at Tannenburg. He was promoted field marshal and became the most popular army commander in Germany. The next year he defeated the Russians

again, in Poland, and was made chief of staff to the whole army. With his friend, General Ludendorff (*p. 282*), he directed German war strategy for the rest of the war. It did not prove successful, but this did not dim his reputation.

In 1925 Hindenburg was elected president of a depressed Germany which was wrestling with unemployment, balance of payments and other problems. In 1933 he had to accept Hitler as candidate for Chancellor of the German state, but in doing so he thought he could keep the demonic dictator under control. He was too old, though, and when he died in 1934, Hitler took over his job as president.

Pinero, Sir Arthur Wing (1855–1934)
English playwright

Sir Arthur Pinero turned out a stream of good plays over fifty years or more. Many of them are still produced today. They include *The Second Mrs. Tanqueray* (1893), *The Gay Lord Quex* (1899), *The Enchanted Cottage* (1922) and *Dr. Harmer's Holidays* (1930). His plays were well constructed, had good plots, and often contained a serious message or moral. Many of the leading parts were well moulded and full of character, giving actors and actresses plenty of scope in which to display their particular talents. For years, theatregoers waited with enthusiasm for 'the latest play by Mr. Pinero'.

Elgar, Sir Edward (1857–1934)
English composer

Apart from Handel, Elgar must be regarded as the greatest English musical composer. His work, which admittedly took years to achieve recognition, is in many instances worthy to be compared with the finest compositions of musical history.

Elgar was born in Worcestershire, a county he loved all his life. He rose to become Master of the King's Musick, a member of the Order of Merit, a baronet, and the recipient of countless honours from all over the world. His compositions were many and varied, but perhaps the loveliest were his violin concerto, his cello concerto, his *Enigma Variations* (a set of musical pieces to illustrate the characters of a number of friends), and his *Introduction and Allegro for Strings*.

Elgar probably enjoyed some, though not all, of his fame. What he did not like was the use put to his compositions, the *Pomp and Circumstance* marches, for they were played time and time again to illustrate the greatness of the British empire and its prowess in war. Towards the end of his life he went home to Worcestershire and died within the sight of the Malvern Hills which he had adored as a boy and missed dreadfully as a man.

Poincaré, Raymond (1860–1934)
French statesman

Poincaré was an economist who had a distinguished career in French government. He was appointed prime minister in 1912, and while in office strengthened ties between France and Britain, largely because of the menace of the Germans under Kaiser Wilhelm II (*p. 286*). In 1913 Poincaré was elected president of France and he held this office right through the First World War.

Most presidents give up politics when they leave office, but Poincaré was prevailed upon to go back to party politics, and in 1922 he was again appointed prime minister, for two years. Once more, in 1926, he was called in to help save France in a financial crisis.

Delius, Frederick (1862–1934)
English composer

Delius was a rare exception in the world of music. His work, wonderful as it is in many respects, shows few traces of the influence of anybody else. Possibly one or two pieces were derived from the inspiration of Grieg (*p. 255*) but on the whole he was absolutely original. His harmony was spectacularly successful, and he could evoke tears with great facility in some of his contemplative studies. His *Walk to the Paradise Garden*, for example, is one of the most moving pieces of music ever written.

In later years Delius went blind, and the world might have lost his last works but for the fact that a young musician, Eric Fenby, went to his home in France and laboriously copied down note by note what the great man was composing in his head but no longer articulating well. One such piece was *Song of Summer*, a wonderful tone poem. He wrote many orchestral and choral works and six operas.

Marie Curie

Curie, Marie (1867–1934)
French physicist

It is interesting to note that although women were until recently thought to be incapable of achieving great things in art or science, the only person ever to win two Nobel prizes was a woman – Madame Curie. She and her husband Pierre were research graduates at Paris towards the end of the last century. They were working in the exciting new field of X-rays and looking for elements that gave off these valuable rays. After years of patient experiment they finally isolated radium, and the discovery bought them tremendous fame. They shared the Nobel prize for physics for 1903.

Pierre Curie was killed in a road accident three years later. Although broken hearted Marie Curie carried on her research work, and the University of Paris made her professor of physics. In 1911, the Nobel foundation awarded her a second prize. Radium is used for many purposes. In medicine its rays can be employed to combat cancer.

The Battle of Jutland in which Earl Jellicoe as British commander-in-chief, established British naval supremacy over the Atlantic

Dreyfus, Alfred (1859–1935)
French martyr to anti-Semitism

This French Jew was deeply involved in a period of strong anti-Semitism in France – but he was by no means the cause. In 1894, when a captain in the army, he was falsely charged with delivering secret papers to a foreign power, court-martialled, dismissed and transported to Devil's Island prison for life.

The storm of protest started by his wife and family, supported by the noted writer Zola, whipped up a period of pro-Jewish and anti-Jewish rivalry lasting several years. After much scandal, he was re-tried, found guilty again, but pardoned, despite the fact that a Count Esterhazy confessed to having given the papers to the enemy. Dreyfus served France with distinction in the First World War and was awarded the Légion d'Honneur after the peace.

Jellicoe, John Rushworth, 1st Earl (1859–1935)
British admiral

It was said that at the Battle of Jutland, in May 1916, Jellicoe, the British commander-in-chief of the Grand Fleet, was the only man who could have won the war in an afternoon. This was an unkind comment on the fact that, when he saw the German fleet withdraw after a heavy engagement, he did not pursue it and destroy it. This may be so, but the German High Seas fleet never again came out in force into the Atlantic in the First World War. Jutland was no great victory, nor a defeat for Britain, but it did establish the superiority of British over German ships.

John Jellicoe had a brilliant career in the navy, and was an expert on gunnery and torpedoes. He was made chief of the naval staff shortly after Jutland, but he failed to crush the submarine menace to convoys coming to Britain, and was superseded.

Pilsudski, Josef (1867–1935)
Polish statesman

Marshal Pilsudski was one of the most famous heroes of Polish history. He had led a campaign during the First World War to get Poland its independence, and he had control of a private army of thousands of men willing to fight and to die for this. He was captured by the Germans and confined until the collapse of the Germans in 1918. Then he returned to Poland, which had been promised statehood by the Allies, and was immediately elected head of state.

For the next fifteen years, although not always in the supreme post, Pilsudski dominated Polish politics, and ruled the country. He gave it back its national pride built up its forces and fought off aggressors who tried to invade.

Allenby, Edmund Henry Hynman, 1st Viscount (1861–1936)
English field marshal

Allenby had a successful army career, and was posted in 1917 as commander of the Egyptian Expeditionary Force to take Palestine and parts of Syria from the Turks. He captured Gaza in 1917 and entered Jerusalem, mounted on a white horse, on 9 December of the same year. The next year he smashed a Turkish army at Megiddo. Thereafter, the Turks gradually withdrew from the whole of the Levant.

Venizelos, Eleutherios (1864–1936)
Greek statesman

Venizelos was the greatest statesman produced by modern Greece. He was prime minister from 1910 to 1915, and two years later he forced the king, Constantine, to abdicate because he would not join the Allied powers in the First World War.

After the war, he fell out of favour for failing to make territorial gains in Asia Minor, but in 1924, 1928–1932 and 1933 he served again as premier, instituting many public works schemes which did much to aid Greece's unemployed.

Kipling, Rudyard (1865–1936)
English writer

Kipling was a young journalist in British India in the days of Queen Victoria, when she was Empress of India and the British flag flew over nearly a quarter of the surface of the earth. He wrote in his spare time as well and sent in verses and stories, usually with a military or imperial twist. An early collection of verse was *Departmental Ditties*, in 1886, and another, of stories, was *Tales From The Hills* (1887).

From 1889, when he came home, he poured out a spate of verse, stories, novels, children's stories, all in an unmistakable style quite peculiar to himself. Among these were *The Light That Failed*, *Barrack Room Ballads*, *The Jungle Book*, *Captain's Courageous*, *Stalky & Co.*, *Kim*, *Just-so Stories* and *Puck of Pook's Hill*.

Kipling loved England, but it seems he was becoming disenchanted with the governing classes. While in 1907 he had accepted the Nobel prize for literature, later he declined all kinds of honours.

Pirandello, Luigi (1867–1936)
Italian playwright

Pirandello lectured in Italian literature at Rome university from 1897 to 1922. During this time he began to write plays which have made him one of the best known of all Italian dramatists. In his work he aimed to create characters of men who built identities for themselves, each person intensely individual and separate from another, but of such characteristics that you could probably find their double somewhere else.

His best known plays were *Six Characters in Search of An Author*, *The Mock Emperor* and *As You Desire Me*.

In 1925 Pirandello formed his own theatrical company and took his plays all over Europe. He was awarded the Nobel prize in 1934.

Gorki, Maxim (1868–1936)
Russian author

Gorki was born Alexei Maximovich Peshkov. He had little education and went into journalism to teach himself. He became a revolutionary and joined the Communist party. When Lenin took over the government of Russia in 1918, he appointed Gorki head of propaganda. Gorki wrote several books, including autobiographies of his earlier days of hardship.

Beatty, David, 1st Earl (1871–1936)
British admiral

Beatty was a typical naval officer, bold, dashing (he wore his officer's cap always at a rakish angle over one eye) and blunt of speech. He won a DSO in the Egyptian War of 1896–1898 by forcing ships up the Nile to help Kitchener in his reconquest of the Sudan. By the time he was only 38 he was a rear-admiral. In the First World War he made himself the idol of the nation by his exploits at the battle of Dogger Bank, where he sank the German battleship, the *Blücher*, and at Jutland where his ship, the *Lion*, was sunk. He became First Sea Lord and chief of the naval staff in 1919 and held the post for eight years.

Chesterton, Gilbert Keith (1874–1936)
English man of letters

G.K.C., as he was known, was a huge man, with massive head, pince-nez spectacles, and jovial personality. He was a brilliant scholar, writer, poet, historian, essayist, novelist and speaker. As poet he wrote, among other things, the splendid narrative poem, *Lepanto*, about the great naval battle between Don John of Austria and the Turks in 1571, and as novelist he invented the character of Father Brown, the cleric detective. G.K.C. also wrote biographies and essays, launched and edited his own paper, *G.K.'s Weekly*.

He had enormous energy, great humour, honesty and forthrightness, and clarity of style. He was also extremely vague. Once he arrived at Didcot Station in Berkshire. He sent a telegram to his wife: 'Am at Didcot. Where ought I to be?'

Kamenev, Lev Borisovich (1883–1936)
Russian communist leader

Kamenev's real name was Rosenfeld. He, like Trotsky, was Jewish born, and had a career of revolutionary activity interspersed with exile in Siberia. He was friendly with Stalin and supported him in his bid to take over the party after Lenin's death in 1924. Stalin was grateful and rewarded him with many high offices.

Then when he married Trotsky's sister, he was accused by Stalin of plotting against him, and was imprisoned. In 1936, Stalin was purging the Communist Party of several elements he thought unreliable, including Field Marshal Tuchachewski, and Kamenev was executed. In fact Stalin despatched the best brains in the party, and Russia was to suffer for it.

Rockefeller, John Davison (1839–1937)
American oil tycoon

With his brother William, Rockefeller founded the Standard Oil Company which for some time controlled the American oil business. He gave some 500 million dollars to medical research, the church, universities, and to establishing the Rockefeller Foundation.

Masaryk, Tomas Garrigue (1850–1937)
Czechoslovak statesman

Masaryk was the father of the Czechoslovak state, as we know it, for in earlier days it had been part of the Austrian empire. When the First World War broke out in 1914, Masaryk, a teacher of philosophy and a member of parliament, organized a campaign to resist the Austrians forcing the Czech people to fight on their side. He became head of a revolutionary council, and at the end of the war, when the Czechoslovak state was created, he became its first president. He stayed in office until 1935, and in that time carried out many useful reforms.

Ludendorff, Erich Friedrich Wilhelm (1865–1937)
German general

Ludendorff was said to have been the brains behind Hindenburg (*p. 278*) who was but a figurehead to amuse the German people and keep their spirits up during the First World War. This is probably an exaggeration, but there is no doubt that the partnership between Hindenburg and Ludendorff when they were in charge of German military strategy in 1917–1918 was largely dominated by Ludendorff. He had been successful in several theatres of war, and the failure of his last efforts on the Western Front in 1918 were said to have come from betrayal by the government and not from faulty strategy.

After the war, Ludendorff played with politics, but he got his fingers burned when he supported Hitler's abortive rising against the government in Munich in 1923.

MacDonald, James Ramsay (1866–1937)
Scottish statesman

Ramsay MacDonald was the first Labour prime minister in Britain. He had risen from the humblest of homes at Lossiemouth in Scotland, become general secretary of the Labour Party, and been elected as member of Parliament for a Leicester seat in 1906. Five years later he was made leader of the Labour Party in the House of Commons, and this really meant that if ever a Labour Government were returned to power, he would become its prime minister. And so it happened, in 1924, but this Labour government had a minority vote and needed Liberal support to stay in office. It fell later in the year, but in 1929 the party did better, and MacDonald again became prime minister.

This time he seemed to be out of his depth. He was unable to tackle the economic difficulties and, in 1931, had to agree to a coalition with the Conservatives under Baldwin.

Rutherford, Ernest, 1st Baron (1871–1937)
New Zealand physicist

Rutherford was the greatest experimental physicist of all time. He split the atom, by bombarding the nucleus of a nitrogen atom with radio-active particles from radium, and obtained a number of nuclei of hydrogen. This great feat, achieved with apparatus costing only a few pounds, opened up a whole new science, nuclear physics, of which he is justly considered the father.

Ernest Rutherford, ebullient, boom-

Ernest Rutherford

ing-voiced, rumbustious, brilliant, patient, far-seeing, became Cavendish professor of Physics at Cambridge in 1919. The University had not seen anything like him before. He dominated nuclear research there for a generation and took a leading part in all the achievements. He gathered about him the most distinguished accumulation of younger brains ever to be assembled in a place of science. He encouraged them, setting a wonderful example by his energy, acute observation and amazing insight. In 1929 he became the first physicist to be created a baron.

Marconi, Guglielmo, Marchese (1874–1937)
Italian scientist

Marconi was the first man successfully to send and pick up radio signals over any distance. He set up a transmitter in Newfoundland, and another in Cornwall, and in 1901 he sent signals across the Atlantic. It was a great day in wireless history; it meant that ships at sea which were in trouble could send for aid swiftly; that armies locked up in ambushes or fortresses by enemy besiegers could signal for help; and that the printed word had lost its dominance in the field of mass communication.

Mustapha Kemal Atatürk and in the background, modern Ankara which he founded

Kemal Atatürk, Mustapha (1881–1938)
Founder of modern Turkey

The Turks, amid intervals of decline, have had periods of greatness and produced outstanding leaders. One of these was Kemal Atatürk who was a soldier in the army in the First World War. He did not like the government of Ottoman rulers and when he saw that Turkey was going to collapse at the end of the war he founded the Turkish Nationalist party. In 1920, a provisional government elected him president of Turkey. This gave him the chance to do what he wanted, which was to re-structure the country and bring it up to date.

Kemal introduced all kinds of useful reforms: he abolished monasteries, old forms of dress, restrictions on women, and he encouraged the use of the Roman rather than the Arabic alphabet. He brought in western type coinage, laws, transport, in fact made his country a 20th century land. Kemal did this great work with the co-operation of a large majority of the Turkish people.

Freud, Sigmund (1856–1939)
Austrian psychologist

Freud was one of the most important influences on life in the present century. He introduced the science of psycho-analysis, that is, investigation of the unconscious mind, and by it brought relief and hope to millions of people with disturbed minds. He began by trying to find out what troubled people by hypnotizing them and thus getting them to reveal emotions normally suppressed. Then he abandoned that technique and tried the free association method, that is, calling up one idea by suggesting another linked to it. In this the patient stops concentrating on any one subject and lets his thoughts wander. Then he tells the analyst whatever comes into his mind. He also talks about dreams he has had, and the analyst puts it all together to get some picture of memories that have been suppressed for one reason or another, causing mental conflict or disturbance. Bringing them into the open usually relieves the tension and removes the conflict.

The possibilities of this science are still enormous and many more have yet to be explored. But there is no doubt of the tremendous value of the science.

Freud studied in Vienna, and was professor of neuropathology there for 36 years. Nazism forced him to leave Austria.

Yeats, William Butler (1865–1939)
Irish playwright and poet
This marvellous Irish genius was perhaps the foremost writer in a veritable galaxy of Irish literary figures who showed the world the potential of the English language, in the earlier years of this century.

Born in Dublin, the son of the well-known painter, John Butler Yeats, young Yeats' first book of verse was published in 1889. Ten years later, he produced *The Wind Among the Reeds*, a collection of verse of astonishing power and imagery.

At the end of the century Yeats helped to found the Abbey Theatre in Dublin, which came to be one of the leading theatres in the world. He wrote plays especially for it, including *Cathleen ni Houlihan*. And he encouraged other playwrights like J. M. Synge. The aim of the group was to show the world the genius of the Irish, and this was important in the fight to win support for the movement for Irish independence from the government of England.

When the Irish won their freedom in 1922 and the Free State was created, Yeats was one of the first of its new senators. The following year his work was rewarded with a Nobel prize.

Grenfell, Sir Wilfred Thomason (1865–1940)
British physician and missionary
Grenfell was a doctor who went to Labrador, off Canada, in 1892, to carry out missionary work among the people, bring hospital treatment, and generally to try to make their lives a little better. He extended his work along the Newfoundland coast. He was particularly anxious to help the fishermen and their families, for fishing in those waters was an extremely dangerous career, and lives were lost and misery resulted frequently.

Chamberlain, Neville (1869–1940)
English prime minister
Neville Chamberlain was the second son of Joseph Chamberlain (*p. 261*). He had been Lord Mayor of Birmingham, and he entered national politics in 1918 in the Conservative party. He at once obtained high office, and when Stanley Baldwin (*p. 293*) resigned the premiership in 1937, Chamberlain was elected to succeed.

Chamberlain loved Britain, but he did not understand foreign policy. He thought he could talk Hitler and Mussolini into leaving the smaller states of Europe alone. He was deeply shocked when Hitler broke his so-called promises and invaded Poland on 1 September 1939, but he braved himself to declare war on Germany two days later.

Chamberlain's direction of the war was sloppy and ineffective, and in the summer of 1940 his own party pressed him to give up the job to someone else. Luckily for Britain – and for the rest of the world – the man who got the job was the greatest Englishman of all time, Winston Churchill.

Trotsky, Leon (1879–1940)
Russian communist leader
Trotsky was Jewish born, and his real name was Lev Davidovich Bronstein. He had an exciting youth as a revolutionary, being caught, exiled to Siberia, escaping to Britain, and returning to Russia, only to be sent to Siberia again. When Lenin set up his first Bolshevik government in Russia in 1917 he appointed Trotsky as commissar for foreign affairs. Trotsky was considered one of the best brains of the communist party, and in some respects he was an abler man than Lenin. They worked well together, and when Lenin died in 1924, most people thought Trotsky would succeed him as head of the party. But Joseph Stalin (*p. 299*) also had strong support and in the end he prevailed. Trotsky was humbled and then banished. He was eventually murdered in Mexico in 1940.

Emperor Wilhelm II

Wilhelm II (1859–1941)
Emperor of Germany (1888–1918)
Friedrich Wilhelm Viktor Albert Hohen-
zollern, Wilhelm II, Kaiser (Emperor) of
Germany, was the grandson of William I
of Germany, whom Bismarck made
emperor in 1871. Wilhelm was an arrogant, cheeky, bullying young man whose
manners did not improve as he got older.
No sooner had he become emperor, than
he began to throw his weight about. He
tested his power by dismissing Bismarck, unquestionably the greatest
statesman Germany ever produced. He
supported nations which quarrelled with
Britain, such as the Boers in South
Africa. And he threatened and bullied
smaller nations in Europe by 'sabre
rattling', that is, war talk.

He was largely responsible for a
localized quarrel in central Europe developing into the First World War in
August 1914. But in the end he was
beaten by the Allies, in 1918. He fled into
exile and was allowed to stay in Holland.

Paderewski, Ignazy Jan (1860–1941)
Polish statesman and pianist
Paderewski began his career as a pianist
and by the end of the 19th century had
become one of the finest performers in
the world. In the First World War he

turned his energies to helping the 'Poland
for the Polish' campaign and toured the
world giving concerts to raise money for
Polish victims of German and Russian
aggression in the war.

After the war, when Poland was being
given statehood, Paderewski was appointed the state's first prime minister,
while Marshal Pilsudski was made commander-in-chief of the Polish armies.

Baden-Powell, Robert Stephenson Smyth, 1st Baron (1857–1941)
Founder of the Scout Movement
'B-P' stood for Baden-Powell, the retired
general, hero of Mafeking in the Boer
War, who in 1908 founded the Boy Scout
Movement. It was also the initials of the
Scout motto, 'Be Prepared'.

Baden-Powell, the son of an Oxford
professor, left the army as a lieutenant
general and with a knighthood. He
settled down to write a book called
Scouting for Boys. It was an account of
an interesting camping holiday he had
organized a year before with some boys,
where they devoted their time to initiative tests, and practising skills of all
kinds like cooking on camp fires, knot-
tying, rope-bridge building and so forth.
The book was a great success and the Boy
Scout Movement, now world wide, arose
from it.

Joyce, James (1882–1941)
Irish author
James Joyce was one of the leading writers
in this century; his greatest works were
written when he was in self-imposed
exile in France.

His work was revolutionary. His novels
break away from conventional forms.
The time sequence is dislocated; much
of the trivia of everyday life which in
other novels would be discarded comes
to the surface. Joyce attempts to capture
the world of the subconscious by letting
the deepest and often half-formulated
thoughts of his characters stream onto the
written page. In *Ulysses*, for example, one
character has long uninterrupted para-
graphs of words running to six or seven
pages. *Ulysses* and *Finnegan's Wake* are

the most complex and brilliant examples of his work.

Alfonso XIII (1886–1941)
King of Spain (1886–1931)

Alfonso was a monarch who got what he deserved. He had come to the throne at birth, for his father died before he was born. As soon as he was old enough to rule, he took over from the council of regency. He did little to rectify the grievances that had been building up under the regency, and his first problems were severe rioting in major cities like Madrid and Barcelona. He kept out of the First World War, but not long after that was over, Spanish forces in Morocco, a Spanish dominion at the time, were soundly defeated by the Moors. This national disgrace provoked further riots. So Alfonso appointed Primo de Rivera (*p. 276*) as prime minister with dictatorial powers.

By this time there was no real parliament as we know it, but in 1927 Alfonso opened a National Assembly. It was, of course, too late. Half of Spain was communist, having had enough of kings and of dictators. In 1931 he had to abdicate, and he retired to live in Italy.

Hertzog, James Barry Munnik (1866–1942)
Boer statesman

Hertzog was a Boer general in the South African War. He did not agree with the surrender to the British in 1902, and he remained anti-British all his life. In the first Union of South Africa government of 1910 he was minister of justice, but he never altered his views, and when Britain and Germany went to war in 1914, he declined to support South Africa's intervention on the British side.

He was prime minister of South Africa from 1924 to 1939, but when Britain and Germany went to war again in 1939, and he tried to keep South Africa away from the British side, he was overruled and driven from office. Despite his anti-British feelings, Hertzog did much for South Africa, and helped the country's modernization programme.

Webb, Beatrice (1858–1943)
English social reformer

Beatrice Webb was the wife of Sidney Webb, and they were among the first socialists in Britain. Indeed, G. B. Shaw (*p. 294*) claimed that he and Sidney invented true communism, and not Karl Marx (*p. 238*). In the 1880s these people began to campaign for the righting of many grievous social wrongs, some of which had grown up from the industrial revolution and had not been put right.

In 1887 Beatrice became a member of the Fabian Society, the first socialist club in the country, and she made her mark as a writer of concise, well-constructed pamphlets on social matters. She had money of her own and spent it freely in the service of socialism.

In 1892 she married Sidney Webb, and they worked together for about the next thirty odd years, writing, lecturing, speaking, campaigning, and in his case standing for, and being elected to, Parliament. They also founded the London School of Economics, the foremost political educational establishment in the world.

Rachmaninov, Sergei (1873–1943)
Russian pianist and composer

Anyone who has any interest in music will have heard Rachmaninov's second piano concerto in C minor. They may also know he composed three other concertos, several symphonies and a lot more music besides. But it is possible that fewer people realize that it was as a concert pianist that Rachmaninov really became famous. In his time he was probably the greatest living pianist. Certainly, the only contenders in the last 50 years were Rubinstein and Richter.

Rachmaninov had composed much of his work in his younger days when he was living in Russia. The second concerto, for example, was said to have been written when he was in a state of acute mental depression, when he felt his life was a total failure. Then, after the 1917 Revolution, he fled to America where he made a home. Over the next generation or so he toured the world giving recitals.

Boris III (1894–1943)
King of Bulgaria (1918–1943)

Boris tried to govern Bulgaria well, but it was not a happy land. Many people wanted to become closer allies of Russia, for there were historic ties with that great land, but Boris was against it. Indeed, he preferred to be allied to the central powers, especially Germany. When the Second World War broke out, Boris tried to keep his kingdom out of it, but German pressure was extremely strong and he caved in, and in 1941 joined Hitler in the attack on Russia. Boris died in 1943.

Rommel, Erwin (1891–1944)
German field marshal

Rommel was one of Nazi Germany's greatest military heroes of the Second World War. He was a member of the Nazi party, which many generals were not, and he went into Poland and into France in Hitler's spectacular invasions and conquests. He was a hero to his soldiers, and he never allowed himself privileges denied the ranks. He was sent to North Africa in command of the German *Afrika Korps* to fight the British and try to drive them into the desert, away from the Suez Canal. At first he was successful, and even his name frightened British troops as one general after another failed to give them inspiration.

Then Montgomery came out, and in October 1942 he launched the first major counter-offensive against Rommel at El Alamein and drove the Germans back a long way. It was a turning point in the war.

Rommel was recalled for duties in Germany, and during a visit to the front in France in 1944 he was severely injured by British fighter planes. When he recovered, he was visited by agents of Hitler's who said he had been involved in the July attempt on Hitler's life. It was in fact true; indeed, Rommel was earmarked to be president of the new Germany, if the attempt succeeded. Rommel was invited to commit suicide or stand trial. He chose suicide, and was given a state funeral.

Ciano, Count Galeazzo (1903–1944)
Italian statesman

Ciano was a diplomat for the Mussolini government in Italy. He made the error of marrying Edda, Mussolini's daughter, in 1930; this brought him to the front of Mussolini's circle. This was in the end to cost Ciano his life.

He was foreign minister from 1936 to 1943, and did as well as he could, with a bullying and strutting father-in-law constantly watching his every move. In the end he was taken by those who succeeded in expelling Mussolini from power, and executed.

Lloyd-George, David, 1st Earl (1863–1945)
Welsh statesman and war leader

Lloyd George was not only the greatest Welshman since Owain Glyndŵr in the fifteenth century, he was also one of the finest war-leaders in British history, equalled only by Pitt the Elder and perhaps a little less remarkable than Churchill.

He came from an extremely humble background, qualified as a solicitor and worked very hard to get into politics, in which he hoped to achieve something for poorer people. He was elected for Caernarvon in 1890, and remained its member until 1945. His early speeches showed him to be one of the best orators in the country. He did not mind what he said or who he hurt, especially if it were the privileged classes.

In 1908 he was appointed chancellor of the exchequer in Asquith's government, and he caused a storm with his reforming policies. He introduced old age pensions, national insurance and super-tax.

When the First World War came he was made Minister of Munitions after the failure to get supplies to the front had caused a scandal, and in that job he galvanized all departments to get the armaments out to France.

In 1916 he became prime minister when Asquith resigned, and for the rest of the war directed all war policy. He quarrelled with many generals, some of

Sir Winston Churchill, Franklin D. Roosevelt and Joseph
Stalin at Yalta

whom he knew to be out of date or tired,
and he spared no one in his drive to get
things done. But no one worked harder
than he.

He remained prime minister for
another four years, but his reputation
was spoiled by the clumsy way he
handled the Irish question – ironically
for a fellow Celt whose people, the
Welsh, had long suffered the same sort of
indignities at the hands of the English
that the Irish (and Scots, too) had. He
left office in 1922.

His last years were spent working in
Wales for his country. He accepted an
earldom only a few weeks before his
death.

Keyes, Roger John Brownlow, 1st Baron (1872–1945)
British admiral

In 1918, some British ships filled with
explosives charged into Zeebrugge harbour in Belgium and blocked it, making
it useless to the Germans. Their commander was Roger Keyes, who had been
director of plans at the admiralty. This
gallant action fired the imagination of the
country, and made Keyes a hero. He
rose to be admiral of the fleet, and in
1940 Churchill called him back from
retirement to organize British com-
mando units preparing for raids on harbours in occupied France.

Roosevelt, Franklin Delano (1882– 1945)
American president (1932–1945)

This Roosevelt, a relative of Theodore
Roosevelt (*p. 265*), was the only American president to serve four terms of
office, although he died during the last
term. It was remarkable for anyone,
more so for him when it is remembered
he had to spend much of his life in a
wheel-chair after an attack of polio-
myelitis.

Roosevelt was a lawyer, like so many
American presidents. He came to prominence as a politician when in 1932 he
offered the American people a New Deal,
that is, sweeping reforms to make the
country rich and strong again after the
calamitous depression of the 1920s and
the slump of 1929. The electorate believed him and put him in office. They
did so again in 1936 and again in 1940.

When the Second World War broke
out and Churchill became British prime
minister, Roosevelt studiously kept out
of the conflict, but equally studiously
offered all sorts of help to Britain short of
war. Finally, he had to bring the Americans in when the Japanese invaded and
smashed the American naval base at
Pearl Harbour in Hawaii in December
1941. Until his death, near the end of the
war in Europe, Roosevelt directed the
entire American war effort.

Benito Mussolini

went round beating up communists and socialists. Then they marched on Rome and demanded of the king, Victor Emanuel, that Mussolini should be allowed to form a government. Reluctantly the king agreed, and the fascist party came to power. For the next twenty-one years (1922–1943) Mussolini ruled the Italians as a dictator. The press was squashed, as was freedom of speech. There were secret police everywhere. The army was led into all sorts of vainglorious expeditions against weaker countries, like Abyssinia in 1935, Albania in 1939 and Greece in 1941.

With typical aggressiveness and empty rhetoric, Mussolini announced, in June 1940, that Italy had entered the war on Hitler's side. Hitler may have welcomed this then, but Italy was to prove a thorn in his side. Italian armies were not the armies of ancient Rome, disciplined, bold and unconquerable. One after the other had to be extricated from some mess or other.

By 1943, enough colleagues of Mussolini's plucked up the courage to arrest him and dismiss him from office as chief of state. The Germans then snatched him from his place of imprisonment, and for a while he ruled a small part of northern Italy, but he lacked firm support, and in 1945, a few days before Hitler's own death, patriots seized him and put him to death.

Laval, Pierre (1883–1945)
French politician

Laval was a brilliant but cunning lawyer and politician who rose to become minister for foreign affairs in 1931. He held several offices up to the outbreak of the Second World War in 1939. Then when France was invaded by the Germans and forced to capitulate, the Germans looked about for members of the French government and other well-known politicians to join them and collaborate in running France as a sort of dependency of Germany. Laval imagined advantages for France in collaborating, though most of his countrymen did not. Many remembered the horrors of the First World War, and in any case did not like the Germans.

Laval was prime minister of the Vichy government (the French government working with the Germans) from 1942 until 1944. After the war, he was arrested, tried and executed for treason.

Mussolini, Benito (1883–1945)
Italian dictator

Mussolini was really a ludicrous figure in European politics, though of course the many millions of Italians who suffered under his oppressive rule would not have found much to be happy about.

This blacksmith's son formed a gang of roughs after the First World War, who

Curtin, John (1885–1945)
Australian statesman

Curtin was a Labour party chief in Australia. He became the leader of the opposition in the Australian Parliament in 1935, and when in 1941 a general election brought his party to power, he became prime minister. This was during a critical period in the Second World War, when Australian troops were fighting gallantly for Britain in North Africa and elsewhere. There was a danger that he might withdraw some Australian forces, and Churchill had many anxious moments over this, but despite their sharp differences of political thought, they got on well.

Hitler, Adolf (1889–1945)
German dictator (1933–1945)

What kind of adjective does one give to a man whose demonic energy took him from a humble role as painter of picture postcards in a Vienna slum to absolute ruler of the German people, all 80,000,000 of them, and then through hideous war to master of the bulk of Europe? How does one adequately describe this man, whose career resulted in the deaths of over 50,000,000 people and the destruction of thousands of cities and towns.

Even at this distance in time, it is hard to comprehend the enormity of his crimes, the magnitude of the miseries he caused, the depths of degradation and beastliness to which he dragged his people who, to their shame, followed him willingly whither he would lead them.

Hitler was the son of an Austrian customs officer. He joined up in the First World War and fought in France where he was gassed and where he was decorated for bravery. After the collapse of the German-Austrian forces, he was one of many men, aimless, jobless and depressed, who wandered about Germany brooding about what was to become of their once great nation. He began to think of the collapse as not being due to any failure in the military sense but rather to a 'stab in the back' at home by politicians corrupted by communists and Jews. So he formed a political party, called the National Socialist German Workers Party, shortened to *Nazi*, to avenge the defeat and to restore German greatness. He discovered various talents in himself at this time, powers of oratory, an ability to put complex issues in very simple terms, demonic energy, and a capability of bending men to his will either individually or in masses.

The party took time to grow and its first attempt to seize power was a failure. But as Germany sank deeper into economic mess and unemployment figures rose to several millions, Hitler's time came, and he bullied his way to the top by offering the only practical solution, one based on terror and blind obedience to his will. He got the aged President

Adolf Hitler

Hindenburg (*p. 278*) to appoint him chancellor, in 1933, as there simply was no one else who could do anything. The next year Hindenburg died and Hitler combined the presidency with the chancellorship, and called himself *Der Führer* (the Leader). In practice it was another word for absolute dictator.

He then set out on a course of political bullying of other nations, and when that failed, military conquest; by 1942 he had mastered nearly all Europe and millions of square miles of Russia. But this had brought him into war with Britain and the United States, and the combined resources of these nations with Russia and other powers, gradually wore down the Nazi military machine, and in April 1945, as Russian shells were falling about the Chancellery in Berlin, in whose basement he was acting out the last scenes of directing a lost war, Hitler took his own life.

This amazing man, who had perhaps brought more misery to the world than anyone before or since, was a vegetarian, loved children, adored animals, did not smoke and remained faithful to his mistress to the end.

Goebbels, Joseph Paul (1897–1945)
German Nazi political leader

Goebbels became minister of propaganda in Hitler's government in 1933, and remained in charge of the Nazi's machinery for indoctrinating the German people with Nazi philosophy right to the end of the regime, which collapsed in May 1945. He was a brilliant journalist and broadcaster who had an uncanny eye for the right moment to say the right thing, or the things people wanted to hear.

Goebbels was also intensely loyal to his leader. When Hitler decided to commit suicide in Berlin at the end of April 1945, Goebbels decided to poison all his children first, give poison to his wife and then take some himself. So it happened: he had no wish to survive his beloved leader.

Wells, Herbert George (1866–1946)
English writer and reformer

H. G. Wells is famous for many things. He was brought up in poverty and spent many years as a draper's assistant. But he had a very lively imagination and a quick eye for observation. He went to college in London and read for a science degree. Thereafter his career took two parallel courses.

He became passionately interested in bettering the lot of his fellow men. He believed men should be happier, have fuller lives, and he thought this would come about through the march of science. He was a Fabian, that is, an early socialist, and he was also a pacifist.

To help get his message across he turned to writing, and produced some of the best novels of the century, including some science-fiction stories that have subsequently proved to be remarkably accurate in their prophecy. Among these are *The War of the Worlds*, *The First Men in the Moon* and *The Time Machine*. He also wrote a marvellously concise history of the world.

Antonescu, Ion (1882–1946)
Rumanian statesman

Antonescu was a brilliant general who had learned soldiering in France. He fought in the Rumanian army in the First World War and then served as military representative in London. In 1937 he was appointed chief of staff of the Rumanian army by King Carol, but he did not like Carol's rule and led a rebellion among the officers against him. It failed, and he was imprisoned.

In 1940 Antonescu was appointed prime minister of Rumania, and in this office he allied his country with the Germans. This gave him the strength to lead a quiet but effective revolt against King Carol who was driven off the throne. Carol's boy son, Michael, was accepted in his place.

Antonescu sent Rumanian divisions against the Russians on the Eastern Front. After the war, he was tried as a collaborator and executed.

Hopkins, Harry Lloyd (1890–1946)
American statesman

A lot of people helped Franklin Roosevelt (*p. 289*) in his conduct of the American effort in the Second World War, but none were so steadfast or so helpful as Harry Hopkins. This wiry but not very strong little man who had given years to welfare work in the United States first of all managed the arrangements whereby America gave Britain ships, aircraft and other supplies for the war against Hitler, in return for the use of British territories in the West Indies for air bases and naval stations. This was called Lend Lease.

But his main role was as special assistant to Roosevelt, in which capacity he undertook all manner of jobs, great and small. Men got to know soon that if you wanted to get through to 'FDR', you tried Hopkins first!

Goering, Herman (1893–1946)
German Nazi leader

Goering had had a brilliantly distinguished career in the German Air Force in the First World War. He was given the highest award for personal bravery, the *Pour le Mérite*, and he became commander of von Richthofen's squadron when that gallant man was killed.

After the war there was a growing movement of people who felt that the army had been 'stabbed in the back' by the home government, or else the war would not have been lost.

Goering joined this, then came to the attention of Hitler (*p. 291*) who made him one of his right hand men. He remained so almost up to the end of the Second World War. In that war, Goering was head of the air force and made many promises about crushing the British, none of which he was able to keep. After the war Goering was sentenced to death at Nuremburg but took poison the night before he was due to be hanged.

Baldwin, Stanley, 1st Earl (1867–1947)
English statesman
Everyone felt comfortable when they saw Mr. Baldwin, with his pipe and his benign smile, when he was prime minister in the gloomy days of the Depression, in the 1930s. They felt everything would be all right. This was the kind of confidence he inspired, and his career was one which amply backed this feeling.

Baldwin spent the first years of his adulthood helping to run his family ironworks. Then he was elected to Parliament for his native town of Bewdley. In 1917 he was appointed financial secretary to the Treasury, and this was the first of a series of offices which took him to the highest, prime minister, in 1923. But a year later the Conservatives were defeated at an election. Baldwin was back again twelve months after that, and he was premier for five years.

In 1935, the National Coalition Government of Ramsay MacDonald (*p. 283*) failed and Baldwin became premier again. In that time he neglected to prepare Britain against possible German aggression, but on the other hand he did a lot for the internal economy of the country and for employment.

Pershing, John Joseph (1860–1948)
American general
General Pershing was America's leading soldier in the First World War. He had fought in the Philippines and in Mexico, and when President Wilson brought the United States into the First World War, Pershing was made commander-in-chief of the American Expeditionary Force. After the war, he became Chief of Staff to the Army, the top military post in the U.S. His memoirs which he published in 1931 were so well received that he was awarded the Pulitzer prize.

Gandhi, Mohandas Karamchand (1869–1948)
Indian leader
Gandhi was a Hindu lawyer who had spent some time studying in England. He became a stern opponent of British rule in India, and he advocated a policy of passive resistance, that is, refusing to do anything helpful, lying down on railway tracks and not moving when engines came along, striking in factories, but always without violence; in fact he advocated anything that could disrupt the normalities of life without resort to fighting. By 1920 he had become almost a god to many Indians who were tired of British rule, and they called him Mahatma, or 'great-souled'. When he was jailed, as he was more than once during his campaign, the movement behind him grew.

After the 1930 Round Table Conference on India in London he became dissatisfied with its progress, and began his process of fasting unto death. He would refuse to touch any food at all for weeks, in the hopes of getting the British to moderate their views.

During the Second World War Gandhi, understandably, tried to persuade Indians not to fight for Britain, and was arrested. Then after the war he emerged again as leader of the independence movement. The Labour government decided to grant this to India, and in 1947 the country was declared two independent dominions, India and Pakistan. Gandhi had always worked for religious tolerance between the various religions of his country, but early in January 1948 a fanatic shot him down, and the whole of the world mourned its loss.

Jinnah, Mohammed Ali (1876–1948)
Pakistani leader

When India was partitioned into India and Pakistan by the British Labour Government in 1947, Mohammed Ali Jinnah, a Moslem statesman, was appointed the new Pakistan's first governor-general. It was no easy task. There was famine. There were many refugees who had been expelled from India, there was rioting in the Punjab, and there was a struggle over who should have the small state of Kashmir.

Jinnah had worked with Gandhi, but increasingly he felt that Gandhi and Nehru were interested only in furthering the Hindu cause, at the expense of the Moslems, who constituted nearly a quarter of the population of the Indian subcontinent. So he felt he had to go it alone, and he directed his policies accordingly. It was a tragedy for Pakistan that Jinnah died so soon after the partition.

Benes, Eduard (1884–1948)
Czechoslovak statesman

Benes had worked with Tomas Masaryk to create the new Czechoslovak state after the First World War. He became its foreign secretary for nearly twenty years, and was elected president after Thomas Masaryk in 1935. In 1938, the Germans under Hitler occupied part of his country, and he resigned rather than allow this. During the Second World War he was president of the provisional government in exile in London, and when the Germans were defeated in 1945 he went back to his country and became president.

Eisenstein, Sergei Mikhailovich (1898–1948)
Russian motion picture director

Eisenstein is one of the greatest names in the story of motion pictures. He came from Riga, in Latvia, which is now part of Russia, and after a short career as a theatrical scene painter, he entered the world of films, in 1922. At once he saw the enormous dramatic possibilities of using crowd scenes in place of individual heroes or villains, and by skilful cutting and editing of filmed crowds he found he could create rising tension in the cinema, leading to taut climax. This was brilliantly executed in the scene on the palace steps, in Odessa, in the film *Battleship Potemkin*, when a crowd of mutineers was mown down by imperial troops.

His striking grasp of the very elements of cinematic drama is demonstrated in his powerful record of the Russian revolution – *October*.

In 1938 Eisenstein made *Alexander Nevski*, and in 1944 *Ivan the Terrible* (*p. 133*), both remarkable films on patriotic and communistic themes.

Maeterlinck, Count Maurice (1862–1949)
Belgian dramatist

Maeterlinck was Belgian born, but spent much of his life in France, where he was greatly influenced by French writers. His early works were largely poetry, and his twelve *Chansons* contained some very beautiful lyric verse. Then he turned to plays, and one of these, *Pélleas et Mélisande* was adapted as an opera by Debussy (*p. 264*). He also wrote essays of great depth and wisdom, and among these were *The Life of the Bee* (1901), *Death* (1912) and *The Life of the Ant* (1930).

Shaw, George Bernard (1856–1950)
Irish playwright, author and wit

G.B.S. was an astonishing man by any standards. Still writing vigorously at 93, still maintaining his rich, Irish brogue after a lifetime in England, and still, in spite of his wealth, claiming to be an original communist. This tall, wiry, humorous Irishman, who believed himself to be greater than Shakespeare, delighted audiences all over the world for half a century with his plays, books, articles and essays. Two of his best known novels are *Love Among the Artists* and *Cashel Byron's Profession*. A prolific playwright, his works include *Candida, Man and Superman, Androcles and the Lion, Pygmalion, Heartbreak House, Back to Methuselah, Saint Joan* and *The Apple Cart*.

He loved to startle people with his

George Bernard Shaw

Jan Christiaan Smuts

remarks. He once said that Lister (*p. 259*) was a half-wit, which was both unkind and untrue. He said he and Sidney Webb had invented communism. And he kept telling the Western world that Russia had far too many problems on her own doorstep to have any time to invade the west, a theory that has so far been proved right.

Shaw did not drink, was a vegetarian, did not smoke, deplored cruelty of any kind, loved a lot of women, but married only once and then for money. Whatever he did or said, it may have exasperated, it may have amused, but it never bored.

Smuts, Jan Christiaan (1870–1950)
South African statesman and general
Smuts was one of the generals in the South African War of 1899–1902 who gave the British so much trouble. After the war was lost for the Boers he worked with Botha (*p. 266*) to make the Union of South Africa a reality.

When the First World War came, he organized South Africa's army so that it could fight with Britain in many spheres. He also dealt with splinter factions at home which seemed to want to fight on the German side.

Smuts was prime minister of South Africa from 1919 to 1924, and again from 1939 to the end of the Second World War. He was a great help to Churchill who consulted him and took his advice on several major strategic matters.

Blum, Léon (1872–1950)
French socialist statesman
Blum was one of the most prominent socialist politicians of the early part of the 20th century, in a land which had many socialists. He was prime minister from 1936 to 1937, and in that very short time effected considerable reforms.

When the Germans invaded and conquered France, they captured him. He had not been popular with the Germans, who thought him a communist, which he was not, and they ill-treated him. But he survived, and after the Second World War became president of France for a short while, in 1946.

Mackenzie King and in the background, the city of Ottawa

King, William Lyon Mackenzie (1874–1950)
Canadian statesman

Mackenzie King was one of Canada's greatest political leaders. He was elected to parliament in 1908 and was made minister of labour the next year. After the First World War he became leader of the Liberal Party, and this party was returned to power in 1921, 1926 and 1935. He was prime minister in each of these ministries, and he exerted a strong influence upon the nations of the commonwealth when the details of the Statute of Westminster were being worked out in 1930–1931. This accorded dominion status with considerable independence to Canada, Australia, New Zealand and South Africa. In fact, the countries were states of their own within the overall commonwealth.

When the Second World War seemed imminent, he tried to get Hitler to withdraw, but when he failed, he brought

Canada wholeheartedly in on the British side, and gave Britain enormous help in men, materials and foodstuffs throughout the war. Mackenzie King represented his country at the United Nations Organization discussions at the end of the war.

Wavell, Archibald Percival, 1st Earl (1883–1950)
British field marshal
Wavell was one of the best soldiers to emerge from Britain in the present century. He was sensitive, learned (he could recite reams of poetry by heart and translate anything from Latin and Greek) and bold. Unfortunately, he very seldom had anything but tough commands to carry out, where there was no hope except for skilful withdrawal.

He was commander in chief of the British forces in the Middle East from 1939 to 1941, at a time when things were not going well for Britain. Shortages of men and materials did not help, and many chances of victory were snatched from him because of this. He was moved to India when the British were being hammered by the Japanese in Burma.

Finally, in 1943 he was made viceroy of India at a time when the anti-British movement, despite the war, was in full swing. He did much of the groundwork which Mountbatten was able to exploit when he took over in 1947.

Pétain, Henri Philippe (1856–1951)
French marshal and statesman
Pétain was the hero of the siege of Verdun in the First World War. He then became commander of the French armies under Marshal Foch (*p. 275*) the Allied Supreme commander. When France was invaded in 1940 by Hitler's armies, Pétain was appointed head of the government when M. Reynaud resigned. He decided to come to terms with Hitler to spare French lives, but it was a sad thing for a warrior who had once been so brave fighting Germany to give in, and Frenchmen were shocked. After the war he was tried, and sentenced to death, but General de Gaulle changed it to imprisonment.

Mannerheim, Baron Carl Gustav Emil von (1867–1951)
Finnish statesman
Mannerheim was a soldier in the Russian army. When the Russian Revolution brought an end to the country's part in the First World War, Mannerheim fled to Finland where he commanded the forces which prevented a similar rising in that country. He was then elected regent of Finland, and held this office for years. He was also made a field marshal in 1933 and in that capacity re-structured the Finnish army so that when it went to war with Russia in 1939 it gave an excellent account of itself, beating the Russians back. After the Second World War Mannerheim was made president of Finland.

Gide, André Paul Guillaume (1869–1951)
French writer
Gide was a distinguished French essayist and writer, who also translated English classics. He wrote important critical studies on all kinds of literary matters, and produced novels, biographies, plays and verse, and was a profound influence on modern French literature. His fiction grapples with the problems of free will and individual morality; his best known works include *Les Caves du Vatican, Les Faux-Monnayeurs* and *L'Immoraliste*. He was awarded the Nobel Prize for literature in 1947.

Litvinov, Maxim Maximovich (1876–1951)
Russian statesman
Litvinov was a right hand man of Lenin in the time of the Russian revolution of 1917. He was an able diplomat who was sent to various meetings and conferences as representative of the new Soviet state. He signed non-aggression treaties with various powers, including France. He also obtained recognition of the Soviet Union by the United States of America.

During the Second World War he was Russian ambassador in Washington, and on his return became deputy commissar for foreign affairs.

Liaquat Ali Khan (1895–1951)
Pakistani leader

Liaquat was a Moslem lawyer who studied in London and then went back to India to try to help in the independence movement. When the British Labour Government gave India its independence in 1947 and partitioned the country into two dominions, India (predominantly Hindu) and Pakistan (Moslem), Liaquat became the first prime minister of Pakistan. He was assassinated in 1951.

Croce, Benedetto (1866–1952)
Italian statesman and historian

This distinguished Italian scholar was buried alive in an earthquake in the island of Ischia in which his parents and sister were killed, and was rescued at the last moment. He became a literary critic and philosopher. He also went into politics and after the First World War was minister of education. He resigned when Mussolini came to power because he could not accept the latter's fascism and dictatorial rule.

When Italy surrendered to the Allies in 1943, and Mussolini was left ruling only a small part of the country, Croce helped to rebuild those institutions in Italy which had been suppressed. He was also the author of several important works, including *History as the Story of Liberty*.

George VI (1895–1952)
King of Great Britain (1936–1952)

Albert Frederick Arthur George Windsor was Duke of York, the second son of George V and Queen Mary. He succeeded to the throne in 1936 quite unexpectedly when his brother, Edward VIII, abdicated because of his wish to marry a divorced woman. So George took on the throne, and one must say he handled it with the greatest skill. Encumbered with an appalling stutter, a desperate shyness, a habit of smoking about 60 or so cigarettes a day, he nonetheless endeared himself to his people in a manner seldom equalled in the history of monarchy anywhere. During the

Second World War he braved the air raids by staying in London and visiting his bombed-out subjects in the burning city. His own home, Buckingham Palace, was damaged by bombs in broad daylight when he was there. He visited all theatres of war and delivered many broadcasts. In 1947 he substituted the title of Head of the Commonwealth for that of Emperor of India.

He died of cancer of the lung in 1952.

Bondfield, Margaret (1873–1953)
English stateswoman

Margaret Bondfield was the first woman in British political history to become a Cabinet Minister. She was also the first chairman of the Trades Union Congress.

She had worked for years as a trade union official, and in 1921 was elected secretary of the National Federation of Women Workers. Two years later her work was rewarded when she became chairman of the Trades Union Congress. Then she went into national politics, and was elected MP for Northampton. In the first Labour Government of 1924 she was appointed Parliamentary Secretary to the Minister of Labour, and in the next Labour Government of 1929 she was Minister of Labour, with a seat in the Cabinet.

Rundstedt, Karl Rudolf Gerd von (1875–1953)
German field marshal

Rundstedt was one of the abler Prussian generals who decided to throw in their lot with Hitler in 1933 when he bullied his way to power in Germany and got Hindenburg (*p. 278*) to appoint him chancellor. He had been chief of the general staff at the end of the First World War and at the outset of the Second World War he had conducted the brilliantly successful invasion and conquest of Poland. He also led the armies which smashed France in the summer of 1940.

In 1944, when France was invaded by the Allies from England, Rundstedt was appointed to command the defence forces there, but he advised Hitler to make peace. For this he was dismissed.

Stalin, Joseph (1879–1953)
Russian leader

Joseph Stalin's real name was Joseph Vissarionovich Dzhugashvili, and he was a Georgian. He got into all kinds of trouble as a young man, and joined the local socialist organization where he read all he could about Marx. He received sentences in Siberia for his activities.

When Lenin became the ruler of Russia in 1917, Stalin was given a high post in the government. And when the leader died in 1924, and most people thought Trotsky (*p. 285*) would get the job as successor, Stalin put in his claim, with the backing of powerful elements of the communist party. He triumphed over Trotsky who had to leave the country. Stalin thereafter ruled Russia with an iron hand, as had Lenin, from about 1929 to the day of his death in 1953. It was a period of prolonged terror, but also of achievement.

When Hitler invaded Russia in 1941, Stalin called upon the people to resist, and they did. They suffered untold miseries and humiliations. Over 20,000,000 were said to have died, and many were permanently injured.

After the war Stalin was determined that the frontiers in Europe should be drawn the way he wanted them, and he dominated the various peace conferences, largely by managing to pull the wool over the eyes of the Americans.

Vargas, Getulio Dornelles (1883–1954)
Brazilian statesman

Vargas was a lawyer who went into politics in Brazil after the First World War to try to rectify the many grievances endured by Brazilians against their governments. He was successful in ousting President Luis in 1930, and getting himself elected provisional president in his place. Then he served two further terms, 1934–1945 and 1951–1954. In the first term, he brought Brazil on to the allied side in the Second World War, denying German submarine and surface craft captains haven or supplies in his country's ports. This was a great help to the Allies.

Mann, Thomas (1875–1955)
German author

Thomas Mann was the leading German novelist of this century. His gifts were recognized by the award of the Nobel prize in 1929. Essentially, Mann was a marvellous storyteller, a true intellectual, and a fine stylist. He was also an implacable opponent of fascism and dictatorship and this appears as a theme in some of his work. After Hitler came to power in Germany in 1933 Mann left his country, went to America and was naturalized an American in 1944.

Mann is best known for his short story *Death in Venice*, his epic novels *The Magic Mountain* and *Doktor Faustus*, and the cycle *Joseph and his Brothers*. He also wrote essays, particularly critical essays on Goethe (*p. 210*) and Schiller (*p. 197*).

Einstein, Albert (1879–1955)
Swiss physicist

Einstein was born German but became a naturalized Swiss in 1894. He was a brilliant mathematician and physicist, and in 1914 he was invited to become professor at Berlin. This meant taking on German nationality again, which he did.

But Einstein also had Jewish blood, and when Hitler came to power in 1933 he was expelled, losing his German citizenship again. He fled to America and stayed there, becoming a naturalized American.

Einstein is of course extremely famous for his theory of relativity. Published in 1905 it says that the speed of light appears to be the same whether an observer is moving rapidly to meet it or to go away from it. He also said that light rays from stars bend as they pass close to the sun, and this was later proved.

Fleming, Sir Alexander (1881–1955)
Scottish bacteriologist

If you get an infection these days, your doctor will probably give you an injection, or a tablet, containing penicillin or a drug of a similar kind, called an antibiotic. This will help your body to fight the germs or viruses causing the infection. You can see how beneficial this is, and you can thank Sir Alexander Fleming, the quiet, patient bacteriologist who was also a professor at St. Mary's Hospital in London.

Fleming began his research into moulds in the 1920s, and in 1928 spotted that the mould penicillium had qualities that brought about the death of germs. So he worked on it, but it needed many years to develop the manufacture of the mould in a form which could be used on a wide scale. By the early years of the Second World War, however, penicillin was available to doctors at the front for injured servicemen, and many lives were saved.

Sibelius, Jean (1865–1957)
Finnish composer

Sibelius was a composer in the grand manner. Although much of his work was written in this century, he has more in common with the heavier orchestral musicians such as Brahms, Liszt and Strauss. He was also very patriotic, and his work has strong Scandinavian and Russian tones. His symphonies are powerful, melodic and sonorous, and *Finlandia*, his best tone poem, is a great favourite with concertgoers and listeners.

Toscanini, Arturo (1867–1957)
Italian conductor

Toscanini was for a long time the most celebrated conductor in the world. That does not mean he was necessarily the best, for there were many different views of his artistry, but he certainly conducted his concerts with dash. He was similar to Sir Thomas Beecham (*p. 302*) but he probably was more dramatic.

His popularity can be judged by the great range of orchestras of which he was either resident or guest conductor, from the New York Philharmonic to the Bayreuth Festival, and from Salzburg Festival to La Scala in Milan.

Horthy, Admiral Miklos von Nagybanya (1868–1957)
Hungarian statesman

Admiral Horthy distinguished himself on the Austrian side in the First World

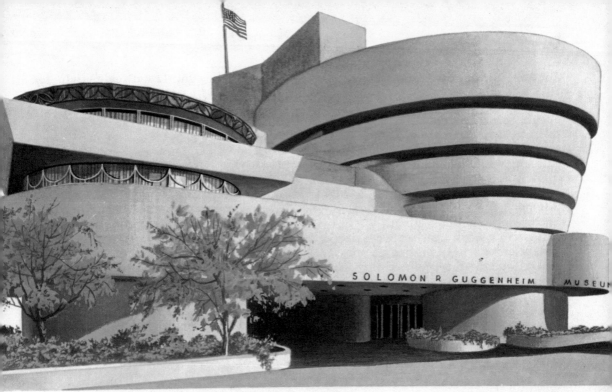

The Guggenheim Museum at Washington, designed by Frank Lloyd Wright

War and eventually became commander in chief of the Austro-Hungarian fleet. After the war, when Hungary split away from Austria and verged on becoming a communist state, Horthy was asked to take charge of the national forces trying to combat this rebellion. In 1920 he was appointed Regent of Hungary, and he held office right up to 1944. This included the days of the conquest of Hungary by Hitler.

Aga Khan, Aga Sultan Sir Mahomed Shah (1877–1957)
Head of Ismaeli Mohammedans
The Aga Khan, an important figure among Indian Mohammedans for many years, as head of their faith, was a great favourite with the British royal family, the government and the public. He was in many ways very Western, having been educated in Europe. He worked for Britain in the First and Second World Wars. He kept a string of horses in England many of which he raced with brilliant success on British racecourses. The Aga Khan was extremely rich: he once had himself weighed against a sack of diamonds belonging to him.

Vaughan Williams, Ralph (1872–1958)
British composer
Vaughan Williams was Herefordshire-born, but of Welsh descent. He was a composer whose work bears little influence of other composers before him. He wrote several symphonies, strong, melodic, sometimes sad, beautifully orchestrated, and always interesting. He also collected folk tunes and orchestrated them most delightfully.

Wright, Frank Lloyd (1869–1959)
American architect
Lloyd Wright was an unconventional architect in his time. He introduced the open plan of building for both private houses and public structures. Many of them looked like 'prairie style' homes such as one would see in the vast areas of the central American plains, where they blended into the landscape.

Lloyd Wright applied revolutionary engineering principles to architecture, and among his buildings are the earthquake-proof Imperial Hotel in Tokyo, Japan and the Guggenheim Museum of Art in New York where the exhibits line the walls of a continuous spiral ramp.

Epstein, Sir Jacob (1880–1959)
British sculptor
Epstein was born in New York, of Russo-Polish Jewish parents. He left America in 1902 and settled in London three years later, after studying art and sculpture in Paris. Then he began to establish himself as a sculptor. Over his next half century he made a name as a highly original genius, whose work was often unconventional but brilliant.

Epstein's work nearly always aroused violent emotions, often hostile ones. His statues outside the new building for the British Medical Association in London were the first. The tombstone to Oscar Wilde in Paris was another. So were *Lazarus*, *Ecce Home*, *Genesis* and, most of all, *Adam*, which was grossly insulted in numerous papers. But they all had fervent supporters, and their quality and power are now universally recognized. He himself was quite indifferent to either view.

Towards the end of his life Epstein began to receive official commissions for work, like the statute to Field Marshal Smuts (*p. 295*) in London's Parliament Square. His portrait busts, though not valued highly by himself, are astonishingly powerful in several instances, such as those of Churchill (*p. 304*), Einstein (*p. 300*), Shaw (*p. 294*) and Lord Fisher (*p. 266*).

Krupp, Gustav von Bohlen und Halbach (1870–1960)
German armament manufacturer
Krupp was synonymous with guns in Germany for a century. Gustav, whose name was von Bohlen und Halbach took the additional name of Krupp when he married the daughter and heir of the second owner of the huge armaments firm. He was an astute businessman and managed to build up the family factories to such an extent that the German government gave him the monopoly of armament manufacture during the First World War. He invented the 'Big Bertha' artillery gun, a huge weapon meant for shelling Paris from the German lines many miles away.

Krupp became fantastically rich. He supported Hitler in his rise to power and provided armaments in the Second World War.

Beecham, Sir Thomas (1879–1961)
British conductor
Up to about 80 years ago the conductor of an orchestra, though obviously an extremely important member of the team, seldom achieved the prominence that conductors do to-day. It was Thomas Beecham who was one of the first to change that. This rich son of the maker of the famous Beecham's pills, created the New Symphony Orchestra in 1906, and for the next generation or so conducted orchestras all over the world with a flamboyance, skill and verve that has seldom been seen before or since.

Beecham was witty, quick tempered, rude, but he was sympathetic, his world was music and its players, and he had an intense desire to please his audiences.

Hemingway, Ernest (1899–1961)
American novelist
Hemingway was a newspaper journalist who had served in the First World War. This experience had greatly disillusioned him about his fellow men and about mankind, and in three brilliant novels, *The Sun Also Rises*, *Men Without Women* and *A Farewell to Arms*, all about the war, he became a leading American novelist, a position he held up to his death.

Hemingway used his skill as a journalist to tell a fine story dramatically and well, and among his novels that were to stand with the greatest of this century were *For Whom the Bell Tolls* (about the Spanish Civil War), *To Have and Have Not* and *The Old Man and The Sea*. He was awarded the Nobel prize for literature in 1954.

Tragically, in 1961, dreading the thought of old age, he shot himself.

Cunningham, Andrew Browne, 1st Viscount (1883–1963)
Scottish admiral
Cunningham was a sailor to his fingertips. He was a brilliant commander in

President John Kennedy and in the background, the
Capitol building, which is the American seat of Congress

chief of the British naval forces in the
Mediterranean in the first years of the
Second World War. He smashed the
Italian fleet at the battle of Cape Matapan
in 1941. Then he became first sea lord in
1943, and remained head of the fighting
end of the Royal Navy until the war
closed.

Kennedy, John Fitzgerald (1917–1963)
President of the United States (1961–1963)
Jack Kennedy was the youngest Ameri-
can ever to be elected president of the
USA. He was also the first Roman
Catholic to hold the office. When he was
assassinated in Dallas, Texas, on 22
November 1963, half way through his

first term of office, the whole nation
mourned.

Kennedy was the second son of
Joseph Kennedy, a multi-millionaire of
Irish descent. As a boy he had all that
rich boys could have. After an academic
training he served in the Second World
War, and as a torpedo boat commander
he was decorated for bravery. When the
war ended, Kennedy went into politics
as a Democrat, and by 1960 had built up
enough support to stand for the presidency. He won with a small majority,
but what is interesting is that the largest
share of his vote came from the younger
people. He was seen to represent the
hopes and dreams of young men and

women, especially coloured people, and they looked to him to build a new world.

During his term he introduced some civil rights laws and he planned others. He handled United States foreign policy with skill and courage, particularly in 1962 when he prevailed upon the Russians to withdraw missiles from Cuba by making it clear he would not hesitate to use nuclear weapons if a war followed.

Kennedy was murdered in 1963 by a single rifle bullet, but the identity of the assassin has never been absolutely established.

Hoover, Herbert Clark (1874–1964)
American president (1928–1932)

Hoover was an engineer who specialized in mining work. In the First World War he became prominent when he headed an organization bringing relief to Belgian nationals suffering because of the war. After the war, when there was poverty and unemployment in many parts of Europe, he was in charge of many relief campaigns. His business sense got him elected as Secretary of Commerce, and in 1928 he felt strong enough in support to stand for president. He was elected and served for one term.

Jahawarhal Nehru

Nehru, Jahawarhal (1889–1964)
Indian national leader

Nehru, an extremely handsome, gifted and quiet scholar, who was educated in England, served Gandhi in the independence movement, got himself frequently arrested for civil disobedience and passive resistance activities, and eventually became secretary of the National Congress. This was the party in favour of independence, and it was on the acquisition of independence to become the leading political party in India. In 1950 Nehru became prime minister and remained in office for fourteen years. In that time he did a great deal for India. He made her name influential in the counsels of the world, and assumed leadership of the nations of the world that were neither in the Western orbit nor the Russian sphere, that is, the Third World. He travelled to many places mediating in this or that dispute, and made himself revered in his own land for his wisdom.

Churchill, Sir Winston Leonard Spencer, KG, OM (1874–1965)
British war leader, statesman, painter and writer

Some have called Churchill the greatest man ever to speak the English language; many more think him the greatest Englishman of the present century. But for him, Britain, Europe, and possibly the rest of the world, might have given way to dominion by Hitler (*p. 291*) and his hordes of conquering Nazi soldiery, who in any case invaded and destroyed a large part of Europe during the Second World War.

Churchill was the son of Lord Randolph Churchill and his wife, the American Jennie Jerome. He was also a descendant of the great Duke of Marlborough (*p. 170*). Like many men destined for greatness, Winston hated school, did badly at it, and only just managed to scrape into a career, in his case the army. He fought in Cuba, in India and with Kitchener in Egypt. Then he went to South Africa in the Boer War as a war correspondent. He had, while in India, taught himself to write good prose, and he had developed a grand, masterly style which captured the greatness of the times in which he was living or about which he was writing. In South Africa he was captured, escaped on a train with a price on his head and returned to England a hero.

Then he went into Parliament, and by 1906 was a junior minister. In 1911 he became first lord of the admiralty and it was largely due to his energy, foresight and persistence that the British fleet was ready, in 1914, to face any comers in the First World War. During the war, Churchill put up several ideas for shortening it, one of which was the bold scheme to take a fleet up the Dardanelles, capture Constantinople and so knock Turkey out of the fighting. It failed, but not through his fault; he was blamed, and was driven from office. So he went to the trenches in France as a colonel.

Churchill returned under more favourable conditions when Lloyd George was prime minister, and he held various offices over the next few years. But he felt himself increasingly at variance with his colleagues over several matters, particularly over India, and then later, in the middle of the 1930s, over British failure to re-arm against Hitler and his aggressive policies. Time and again he warned Britain to be ready to deal with the Nazis, but no one listened.

In 1939, Britain declared war over Hitler's invasion of Poland. Churchill was brought back as first lord of the admiralty and again he organized the fleet so that it would play its role. Then in May 1940, when France was about to collapse before the Germans, Chamberlain, the prime minister, was compelled to resign for his lack of leadership, and Churchill was sent for by the king, George VI, to form a government. His hour had come.

By his stirring inspiration and his magnificent speeches invoking all the best qualities of the British people, and his more practical direction of the nation's war effort, from grand strategic plans down to the smallest but still important

Sir Winston Churchill

details, he took the country through five years of hardship and loss to ultimate victory. Without his leadership, the British might well have given way and surrendered to Hitler.

After the war, Churchill was in opposition for six years. Then the Conservatives were returned and he was prime minister again, until 1955. By this time he was 80 and he knew it was time to go. He had had a wonderful innings and had left his mark not only on politics and soldiering, but also in quite different fields. His authorship developed enormously. His memoirs of the Second World War, in six volumes, earned him the Nobel prize for literature. He had also been painting for many years, with vigour and a strong sense of colour, and he had been elected an honorary academician extraordinary by the Royal Academy.

Loaded with honours and revered throughout the world, Winston Churchill died at the grand age of 90, and was given a solemn state funeral.

Maugham, William Somerset (1874–1965)
English writer

Somerset Maugham trained to be a doctor at St. Thomas's Hospital in London, and he practised for a while. He also began to write novels, and his first, *Liza of Lambeth*, was published soon after he qualified.

Then he decided to give up medicine and concentrate on writing. He developed enormously, and over a long life turned out a large quantity of novels, plays and short stories of the highest quality. They were consistently good in plot, characterization, drama and descriptive power. Many of the novels, like *Of Human Bondage*, *The Moon and Sixpence* and *The Razor's Edge* were runaway best-sellers. Most of his plays ran for months and months to packed houses, and are still very popular today. His short stories, collected in five volumes, are among the best ever written in English.

Maugham was, however, a cynic. He had little time for the frailties of men, and he could see few virtues in women at all. His writings portray both sexes at their weakest and most vulnerable. He also used incidents from real life, some of them given to him in confidence, and made little attempt to disguise where he got them from.

Schweitzer, Albert (1875–1965)
French medical missionary, theologian, philosopher and musician

Schweitzer was educated at Paris and Berlin universities, and entered the church at Strasbourg. He went on to become professor of religious philosophy at Strasbourg university. While he was studying, and later teaching, he also studied music, specializing in the organ, to the extent that he became one of the finest organists in the world. In 1908 he published a remarkable book about Bach (*p. 177*).

In 1905, Schweitzer gave up his theological career to study medicine, and when he qualified a few years later he left Europe to set up a hospital in French Equatorial Africa, at a small place called Lambarene. This institution was built, equipped and staffed by Schweitzer from his own funds and such as he could raise elsewhere. Most of the latter were earned by periodic returns to Europe for triumphant organ recitals.

This amazingly saintly man was awarded the Nobel Peace Prize in 1952.

Le Corbusier (Charles Édouard Jeanneret) (1887–1965)
Swiss architect

Le Corbusier was the pseudonym for Charles Édouard Jeanneret, a revolutionary Swiss architect who was a pioneer of functionalism in building, believing that a building's beauty derived from functional design. To achieve this, and thereby maintain aspects of beauty and proportion, Le Corbusier used innovations such as glass facades and elevated traffic passages. He used concrete and steel and made them look more than just two heavy and uninteresting materials.

Le Corbusier worked chiefly in Paris where there are several of his original designs. He also devised town centre schemes for Buenos Aires, Marseilles and Barcelona.

Eliot, Thomas Stearns (1888–1965)
American born poet

T. S. Eliot was a young American poet who came to settle in England in 1914. He had had a wide education in America and Europe, in philosophy, French language, English literature and history.

Eliot, who had already written some poetry which was known only to friends, took work as a schoolmaster and then entered a bank where he stayed for some years. Later on, he became a director of a well-known publishing company.

His verse was first appreciated widely when in 1917 he produced *Prufrock and Other Observations*, which was championed by Bertrand Russell (*p. 309*) among others. It was recognized as being of the highest skill and beauty, and when in 1922 he published another book of verse, *The Waste Land*, his reputation became an international one.

Thereafter, Eliot was to be among the leading poets in the English language right to his death. He also wrote several distinguished plays – *Murder in the Cathedral*, about the death of Thomas à Becket, was in blank verse – and a number of works of literary criticism. In 1948 he was awarded the Nobel prize for literature. He had taken British nationality in 1927.

Attlee, Clement Richard, 1st Earl (1883–1967)
British Labour statesman

'Clem' Attlee was a remarkable man. Born of a good family and educated well, he nonetheless acquired early in life a devotion to the interests of the lower

Clement Richard Attlee

classes. Before the First World War, in which, incidentally, he was to serve with great distinction, he gave a long period of service in the betterment of the poor in Stepney. In 1922, he became a member of Parliament and was parliamentary secretary to Ramsay MacDonald (*p. 283*), Labour's first prime minister. Before the outbreak of the Second World War, Attlee had worked his way to becoming Leader of the Opposition in the Commons, and so was given high office in Churchill's wartime national government. In 1942 Winston made Attlee deputy prime minister.

When the European war was over, the country elected a Labour government. Attlee became prime minister and held power for six momentous years in British social history. It was no easy task. The country was greatly impoverished through its exertions to save Europe from the Hitler tyranny. He laid the foundations of the National Health Service, introduced nationalization projects, and provided effective leadership despite the conflicting personalities of his colleagues.

In 1951 he was defeated in the general election, and became Leader of the Opposition again. He retired in 1955, accepted his well-earned earldom and spoke frequently in the House of Lords.

Bruce, Stanley Melbourne, 1st Viscount (1883–1967)
Australian statesman

Bruce was prime minister of Australia from 1923 to 1929. Then he went to the League of Nations to represent Australia, and in 1935 was elected president of the League by the other delegates. His wise statesmanship had endeared itself to politicians all over the world. His pro-British feelings earned him appointment as Australian high commissioner in London from 1933 to 1945, and it was particularly valuable for the British that he was there, for he facilitated the arrangements whereby Australian divisions came to fight in the Second World War on the Allied side. Churchill asked the Australians to let Bruce sit on the British War Cabinet.

Donald Campbell and one of his high-speed land vehicles

Campbell, Donald (1921–1967)
British land and water speed record holder

Donald Campbell was the son of Sir Malcolm Campbell who, in 1935, was the first man to drive a racing car faster than 300 mph. For years, Sir Malcolm was very famous, and the boy grew up in his shadow. He longed to do as well, better if possible, but was not encouraged while his father remained alive. Then, after 1949, Donald Campbell came into his own.

With a fine team of engineers, and backed by individuals and companies willing to finance him, he embarked on a splendid record breaking career on land and water. He broke the water speed record first in 1955, and by 1964 had reached 276 mph. Then, in 1967, on Lake Coniston in Westmoreland, his last attempt to edge this speed higher still ended in tragedy when his speed craft blew up, killing him instantly.

Keller, Helen Adams (1880–1968)
American blind, deaf-mute author

Imagine being struck down in childhood with an illness that leaves you blind, deaf and dumb. This happened to Helen Keller when she was six. So her parents took her to Alexander Graham Bell (*p. 266*) the inventor of the telephone, and asked his help. He recommended a part-blind teacher from the Perkins Institute in Boston. This was Ann Sullivan, and she got busy teaching Helen all kinds of things. Helen had a quick brain, and this enabled her to some extent to get over her appalling disability. Her progress was amazing. By the time she was 20 she was writing fluently on many subjects. And in 1904 she won an honours degree.

Helen Keller discovered that there were many people like her and she decided to devote her life to their welfare. She wrote books, articles and papers on her own story and her thoughts about it, and she also lectured. This brought comfort and encouragement to many who might otherwise have led a silent, empty existence.

King, Martin Luther (1929–1968)
American Negro leader

This minister of the church founded the Southern Christian Leadership Conference, a movement which aimed to achieve civil rights for American Negroes. He advocated no violence whatever, and set a splendid example to his colleagues – and to many others involved in the black struggle in the United States, by his patience, kindness, wisdom and restraint.

Americans of all colours came to respect Martin Luther King, who was awarded the Nobel Peace Prize in 1964, and the world was appalled to hear on 4 April 1968 that at Memphis a white fanatic had shot him and wounded him so badly that he died shortly afterwards.

Eisenhower, Dwight David (1890–1969)
American president and general (1853–1961)

'I Like Ike' was a catchphrase in the United States in the last generation. It referred to Eisenhower, whose nickname was 'Ike' and who was one of the most popular men in the land. With his beaming smile, his kind, quiet, reassuring voice, he embodied the solid, reliable father-figure that so many Americans longed for.

Eisenhower was a professional soldier. By 1942 he was a general, but he had had no major battle experience. All the same, Roosevelt (*p. 289*) picked him as commander of the American forces in Europe in the Second World War. Eisenhower was an able leader of men, and seemed to be just the person to take over supreme command of all the Allied forces in Europe at the time of the invasion of France in 1944. It proved true, for he led them to victory in 1945.

In 1952 his popularity was still high and he won the presidential elections as a republican candidate. He repeated this success in 1956.

Alexander, Harold Rupert Leofric George, 1st Earl (1891–1969)
Irish field marshal

Alex, as everyone in the army knew him, was a polished, erudite, courageous and charming gentleman-soldier, whose gifts as a commander in the field were seldom equalled in the story of the Second World War. Nothing ever worried him, or if it did, nobody ever knew it.

Gallant as any man in uniform, he won a DSO in the First World War and ended up a colonel before the age of 30. He helped get the men out of Dunkirk in 1940, when France collapsed in the Second World War, and was the last man to leave. In 1942 he was made commander in chief in the Middle East, and with Montgomery as his deputy, he cleared the enemy out of North Africa completely. Then he went to Italy and drove the Germans up into the Alp districts, entering Rome on 4 June 1944.

After the war he was made Governor General of Canada, and endeared himself to Canadians. He came home and was minister of defence in Churchill's peace time government.

Russell, Bertrand Arthur William, 3rd Earl (1872–1970)
British philosopher

Bertrand Russell was one of the most original and brilliant thinkers of the last century or so. His career spanned nearly 100 years and during it he expressed a wide variety of beliefs, many of which landed him in a lot of trouble. He was a mathematician at Cambridge for many years, but when during the First World War, he spoke out against fighting, he was dismissed as fellow of Trinity College. He also went to prison for his views.

After the war he visited Russia and was not impressed by the practical application there of the teachings of Karl Marx (*p. 238*) in whose theories he believed. He was opposed to many of the moral and matrimonial conventions of Western Europe, and he earned a good deal of abuse for his attacks on them.

Russell wrote many learned works, including a *History of Western Philosophy*, *Human Knowledge: Its Scope and Limits* and *The Analysis of Matter*. He was awarded the Nobel Prize in 1950 and the Order of Merit in 1949. In his last years he campaigned vigorously against nuclear weapons and the war in Vietnam; he sat outside No. 10, Downing Street, in protest, and was arrested and imprisoned often.

Kerensky, Alexander Feodovorich (1881–1970)
Russian statesman

Kerensky was a democratic politician who supported a moderate reform of the Russian government. In 1917, when a series of disasters on the Russian front against the Germans, led to a collapse of authority at home and a curtailment of Czar Nicholas II's powers, Kerensky became prime minister of the new revolutionary government. He governed well for about six months, but certain elements in and outside it were anxious to carry the revolution further, expel the royal family and set up a Communist state. Led by Lenin (*p. 270*) they overthrew Kerensky's government and he had to flee for his life. He went to Paris and then to the United States where he lived for many years lecturing and writing about the great Russian revolution and about social democracy.

Bruening, Heinrich (1885–1970)
German statesman

Bruening was a statesman who understood a lot about finance. In 1930 Hindenburg (*p. 278*) made him Chancellor of Germany with the task of sorting out the severe financial depression into which the nation had fallen. Bruening might have succeeded, but Hitler (*p. 291*) was by then bent on achieving the chancellorship himself, and his Nazi party did everything it could to obstruct Bruening.

When Hitler did become chancellor in 1933, Bruening left the country and lectured in America. After the Second World War, he gave evidence in the famous Nuremburg Trials of the Nazi War leaders.

Salazar, Antonio de Oliviera (1889–1970)
Portuguese dictator

There are many who did not like the repressive and harsh nature of Salazar's government in Portugal – yet this man was quite unique in twentieth century power politics. He was appointed prime minister of Portugal in 1932, and minister

President Charles de Gaulle and in the background, the Arc de Triomphe

of war and foreign affairs in 1936, and he held on to both right to the end of his life. He survived many attempts to unseat him; he earned the dislike of many of his people and the hatred of many more people outside Portugal. He restructured the country, gave it a new constitution, kept it out of the Second World War, and preserved its colonial empire in Africa, the Far East and elsewhere.

De Gaulle, Charles André Joseph Marie (1890–1970)

French leader and President of France (1958–1969)

De Gaulle means 'of France', and no more appropriate surname could fit the achievements of General de Gaulle, if it had been invented for him. This patriotic and gallant French soldier, who became an expert in mechanized warfare in the 1920s and tried to get the French government to modernize its armies, was a general early in the Second World War. When France was overrun by Nazi Germans in 1940, de Gaulle left to go to England on a mission to get help. In his absence, the French surrendered to Hitler, but he refused to accept this. He made himself head of a Free French National Committee in London, with one aim – to get back to France and drive the Germans out.

In 1944 the Allies expelled the Germans from France and he entered Paris in triumph, but walking on foot. After the war, the French people elected him prime minister, but in 1946 he was ousted. He remained in political exile for thirteen years, watching one government after another come to office and fall, as every one failed to tackle the nation's problems. In 1958 he was returned to power this time as president, and headed the government and the country, almost as a dictator, for ten years. In that time he lifted French prestige to great heights, and made his own reputation as a world statesman.

Nasser, Gamel Abdel (1918–1970)

Ruler of Egypt (1956–1970)

At first, when Colonel Nasser seized power in Egypt, soon after the revolution which got rid of the last king, Farouk, in 1953, few realized his serious intentions, when he threatened to smash the Israelis and drive them into the sea.

But after a while, when it seemed he had a firm grip on power in Egypt and was actually doing something to modernize the country, people began to take notice. He began to become important among the counsels of the nations who

make up the Third World, those countries committed neither to the Russian nor the American sphere of influence.

Even when he lost the Six Day War of 1967, his regime did not falter. When he died in 1970, he was greatly mourned. He had revolutionized his country and made it a political power to be reckoned with.

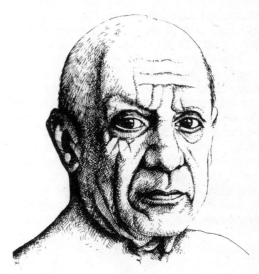

Pablo Picasso

Picasso, Pablo Ruiz y (1881–1972)

Spanish painter

Picasso was a Spanish artist who in his time was regarded by many as the greatest living painter. Throughout his life his work was full of vigour, colour and technical brilliance.

His pictures still fetch enormous prices in auction rooms. Picasso was a pioneer of abstract art, who radically altered the traditions of painting during the long period he was working. Early influences were gained in Paris, where the Post-Impressionists were active; his work was fairly representational, featuring actors and harlequins. He then introduced Cubism, a style of art which interpreted objects in three dimensions, as planes of cubes and other rectilinear shapes. A series of Spanish subjects – pictures of bull-fighting – culminated in the terrifying painting *Guernica*, depicting the horrors of the Spanish Civil War in 1936.

Manstein, Fritz Erich von (1887–1972)
German field marshal

Manstein was Rundstedt's chief of staff in the Polish campaign in 1939, at the outbreak of the Second World War. When Rundstedt went to France in 1940, Manstein accompanied him and was the brains behind the skilful plan to envelop and cut to pieces the French forces. When Hitler invaded Russia in 1941, Manstein was given an army and although not an expert in armoured warfare used it with the greatest skill.

The German success was stemmed in 1942 by the collapse of the 6th Army at Stalingrad, and thereafter the story was one of retreat after retreat, punctuated occasionally by a local advance or two. Manstein had command in the southern sector and managed to extricate his forces with tremendous skill, so that they could fight again, as they did on many occasions. Sometime in 1944, when he felt he could not obey a hopelessly impractical order of Hitler's, he was sacked.

Nkrumah, Kwame (1909–1972)
Ghanaian statesman

Nkrumah was called by his people 'The Redeemer'. He was a lawyer and politician who in 1949 formed the nationalist movement, the Convention People's Party, with the express object of obtaining complete independence from British rule in his homeland, then called the Gold Coast. He endured several misfortunes, including a term in jail for his activities, but such was his dynamic leadership that he won over nearly the whole population to his side and in 1957 he became the first prime minister of the independent state of Ghana.

Nkrumah was interested in all black countries obtaining their independence and he did much to further nationalist movements in other lands in Africa. But at home, despite enormous strides in industrialization and political development, Nkrumah made himself increasingly hated by virtue of his dictatorial behaviour, and in 1966 his regime was overthrown by the army. He was granted asylum in Guinea and died in 1972.

Casals, Pablo (1876–1973)
Spanish cellist and conductor

Casals has been called the greatest cellist of all time. He was also a conductor of great originality and verve. He spent his youth in his native Spain and toured the musical centres of the world giving recitals. But when General Franco established his dictatorship in Spain in 1937–1938, Casals, a man of peace, left the country to live in France. Unfortunately, he refused to play in public for years, except in very special circumstances.

Casals adored the music of Bach more than of any other composer – understandably – and he gave it a new meaning with his vigorous and unorthodox interpretation when he conducted it. One feels that the great composer would certainly have approved.

Inönü, Ismet (1884–1973)
Turkish statesman and leader

Inönü worked with Kemal Atatürk (*p. 284*), the founder of modern Turkey. He had been an officer in the Turkish army in the First World War, and became Atatürk's chief of staff in 1919 when that great leader defeated the Greeks.

Atatürk appointed Inonu prime minister in 1923 and he held office until 1937, during which time he did much to put into action Atatürk's great schemes to modernize Turkey. When Atatürk died in 1938, Inönü was elected president in his place with a huge majority. He held office throughout the Second World War, kept Turkey out of it despite many blandishments by Nazi Germany, and retired in 1950.

Inönü agreed to serve as prime minister from 1961 to 1965 to help the country out of an awkward internal situation.

Ben Gurion, David (1886–1973)
Israeli statesman

Ben Gurion was born in Poland. He emigrated after much difficulty to Palestine in 1906 and worked slowly for the building of a Jewish state in the land. He created the first trade union in Palestine in 1915. Once the state was created after the First World War, Ben Gurion became secretary of the General Federation of Jewish Labour, which is like being secretary of the trades unions. He headed the Labour party from 1930 to 1955. In 1948, during a bitter campaign against the British police troops in Palestine, he proclaimed the independent state of Israel, and shortly afterwards effected the withdrawal of the British altogether. Ben Gurion was Israeli prime minister from 1948 to 1953, and 1955 to 1963. He was a revered and much loved leader of his country.

Coward, Sir Noel (1899–1973)
English actor, writer and composer

Actor, singer, producer, playwright, poet, composer, lyric writer, film star: Coward was all these and to the highest degree.

Born in London, he went into the theatre as a very young lad – and stayed there until the end of his life. He started to write plays when still in his teens and he went on taking whatever parts he could get, hoping one day to be recognized for what he was, a genius.

In 1924 he produced his play, *The Vortex*, which shocked many people because one of its characters became a drug addict. But it established him. Thereafter, nearly everything that he did was successful. *Hay Fever*, *Private Lives*, *Blithe Spirit*, *Bitter Sweet*, *Cavalcade* and many more, played to full houses; some plays, such as *Bitter Sweet*, contained melodies that were sung, whistled and hummed by people everywhere.

His plays were filled with wit, commonsense and often serious moral pointers. His films, some of which he wrote, produced and acted in, such as *In Which We Serve*, were among the most popular of their time.

Auden, Wystan Hugh (1907–1973)
English born poet

W. H. Auden, as he liked to be known, was born in England and educated at Oxford, the one city he loved most of all, where he died in 1973. As a young man he was very forceful, and he was brilliant, too; he gathered round him a group of

Noel Coward

friends, all of whom were to become first class writers, such as Stephen Spender, Cecil Day Lewis and Christopher Isherwood. These authors and poets were disillusioned with Britain in the 1930s, with its unemployment figures running into millions, and the misery which followed; they sought a new world. This got them a reputation for being communist.

In 1939, Auden emigrated to America and became an American citizen. But he never lost his love for Britain, especially Oxford. His output of verse was extensive and brilliant. It was probably more simple and direct than that of many contemporaries. *Poems* appeared in 1930, and the *Dance of Death* in 1933, establishing him in the front rank of British poets. He also worked on plays and books, and was part author (with Isherwood) of *The Ascent of F.6*, a taut drama that has often been produced on stage and on radio and television.

Index